THE USE OF COMPARATIVE LAW BY COURTS

Académie internationale de droit comparé
International Academy of Comparative Law

The Use of Comparative Law by Courts

XIVe Congrès international de droit comparé
XIVth International Congress of Comparative Law
Athènes/Athens 1997

Edited by

ULRICH DROBNIG
Professor and Director Emeritus
Max-Planck-Institute for Foreign Private
and Private International Law, Hamburg

and

SJEF VAN ERP
Professor of civil law and European
private law, University of Maastricht;
Deputy justice Court of Appeals 's-Hertogenbosch;
deputy judge District Court of Amsterdam

KLUWER LAW INTERNATIONAL
THE HAGUE / LONDON / BOSTON

A C.I.P Catalogue record for this book is available from the Library of Congress.

ISBN 90-411-1044-5

Published by Kluwer Law International,
P.O. Box 85889, 2508 CN The Hague, The Netherlands

Sold and distributed in North, Central and South America
by Kluwer Law International,
675 Massachusetts Avenue, Cambridge, MA 02139, USA

In all other countries, sold and distributed
by Kluwer Law International, Distribution Centre
P.O. Box 322, 3300 AH Dordrecht, The Netherlands

Printed on acid-free paper

Kluwer Law International incorporates the publishing programmes of
Graham & Trotman Ltd, Kluwer Law and Taxation Publishers,
and Martinus Nijhoff Publishers.

Printed and bound in Great Britain by Antony Rowe.

Table of Contents

PART TWO: NATIONAL REPORTS

Preface

In our quickly integrating world, comparison of the various divergent national laws is of ever-growing importance. Practitioners advising on trans-border legal transactions; legislators preparing major legislation requiring special expertise; officers of international organizations preparing conventions or legislation unifying aspects of the legal systems of member countries – all of these must employ the methods of comparative law in order to achieve optimal solutions.

In addition to these traditional users, judges are slowly beginning to recognize the usefulness of comparative law. If courts are confronted with novel issues; if they wish to depart from a judicial practice which no longer conforms to present-day conceptions of justice, morality or equality; if, due to the small size of a country, there is very little judicial precedent – in all these (and other) cases, an open-minded judge would be well-advised to look at foreign law, be it legislation or case-law, in order to find inspiration for the best decision. Comparative legal analysis enlarges the spectrum of choice as well as the various arguments for and against a particular solution.

The fifteen reports collected in this volume offer an interesting cross-section of contemporary court practice in twelve countries situated in all corners of the world. The reports illustrate well the impact of divergent traditions, attitudes and surrounding circumstances. Of special interest are both the role of comparative law and the comparative method employed in the practice of a supranational court, i.e. the European Court of Justice.

While, for one reason or another, not all of the national reports submitted to the XIVth International Congress of Comparative Law and covered by the General Report are to be found in this collection, the editors have tried to compensate for this by adding three new reports (i.e. those from Iceland, Israel and Luxembourg) presenting the typical problems courts are confronted with in small countries.

We hope that the book will not only illustrate present-day judicial practice in a variety of countries, but also inspire further research and encourage judges to use comparative enquiry as a means of improving the law.

U. Drobnig *J.H.M. van Erp*

PART I

GENERAL REPORT

ULRICH DROBNIG

The Use of Comparative Law by Courts

I. Introduction

1. – The *present topic* is a sequel to the earlier subject dealing with the "Use of Comparative Law by the Legislature" which was discussed 12 years ago at the XIth Congress of the Academy in Caracas (1982).[1] The same topic as the present one had already been discussed by the Academy at an earlier occasion, namely at the VIIth Congress 1966 in Uppsala.[2] However, at that time the basis of discussion was extremely small: only five national reports had been delivered.

What today might seem like a repetition, is in reality a very different venture. No fewer than 15 national reports were delivered to me, some of them of very substantial scope; in addition, I asked for and received two brief notes from small countries. This fact alone accounts for a much broader and more differentiated picture. In addition, the national reports themselves are of very high quality and have been a rich source of inspiration.

2. – It is, of course, neither possible nor my function to summarise the *15 national reports and two notes* as such.[3] However, it appears to be useful to

[1] A general report was neither presented nor published.

[2] See the general report by *Baudouin*, L'usage qui est fait en jurisprudence du droit comparé, in Rapports Généraux au VIIe Congrès International de Droit Comparé (Uppsala 1966) (Stockholm 1968) 125-135.

[3] For interested readers, a short because accidental list of references to published reports is given: AUSTRALIA: *J. Chen*, The Use of Comparative Law by Australian Courts: *Tay and Leung* (ed.), Australian Law and Legal Thinking in the 1990s (1994) 60-82; FRANCE: *Legeais*, L'utilisation du droit comparé par les tribunaux: Rev.int.dr.comp. 1994, 347-358; GERMANY: *U. Drobnig*, The Use of Foreign Law by German Courts: *Jayme* (ed.), German National Reports in Civil Matters for the XIVth Congress of Comparative Law in Athens 1994 (Heidelberg 1994) 5-24; ISRAEL: *Sanilevici*, The Use of Comparative Law by Israeli Courts: *Rabello* (ed.), Israeli Reports to the XIV International Congress of Comparative Law (Jerusalem 1994) 43-74; ITALY: *Taruffo*, The Use of Comparative Law by Courts: *Associazione Italiana di Diritto Comparato* (ed.), Rapports Nationaux Italiens au XIVe Congrès International de Droit Comparé/Italian National Reports to the XIVth International

U. Drobnig and S. van Erp (eds.), The Use of Comparative Law by Courts, 3–21

present their geographical distribution and also to localise very briefly the legal orders covered by reference to the macro-comparative division of the legal systems of the world.

Five reports were received from the *Americas*; among these one from South America (scil. Brazil) and four from North America, namely two each from Canada and the United States.

The two *Asian* reports came from the outer borders of this continent, *i.e.* from Israel and from Japan. And, of course, one only from *Australia*.

Seven reports and two notes were received from *Europe*. They cover eight countries, i.e. France, Germany, Greece, Iceland, Italy, Luxembourg, the Netherlands, and the United Kingdom; and, in addition, the European Union as a supranational entity.

By the 15 reports and the two notes, the major families of law are well represented. Represented are not only the "heads" of these families but also some of their off-spring. This introduces not only a welcome "sociological distinction" between "parent" and "off-spring" but also, as will be demonstrated, a relevant legal differentiation.

Finally, it must be added that the level of inquiry achieved in the various reports differs considerably. Some reporters, e.g. those from France and Italy, note expressly that no earlier research was available to them; by contrast, most other reporters apparently were able to integrate into their own research efforts earlier undertaken by others.

3. – In the context of the present paper as well as the national reports, the *term "comparative law"* must be qualified in several respects.

First, according to practical experience in all the countries, most courts which refer to foreign law, be it statutes, court decisions or writings, do not really undertake a comparison of law, utilising the methods and standards applied by academics. Often the courts refer to individual sources of foreign law without indicating why a particular country was selected; sometimes such references appear to be rather accidental. Nevertheless, all references of this kind count as comparative efforts since they demonstrate that the courts are aware of solutions to legal problems which differ from those of their domestic law.

Secondly, in some countries there are general limits of a procedural nature which prevent courts – or, rather, certain courts – from taking into account foreign law. The decisions of the French *Cour de cassation*, of the Dutch *Hoge Raad* and of the Greek *Areopag* generally do not contain any references at all. Citations, including references to foreign law, may well be found in the well-reasoned opinions of the Attorney-Generals of those countries, provided they are published; this is done in the Netherlands but not regularly in France. Can a connection be established between the

Congress of Comparative Law (Milano 1994) 49-59. References to these reports refer to the printed version published in this volume.

comparative elements of such an advisory opinion and the holding of the respective supreme court, provided it follows the Attorney-General's opinion? The Dutch report has argued in favour of this approach without concealing the obvious doubts which must persist.[4] It would seem to me that one may accept that suggestion only where an unambiguous connection between the opinion and the decision can be established, if, *e.g.*, the court expressly refers to the corresponding part of the Attorney-General's opinion.

Thirdly and by contrast, in my view there is no longer an identifiable connection between foreign law and a court decision, where the court refers to a domestic book or article which, while being based upon comparative research, "translates" foreign law into the legal culture of the *forum* state.[5] This may be distinguished from those cases in which a court refers to a domestic publication which describes and analyses foreign law without such "translation".

4. – There is some divergence of opinion as to the *proper object* of comparative efforts by the courts.

The Italian and the Dutch reporters insist that only domestic law, substantive as well as procedural, should be the proper object of comparative efforts in the present context. Thus they exclude the conflict of laws and certain rules of international criminal law, as well as the application of treaties and conventions.[6] To my mind, this is too narrow a delimitation.

It is true that the application of foreign law if directed by the conflicts rules of the *forum* state is not relevant in the present context. That application is ordered by the *lex fori* and therefore lacks that element of voluntary regard to foreign law which, in my view, is the equivalent of a legislator's or a scholar's voluntary research in foreign law. Further, the application of foreign law to the facts of a case does not involve that element of interaction between foreign and domestic law, that is the special purpose of comparison in the present context. This limit has been acknowledged by most reporters.[7]

However, applying foreign law as directed by a domestic conflicts rule does not exclude all aspects of private international law and of other rules dealing with foreign countries from the impact of comparative inquiry. There are several problems where the proper application of a conflicts rule involves a comparison of domestic and foreign law, as we will see. The same applies to some degree to other branches of "foreign relations law" as well, such as aspects of extradition.

---

[4] The Netherlands report *infra* p. 243 calls these cases "hidden use of comparative law"; but see the qualifications at p. 247, 250 and 251.

[5] This is described in the Italian report p. 50 and mentioned in the Japanese report p. 224.

[6] Italian report p. 51-52; Netherlands report *infra* p. 237.

[7] The only exceptions are the reports on United States law by Prof. *Clark* and the United Kingdom report (p. 254, 266-268; *cf.* also the statistical data at p. 263-265).

In sum, this report does not exclude *a priori* any field of law from comparison, provided that the rules of foreign law are considered by the deciding court as having, potentially or actually, an impact on the contents of the relevant domestic rule of law to be applied for the solution of the case at hand.

II. NECESSARY AND VOLUNTARY RECOURSES TO FOREIGN LAW

5. – I had suggested to *classify* court practice *into three groups*, depending on the respective motivation for the use of foreign law; many national reports have adopted this classification.

The first group deals with cases involving those rules of national law that can only be applied with the help of foreign law; in these cases comparison is necessary (*infra* A).

In the two other groups, by contrast, recourse to foreign law is less indicated or even completely voluntary. It is less voluntary where the application of legal rules is at issue that have an international element (*infra* B). Regard to foreign law is least indicated in the third group which comprises rules of a completely domestic character (*infra* C).

Generally speaking, therefore, one may expect for the three groups a decreasing willingness of the courts to consider foreign law. We will presently see, whether that hypothesis is well founded.

A. Necessary Comparison

6. – In the present context of "measuring" the motivation of courts to pay attention to foreign law, this first group requires only little attention. Recourse to foreign law and in some cases even true comparison is inevitable for the proper application of the rules which fall into this group.

i. General Principles of Law

7. – In Germany and Greece, the *generally recognised rules of public international law* are, by constitutional commands,[8] directly applicable in these two countries and have even priority over national law. These constitutional provisions confront the courts with the task of identifying the relevant "general rules". This task is in Germany the monopoly of the Federal Constitutional Court, whereas in Greece any court may do it, although such matters may also be brought before a Special Supreme Court. The German Federal Constitutional Court has performed the task of ascertaining whether unwritten rules of public international law are recog-

[8] German Constitution art. 25; Greek Constitution art. 28 par. 1.

nized by the majority of countries in an exemplary fashion; it has undertaken comprehensive inquiries and comparisons of the views that are held of the relevant rules in a great number of foreign countries.[9] The Greek report, by contrast, reveals that the necessary comparative analysis is seldom undertaken; rather, the courts simply assert or negate the general character of a relevant unwritten rule of international law without comparative analysis. Even the Special Supreme Court, which has been seized of only one case, rendered its decision without undertaking the necessary comparison.[10]

8. – A somewhat different illustration of the comparative impetus that is due to "*general principles of law*" is furnished for the field of private law by Brazil. According to an express provision, gaps in domestic private law may be filled by "analogy, the usages or general principles of law".[11] Such general principles are to be ascertained by comparative law. Unfortunately, the Brazilian report does not specify in which fields and in which ways the courts do accomplish that comparative analysis. It is merely said that the main source of inspiration is French law.[12]

9. – The most fascinating use of "*general principles*" is to be found on a supranational level in the European Union.

According to certain provisions in the founding conventions of at least two of the original Communities, the delictual liability of the Union for damage caused by the Community or its agents is to be determined "in accordance with the general principles common to the laws of member states."[13] The European Court of Justice therefore is required to analyse in each relevant case the detailed rules of tort law as they have been developed in the 12 member states. Most of these rules are to be gathered from court practice, a very laborious undertaking, as any comparative private lawyer will appreciate.

Of special interest is the way in which the European Court distils a general principle from the 12 national tort laws. The arithmetic common denominator is usually accepted but not always. The Court may choose, as Mr. Justice *Kakouris* puts it, "the most appropriate rule".[14] Such selection seems to be made, in particular, if the relevant national rules are strongly diverging or if there are no rules in an important field, like tort liability of a state for illegal legislative acts.[15]

---

[9] Cf. the German report *infra* p. 130 with references.

[10] Cf. the Greek report *infra* p. 166-168.

[11] Introductory Law to the Civil Code art. 4.

[12] Brazilian report p. 7-8.

[13] Treaty on the European Economic Community art. 215 par. 2; Treaty on the European Atomic Community art. 188 par. 2.

[14] Report on the European Court of Justice *infra* p. 100 no. 15.

[15] For details, cf. *ibidem* p. 100 no. 15-16.

ii. Examples from the conflict of laws

10. – Certain rules of the conflict of laws require for their proper application a comparative analysis. Since this leads into a special field, I shall be very brief.

11. – One illustration is furnished by the famous problem of *characterisation*. According to the traditional and widely accepted view, the characterisation of a foreign legal institution or rule that is unknown to the *forum* state must start from the *lex fori*. There is broad agreement, however, that this must be preceded by a description and evaluation of the foreign institution or rule according to its meaning and purpose. In truth, therefore, a comparison of the foreign institution or rule with the nearest equivalent institution or rule of the *lex fori* is necessary.[16]

12. – *Public policy clauses* are another illustration. They require the judge to juxtapose the rule of foreign law which is applicable according to his ordinary conflicts rules, with the fundamental principles of his own law.[17]

13. – A third illustration: some modern conflict rules expressly provide for a comparison between two legal systems and declare applicable the one which is more favourable for a specific party. Recent examples are two provisions of the Convention of member states of the European Union on the law applicable to contractual relationships (the Rome Convention) of 1980. Article 5 protects the consumer and art. 6 the worker by assuring to both of them the minimum protection of a specific legal system if a choice-of-law clause by the parties would make applicable a less favourable legal system.[18]

B. Legal Rules with an International Element

14. – In this second group, comparison is no longer an indispensible prerequisite for the proper application of a national rule, as it is in the first group. However, a variety of international elements or links to foreign countries make it appropriate to use the comparative method. The following six sub-classes are arranged according to the extent of links with foreign countries, in a descending order.

i. Uniform international rules

15. – A very strong international element attaches to those rules of national law that are based on international agreements providing uniform, self-

---

[16] Cf. the Canadian report by *Glenn infra* p. 63-64; the German report p. 130; and Greek report p. 174-175.

[17] Cf. the German report p. 137; French report p. 115; Greek report p. 175-176, 179.

[18] The Greek report p. 177-180 mentions these examples.

executing rules in various fields of law, or in such international instruments themselves (depending on the necessity *vel non* of transformation). To which degree have courts accepted this possibility or moral, if not even legal obligation which is expressed by certain formulas which are currently used in international agreements in order to secure the desired uniformity of interpretation in all contracting states? For many conventions, the relevant decisions of national courts are conveniently accessible.[19]

16. – A preliminary point may be mentioned in passing which, although beyond the scope of this paper, has an indirect impact. Countries following a *strictly dualistic approach* in public international law need a special rule of interpretation in order to preserve conformity, as far as possible, of the national regulation with the international agreement which is not binding upon the citizens.[20] This general approach to treaty obligations restricts, of course, although it does not entirely exclude, the willingness of the courts to strive for their uniform interpretation.

17. – A broad willingness to consider the attitude and practice of other contracting states in the interpretation of international uniform law is to be found in *Germany*.

The Federal Supreme Court has held that the interpretation of international uniform rules has to pursue, beyond the traditional methods of interpretation, a further purpose, *i.e.* to guarantee to the extent possible a uniform interpretation in all contracting states. Consequently, the interpretation of the rules should be autonomous because recourse to the meaning of the corresponding national legal notions would endanger the uniformity of the rules, *i.e.* the primary aim of the international treaties. In case of doubt a rule of uniform law retains the same meaning as attaches to the corresponding rule in that country from which the uniform rule was derived. Furthermore, the need for uniform interpretation would speak in favour of giving the wording of the uniform provisions more weight than usual in the process of interpretation.[21]

Two decisions merit special attention because they demonstrate the need as well as the limits of the comparative method in interpreting international uniform laws. In November 1956 the Federal Supreme Court had to decide on the question whether a presumption laid down by the Geneva Uniform Law of Bills of Exchange of 1930 art. 31 par. 4 is or is not rebuttable. This issue is very controversial in all contracting states. The court cited contradictory decisions from six countries, both views balancing each other in

[19] See especially Unidroit, Jurisprudence de droit uniforme (1959-1971); Unidroit, Revue de droit uniforme (since 1972).

[20] Australian report p. 35-36; English report p. 268-270; cf. also Greek report p. 169-172 on the slow change from the former to the present position.

[21] German report p. 132.

numbers. Among the cited decisions, three originated from French appellate courts; the Federal Supreme Court adopted their view that the presumption established by the provision is rebuttable. However, ten months earlier the French Court of Cassation had overruled those French cases; and four years later a plenary decision of the French Court of Cassation confirmed that decision, most probably also without any knowledge of the contrary German ruling. Another ten months later the German Federal Supreme Court confirmed its decision of 1956, apparently still in ignorance of the latest French decisions.[22] This case study illustrates both the need for an interpretation of uniform international rules using foreign law as well as the technical problem of a rapid exchange of information.

18. – Some instances of comparative interpretation have been mentioned in *other reports* but without details.[23] For Greece it is reported that, although the former dualistic conception had been abrogated by the Constitution of 1975, the courts are still influenced by it and therefore only very rarely look to foreign interpretations.[24]

ii. European Community Law

19. – Primary as well as secondary law of the European Union/Community is – as supranational law – uniform law of a specific quality. On the other hand, the division between regulations and directives delimits two spheres of secondary community law, one part of which deploys direct effects, whereas the other part has merely indirect effects. Since this type of supranational law is valid for a specific region only, this report will and must exercise restraint, since also most national reports from member states do not deal with this special topic.

A distinction must be made between the recourse to comparative methods by the courts of the member states (*infra* no. 20) and by the European Court of Justice (*infra* no. 21).

20. – On the level of the *member states*, one decision from the German Federal Constitutional Court is of major interest because it deals with objections against the progressive and law-making function of the European Court of Justice; the Constitutional Court underlined: "The Treaties constituting the European Communities have to be interpreteted in the light of common European legal tradition and legal culture, too." Referring to Roman law, to the English common law, the Continental *jus commune* and French administrative law, the German court justified the law-creating role of the European Court. In an earlier decision the Constitutional Court had,

[22] Cf. German report p. 132-133.

[23] Australian report p. 46-48; Canadian report p. 65; English report p. 268-269; Netherlands report p. 248-249.

[24] Greek report p. 169-172.

however, also pointed out certain limits to the transfer of sovereign rights to the European Communities according to German Constitution art. 24, and it had based its ruling, *inter alia*, on the legal situation existing in Italy.[25]

21. – Of general relevance at least for the European Union is the description which Mr. Justice *Kakouris* has given of the rôle of comparative law for the decision-making of the *European Court of Justice* in applying Community law. This analysis relates to all the fields of European law *outside* the aforementioned specific provisions of two of the Treaties directing the Court to apply the general principles of tort law common to the member states (*supra* no. 9).

One source from which the European Court draws is public international law. By emphasising the autonomy of Community law, the Court refuses to subject the Community itself or its relationship with the member states to the general rules of public international law. However, the Court feels free to refer to such rules in aid of the interpretation of Community law or for filling its gaps. The Court feels entitled to invoke the European Convention on Human Rights since all member states have ratified it.[26]

Much more relevant for the character and contents of Community law and also for its relationship with the member states is the very central rôle which comparison with the laws of the member states plays in the practice of the European Court. As Mr. Justice *Kakouris* assures us, such comparative inquiries are undertaken in almost every case, although usually this does not appear from the reasons of the decisions; often, however, the Attorney-General's opinion reveals this material, and these opinions are published together with the decision. The report emphasises that the Court's comparative inquiry is not the only and not even the primary method of the Court's interpreting Community law.

Comparative interpretation is subject to teleological interpretation. The reporter explains the relationship between these two methods of interpretation by distinguishing between two steps searching for the *telos* of a rule of Community law: In the first place, the purpose of such a rule is searched in the laws of the member states; and that is an application of comparative law proper. But if this inquiry is not conclusive (*e.g.*, because relevant rules are lacking or the existing ones are hopelessly contradictory) or if the common legal denominator is not adequate for the purposes of Community law, then the Court must directly inquire into the common convictions in order to find a common denominator on a level beyond that of the laws of the member states. In the words of Mr. Justice *Kakouris*, the Court "doit

[25] German report *infra* p. 134.
[26] Report on the EuCJ *infra* p. 102.

agir comme si elle était la conscience de l'Europe" and this implies a creative element.[27]

iii. Rules shared with other countries

22. – This section comprises two rather different classes of situations which the title cannot equally well express. The first class to which the title alludes refers to a common set of unwritten rules, the typical example being the Anglo-American common law. The equivalent phenomenon on the level of codification or legislation is the wholesale reception of a foreign legal system or of major parts of it, or the full or partial adoption of individual provisions. I will first deal with the special situation of an unwritten common law (*infra* no. 23) and then with adopted legislation (*infra* no. 24-26).

23. – Three out of the five reports from *Ango-American countries* – with the characteristic exception of the two United States reports – emphasise the predominant rôle of comparison with other major common law countries. The common heritage of the common law as understood in England was so strong in Australia, that until the 1970s the unwritten law in force in Australia was thought to be English law because this had been received in the country and because the Privy Council as the final appellate court was located in England and manned with English Law Lords.[28] And the Anglo-Canadian report discloses a "major difficulty of deciding what, in law, is foreign" because the common law is not bound up with, nor limited to, one particular country.[29] Only in the last two decades a certain emancipation of Australian and Canadian law from English law may be observed, one of the reasons being the increasing integration of English law into European law, another, a higher degree of consumer protection in Australia, and a third, more independent legislation.[30]

Nevertheless, much stronger than some decentralising trends is the unity and cohesion of the common law. This is confirmed by some figures: In the decade between 1983 and 1992, more than 80% of foreign cases cited by published Australian decisions were English cases.[31] A comparable count by the English reporter for six years in the period between 1972 and 1993 discloses that between 65 and 75% of the references to foreign law are to common law jurisdictions.[32]

---

[27] *Ibidem infra* p. 102-107, and, in particular, p. 103-104.

[28] Australian report *infra* p. 27-29.

[29] Anglo-Canadian report p. 59.

[30] Australian report p. 5.

[31] *Ibidem* p. 27.

[32] *Cf.* English report p. 263-265; the references in conflict cases and to EC-law and the decisions of the European Court of Justice are discounted.

24. – The nearest equivalent to a common unwritten is a common written law. This situation – combined with a very small size country – can be found in *Luxembourg*. The French five major codes are in force in this country, although without the major amendments and revisions they have undergone in France. Other legislation is patterned either on French or on Belgian models. Since there is no law faculty in the country, law students must study abroad and they do so either in France or in Belgium. A last factor is a very small number of judicial decisions by Luxembourg courts which, moreover, are rarely published.

The combination of all these special factors means in practical terms that very few judicial decisions would *not* contain references to foreign law, especially French but also Belgian law.[33]

On the basis of legal history one might expect a similar phenomenon for Brazil and for Quebec. But that expectation is only fulfilled for *Quebec*, although the report makes this important point only in passing.[34] By contrast, the main source of inspiration for *Brazilian* law is not Portuguese law but has been French law in the past and in the last 50 years other European legal systems and partly American law.[35] *Iceland*, a former colony of Denmark, still shares much of the legislation with that country. References are also made to Danish cases.[36]

25. – The *Greek* Civil Code of 1946 has been strongly influenced by German, French and Swiss law; these legal systems are therefore also used for the interpretation of the Code. The primary source is German law because it codified the law of the pandects which was regarded as a modern form of the Roman-Byzantine law that had been governing in Greece until 1946. Such recourse is particularly strong where the text of a Greek Code provision is identical with, or very similar to, a foreign provision.

Administrative law that was not codified had to be developed by the decisions of the Council of State which in the beginning followed closely its institutional model, *i.e.* the French *Counseil d'Etat*.[37]

26. – In *Australia* and *Germany*, similar references to provisions (and the case law) of a foreign country which served as a model for a specific domestic provision, occasionally occur.[38] In Australia, the most frequent occasion is furnished by legislation in the areas of commerce and economic regulation. Since this legislation is often patterned on United States stat-

---

[33] Note on Luxembourg *infra* p. 231, 233.
[34] Franco-Canadian report p. 93.
[35] Brazilian report p. 8, 13-16.
[36] Note on Iceland, *infra* p. 189-194.
[37] Greek report p. 158, 161-162, 183-185, 186-187.
[38] German report p. 134.

utes, American case law applying those statutes has been used as an aid for the interpretation of equivalent Australian legislation.[39]

iv. Maritime and air law

27. – Closely related to the preceding section, maritime and air law are fields with rather strong international and foreign links. Only few reports mention these fields. The *German* report emphasises the dominant position of English law for maritime matters.[40]According to the *Italian* report, maritime and air law are the only fields in which Italian courts will cite foreign legislation and "even" cases, especially in construing certain typical contract clauses.[41]

v. Conflict of laws

28. – In shaping new conflict of laws rules the *German* Federal Supreme Court has often referred to foreign conflict rules. One of the reasons for this openness towards foreign legal systems is obviously that the German statutory rules of conflict of laws contain many gaps. When creating a conflicts rule concerning collisions of ships in the territorial sea, the Federal Supreme Court supported the reference to the law of the place of collision by the argument, *inter alia*, that this rule is also accepted in various foreign countries; a decision in favour of this rule therefore promotes the international uniformity of judicial practice in this field. The same reason is invoked in another decision of the Federal Supreme Court in which it held that certain traffic accidents occurring abroad are subject to the law of the common residence of the tortfeasor and the injured driver.[42]

Of special interest is another application of the comparative method, *i.e.* to specify the German public policy clause. In examining the question whether the German public policy clause should be used against the application of foreign law, the Federal Supreme Court has in numerous cases given a broad comparative overview over the legal rules applied in different countries. The court tried to determine whether the foreign rule in issue represented one of the "typical" solutions used on the international scene, even if this idea was unknown in Germany. In most cases such a comparative survey saved the foreign rule from being disregarded as being contrary to German public policy. This procedure was used, for instance, to evaluate contracts with American attorneys stipulating contingent fees, in a case of unfair competition, in evaluating a one-year period for contesting the

---

[39] Australian report *infra* p. 33-34.

[40] German report p. 135-136; *cf.* also the Anglo-Canadian report p. 66-67.

[41] Italian report, original version p. 15-16; *cf.* also the German report p.137.

[42] German report p. 136.

legitimacy of a child, and as to the rule of Islamic law concerning paternal custody over minors.[43]

vi. Extradition

29. – In the law of extradition, *German* courts have used the same method, *i.e.* to determine an international standard with the help of comparative law.

In one case an arrested person objected to his extradition to a country that is still providing for the death penalty whereas the German constitution has abolished it. The Federal Constitutional Court refused to accept this argument since numerous "civilized countries and among them the leading democracies of the Western world" have retained the death penalty. A country like the Federal Republic of Germany could not enforce its own legal solution without regard to these facts.

Two other cases were dealing with foreign criminal trials which had been conducted in the absence of the accused; such procedure is contrary to German law. In a first case the Federal Supreme Court stated that the sentence of the foreign court is valid according to the law of the country requesting the extradition. And German public policy would only be affected if the trial in the absence of the accused would violate "high-ranking principles, that are recognized by all countries in which the rule of law prevails". In the given circumstances, however, this was not the case.

In 1982 the Federal Constitutional Court added a further criterion for the examination of cases in which an accused was sentenced in his absence, *i.e.* the procedural minimum standard of public international law which has to be taken into consideration according to German Constitution art. 25. The court referred to the decisions of three European countries to show that the application of such standards is justified in extradition cases.[44]

This court practice concerning extradition applies the same method as the decisions regarding German public policy in the conflict of laws. Also in extradition cases international standards are used to specify the public policy clause. Rules of foreign countries differing from or even contrary to German law are measured against these international standards. If the court comes to the conclusion that the foreign rule corresponds to a typical solution which is used in a number of foreign countries that share the same political ideas as Germany, the foreign provision will be saved from being disregarded as contravening German public policy. This comparative interpretation of the public policy clause is welcome, because it eliminates the parochial character of the clause and it tends to narrow and internationalize its application.

---

43 *Ibidem* p. 137.

44 *Ibidem* p. 137-138.

C. Legal Rules of a Purely Domestic Character

30. – The most interesting class of cases concerns rules of a purely domestic character. Amazingly and unfortunately, this class where the willingness to look to foreign law will be very modest, is hardly represented in the national reports. Nevertheless, the few cases that are mentioned are of particular relevance since often comparative law is used either to abrogate existing national rules or to fill gaps, although sometimes also for merely decorative purposes.

31. – The *abrogation* of existing written or unwritten rules can be exemplified by one Australian and a series of German cases.

The *Australian Mabo*-case stands for a particularly far-reaching abrogation of a well-settled common law rule. The decision by the High Court of Australia (1992) recognised land rights of the pre-colonial inhabitants of the country which, under the common-law doctrine of *terra nullius*, had been denied for over two centuries. Relying upon an array of 14 foreign cases, *inter alia* an opinion of the International Court of Justice (in the Western Sahara case of 1975), the High Court brought the common law in line with recent developments in foreign and in international law.[45]

In three *German* decisions the comparative method was used to justify a deviation from the clear statutory wording of German Civil Code § 253 , which excludes generally compensation of moral damages. In an early decision in which the Federal Supreme Court disregarded this rule in a case of invasion of personal privacy, it justified its conclusion by referring shortly to Swiss law. Shortly afterwards the Court gave a more comprehensive justification for its recourse to foreign law in a case in which the defendant, a newspaper publisher, argued that the preceding decision endangered the freedom of the press:

> "....., in almost all legal systems in which the value of the individual has the central position in the legal system as in ours, the compensation of moral damage is recognized as the adequate private law sanction for invasions of privacy."

Finally, redress was sought against this "judge-made" law from the Federal Constitutional Court. This Court based its confirming decision on the corresponding "development of the law in other countries of the Western world" and on the fact that the case-law of the German courts as to this question has succeeded to establish a legal situation "that is in broad conformity with this international development of the law".[46]

---

[45] *Cf.* the broad analysis of the decision in the Australian report *infra* p. 42-45.

[46] *Cf.* German report p. 139.

32. – The *filling of a gap* with the help of comparative law can be demonstrated by only two closely related examples. In both, a child claimed a new head of damages, namely for its "wrongful life". The German Federal Supreme Court was not only using this American legal term, but also discussed English and American decisions on this topic, most of them refusing such a claim. The Federal Supreme Court reached the same result, obviously under the influence of the foreign case-law.[47] A similar Israeli case was decided in the same sense, also relying strongly on American and English cases.[48]

33. – In the discussion, attention was drawn to a third "function" of voluntary recourse to foreign law, namely *ornamental purposes*. One of the reports confirms that occasionally references to foreign law are inserted into a judicial opinion, not as a necessary element of the court's reasoning but in order to illustrate the judge's learning (*infra* no. 36 at n. 50). It goes without saying that such tributes to comparative learning are a superfluous ornament at best and may even do a disservice to the serious study of comparative law.

III. Methods of Judicial Comparison

34. – The practical ways used by the courts in taking recourse to foreign law are an important aspect that should not be neglected.

i. Contents or effect of foreign rules

35. – One important initial question is, whether the courts direct their attention solely to the contents of a foreign rule or whether they regard also, or even exclusively its effects. Apparently, the courts mainly look to the *contents* of the foreign rule.

A few exceptions to this general attitude may, however, be found in decisions of the *German* Federal Constitutional Court. In two cases, the effects of a foreign legal provision were taken into account, and in both cases even exclusively. Both cases were concerned with the constitutionality of German statutes. The court endeavoured to assess the consequences of a decision declaring the relevant statute unconstitutional by examining the legal situation in such countries which had adopted a different legal solution. Also a recent ruling (dealing with a new legal regime for abortions) made a general reference to experiences with different legal solutions abroad; however, the court expressed some reservation "because the

[47] German report p. 139-140.
[48] Israeli report p. 218-219.

uncertain degree of comparability of the circumstances" qualifies the relevance of such experiences.[49]

For practical reasons it is, however, difficult to generalize such an approach for other courts, desirable as it is.

ii. Weight of comparative arguments

36. – The weight of foreign solutions is always limited. All reports agree that no court bases its decision solely on a foreign rule. The recourse to foreign law furnishes but a supplementary element for the court's reasoning. The Italian report even reduces the weight of such references to a merely "ornamental function."[50]

But even within these limits it is difficult to draw general conclusions about the relative weight of foreign law. The references to foreign legal materials are sometimes extremely short. If courts cite foreign decisions, in most cases they describe only their results, and rarely also their reasoning. Courts are, apparently, proceeding pragmatically and largely disregard the state of the art of the academic comparison of law.

iii. Countries chosen for comparison

37. – Where comparison is made with respect to rules with an international element (*supra* II B), that international element will very often indicate the countries that offer themselves for useful comparison.

For other cases, the selection of countries differs widely and appears sometimes to be rather accidental. Often only one foreign legal solution is mentioned by the court, without indicating the criterion used for the choice of that particular legal system. Occasionally, an overview over more than one foreign legal solution is given. Very seldom can one find descriptions of the legal situation in geographical or political units, which are then often oversimplistic.

Geographically broader findings will have a stronger persuasive value than others. This may be one reason why the German and the Italian Constitutional Courts like to refer to particular groups of countries, *e.g.* to the liberal or the Western democracies, to the peoples with a common cultural heritage or to the Western European countries.[51]

Whether the choice of the countries used for comparison is determined or limited by practical problems of access to information can unfortunately not be said. Several reports refer to problems of linguistic and documentary access. Some reports seem to imply that references to those countries are preferred which are most progressive in certain fields. For many fields of modern commercial law, the United States may qualify in this respect.[52]

[49] German report p. 141-142.
[50] Italian report, original version p. 19.
[51] German report p. 143; Italian report p. 54.
[52] *Cf.* Brazilian report p.16.

iv. Sources of information

38. – The ideal solution is a multi-jurisdictional court such as the European Court of Justice where each member state is represented by one judge. Mr. Justice *Kakouris* vividly describes the result: "un droit comparatif vivant se trouve autour de la table des délibérés."[53] On the Canadian Supreme Court, three out of the nine judges are lawyers from Quebec,[54] which must have a similar effect.

Comparative literature written in the court's language is another helpful source of information. The recourse to comparative literature has the additional advantage that one may expect, at least in general, a balanced account of the foreign law in question; that assists the courts to guard against prejudiced, one-sided information.

In which other ways do the courts obtain access to foreign legal material? A few supreme courts have research services, *e.g.* the European Court of Justice and the Japanese Supreme Court.[55] Supreme Courts may be entitled to ask official agencies to seek the necessary information. The German Federal Constitutional Court once asked the Ministry of Foreign Affairs for reports about the legal situation in 16 countries. The reports were delivered by the German diplomatic representations, in fact, most probably, by local attorneys, who regularly advise the representation. In another case foreign legal experts were heard in court, and the court asked for a statement by a private international association.[56]

It is difficult to establish the rôle of the attorneys of the parties in the obtaining of foreign legal materials. There is, however, some basis for the assertion that this source of information is important in cases where a high amount is in controversy.

IV. Justifications for the Use of Foreign Law

39. – A general postulate, such as *Zweigert*'s characterisation of comparative law as a "universal method of interpretation",[57] appears to be too undifferentiated.

40. – It is necessary *to distinguish* according to the extent to which a provision or rule of national law is related to provisions of international, European or foreign law, in conformity with the general idea underlying the

[53] Report on the EuCJ p. 106 no. 37.
[54] Anglo-Canadian report p. 69 n. 39.
[55] Report on the EuCJ p. 106; Japanese report p. 225.
[56] German report p. 144.
[57] *Zweigert*, Rechtsvergleichung als universale Interpretationsmethode: RabelsZ 15 (1949/50) 5-21 (esp. 9).

structure of the present report in chapter II. This helps in ascertaining the different justifications for the recourse to foreign law.

41. – The cases of *necessary comparison* (see *supra* II A) are self-explanatory and do not require any justification.

42. – *Voluntary comparison* with respect to norms with an international element (see *supra* II B) comprises quite different situations that have to be analyzed depending on the kind of foreign link which the relevant national provision has.

43. – For provisions which are based on *international uniform rules* (see *supra* II B i), the comparison with the laws of the other contracting parties has to be considered as required in order to preserve the uniformity which is intended and at first achieved by agreeing upon uniform rules. Therefore the task of comparison is, basically, the performance of a duty which derives from public international law.

44. – For *European law* (*supra* II B ii), the preceding argument of preserving uniformity is even more compelling.

45. – The linkages of maritime law, conflict of laws and the law of extradition (see *supra* II B iv-vi) with foreign countries and international situations suggest a two-fold regard of foreign law: first, as in other cases, to reach, especially in the fields of maritime law and conflict of laws, uniformity of judicial decisions, and thereby an implicit harmonisation of laws. Secondly, notably in the conflict of laws and in the law of extradition, to internationalize the interpretation and application of the public policy clauses; rules of foreign law should only in those cases be disregarded in which these rules are violating international standards.

46. – Where *rules are shared* or *provisions were adopted from* or inspired by *foreign legal systems* (see *supra* II B iii), two different justifications for looking to foreign law offer themselves. In the first case of shared rules, as typified by the common law, it is the common legal basis which justifies looking over the borders. This common element is so strong that the other jurisdictions which follow the same stream are not even perceived as having a "foreign" law; and recourse to that law is not felt as being an exercise in comparative law.

The situation is very different if the interpretation of a single adopted rule only is involved. This may be understood and justified on a narrow technical ground, namely as a resort to the legislative history of the adopted provision.

47. – Matters are quite different with respect to *purely domestic rules* or provisions (see *supra* II C). In these cases, recourse to foreign law is exceptional, and here it is more difficult to explain its necessity and to justify its application. The survey of the sparse case law suggests a distinction according to two different functions which comparative law may fulfill with respect to these genuinely "domestic" provisions: first, legal comparison helps to fill gaps in national law, especially if novel problems are arising in more than one country. Secondly, comparative law may assist in scrutinising and, if need be, even "overruling" the relevant rule or statutory provision. Both cases demonstrate the creative development of law by judges, either by filling legal gaps, or by overcoming an outmoded positive rule.

V. Why the Differences?

48. – If one discounts all variations which are due to differing degrees of accessibility of the relevant material on the use of foreign law by courts, *one major difference* as to the intensity of comparative research remains: Some countries like the United Kingdom, the United States and Japan are much less open to genuinely foreign law (apart from the other common jurisdictions) than other countries.

As history shows, this phenomenon is not to be explained merely by size. Until well into the 19th century United States courts were quite willing to look to foreign law.[58] The same is true for Japan in the first three decades of this century.[59] For the present abstinence another reason is given by the reporters: today there are so many cases of *domestic* courts that it is superfluous to look abroad.[60] The English report expresses this by quoting a judge as saying: "Why bother with foreign law when we have so much material of our own."

This observation cannot be better confirmed than by the note on Luxembourg: it is the dearth of domestic cases which drives the courts to French or Belgian law. And also the Israeli report asserts that the relatively frequent recourse to foreign law is due to the relatively scarce local case law.[61]

Nevertheless: there remain the cases of necessary comparison and those many rules and provisions with an international element. And even for purely domestic rules, comparative law may assist in overcoming an outdated rule or provision or it may assist in filling a gap existing in the national legal system.

---

[58] American report by *Levasseur* p. 317-323.

[59] Japanese report p. 224.

[60] American report by *Levasseur* p. 333; Japanese report p. 224, 228.

[61] Israeli report p. 220-221.

PART II

NATIONAL REPORTS

JIANFU CHEN*

The Use of Comparative Law by Courts: Australian Courts at the Crossroads**

INTRODUCTION

Australian law, in its origin, is predominantly English law brought to Australia with the early colonists as their 'birthright', in part based on a denial of the indigenous presence.[1] Indeed, Australian law, as a law distinct from its English source, is still in a process of emergence. The emergence of Australian law is marked by, first, a gradual departure from the domination of English influence through a series of evolutionary events; secondly, the increasing influence of wideranging international and comparative jurisprudence and; thirdly, a continuing search for Australian solutions to Australian problems. Essentially, English law forms the 'skeleton' of Australian law, but the emerging Australian law is taking its shape by absorbing experience from various jurisdictions as well as international and comparative jurisprudence. It is in this process that comparative law becomes important not just for academics but also for judges and practitio-

* Senior Lecturer, School of Law and Legal Studies, La Trobe University, Australia.

** See List of Abbreviations at end of Chapter.

[1] Until very recently, Australia was regarded as a *terra nullius*. Under common law, such a territory was acquired by the colonists by 'settlement' and, upon settlement, English law, common law and statute law, was received into Australia denying any pre-existing Aboriginal laws. See James Crawford, *Australian Courts of Law*, 2nd edition, Melbourne: Oxford University Press (1988), ch.2; and Marion Pascoe, 'The Diffusion of Juridical Models', in Alice Tay (ed.), *Australian Law and Legal Thinking Between the Decades: A Collection of 33 Australian Reports to the XIIIth International Congress of Comparative Law*, University of Sydney (1990), at 1-9. The doctrine of *terra nullius* was only formally rejected by the High Court of Australia in 1992 in *Mabo & Others v. State of Queensland* (1992) 107 ALR 1; (1992) 175 CLR 1; and (1992) 66 ALJR 408.

U. Drobnig and S. van Erp (eds.), The Use of Comparative Law by Courts, 25–57

ners.[2] The use of comparative law by Australian courts is examined from this perspective.[3]

Because of the nature of federalism in Australia and the common law tradition, the absorption of international jurisprudence has not been without controversy. This is particularly so when Australian courts attempt to use international human rights jurisprudence. Yet, it has been in the human rights area that Australian courts have been engaged in extensive discussions on the use of international and comparative law.

This report is divided into three parts. Part I examines changing attitudes of Australian courts towards English law and comparative law in general. Part II analyses the status of international law in the Australian domestic legal system and the use of international human rights jurisprudence by Australian courts. Part III discusses three recent High Court decisions to illustrate the extent and limits to which international and comparative jurisprudence may be used by Australian courts.

I. THE USE OF COMPARATIVE LAW FROM A HISTORICAL PERSPECTIVE

A. An overview

Until the 1970s, English law exerted an almost exclusive influence over Australian judge-made law. This is partly because of the fact that the Privy Council in England remained the final appellant tribunal until the 1970s for federal matters and until 1986 for state matters, and partly because of the self-imposed obligations of the High Court to follow the precedents of the House of Lords.[4] Through a series of evolutionary events, the last residual constitutional tie with Great Britain was cut in 1986 by the Australian Acts

[2] See e.g. Sir Anthony Mason, 'Changing the Law in a Changing Society', (1993) 67 *ALJ* 568, at 574. Sir Anthony was then Chief Justice of the High Court of Australia.

[3] Following the suggestion of the General Reporter for this topic, 'the use of comparative law' is taken to mean the consideration by courts of any 'foreign law'. 'Foreign law' in an Australian context includes also international law, both customary law and conventional law to which Australia is a party but where no domestic implementing law has been made. It should also be pointed out that this report deals with the use of 'foreign law' to resolve domestic disputes not necessarily foreign-related; it does not deal with rules of private international law.

[4] See generally James Crawford, 'Australian Law After Two Centuries', (1988) 11 *Syd.L.Rev.* 444; Justice J. Toohey, 'Towards an Australian Common Law', (1990) *Aust.B.Rev.* 185; Ross Parsons, 'English Precedents in Australian Courts', (1949-50) 1 *U. of W.A.Annul.L.Rev.* 211; Alex C. Castles, 'The Reception and Status of English Law in Australia', (1963) *Adel.L.Rev.* 1; and Harold Luntz, 'Throwing Off the Chains: English Precedent and the Law of Torts in Australia', in M P Ellinghaus, A J Bradbrook & A J Duggan (eds.), *The Emergence of Australian Law*, Sydney: Butterworths (1989), at 70-88.

1986.[5] Thereafter and increasingly, Australian courts have paid serious attention to decisions from other common law jurisdictions as well. However, until this day, English influence remains the strongest: in the judgments reported in the *Australian Law Reports* from 1983 to 1989, 1114 non-Australian cases were judicially considered by judges, of which 85% were English.[6] Again, of the 680 foreign cases considered in judgements reported in the *Australian Law Reports* from 1991-1994, some 83% were English cases.[7] Other foreign cases consist mainly of decisions from Canada, New Zealand and the United States.[8] These tables also indicate a decline in judicial consideration of decisions from other jurisdictions: from 1983 to 1987, of all cases as contained in the 'Table of Cases Judicially Considered' in the *Australian Law Reports*, 65% were Australian cases.[9] The percentage of Australian cases increased to 75% during 1987-1989.[10] An assessment of that Table for 1991-1994 reveals a similar percentage (74.8%).[11] However, since the bulk of foreign cases are English, such a decline is more precisely a reflection of the decrease of English influence over Australian judge-made law.

The frequent judicial consideration of non-Australian cases contrasts strongly with the discussion of non-Australian statutes by Australian judges in their decisions. Only an insignificant number of foreign statutes is listed in the 'Table of Statutes Judicially Considered' in the *Australian Law Reports*. A study of the use of comparative law by courts is therefore mainly a study of the use of foreign judicial decisions. In this Part, we shall then concentrate on changing attitudes of Australian Courts towards foreign cases.

B. Conformity with English law upheld

Since Australia was treated as a settled colony, English common law and rules of equity were substantially received in each of the colonies (now States).[12] Some British statutory law, if appropriate to the new colonies,

[5] Australia (Request and Consent) Act 1985 (Cth); the Australia Acts (Request) Act 1985 passed by the Parliament of each State; and Australia Act 1986 (U.K.). These Acts severed the residual constitutional (legislative, executive and judicial) links between Australian States and the United Kingdom. The evolutionary events will be discussed below.

[6] Toohey, *supra* note 4, at 187.

[7] Based on my calculation of cases listed as 'judicially considered' in *Australian Law Reports Cumulative Supplement Index and Tables Volumes 101-120 (1991-1994).*

[8] *Ibid.*

[9] Crawford, *supra* note 4, at 446.

[10] Toohey, *supra* note 4, at 197.

[11] See *supra* note 7. Of course, the percentage of non-Australian cases cited as contrast with 'considered' would be much higher.

[12] For detailed discussions, see Crawford, *supra* note 1, at 14. Although the pre-condition of reception was that such law would be 'suitable' to be received and applied in conditions of the colonies, little scrutiny of local conditions was actually carried out carefully by courts

was also received. However, English law has not only provided a foundation for Australian law, English decisions were also followed in Australian courts as a matter of course after the date of reception.[13] As a result, 'the initial reception flowed without much distinction into the assumptions of precedent.'[14]

There are several reasons for the authoritative status of English judgments in Australian courts. Initially, common solutions to common problems within the British Empire were thought to be possible and, therefore, uniformity and harmony of law in the British Empire were emphasised.[15] Such uniformity within the Empire was upheld by the Privy Council as being 'of utmost importance.'[16] This view was echoed in Australia in the following words:

> "Diversity in the development of the common law (using that expression not in the historical but in the very widest sense) seems to me to be an evil. Its avoidance is more desirable than a preservation here of what we regard as sounder principle."[17]

Secondly, until quite recently, the Privy Council was still the final appeal court from Australian courts. Naturally, uniformity within the British Empire has meant the conformity with the common law *as declared* in England. It should not be surprising that such conformity was seen, as noted by Sir Anthony,[18] as 'a virtue, if not a necessity.'

As a result, not only were both judgments of the Privy Council binding on Australian courts and decisions of the House of Lords in the absence of Australian authority followed by Australian courts, but also, in the cases of conflict between the High Court of Australia and the House of Lords, the latter instead of the former was to be followed.[19] Further, decisions of the English Court of Appeal were ordinarily followed by Australian courts and

---

in practice to test 'suitability'. See Alex C. Castles, *An Australian Legal History*, Sydney: Law Book Company Ltd (1982), at 507.

13 In the case of statutory law, British Parliament, by virtue of dominion and control over the colony, was also able to pass 'paramount force' statutes for Australia after the date of reception. See Crawford, *supra* note 1, at 15.

14 *Ibid*.

15 Paul E von Nessen, 'The Use of American Precedents by the High Court of Australia, 1901-1987', (1992) 14 *Adel.L.R.* 181, at 182.

16 '[I]t is of the utmost importance that in all parts of the Empire where English law prevails, the interpretation of that law by the courts should be as nearly as possible the same.': *Trimble v Hill* [1879] 5 App Cas 342, at 345, quoted in Luntz, *supra* note 4, at 71.

17 *per* Justice Dixon in *Wright v Wright* (1948) 77 CLR 191, at 210.

18 See Sir Anthony Mason, 'Future Directions in Australian Law', (1987) 13 *Monash U.L.R.* 149, at 150-1.

19 '... it should now be formally decided that it will be a wise general rule of practice that in cases of clear conflict between a decision of the House of Lords and of the High Court, this court, and other courts in Australia, should follow a decision of the House of Lords upon matters of general legal principle.': *per* Latham CJ in *Piro v W. Foster Co. Ltd.* (1943) 68 CLR 313, at 320.

not normally departed from by the High Court of Australia.[20] Hence, a judge in the Supreme Court of Victoria said in 1975:

> "I cannot find, nor can I remember, nor have I been referred to any decision of the [English] Court of Appeal that this court has not followed except where the High Court or the House of Lords has expressed a contrary opinion. In my judgment a decision of the [English] Court of Appeal should be departed from in this court only in exceptional circumstances."[21]

The logic of the time was that 'it is the same law in England as in Australia, and we must avoid divergent interpretation of it at all costs.'[22]

C. Changing attitude towards English precedents

Exceptions to the conformity with English law did, however, exist before the final abolition of all appeals to the Privy Council by the Australian Acts 1986. In fact, there was a series of evolutionary events that gradually led to the departure from English domination and the emergence of Australian law.

The change of attitude towards English precedents first occurred in the 1960s in *Parker v R*.[23] Although the case was seen by some as 'unfortunate' and only justified as furthering a perceived 'purity of doctrine' rather than asserting independence of English law,[24] *Parker* nevertheless 'shattered a long Australian tradition'.[25] Sure, there were many other occasions in which the High Court departed from the House of Lords.[26] However, so long as the Privy Council remained the ultimate court of appeal, Australian judges would naturally look to English decisions for guidance.[27]

---

[20] Luntz, *supra* note 4, at 70. As late as 1975 it was still asserted that in the absence of authority of the High Court of Australia, State Supreme Courts should follow the decisions of the English Court of Appeal: *per* Barwick CJ in *Public Transport Comm (NSW) v J Murray-More (NSW) Pty Ltd* (1975) 132 CLR 336, at 341. In the same case (at 349), Gibbs J went further to say that decisions of the English Court of Appeal should be treated by State Supreme Courts as binding authorities.

[21] *per* Starke J in *Pratt Goldsmith v Pratt* (1975) VR 378, at 391.

[22] Parsons, *supra* note 4, at 215.

[23] (1963) 111 CLR 610. In this case, the High Court declined to follow the House of Lords' decision, *DDP v Smith* [1961] AC 290.

[24] See comments referred to in Crawford, *supra* note 4, at p.445, and in Luntz, *supra* note 4, at 76.

[25] A.R. Blackshield, 'The High Court: Change and Decay', (1980) 5 *Legal Service Bulletin* 107, at 107.

[26] For a brief chronology of some of the significant departures, see Toohey, *supra* note 4, at 193-195; Luntz, *supra* note 4, at 76-78.

[27] Sir Anthony Mason, 'Jurisdictional and Procedural Constraints on the Evolution of Australian Law', (1984) 10 *Syd.L.Rev*. 254, at 256.

The gradual abolition of appeals[28] to the Privy Council gave Australian courts a greater degree of freedom to pursue an indigenous approach that would be more suitable to Australian local conditions and depend less on analysis of English law. Further, the U.K membership of the European Community and the likelihood of European influence on English law, the greater consumer (rather than commercial or maritime) orientation in Australian law, and the much more independent development of Australian statutory law all added to the need for a close examination of Australian local conditions.[29] The failure of the Privy Council to appreciate local conditions also led to some strong criticisms.[30] For instance, in *Viro v R*,[31] Murphy J noted that the Privy Council paid little attention to local conditions of the components of the British Empire and imposed limits on local legislatures. Further, his Honour went on:

> "More importantly, the great body of common or decisional law was under the Privy Council's control. The appeal (as of right or by leave) to the Privy Council thus enabled the United Kingdom to control the interpretation of colonial legislation and the development of decisional law. Consequently, *a significant part of Australian law has been made in the United Kingdom rather than in Australia and, inevitably, much of this law was evolved to meet changing conditions in the United Kingdom and to facilitate its emergence as a world power*."[32] (Emphasis supplied)

These factors then led to the historical ruling of the High Court in *Viro*, and a definite statement in *Cook v Cook*,[33] regarding the authority of English decisions and the status of cases from other common law jurisdictions.

In *Viro*,[34] a case regarded as the climax of the assertion of national and judicial independence,[35] the High Court declared that it no longer regarded itself as bound by the decisions of the Privy Council, that State Courts would be bound to follow decisions of the High Court, and that State Supreme Courts might regard themselves as bound by decisions of the Privy Council only when there was no relevant decision of the High Court, no matter when decided.

---

[28] Appeal to the Privy Council was abolished in stages, first in federal matters, then appeal from the High Court, and finally appeal from State Supreme Courts: Privy Council (Limitation of Appeals) Act 1968 (Cth); Privy Council (Appeal from the High Court) Act 1975 (Cth); and Australia Act 1986 (Cth and Imp) (S.11).

[29] See e.g. Mason (1984), *supra* note 27, at 256; Sir Anthony Mason, 'The Use and Abuse of Precedent', (1988) 4 *Aust.B.Rev.* 93, at 107; and Toohey, *supra* 4, at 196-197.

[30] For instance, the above mentioned *Parker* case was overturned by the Privy Council: *Parker v R* (1964) 111 CLR 665.

[31] (1978) 18 ALR 257.

[32] *Id.*, at 313.

[33] (1987) 61 ALJR 25.

[34] *Viro v R* (1978) 18 ALR 257.

[35] Blackshield, *supra* note 25, at 107.

In the joint decision by Mason, Wilson, Deane and Dawson JJ. in *Cook*, their Honours continued the process started in *Viro*:

> "There is one further matter which should be mentioned. In the Full Court of the Supreme Court Matheson J., having expressed the view that the comments of Latham C.J. and Dixon J. in relation to the reduced content of the duty of care were 'only dicta', regarded himself as constrained to accept the reasoning of the majority of the English Court of Appeal in *Nettleship v. Weston*... In support of that approach, his Honour referred to a number of statements in cases in this and other courts in which it has been said that in the absence of controlling authority a State Supreme Court, including a 'Supreme Court on appeal', should, as a general rule, follow decisions of the English Court of Appeal. ... Whatever may have been the justification for such statements in times when the Judicial Committee of the Privy Council was the ultimate court of appeal or one of the ultimate courts of appeal for this country, those statements should no longer be seen as binding upon Australian courts. The history of this country and of the common law makes it inevitable and desirable that the courts of this country will continue to obtain assistance and guidance from the learning and reasoning of United Kingdom courts just as Australian courts benefit from the learning and reasoning of other great common law courts. Subject, perhaps, to the special position of decisions of the House of Lords given in the period in which appeals lay from this country to the Privy Council, the precedents of other legal systems are not binding and are useful only to the degree of the persuasiveness of their reasoning."[36]

In short, no Australian court is bound as a matter of precedent by non-Australian decisions, no matter how influential they might be.[37] Further, the value of English decisions, like judgments from other common law jurisdictions, depends on how persuasive they are in their reasoning with the decisions of the House of Lords before 1986 as possible exceptions.

This statement was made in general terms, covering not only English decisions, but also precedents from all other legal systems. This statement therefore lays down an authoritative principle guiding the use of comparative law by Australian courts.

D. The use of comparative law by Australian courts

With this historical background, some general features regarding the use of comparative law by Australian courts can now be sketched.

---

[36] (1987) 61 ALJR 25, at 30-31.

[37] Crawford (1988), *supra* note 4, at 450.

To start with, there are ambiguities in the statement of the High Court in *Cook*.[38] These ambiguities, however, should not diminish the significance of the statement in enhancing the development of Australian law as distinct from English law. What is important is that the rules as laid down in the above statement establish the precondition for an Australian jurisprudence.[39] These rules enable Australian courts to use wide international and comparative jurisprudence in developing an 'Australian law':

> "In formulating principles of judge-made law and in interpreting municipal statutes we have had a close eye to what is happening elsewhere. We constantly look to relevant principles of comparative law and to the decisions of international and national tribunals. Naturally we look primarily to decisions in other common law jurisdictions. But our researches do not stop there. Sometimes it is desirable to ascertain what other systems of law have to say about a particular legal problem. Legal problems, because they often reflect human problems, are not unique to any one system of law. And the appropriate answers must be moulded, at least in part, by reference to experience and, in large measure, experience is common to all peoples."[40]

It is also under these rules that some Australian courts are willing to entertain challenges even to long-standing doctrines of the common law as developed in England.[41]

But the use of comparative law is not without 'discrimination'. As Sir Anthony Mason has pointed out,[42] if Australian authority can be found for a fairly straightforward proposition, it should be cited in preference to English authority. Although it is acknowledged that Australian and English laws are taking different paths, in particular as a result of English membership of the EC and therefore the European influence on English law,[43] it has been explicitly warned that there is no reason to distance Australian courts from the continuing evolution of the law in England.[44] The greater

---

[38] The statement made by the High Court in *Cook* contains at least two ambiguities: a/ What is the 'special position of the decisions of the House of Lords', which is qualified by the expression 'perhaps'? b/ The expression 'useful only to the degree of the persuasiveness of their reasoning' also presents ambiguities. How persuasive should they be – wholly, partially or only slightly – before an Australian court can rely on them? See 'Statement by High Court on respect to be paid to precedents of other legal systems', (1987) 61 *ALJ* 263, at 264.

[39] Crawford (1988), *supra* note 4, at 450.

[40] See Sir Anthony Mason, 'The Relationship Between International Law, National Law, and its Application in National Courts', (1992) 18 *Commonwealth Law Bulletin* 750, at 753. See also Mason (1987), *supra* note 18, at 154.

[41] See Luntz, *supra* note 4, at 86. See further discussions in Parts II & III of this report.

[42] Sir Anthony Mason, 'The Role of Counsel and Appellate Advocacy', (1984) 58 *ALJ* 537, at 540.

[43] See e.g. Mason (1988), *supra* note 29, at 107-108; and Toohey, *supra* note 4, at 196.

[44] Mason (1987), *supra* note 18, at 154.

value of reasoning in judgments of common law courts, especially, courts of Canada, New Zealand and the United States, than those of other jurisdictions, has also been emphasised.[45] Even among common law jurisdictions, Canadian and especially New Zealand authorities are perceived as presenting less difficulties than those from United States courts, since the latter have long departed from English law and often apply different principles in different jurisdictions.[46]

However, American influence is increasing and will continue to increase, particularly in constitutional interpretation and in the area of restricted trade practice.[47] The increasing American influence in these areas of law can be explained by a number of factors. First, the Australian Constitution is partly based upon the American Constitution, both in form and substance. In the early years of constitutional interpretation, the High Court enthusiastically embraced American constitutional doctrines.[48] Although American influence decreased since the *Engineers* case in which the previous High Court's attitude towards American case law was re-assessed,[49] leading American constitutional cases continued to be considered seriously by the High Court.[50] Secondly, English influence over Australian legislation was not institutionalised and, therefore, European and North American ideas of and approach to legislation began to influence Australian legislation as early as the 19th century.[51] As a result, North American legislation models, in particular in trade practice, consumer protection, freedom of information, securities regulation, corporations laws, bankruptcy law and environment law, have been increasingly accepted and adopted in Austra-

---

[45] Mason (1984), *supra* note 27, at 257; and Toohey, *supra* note 4, at 197. See also *supra* notes 6-11.

[46] Mason (1984), *supra* note 27, at 257. On using American judgments, Sir Anthony has said: 'There is simply no point in referring to United States authority unless it demonstrates universal and unqualified acceptance of a particular rule of common law or of equity or unless it offers an illuminating exposition of principle, such as the judgments of Justices Holmes, Cardozo, Brandeis and Learned Hand provide.': Mason (1984), *supra* note 42, at 539. He has also warned: 'American case law is a trackless jungle in which only the most intrepid and discerning Australian lawyers should venture. It is possible to find American authority to support almost any conceivable proposition of law. ... It is essential therefore to use American authority with care and discrimination.': Mason (1988), *supra* note 29, at 108-109.

[47] Mason (1984), *supra* note 27, at 257. For an empirical study of the use of American precedents by the High Court during 1901-1987, see von Nessen, *supra* note 15.

[48] See Table 1 in von Nessen, *supra* note 15, at 194; and Jerome B. Elkind (ed.), *The Impact of American Law on English and Commonwealth Law*, St. Paul, Minnesota: West Publishing Co. (1978), especially at 17-19.

[49] *Amalgamated Society of Engineers v. Adelaide Steamship Co. Ltd.* (1920) 28 CLR 129.

[50] See discussions in Elkind, *supra* note 48, at 19-20; and Brian Galligan, *Politics of the High Court*, St Lucia, Queensland: University of Queensland Press (1987), at 96-102.

[51] Toohey, *supra* note 4, at 186.

lia.[52] Naturally, Australian judges would look into American doctrines in interpreting these statutes.

Although it is mainly in the criminal law area that Australian courts started the process of departing from English domination and later resolved the conflict of authority between English decisions and Australian cases,[53] a quick survey of the *Australian Law Reports* indicates that foreign cases other than English are much more often cited in areas of constitutional law, civil and commercial law than in criminal law. Also, the High Court appears to lead the way in using international and comparative law. For instance, a survey regarding the use of American precedents by Australian courts indicates that the High Court much more frequently uses American precedents than do the State Supreme Courts of Victoria and New South Wales – two most representative Australian State Courts.[54]

Finally, in formulating an 'Australian' law,[55] Australian courts have paid great attention to general international developments and to conforming with international standards. As Sir Anthony has recently pointed out after discussing recent Australian legal developments:

> "It is one thing to say of the developments which I have mentioned that they have no precise counterpart in English law and that they are distinctive in that sense. But it would be quite another thing to say that we are bringing into existence by judicial decision a body of law in this country which has definite characteristics that set it apart from the law as it exists elsewhere. Our common law is, despite variations, very similar to the common law as it exists elsewhere. Furthermore, ease of communication and growing familiarity with other countries and their cultures, as well as the internationalisation of commerce and politics, are encouraging a greater unity and harmony of legal rules throughout the world. So the trend is towards similarity rather than distinctiveness."[56]

Indeed, it is in this sense that Sir Anthony has emphasised the importance of comparative law.[57]

There are however difficulties and obstacles in bringing Australian law into unity and harmony of legal rules internationally. The use of 'interna-

---

[52] Toohey, *supra* note 4, at 186-187; Mason (1987), *supra* note 18, at 149; Pascoe, *supra* note 1; and von Nessen, *supra* note 15, at 184-185. See also Elkind, *supra* note 48, *passim*.

[53] See e.g. *Parker v R* (1964) 111 CLR 665; *Viro v R* (1978) 18 ALR 257. More recently: *R. v. Judge Bland; Ex parte Director of Public Prosecutions* (1987) V.R 225; and *Wilson v. R* (1992) 107 ALR 257.

[54] See von Nessen, *supra* note 15, at 203-206.

[55] The term 'common law in Australia' formally replaced that of 'English common law' following an amendment to s.80 of the Commonwealth *Judiciary Act 1903* in 1988.

[56] Mason (1993), *supra* note 2, at 573. See also Sir Anthony Mason, 'The Influence of International and Transnational Law on Australian Municipal Law', (1996) 7 *Pub.L.Rev* 20, and 'An Australian Common Law', (1996) *Law in Context* 81.

[57] Mason (1992), *supra* note 40, at 753.

tional law' by Australian courts is controversial. The issue becomes particularly so in the area of human rights protection, to be discussed below.

II. THE USE OF INTERNATIONAL HUMAN RIGHTS JURISPRUDENCE

A. The status of international law in the Australian domestic legal system

Unlike their status in many other countries, international treaties ratified by the Australian Government do not automatically become part of Australian domestic law and, therefore, treaties are not binding in themselves in the domestic legal system. This position has been stated by the High Court unambiguously:

> "It is a well settled principle of the common law that a treaty not terminating a state of war has no legal effect upon the rights and duties of Australian citizens and is not incorporated into Australian law on its ratification by Australia. ... To achieve this result the provisions have to be enacted as part of our domestic law, whether by Commonwealth or State statute."[58]

Furthermore, an Australian court will only apply a rule of customary international law so long as it is consistent with municipal statutes and common law principles as finally declared by national courts.[59]

Technically, it is the strict separation of powers between the Legislature and the Executive and the division of powers between the Commonwealth and States that prevent treaties ratified by the Australian Government taking direct effect in Australia.[60] Ideologically, however, international law is perceived by common law lawyers as being too general and vague to be applied precisely. On this point, Justice Kirby, in his extra-curial writing, puts it thus:

> "For me, as for most judges and lawyers of this century, brought up in the common law, international law was a vague *mélange* of political statements and motherhood principles – not to be compared with the precise, renewable and generally just rules of municipal law made by

---

[58] *per* Mason J (as he then was), in *Koowarta v. Bjelke-Petersen* (1982) 39 ALR 417, at 459. Reference to early authorities has been omitted from the above quotation.

[59] Mason (1992), *supra* note 40, at 750.

[60] For further discussions, see James Crawford & W.R. Edeson, 'International Law and Australian Law', in K.W. Ryan, (ed.), *International Law in Australia*, 2nd ed., Sydney: The Law Book Company (1984), at 71-135; and Andrew Byrnes and Hilary Charlesworth, 'Federalism and the International Legal Order: Recent Developments in Australia', (1985) 79 *Am.J.Int'l.L.* 622.

> legislatures answerable to the people and judges accountable in the courts."[61]

Precisely for these reasons, international law, whether conventional or customary, had not made a significant influence upon the development of Australian law until very recently.[62]

This does not, however, mean that international law has no role to play in the Australian domestic legal system. In fact, the common law is always flexible in accommodating international, at least customary, law. This flexibility can also cause problems and ambiguities. For instance, Crawford and Edeson have identified three different propositions, each of them was supported by the same authority – *Chow Hung Ching v. R.* (1949) 77 CLR 449 – that international law is a part of domestic law; that it is not a part of the law but may nevertheless be applied by the courts and that it is merely one of the sources of municipal law, relevant in legal reasoning but lacking more direct applicability.[63]

Even when an international obligation of Australia is embodied in the domestic law, Australian courts will still face many problems. Indeed, the relationship between an instrument embodying an international obligation of Australia and a municipal statute dealing with that subject matter became a major issue in a recent case in the Federal Court of Australia.[64] In the course of judgment, Gummow J identified six possible situations of tension between international obligations and Australian municipal law:

> "First, there is the basic proposition that if the international obligation involves enforcement in the courts which is not already authorised by municipal law, legislation is needed to make the necessary changes in the obligation; it is for the Parliament and not the Executive to make or alter municipal law. ...
>
> Secondly, not all legislative approval of treaties or other obligations entered into by the Executive renders the treaty binding upon individuals within Australia as part of the law of the Commonwealth, or creates justiciable rights for individuals. An example is s 3 of Charter of the United Nations Act 1945 (Cth). This simply states that the Charter is 'approved', something insufficient to render the Charter binding on individuals in Australia. ...
>
> Thirdly, the Parliament may make no attempt to incorporate expressly into domestic law the terms of a convention which has been ratified by

---

[61] Justice Michael Kirby, 'The Australian Use of International Human Rights Norms: From Bangalore to Balliol – A View from the Antipodes', (1993) 16 *UNSW.L.J.* 363, at 364.

[62] Gillian Triggs, 'Customary International Law and Australian Law', in Ellinghaus, Bradbrook & Duggan (eds.), *supra* note 4, at 376.

[63] See Crawford & Edeson, *supra* note 60, at 77-78.

[64] *Minister for Foreign Affairs and Trade and Others v Magno and Another* (1993) 112 ALR 529.

> Australia. Nevertheless, the terms of the convention may be resorted to in order to help resolve an ambiguity in domestic primary or subordinate legislation. ... This is on the footing that, *prima facie*, the Parliament should be taken as intending to legislate in conformity and not in conflict with international law. ...
>
> Fourthly, in some cases, notwithstanding the absence in the statute of any reference to a particular international obligation, it may be evident that the statute adopted the nomenclature of a Convention in anticipation of subsequent Australian ratification. If so, where the language of the statute is ambiguous it is permissible to refer to the provisions of the Convention to assist resolution of an ambiguity, but not to displace the plain words of the statute. ...
>
> Fifthly, difficult questions of administrative law and of judicial review arise where, whilst the international obligation or agreement in question is not in terms imported into municipal law and the municipal law is not ambiguous, nevertheless, upon the proper construction of the municipal law, regard may be had by a decision maker exercising a discretion under that law to the international agreement or obligation. If that agreement or obligation is misconstrued by the decision maker, is there reviewable error of law? Or is the 'error' to be classified as factual in nature? If the latter is correct, the scope for judicial review will be narrowed. The question is unresolved. ...
>
> Finally, in other cases, an expression used in a law made by the Parliament may have given to it expressly in that law the meaning it bears in a particular convention. ... In cases falling within this last category, where the treaty or other international obligation is 'referred to' within the meaning of s15AB(2)(d) of the Acts Interpretation Act 1901 (Cth), consideration may be given to it not only to determine provisions which are ambiguous or obscure, but for the wider purposes spelled out in s15AB(1). It may be sufficient to attract to s15AB that the agreement, whilst 'not referred' to in the statute itself, was referred to in the second reading speech."[65]

These propositions define fairly clear the role of international law in interpreting domestic statutes. Its role in interpreting common law principles is, however, unclear. Indeed, it is in areas of common law that the use of international law, especially international human rights law, has caused great controversies.

[65] *Id.*, at 534-5. Reference to various English and Australian authorities have been omitted in the above quotation. S.15AB of the Acts Interpretation Act 1901 (Cth) defines the use of extrinsic materials for the purpose of statutory interpretation. S.15AB(2)(d) allows the court to take into consideration any treaty or other international agreement that is referred to in the Act, in the ascertainment of the meaning of the provision.

B. International law and human rights in Australia

Australia is a country without a Bill of Rights, nor does the Australian Constitution provide many provisions directly conferring individual rights.[66] Human rights are therefore principally protected by traditional methods of common law in Australia.

Common law protection of human rights tends to be negative rather than positive (i.e. civil liberties are treated as residual rather than as positive rights). Deficiencies of such negative protection, in particular in relation to the protection of vulnerable groups, have been well recognised in Australia.[67]

Positive protection of human rights can however be found in many international treaties ratified by the Australian Government. The problem is that, as discussed above, international treaties cannot be enforced by courts directly without enabling legislation made by Parliament. Among all major international treaties ratified by the Australian Government, only rights as contained in racial and sex discrimination conventions can be said to have been translated into domestically enforceable rights through enabling legislation passed by the Parliament.[68]

Furthermore, without the vehicle of international treaties, issues relating to human rights protection in Australia are largely out of the jurisdiction of the federal Government under the Commonwealth Constitution. Without amending the Constitution,[69] the most suitable power for human rights

---

66 Provisions most directly concerned with individual rights are to be found in only four sections – s.51(31) (just compensation for property acquisition), s.80 (trial by jury), s.116 (freedom of religion) and s.117 (no discrimination against residents in different State). Other provisions can only be seen as having a potential for human rights protection, rather than directly conferring rights on individuals.

67 See e.g. Marcus Einfeld, 'Human Rights Australia and the Justice System', (1989) *L.Institute J.* 738.

68 See Sex Discrimination Act 1984 (Cth) (implementing International Convention on the Elimination of All Forms of Discrimination Against Women) and Racial Discrimination Act 1975 (Cth) (implementing International Convention on the Elimination of All forms of Racial Discrimination). Both Acts create legally enforceable rights. Other major international human rights conventions ratified by Australia are scheduled in Human Rights and Equal Opportunity Commission Act 1986, which allows the Commission to conduct enquiries and to conciliate the complaint, but no enforceable legal rights are created. For further discussions, see Peter Bailey, *Human Rights: Australia in an International Context*, Sydney: Butterworths (1990), ch.5; Beth Gaze & Melinda Jones, *Law, Liberty and Australian Democracy*, Sydney: Law Book Company Ltd (1990), at 54-56.

69 Under s.128 of the Commonwealth Constitution, legislation proposing the amendment must be passed by an absolute majority of each House of the Commonwealth Parliament, or twice by one House with an absolute majority on two occasions at least three months apart. The legislation then shall be submitted to the voters in a referendum within six months. To pass a referendum, it must command acceptance by both an overall majority of voters and by a majority of voters in a majority of States. The record of constitutional referendum in Australia has not be impressive; only eight referenda out of 42 put to the voters were successful and many proposals for constitutional change never made it to referendum.

legislation is through the s.51(xxix) 'external affairs' powers to incorporate international treaties into domestic law. Through a series of litigation in the High Court,[70] it can now be said that the only legal limit on incorporating international treaties is that legislation must be in conformity with the treaty. However, various political considerations have prevented the full implementation of Australia's obligations under international treaties and conventions.[71]

C. The use of international human rights jurisprudence

What can courts do without a Bill of Rights nor the incorporation of international treaties into Australian domestic law? Could courts of law use international human rights jurisprudence to aid their interpretation of express provisions in the Constitution; to imply constitutional protection of human rights into the Constitution; and to fill out the gaps in common law and to deal with ambiguities and vagueness in the statutes and common law? Indeed, these are some of the controversial issues that have faced the Australian courts for some time.

The lead to use international human rights jurisprudence, in particular that as expressed in the leading international human rights instruments such as the *Universal Declaration of Human Rights*, the *International Covenant on Civil and Political Rights* and the *International Covenant on Economic, Social and Cultural Rights*, in deciding domestic issues, was taken by a High Court justice, Justice Lionel Murphy.[72] His view however was not embraced by most members of the Court of his time.[73]

Justice Michael Kirby, until recently President of the Court of Appeal of the Supreme Court of NSW and now a justice in the High Court, is perhaps now the strongest advocate for the use of international human rights jurisprudence in judicial decision-making. He has done so both in his curial and extra-curial writing.[74] His advocacy comes from his strong commitment to

---

[70] E.g. *Koowarta v Bjelke-Petersen* (1982) 39 ALR 417; and *Commonwealth v. Tasmania* (the *Franklin Dam* case) (1983) 46 ALR 625. For further discussions, see L Zines, *The High Court and the Constitution*, 3rd edition, Sydney: Butterworths (1992), ch.13; and Peter Hanks, *Constitutional Law in Australia* (2ed ed.), Sydney: Butterworths (1996), at 414-432.

[71] See Bailey, *supra* note 68, ch.3; and Gaze & Jones, *supra* note 68, at 53-54.

[72] See Kirby (1993), *supra* note 61, at 375-377. See further A. R. Blackshield, *et al*, (eds), *The Judgments of Justice Lionel Murphy*, Sydney: Primavera Press (1986); Jean and Richard Ely, (eds.), *Lionel Murphy: The Rule of Law*, Sydney: Akron Press (1986); and Jocelynne A. Scutt, (ed.), *Lionel Murphy: A Radical Judge*, Melbourne: McCulloch Publishing Pty Ltd (1987), esp. chapter 10.

[73] *Ibid*; and *Final Report of the Constitutional Commission*, Vol. One, Canberra: Australian Government Publishing Service, 1988, at 445.

[74] Justice Kirby has written extensively and spoken widely on domestic application of international human rights jurisprudence. The following are some of his extra-curial writings directly discussing the use of international human rights: 'The Role of the Judge in Advancing Human Rights by Reference to International Human Rights Norms', (1988) 62

the implementation of the Bangalore Principles,[75] principles adopted and re-affirmed by participants to a series of judicial colloquiums organised by the Commonwealth Secretariat.[76] These Principles recognise that international law is not directly enforceable by national courts in many common law countries unless it is incorporated into the domestic legal system by legislation; acknowledge that judges must give effect to national law when it is clear but inconsistent with international law; but call for judges to have regard to international obligations for the purpose of removing ambiguity or uncertainty from national constitutions, legislation or common law.[77] Based on these principles, Justice Kirby has said:

> "When I returned to Australia with the Bangalore Principles it seemed to me that they provided a timely corrective to the insularity to which any legal system is prone, but to which the Australian legal system, in particular, seems always susceptible. If the organised institution of the international community reached conclusions upon issues analogous to those arising in my Court, and if the local law on the point is uncertain or ambiguous, it seemed (after Bangalore) self-evident that a judge would wish to inform himself or herself upon the thinking of jurists tackling like problems and drawing upon the developing jurisprudence of the international community."[78]

This he also translates into actual judicial decision-making. Among various decisions in which his Honour drew international human rights jurisprudence to his legal reasoning was the case, *Jago v District Court of New South Wales & Ors*, in which his Honour said:

> "I regard it to be at least as relevant to search for the common law of Australia applicable in this State with the guidance of a relevant instrument of international law to which this country has recently subscribed, as by reference to disputable antiquarian research concerning the procedures which may or may not have been adapted by the itinerant justice in

---

ALJ 514; 'Judges and the Use of International Human Rights Law', (1993) 5 (3) *The Sydney Paper* 9; 'Human Rights – Emerging International Minimum Standards', (1993) 19 (no.3) *Commonwealth Law Bulletin* 1254; 'The Australian Use of International Human Rights Norms: From Bangalore to Balliol – A View from the Antipodes', (1993) 16 *UNSW.L.J.* 363; 'The Impact of International Human Rights Norms: "A Law Undergoing Evolution"', (1995) *UWA L.Rev.* 30. Reference to cases in which Justice Kirby applied international human rights law can be found in these papers.

[75] 'Report of Judicial Colloquium on the Domestic Application of International Human Rights Norms, Bangalore, India – Chairman's Concluding Statement'. A text of the Statement is annexed to Justice Kirby's paper in (1988) 62 *ALJ* 514, at 531-34.

[76] See Kirby, 'Human Rights – Emerging International Minimum Standards', *supra* note 74, at 1265-6; and 'Abuja Confirmation of the Domestic Application of International Human Rights Norms', (1992) *Commonwealth Law Bulletin* 198-303.

[77] See Principles 4, 7 & 8.

[78] Kirby, 'The Australian Use of International Human Rights Norms: From Bangalore to Balliol – A View from the Antipodes', *supra* note 74, at 366.

> eyre in parts of England in the reign of King Henry II. Our laws and our liberties have been inherited in large part from England. If an English or Imperial statute still operate in this State, we must give effect to it to the extent provided by the Imperial Acts Application Act 1969. ...But where the inherited common law is uncertain, Australian judges, after the Australia Act 1986 (Cth) at least, do well to look for more reliable and modern sources for the statement and development of the common law. One such reference point may be an international treaty which Australia has ratified and which now states international law."[79]

His Honour then continued to discuss the significance of the International Covenant on Civil and Political Rights for Australia.

Jago was then appealed to the High Court. The decision was upheld, but the issue of using international human rights jurisprudence was not discussed.[80] However, the highest judicial tribunal in Australia, the High Court of Australia, did in many occasions draw heavily international and comparative jurisprudence in its reasoning and decision-making.[81] Most importantly, unmistaken endeavour of the High Court in its efforts to use international and comparative human rights jurisprudence to resolve domestic disputes began to emerge since 1992. Several landmark decisions have been handed down by the High Court, some remaining controversial,[82] other even contentious,[83] but all of them breaking new grounds for legal developments through the use of international and comparative law.

III. International and comparative law in the High Court – A case study

A. The High Court and legal developments in Australia

In this Part, we will analyse three recent High Court decisions to illustrate the extent and limits to which Australian courts may use comparative law in their judicial decision-making.[84] It is submitted that the decisions of the High Court may not reflect perfectly the influence or the receptiveness of

---

[79] (1988) 12 NSWLR 558, at 569.

[80] (1989) 87 ALR 577.

[81] See e.g. *Street v Queensland Bar Association and Others* (1989) 88 ALR 321; *Polyukhovic v The Commonwealth of Australia and Another* (1991) 101 ALR 545; *Leeth v Commonwealth*, (1992) 107 ALR 672. See also Mason (1992), *supra* note 40, at 753-4; and Mason (1996), *supra* note 56.

[82] *E.g. Australian Capital Television Pty Ltd and Others v Commonwealth of Australia* (1992) 108 ALR 577; *Nationwide News Pty Ltd v Wills* (1992) 108 ALR 681.

[83] *E.g. Mabo and Others v State of Queensland* (1992) 107 ALR 1; and *Minister for Immigration and Ethnic Affairs v Teoh* (1995) 128 ALR 353.

[84] i.e. *Mabo v. Queensland* (1992) 107 ALR 1; *Dietrich v. R* [1992] 109 ALR 385; and *Minister for Immigration and Ethnic Affairs v Teoh* (1995) 128 ALR 353.

international and comparative law in Australian courts. Nevertheless, the fact that the High Court is the final appeal court for both common law matters and the interpretation of Australian state statutes gives an especially important status to High Court's decisions in the Australian legal system. Furthermore, as Sir Anthony Mason has recently pointed out, it has often been the case and it is generally expected that if any significant change is to be made to the principles of judge-made law, it is the High Court rather than the intermediate courts of appeal that would make that change.[85] How relevant principles of law are to be formulated is also to be decided by the High Court.[86] In other words, the High Court assumes a leadership in judicial decision-making in Australia.

The choice of the three cases also needs explanation. As already pointed out, the High Court has on many occasions made use of international and comparative law. Indeed, in its landmark decisions on freedom of political communication,[87] a large body of Canadian and US decisions and decisions of the European Court of Human Rights were considered.[88] The level of freedom propounded by the Court was closely modelled upon that applied in the United States.[89] The following three cases are chosen because, not only a large body of foreign decisions were considered, but how these decisions and international law can be used by Australian courts was also discussed. These discussions well illustrate the extent and limits to which Australian courts may use international and comparative jurisprudence.

B. The Mabo *decision*[90]

Mabo is a case in which five residents of the Murray Islands in Torres Strait sought a High Court declaration that, upon annexation to Australia, pre-existing land rights were not lost. *Mabo* presented the first opportunity for the High Court to confront the central question of the existence and the nature of native title in Australian law and, for the first time in Australia, to recognise a native title for Aboriginal Australians. In retrospect, it could

---

[85] Sir Anthony Mason, 'The Role of the Courts at the Turn of the Century', being the Fifth Annual Oration in Judicial Administration, delivered on 5 November 1993 in Melbourne.

[86] Sir Anthony Mason, 'The Tort Law Review', (1993) 1 *Tort L.Rev.* 5, at 5.

[87] *Australian Capital Television Pty Ltd and Others v Commonwealth of Australia* (1992) 108 ALR 577; and *Nationwide News Pty Ltd v Wills* (1992) 108 ALR 681.

[88] See particularly Mason CJ in *Australian Capital Television* case; Brennan J in both cases and Deane and Toohey JJ in the *Nationwide News* case.

[89] See *Australian Capital Television* case, *per* Mason CJ, at 597-8. It is precisely because of this, that the decisions have been severely criticised by some academics, as the American model was rejected by the Founding Fathers of the Australian Constitution and the American model was derived from an express guarantee not from general notions of representative democracy. See e.g. Peter Creighton, 'The Implied Guarantee of Free Political Communication', (1993) 23 *U.W.A.L.Rev.* 163, at 168.

[90] *Mabo v. Queensland* (1992) 107 ALR 1.

have well been a low key decision had the High Court relied on a long-standing common law doctrine of exclusive Crown ownership of all land in Australia. Instead, the High Court unambiguously attempted to integrate the claims of justice, Aboriginal human rights, international law, and Australian common law in a single decision.[91] By doing so, it demonstrates how common law could accommodate modern developments of international law and, therefore, re-shape common law itself. Indeed, and on the face, the case was decided largely on the basis of foreign and international law: In the judgement, 14 cases were approved. Among them, three were English, four Canadian, two New Zealand, one U.S. and one International Court of Justice case. Only three were Australian.[92]

The principal decision was delivered by Brennan J, concurred by Mason CJ and McHugh J. The use of international and comparative law to bring the Australian common law into line with international developments can be summarised as follows:

There was a common law doctrine, upon which the defendant's argument relied, that when the territory of a settled colony became part of the Crown's dominions, the law of England so far as applicable to colonial conditions became the law of the colony and, by that law, the Crown acquired the absolute beneficial ownership of all land in the territory so that the colony became the Crown's demesne and no right or interest in any land in the territory could thereafter be possessed by any other person unless granted by the Crown.[93] This theory, as Brennan J declared, invites critical examination. The task for the High Court Justices was not an easy one. On the one hand,

> "Judged by any civilised standard, such a law is unjust and its claim to be part of the common law to be applied in contemporary Australia must be questioned."[94]

and on the other hand:

> "In discharging its duty to declare the common law of Australia, this court is not free to adopt rules that accord with contemporary notions of justice and human rights if their adoption would fracture the skeleton of the principle which gives the body of our law its shape and internal consistency."[95]

---

[91] Gerry Simpson, 'Mabo, International Law, Terra Nullius and the Stories of Settlement: An Unresolved Jurisprudence', (1993) *Mel.U.L.Rev.* 195, at 196. See also Peter Bailey, 'How Are You Going, Mate, Without a Bill of Rights?', a paper presented to ALTA Conference, Christchurch, New Zealand, October 1993.

[92] See *Mabo v. Queensland* (1992) 107 ALR 1, at 6. It should be pointed out that a much larger number of foreign cases were considered by various justices in their judgments.

[93] See *Mabo v. Queensland* (1992) 107 ALR 1, at 15-18.

[94] *Id.*, at 18.

[95] *Id.*, at 18.

What the court has to do is then to modify, but not to destroy, common law and therefore 'to bring it into conformity with contemporary notions of justice and human rights.'[96]

Brennan J then proceeded to examine the basis of that theory, ie. Australia was *terra nullius* before the European settlers arrived. Here his Honour collected and examined a large body of cases decided in various common law jurisdictions as well as scholarly research. Relying particularly on Advisory Opinion on Western Sahara,[97] his Honour declared:

> "If the international law notion that inhabited land may be classified as *terra nullius* no longer commands general support, the doctrines of the common law which depend on the notion that native peoples may be 'so low in the scale of social organisation' that it is 'idle to impute to such people some shadow of the rights known to our law' can hardly be retained. If it were permissible in past centuries to keep the common law in step with international law, it is imperative in today's world that the common law should neither be nor be seen to be frozen in an age of racial discrimination."[98]

His Honour continued:

> "The expectations of the international community accord in this respect with the contemporary values of the Australian people. The opening up of international remedies to individuals pursuant to Australia's accession to the Optional Protocol to the International Covenant on Civil and Political Rights brings to bear on the common law the powerful influence of the Covenant and the international standards it imports. *The common law does not necessarily conform with international law, but international law is a legitimate and important influence on the development of the common law, especially when international law declares the existence of universal human rights.*"[99] (Emphasis supplied)

To bring the common law into conformity with international standards and, at the same time, not to fracture a skeleton principle of the common law, his Honour made a distinction between the Crown's title to a colony and the Crown's ownership of land in the colony.[100] Again, after examining many cases decided in other common law jurisdictions, his Honour concluded that a mere change in sovereignty does not extinguish native title to

---

[96] *Id.*, at 19.

[97] [1975] 1 CJR 12.

[98] *Mabo v. Queensland* (1992) 107 ALR 1, at 28.

[99] *Id.*, at 29.

[100] It is to be noted that, in the case of *Milirrpum v. Nabalco* [1971] 17 F.L.R. 141 at the Supreme Court of Northern Territory, Blackburn J refused to separate sovereignty from land rights issues and therefore rejected the concept of native title. The arguments by the State of Queensland followed the *Milirrpum* case quite closely.

land.[101] Since the notion 'native title' was recognised for the first time by Australian law, his Honour then continued to define the nature and content of 'native title'. Here again, a large body of foreign law, particularly cases from Canada, New Zealand and the United States, was collected and examined.[102]

Other justices also placed reliance on the compelling authority of the jurisprudence from Canada, New Zealand and the United States. In particular, the recognition of the concept of 'native title' placed particular reliance on the Supreme Court of Canada's decision in *Calder*,[103] and the nature, content and extinguishment of native title are all founded upon the pragmatic compromise declared by Chief Justice Marshall of the U.S. Supreme Court in *Johnson v. McIntosh*.[104] Professor Bartlett has therefore commented:

> "What determined the result in Mabo was not emotive pronouncements nor early *obiter dicta*, but the overwhelming dictates of the jurisprudence in every other part of the common law world."[105]

The use of international and foreign law in the *Mabo* case apparently goes beyond clarifying ambiguities or filling gaps in the common law; it actually overturned a long-standing and established doctrine of common law in Australia and, therefore, established new rules for Australia. The holding of the High Court in *Mabo*, as Justice Kirby has commented, represents an extremely bold step:

> "It pointed the way to the future development of the Australian common law in harmony with developing principles of international law, just as the Bangalore Principles had suggested."[106]

C. The Dietrich *case*[107]

In this case, the applicant was charged of three counts of drug trafficking offence. The trial in the County Court lasted about 40 days and during the entire period, he was unrepresented (as the Legal Aid Commission would only provide assistance if he pleaded guilty which he would not). He was convicted of one count of importing into Australia not less than a trafficable quantity of heroin in contravention of s.233B(1)(b) of the Customs

---

[101] *Mabo v. Queensland* (1992) 107 ALR 1, at 41.

[102] See *id.*, at 42-51.

[103] *Calder v Attorney-General of British Columbia* [1973] SCR 313.

[104] (1823) 8 Wheat 543. See Richard H Bartlett, 'The Mabo Decision', in *The Mabo Decision*, Sydney: Butterworths (1993), at xi-xii.

[105] *Ibid.*, at xii.

[106] Kirby, 'The Australian Use of International Human Rights Norms: From Bangalore to Balliol – A View from the Antipodes', *supra* note 74, at 386.

[107] *Dietrich v. R* [1992] 109 ALR 385.

Act 1901 (Cth). He then appealed to the Court of Criminal Appeal for leave to appeal against the conviction on the ground that every indigent accused charged with an indictable offence was entitled to counsel provided at the expense of the State and that the failure of the trial judge to appoint counsel for the applicant was a miscarriage of justice requiring that the conviction be quashed. The Court of Criminal Appeal refused leave. It is from the order refusing leave that the applicant sought special leave to appeal to the High Court.

The sole ground of the application is that the applicant's trial miscarried by virtue of the fact that he was not provided with legal representation. The difficulties for the applicant to rely on this ground are apparent. Earlier in 1979 in a similar situation, the High Court had decided quite clearly that:

> "... an accused does not have a right to be provided with counsel at public expense. He has, of course, a right to be represented by counsel at his own or someone else's expense. He has no absolute right to legal aid."[108]

One of the central questions in *Dietrich* is, to what extent can international and comparative law affect domestic law.

The High Court first re-affirmed the status of an international treaty ratified by the Australian government without enabling legislation in the domestic legal system:

> "Ratification of the ICCPR [International Covenant on Civil and Political Rights] as an executive act has no direct legal effect upon domestic law; the rights and obligations contained in the ICCPR are not incorporated into Australian law unless and until specific legislation is passed implementing the provisions. No such legislation has been passed. This position is not altered by Australia's accession to the First Optional Protocol to the ICCPR, effective as of 25 December 1991, by which Australia recognises the competence of the Human Rights Committee of the United Nations to receive and consider communications from individuals subject to Australia's jurisdiction who claim to be victims of a violation by Australia of their covenanted rights."[109]

The Court then went on to discuss the *Jago* approach. Although the *Jago* approach was not expressly affirmed, the Court did not reject it either:

> "In *Jago v District Court of New South Wales* (1988) 12 NSWLR 558 at 569, Kirby P expressed the view that, where the inherited common law is uncertain, Australian judges may look to an international treaty which Australia has ratified as an aid to the explication and development of the common law. As a suggested example of this approach, the applicant points to the status accorded to the ECHR [European Convention for the

---

[108] *McInnis v. R* (1979) 27 ALR 449, *per* Barwick CJ, at 453.

[109] *per* Mason CJ and McHugh J in *Dietrich v. R* (1992) 109 ALR 385, at 391.

Protection of Human Rights and Fundamental Freedoms] in English law. In common with the status of the ICCPR in Australian law, the ECHR is not part of English domestic law and thus rights contained in the ECHR cannot be enforced directly in English courts; furthermore, if domestic legislation conflicted with the ECHR, English courts would nevertheless be required to enforce the legislation. However, it is 'well settled': *R v Home Secretary; Ex parte Brind* [1911] 1 AC 696, *per* Lord Bridge of Harwich, at 747-8, that, in construing domestic legislation which is ambiguous, English courts will presume that Parliament intended to legislate in accordance with its international obligations. English courts may also have resort to international obligations in order to help resolve uncertainty or ambiguity in judge-made law: *Derbyshire Country Council v. Times Newspapers Ltd* [1992] 3 WLR 28, per Balcombe LJ at 44.

Assuming, without deciding, that Australian courts should adopt a similar, common-sense approach, this nevertheless does not assist the applicants in this case where we are being asked not to resolve uncertainty or ambiguity in domestic law but to declare that a right which has hitherto never been recognised should now be taken to exist. Moreover, this branch of the applicant's argument assumes that Art 14(3)(d) of the ICCPR supports the absolute right for which he contends. An analysis of the views of the Human Rights Committee on communications submitted to it relating to Art 14(3)(d) reveals little more than that the Committee considers that legal assistance must always be made available in capital cases: *Pinto v Trinidad & Tobago* CCPR/C/39/D/232/1987. However, the European Court of Human Rights has approached the almost identical provision in the ECHR by emphasising the importance of the particular facts of the case to any interpretation of the phrase 'when the interests of justice so require': *Monnell and Morris v United Kingdom* (1987) 10 EHRR 205 at 225; *Granger v United Kingdom* (1990) 12 EHRR 469 at 408-2. As will become clear, that approach is similar to the approach which, in our opinion, the Australian common law must now take."[110]

Here again, a large body of U.S., U.K. and Canadian cases and cases of the European Court of Human Rights were collected and considered. International and comparative jurisprudence was clearly taken as one of the reasons that *McInnis* had to be reconsidered.[111] For instance, Deane J considered a number of U.S cases and concluded:

"The reasoning in those United States judgments is, in my view, compelling in its analysis of the significance of lack of legal representation

[110] *Dietrich v. R* (1992) 109 ALR 385, at 392-3. The *Jago* approach was also allowed by Toohey J, at 434. Art 14(3)(d) of the ICCPR provides an accused a right to have legal assistance in a criminal trial.

[111] *Dietrich v. R* (1992) 109 ALR 385, at 443-4.

> by reason of poverty to the law's fundamental requirement that a criminal trial be fair. Similar reasoning has prevailed in the highest courts of the common law jurisdiction of the Republic of Ireland: See *The State (Heady) v Donoghue* [1976] IR, at 350-1, 354-5, 357, 363-4, and India: See *Hoskot v State of Maharashtra* [1979] i SCR (India) 192, at 204-8; *Hussainara Khantoon v Home Secretary* [1979] 3 SCR (India) 760, at 765. It should now be accepted and applied in this court."[112]

His Honour then continued to point out that it is relevant in deciding the present case to note that Australia, as a nation, is a party to the International Covenant on Civil and Political Rights.[113]

An important point regarding the use of international and comparative jurisprudence was discussed by Brennan J in his dissenting judgment. Here his Honour continued the discussion regarding changes or modifications to be made to common law as his Honour had earlier expounded in *Mabo*:

> "Where a common law rule requires some expansion or modification in order to operate more fairly or efficiently, this court will modify the rule provided no injustice is done thereby. And, in those exceptional cases where a rule of the common law produces a manifest injustice, this court will change the rule so as to avoid perpetuating the injustice."[114]

Changes to the common law must not only be in conformity with contemporary values but also conform with the 'skeleton of principle which gives the body of our law'.[115] In this case, Art 14(3)(d) ICCPR is held as a concrete indication of contemporary values,[116] but the change can not be made by judges alone:

> "Although this provision of the Covenant is not part of our municipal law, it is a legitimate influence on the development of the common law. Indeed, it is incongruous that Australia should adhere to the Covenant containing that provision unless Australian courts recognise the entitlement and Australian governments provide the resources required to carry that entitlement into effect. But the courts cannot, independently of the Legislature and the Executive, legitimately declare an entitlement to legal aid."[117]

At the end, *McInnis* was reconsidered and a new approach adopted: Although the Court stopped short of recognising a right to legal counsel at public expense, it held that, in the absence of exceptional circumstances, a trial should be adjourned, postponed or stayed until legal representation

[112] *Id*, at 414.
[113] *Id*, at 416.
[114] *Id*, at 402-3.
[115] *Id*, at 403.
[116] *Id*, at 404.
[117] *Id*, at 404.

became available if an indigent accused, charged with a serious offence, was unable to obtain legal representation without his or her own fault. What the *Dietrich* case has achieved then is a demonstration of the capacity of the common law in taking a new approach to similar situations in light of contemporary human rights values and, therefore, to modify (but not to change) the common law. Furthermore, as Einfeld J has observed:

> "Whilst authoritatively determining that treaties ratified only by the executive government do not, *per se*, become part of domestic law, *Dietrich* seems to make clear that the statutory approval or scheduling of treaties is not to be ignored as merely platitudinous or ineffectual, but must be given a meaning in terms of the parliamentary will. Thus when the Australian Parliament endorses and acknowledges a treaty by legislation, there being no contrary statutory or clearly applicable common law provision in relation to the matters contained in the treaty, it approves or validates the treaty as part of the law which ought as far as possible to be applicable to and enforceable on or by Australians and others in the country to whom it is available. ... This is not applying international law domestically by reason of a treaty itself or even by reason of Australia's ratification of it. It is applying the law and intent of parliament."[118]

D. The Teoh *decision*[119]

The *Teoh* case concerned the role of international treaties, ratified by Australia but not incorporated in domestic law, in administrative decision-making. In this case, Mr. Teoh, a Malaysian citizen married to an Australian woman, was denied a permanent entry permit and faced deportation. The rejection of his application for a resident status was grounded on the fact that he was convicted of six counts of being knowingly concerned in the importation of heroin and of three counts of being in possession of heroin, thus failing to meet the 'good character' requirement for immigration. At the time of the deportation order, there were seven children in the Teoh's family, three children of the marriage and four of Mrs Teoh's previous relationships. Most of the children were then under 10 years old with the youngest being born on 20 March 1992. The severely adverse consequences for the family and the children as a result of the deportation were not disputed. The contentious issue was whether the UN Convention on the Rights of the Child, in particular Arts 3 & 5, which requires the best interests of the child to be the primary consideration in all actions concerning children, had any role in the decision-making under the Migration Act.

---

[118] per Einfeld J in *Minister for Foreign Affairs and Trade and Others v Magno and Another* (1993) 112 ALR 529, at 572-3.

[119] *Minister for Immigration and Ethnic Affairs v Teoh* (1995) 128 ALR 353.

That Convention was ratified by Australia on 17 December 1990 and entered into force for Australia on 16 January 1991. The Convention was declared to be an international instrument relating to human rights and freedoms for the purposes of the Human Rights and Equal Opportunity Commission Act 1986 (Cth) by the Attorney-General of the Commonwealth pursuing to Art 47 of the 1986 Act.[120] The Convention is otherwise not incorporated into domestic law.

The High Court, by a four to one majority, ruled that ratification of an international treaty gave rise to a legitimate expectation, in the absence of statutory or executive indications to the contrary, that decision-makers would act in conformity with the treaty. At the same time the High Court also made it clear that treaties to which Australia is a party do not create legally enforceable rights and duties unless their provisions have been incorporated into municipal law by legislation. Nevertheless, *Teoh* reaffirms that unincorporated treaties may aid statutory interpretation and guide the development of the common law.[121]

What is perceived of as a 'new way', in addition to providing guidance for statutory interpretation and common law development, in which treaties affect domestic law is the majority decision on the impact of international treaties on the exercise of government discretion, more specifically, on the notion of 'legitimate expectation' as part of the 'procedural fairness' requirement.[122] According to the High Court,

> "ratification by Australia of an international convention is not to be dismissed as a merely platitudinous or ineffectual act, particularly when the instrument evidences internationally accepted standards to be applied by courts and administrative authorities in dealing with basic human rights affecting the family and children. Rather, ratification of a convention is a positive statement by the Executive Government of this country to the world and to the Australian people that the Executive Government and its agencies will act in accordance with the Convention. That positive statement is an adequate foundation for a legitimate expectation, absent

---

[120] See Commonwealth of Australia Gazette GNI, 13 January 1993 at 85-107.

[121] *Minister for Immigration and Ethnic Affairs v Teoh* (1995) 128 ALR 353 at 361-3 *per* Mason CJ & Deane J.

[122] See Kirby (1995), *supra* note 74, at 47; Penelope Mathew, 'International Law and the Protection of Human Rights in Australia: Recent Trends', (1995) 17 *Syd.L.Rev.* 177, at 201; and Susan Roberts, 'Minister for Immigration and Ethnic Affairs v Ah Hin Teoh: The High Court decision and the Government's reaction to it', (1995) 2 *AJHR* 135, at 136. For detailed discussion on 'legitimate expectation' and procedural fairness, see Pamela Tate, 'The Coherence of "Legitimate Expectation" and the Foundations of Natural Justice', (1988) 14 *Monash U.L.R.* 15; and Margaret Allars, 'One Small Step for Legal Doctrine, One Giant Leap Towards Integrity in Government: *Teoh*'s Case and the Internationalisation of Administrative Law', (1995) 17 *Syd L Rev* 204.

> statutory or executive indications to the country, that administrative decision-makers will act in conformity with the Convention..." [123]

However, such a legitimate expectation is not a legally enforceable right. Thus,

> "The existence of a legitimate expectation that a decision-maker will act in a particular way does not necessarily compel him or her to act in that way. That is the difference between a legitimate expectation and a binding rule of law."[124]

The effect of the existence of such a legitimate expectation on administrative decision-making is that 'if the decision-maker proposes to make a decision inconsistent with a legitimate expectation, procedural fairness requires that the persons affected should be given notice and an adequate opportunity of presenting a case against the taking of such a course.'[125]

Although *Teoh* creates a new mechanism for international law to affect domestic legal development, it is, as compared with *Mabo*, not a radical decision in any sense but a half-way compromise. *Mabo* has already decided that international law is a legitimate and powerful influence on the development of the common law. *Mabo* has thus foreshadowed further developments in common law in conformity with international law. *Teoh* does not in any way fracture any skeleton of the common law;[126] it adds one more dimension to the requirement for procedural fairness as a result of government actions in ratifying international treaties, and thus showing its willingness to uphold fundamental human rights standards. *Mabo*, as already discussed above, goes much beyond clarifying ambiguities or filling gaps in common law; it actually overturned a long-standing and established doctrine of common law and thus led to some far-reaching legal and practical consequences. Even here, *Mabo* can not be seen as a radical decision; it has done what had been done many years ago in some other common law jurisdictions such as the United States, Canada and New Zealand.[127] Further, *Teoh* and *Dietrich* share a similar approach in the sense that both cases try to find a middle way between creating legally enforceable rights and total ignoring of ratified but unimplemented treaties. In short, *Teoh* is a natural, logical, and perhaps inevitable, development from *Mabo* and *Dietrich* with a less radical and less uncertain result. It is a small step in legal doctrinal development, but it offers an excellent oppor-

---

[123] *Minister for Immigration and Ethnic Affairs v Teoh* (1995) 128 ALR 353 at 365 *per* Mason CJ & Deane J.

[124] *Ibid.*

[125] *Ibid.*

[126] In an excellent analysis, Allars has convincingly argued that *Teoh* represents a very small step in doctrinal development in administrative law. See Allars, *supra* note 122.

[127] See *supra* note 105.

tunity for a giant leap towards integrity in government.[128] Yet *Teoh*, as Justice Kirby has commented, confirms that the age of the impact of international and comparative law on Australian municipal law has arrived. It presents an inevitable development suitable for the approaching millenium.[129] However, *Teoh* has not only attracted media interests and criticisms, but also strong responses from the Australian Government.

E. Government responses to the Teoh *decision*

The Government response was swift. A joint statement by the Minister for Foreign Affairs and the Attorney-General was issued a little more than a month after the *Teoh* decision. The intention of the Joint Statement was to provide a clear executive indication that 'entering into an international treaty is not reason for raising any expectation that government decision-makers will act in accordance with the treaty if the relevant provisions of that treaty have not been enacted into domestic Australian law.'[130] The Joint Statement also made it clear that 'It is not *legitimate*, for the purpose of applying Australian law, to expect that the provisions of a treaty not incorporated by legislation should be applied by decision-makers.' (emphasis added). Finally, the Joint Statement foreshadowed the government's intention to legislate to enforce the statement and 'put beyond any doubt' the status of the unlegislated international obligations. A Bill to that effect was indeed introduced into the Parliament in later June 1995.

The substantive provision of the Bill is as follows:

> "5. The fact that Australia is bound, or a party to, a particular international instrument, or that an enactment reproduces or refers to a particular international instrument, does not give rise to a legitimate expectation, on the part of any person, that:
>
> (a) an administrative decision will be made in conformity with the requirements of that instrument; or
>
> (b) if the decision were to be made contrary to any of those requirements, any person affected by the decision would be given notice and an adequate opportunity to present a case against the taking of such a course."

The justification advanced by the Government for the executive and legislative intervention is that the *Teoh* decision has introduced 'a great deal of uncertainty' into government activities. The Government also takes the

---

[128] See Allars, *supra* note 122.

[129] Kirby (1995), *supra* note 74, at 48.

[130] See *Joint Statement* by the Minister for Foreign Affairs, Senator Gareth Evans and the Attorney General, Michael Lavarch on 10 May 1995, in *Ministerial Document Service*, no.179/94-95, 11 May 1995, at 6228-6230.

view that *Teoh* has created a new way in which treaties could affect administrative decisions and, thus, provided a means of usurping the legitimate role of Parliament in law-making. The government action is therefore to 'restore' the pre-*Teoh* position of treaties in domestic law.[131] Hence, the justification of the Government action is grounded on the presumption that *Teoh* radically departs from previous common law position and, consequently, creates great uncertainties in Government administration.[132]

SOME CONCLUDING REMARKS: AUSTRALIAN COURTS AT THE CROSSROADS

Sir Anthony has recently pointed out:

> "We live in an age in which not only academics but also judges and practitioners are looking to developments in other countries."[133]

Indeed, the thinking of judges, lawyers and scholars about international and comparative law has changed.[134] There is no doubt that Australian courts will continue to look to developments in other countries. However, the road ahead for Australian courts in using international and comparative law is uncertain.

First, until this day, the term 'other countries' mainly means 'other common law countries'. This should not be surprising: The emerging Australian law is moving away from the domination of English influence, but not from the 'skeleton' of the common law which originated from English law. The relevance of decisions from common law countries derives directly from the common legal heritage and shared culture and tradition among these countries. However, there is an open question, that is what is the role of Civil law and Asian law. Sir Anthony Mason has recently discussed factors that would affect the judiciary and the develop-

---

[131] See the *Joint Statement*, *id*; the *Administrative Decisions (Effect of International Instruments) Bill* 1995 – *Explanatory Memorandum*; and *Second Reading Speech*, *Daily Hansard* (21 September 1995), House of Representatives, 1435-1439.

[132] I have elsewhere argued against and rejected these justifications. See Jianfu Chen, 'Anti-Teoh Bill: A Wrong Course for a Wrong Reason, and a Wrong Message', a paper presented to the 50th Anniversary of the Australasian Law Teachers' Association Conference, La Trobe University, 28 September – 1 October 1995; and 'Taking International Obligations More Seriously', in Martin Chanock & Lee Ann Marks (eds.), *Cross Currents: Internationalism, National Identity & Law*, La Trobe University, 1995, at 181-193. The Bill has also been criticised by many others. See eg 'Ex-judge warns of treaty Bill hypocrisy', *The Australia*, 12 May 1995, at 2; 'Rights chief condemns bid to neutralise Teoh ruling', *The Australia*, 17 May 1995, at 2; 'Parliament need role in treaties, says Kirby', *The Weekend Australia*, 27 May 1995, at 12. It should be noted that the Bill lapsed as a result of the 1996 parliament election.

[133] Mason(1993), *supra* note 86, at 9.

[134] See Mason (1996 in *Law in Context*), *supra* note 56, at 87.

ment of Australian law. One of these factors is Australia's closer identification with Asia.[135] In a separated paper, he further suggests that the use of Civil law will also be increased as a result of the move towards internationalisation and a rich tradition in some legal concepts in Civil law.[136] If that is so, to what extent will Australian judges take into consideration Civil law and Asian law in their future judicial decision-making? and how?

Secondly, there is a lack of a clear and general theory guiding the use of international and comparative law; such a use is often subject to the discretion of individual judges since the value of foreign decisions depends on the 'persuasiveness' of the decisions and the application of international standards involves the exercise of value judgment and policy consideration by individual judges.

There is no doubt that strict legalism has gone and is now a thing of the past.[137] It is now well recognised that judges do make law.[138] It is also recognised that the doctrine of precedent is as much an attitude of mind as it is a legal doctrine.[139] All this means that courts in Australia will attempt to settle the rules right rather than just following settled rules. To do so, judges in Australia will continue to seek assistance from international and comparative law just as they have done in *Mabo, Dietrich* and *Teoh* and in many other cases. However, the use of international law by Australian judges is less settled than the use of foreign decisions from other common law countries, as Justice Kirby has recently pointed out:

> "[I]t remains a question as to whether it is legitimate for Australian judges to have regard to human rights standards, expressed in international conventions, either:
>
> (a) where such conventions are ratified by Australia; or

---

[135] Mason (1993), *supra* note 85.

[136]See Mason (1996 in *Law in Context*), *supra* note 56, at 90.

[137] It was once asserted that 'there is no other safe guide to judicial decisions in great conflicts than a strict and complete legalism': Quoted in Mason (1987), *supra* note 18, at 155. Under this strict legalism doctrine, it was also asserted that 'in most matters it is more important that the applicable rule of law be settled than it be settled right.': Quoted in Mason (1988), *supra* note 29, at 94. See also David Wood, 'Adjudication and Community Values: Sir Anthony Mason's Recommendations', in Ellinghaus, Bradbrook and Duggan (eds.), *supra* note 4, at 89-103.

[138] See e.g. Mason (1987), *supra* note 18, at 158; M McHugh, 'The Law Making Function of the Judicial Process', Part I in (1988) 62 *ALJ* 15 and Part II in (1988) 62 *ALJ* 116; and Kirby, 'The Australian Use of International Human Rights Norms: From Bangalore to Balliol – A View from the Antipodes', *supra* note 74, at 372.

[139] Sir Anthony Mason, 'The courts and their role in changing the law today', in Alice E.-S. Tay and Eugene Kamenka (eds.), *Law-making in Australia*, Melbourne: Edward Arnold (Australia) Pty Ltd (1980), at 11.

(b) (even if not ratified) where the rules stated have come into force and have come to express international customary law. '[140]

Although the use of international law for statutory interpretation seems to be well accepted:

> "We accept the proposition that the courts should in a case of ambiguity, favour a construction of a Commonwealth statute which accords with the obligations of Australia under an international treaty."[141]

Its use to cause modifications or changes to the common law remains very controversial. As discussed earlier, Justice Kirby believes that it is legitimate to use international law to clarify ambiguities or to fill the gaps in the common law. Sir Roland Wilson, a former justice of the High Court and now the president of the Human Rights and Equal Opportunity Commission, also asserts that resource to international law is just as relevant to the moulding of the common law as it is to statutory interpretation.[142] In the view of Sir Anthony Mason, the development of international human rights law is one of the factors that have reduced the distinction between international and domestic law. For him, the existence of an inconsistent international rule with a common law principle would present an invitation to re-examine the common law principle.[143] Justice Dawson of the High Court, however, has doubts regarding the use of international law in resolving ambiguities in the common law. His Honour said in *Dietrich*:

> "There is authority for the proposition that, in the construction of domestic legislation which is ambiguous in that it is capable of being given a meaning which either is consistent with or is in conflict with a treaty obligation, there is a presumption that Parliament intended to legislate in conformity with that obligation: See *R v Home Secretary; Ex parte Brind* [1991] 1 AC 696, esp at 747-8. Whether that approach may be extended beyond statutory interpretation to the resolution of uncertainty in the common law is not so clearly established ...' [144]

In his Honour's view, it would be sufficient to preclude the reliance on international law if the use of it is to cause a fundamental change to the common law.[145]

For Justice Brennan, international law shall only be used to modify the common law and to change the common law only in exceptional cases.[146]

---

[140] Kirby, 'Human Rights – Emerging International Minimum Standards', *supra* note 74, at 1266; Kirby (1988), *supra* note 74, at 515.

[141] *per* Brennan, Deane, Dawson JJ in *Chu Kheng Lim and Others v Minister for Immigration, Local Government and Ethnic Affairs and Another* (1993) 110 ALR 97, at 123.

[142] Sir Roland Wilson, 'The Domestic Impact of International Human Rights Law', (1993) 19 *Commonwealth Law Bulletin* 1246, at 1249.

[143] Mason (1992), *supra* note 40, at 750-1.

[144] *Dietrich v. R* (1992) 109 ALR 385 at 426.

[145] *Id*, at 426.

Thirdly, the use of international and comparative law by Australian courts has attracted many severe criticisms from some media commentators as well as some scholars and practitioners.[147] It is unclear to what extent will these criticisms affect the future approach by Australian courts in their use of international and comparative jurisprudence. Most importantly, the Australian Government's swift and strong response to the *Teoh* decision has a potential effect of setting back the natural development which has occurred in Australian courts;[148] its signal was also clear, that is to discourage the approach that has been taken by Australian courts. Although the Bill to displace the *Teoh* decision has lapsed as a result of the 1996 election and the new Government has not yet re-introduced the Bill to the Parliament, it is important to note that the new Government (then in Opposition) supported the previous Government's responses to the *Teoh* decision.[149] It is expected that the new Government will, at some stage, introduce certain limitations on the effects of international and comparative law on domestic law.

Clearly, the future for Australian courts to use international and comparative law in domestic legal development is uncertain and unstable. But one thing is clear, as Sir Anthony has recently pointed out:

> "judges and lawyers in this country and in other jurisdictions are developing a growing familiarity with comparative law and showing a greater willingness to borrow from other legal systems. Ultimately the new spirit will facilitate the moulding of rules of international law suited to incorporation into national law and create a climate in which acceptance by national courts is more readily attainable."[150]

List of Abbreviations:

AC: Appeal Cases (English)
Adel.L.Re.: Adelaide Law Review
AJHR: Australian Journal of Human Rights
ALJ: Australian Law Journal
ALJR: Australian Law Journal Reports
ALR: Australian Law Reports
Am.J.Int'l.L.: American Journal of International Law

---

[146] See *supra* note 114.

[147] For a summary of these criticisms, see Kirby (1995), *supra* note 74, at 40-42.

[148] See Kirby (1995), *supra* note 74, at 48; and Mathew, *supra* note 122, at 203.

[149] The Bill was only opposed by the minor Parties in the Parliament. See The Parliament of the Commonwealth of Australia, *Administrative Decision (Effect of International Instruments) Bill 1995*, Report by the Senate Legal and Constitutional Legislation Committee, 1995. See also the Second Reading debate, *supra* note 131. For recent developments, see the Joint Statement of 25 February 1997 by the Minister for Foreign Affairs and the Attorney-General and Minister for Justice, which has so far caused exactly the same controversies as the earlier Joint Statement.

[150] Mason (1992), *supra* note 40, at 754.

App Cas.: Appeal Cases (English)
Aust.B.Rev: Australian Bar Review
CLR: Commonwealth Law Reports (Australia)
F.L.R.: Federal Law Reports
ICCPR: International Covenant of Civil and Political Rights
L.Institute J.: Law Institute Journal (Australia)
Mel.U.L.Rev: Melbourne University Law Review
Monash U.L.R.: Monash University Law Review
NSWLR: New South Wales Law Reports (Australia)
Pub.L.Rev: Public Law Review (Australia)
SCR: Supreme Court of Canada Reports
Syd.L.Rev: Sydney Law Review
Tort L.Rev: Tort Law Review (Australia)
U. of W.A.Annul.L.Rev.: University of Western Australia Annual Law Review
U.W.A.L.Rev.: University of Western Australia Law Review
UNSW.L.J: University of New South Wales Law Journal
VR: Victorian Reports (Australia)

H. PATRICK GLENN[*]

The Use of Comparative Law by Common Law Courts in Canada[**]

INTRODUCTION

Sources of law are defined widely by common law courts in Canada and the use of foreign sources, which would be seen as a process of comparative law in some jurisdictions, is often seen within Canada as simply the process of legal reasoning itself. Since this process is inherently comparative there is no need to expressly designate it as such. This attitude may be seen as flowing from the major difficulty of deciding what, in law, is foreign. In some jurisdictions foreign law is defined by implication through a national and legislative definition of domestic law.[1] In common law Canada a national and legislative definition of law has not been possible, for essentially three reasons.

The first of these reasons is the influence of the common law tradition, as it emerged from English legal history and the practice of the British Empire and Commonwealth. While the judge played a prominent role in the common law tradition, the notion of judicial law-making and *stare decisis* was absent from that tradition through most of its history. Courts and judges were open to a multiplicity of sources and reflective of the society within which they functioned. National closure occurred to some extent in nineteenth and twentieth century England but elsewhere in the Empire and Commonwealth there was inherent resistance to the idea of *stare decisis* and the notion of national, judicial law-making. Common law sources thus tended to float freely about the Empire and later the Commonwealth. Efforts to create lines of uniform and strictly binding jurisprudence common to these political entities were unsuccessful. The result was a common law, now existing throughout the contemporary Commonwealth,

[*] Faculty of Law and Institute of Comparative Law, McGill University, Canada
[**] See List of Abbreviations at end of Chapter.
[1] For the effect of the process of harmonization of laws on the distinction between foreign and domestic law see H.P. Glenn, "Harmonization of Law, Foreign Law and Private International Law": (1993) 1 Eur. Rev. Priv. L. 47, notably at p. 56.

U. Drobnig and S. van Erp (eds.), The Use of Comparative Law by Courts, 59–78.

inspired largely by English decisional sources but yielding to local jurisprudence where local circumstances dictated. Blackstone's declaratory theory of law was the major instrument in this process. It allowed judges to pick and choose amongst local and distant common law sources, in the search to declare the common law in its truest form. In Canada this has meant frequent use of non-Canadian common law sources, widespread inter-provincial citation of case law, and the rejection of a federalized court system in which each level of government (federal and provincial) would have its own court system and attendant common law.[2]

The second reason for adoption of an informal and inclusive concept of sources of law has been the co-existence within Canada of both civil and common law traditions. While nine of the provinces received the common law as it had been developed in England, Quebec received the *ancien droit français* and the civil law tradition is alive and well within Quebec today.[3] In some parts of Canada there has been relatively little practical contact between these two traditions, but judicial practice, professional structures and legal education have been open to their mutual influence. The Supreme Court of Canada, in particular, has been pre-occupied throughout its history with the reciprocal influences of the civil and common laws and has demonstrated its willingness to contribute to a process of cross-fertilization. This tendency has been accelerating in recent years. As well, the circumstances of contemporary legal practice and the development of multi-jurisdictional law firms has stimulated greater awareness of the contribution of both common and civil laws to legal problems of national or inter-provincial dimensions. Finally, a number of law faculties have undertaken multi-traditional or multi-lingual training.[4]

Finally, Canadian common law courts have been open to a multiplicity of sources because of the existence within Canada of a recognizable aboriginal legal tradition. While the aboriginal population of Canada is recognized in public international law as subject to Canadian sovereignty, this has not gone uncontested within Canada and the acceptance of Canadian sovereignty does not entail the exclusive application of the law of the

---

[2] Cf. the position which has prevailed in the United States, where a federalized court system is accompanied by a widely accepted notion of individual state common laws. In contrast, the unitary court system of Canada, replicated in each province, is based on the general or unitary competence of provincial superior court judges, who are appointed by the federal government. This single judiciary, competent in both federal and provincial matters, is thus a major continuing source of a single common law, existing in and beyond Canada.

[3] The Civil Code of Quebec replaced the Civil Code of Lower Canada of 1866 on January 1, 1994.

[4] In particular, the Faculties of Law of McGill University and the University of Ottawa offer both civil and common law degrees; the Faculties of the Universities of Moncton and Ottawa offer common law programmes in French, as McGill University offers the civil law in English; a number of Faculties have developed student exchange programmes; and the Federal Government has sponsored an annual summer programme in which students from both legal traditions undertake comparative legal studies.

Canadian State, and of Canadian judges, to the aboriginal population. Canadian courts are now engaged in an ongoing process of defining the law applicable to aboriginal populations and it is the common law which is adapting, through its judges, to aboriginal sources.

Given these general considerations which may be seen as affecting the use of comparative law by common law courts in Canada, the more precise features of this practice will be examined by considering successively: I The Views of Legal Writers; II Judicial Practice; III Methods of Judicial Comparison; IV Limits of Judicial Comparison; and V Justifications of Judicial Comparison.[5]

I. THE VIEWS OF LEGAL WRITERS

The debate in Canada on the use of sources which are in some measure foreign has not, in general, been in terms of the use of comparative law. It has been a debate in the language of more immediate contexts, such as the role of national *stare decisis* or the importance of international human rights standards in the interpretation of domestic human rights norms. Opinions on the use of non-local sources have varied from one context to another.

The most persistent and long-lasting debate has been with respect to the continuing relevance and authority of English case law. Since the nineteenth century there has been present in Canadian doctrinal writing a strong current in favour of a national concept of *stare decisis*, which would look essentially to the Supreme Court of Canada and provincial appeal courts as sources of domestic law. This view is implicitly if not explicity opposed to continuing adherence to English and Commonwealth authority, though it often would recognize English and Commonwealth authority as continuing to have (some) persuasive authority. In the nineteenth century this view was perhaps best represented by A.H.F. Lefroy, whose scientific view of the common law was based on the view that individual cases alone were binding.[6] The movement of Canada towards political and legal independence was inevitably accompanied by a reinforcement of this view. Mid-twentieth century Canadian writers called regularly for elevation of

---

[5] In accordance with the analysis proposed by Professor Ulrich Drobnig, General Reporter for the subject *The Use of Comparative Law by Courts*, XVth International Congress of Comparative Law.

[6] See R.C.B. Risk, "A.H.F. Lefroy: Common Law Thought in Late Nineteenth-Century Canada: On Burying One's Grandfather": (1991) 41 U.T.L.J. 307. Lefroy exhibited the usual ambiguity of the age, in insisting on the binding character of local law and in using a limited range of literature and ideas, while retaining an "unbounded loyalty" to Britain and British models. *Ibid.*, at p. 316.

Canadian sources and abandonment of the habits of Empire.[7] In its more extreme form this view would recognize common laws for each of the Canadian common law provinces as well as at the level of the Federal government.[8]

It cannot be said that this doctrinal movement has been entirely succssessful. The movement was in no way original, representing a phenomenon which had largely played itself out in many jurisdictions in the eighteenth, nineteenth and early twentieth century; it underestimated the ongoing attachment of Canadian common law lawyers to Commonwealth sources of law; and it has failed completely to address the late twentieth century phenomenon of globalization. Throughout the twentieth century the view thus continued to be stated that the common law possessed an underlying unity of principle which justified use of Commonwealth authorities generally,[9] as well as those of the United States.[10] As will be seen, these later views have received and continue to receive major support from Canadian judicial practice. Perhaps most importantly, Canadian common law doctrinal writing continues to make extensive use of decisional law drawn from the contemporary Commonwealth, the U.S.A., and on occasion from civil law jurisdictions including Quebec.[11]

The second major area of doctrinal debate relates to the use of international human rights standards in the interpretation of domestic human rights norms. In this regard there appears to be near unanimity amongst legal writers that resort to foreign and international human rights instruments will re-inforce implementation of human rights within Canada.[12]

---

[7] See, for example, G. Kennedy, "Stare Decisis – Five Recent Judicial Comments": (1951), 29 Can. Bar Rev. 92; H. Read, "The Judicial Process in Common Law Canada": (1959), 37 Can. Bar Rev. 265.

[8] See, for support for such a view by a contemporary Canadian constitutional lawyer, P. Hogg, *Constitutional Law of Canada*, (3rd ed., Toronto, 1992), p. 177.

[9] See W. Jackett, "Foundations of Canadian Law in History and Theory," in O.E. Lang (ed.), *Contemporary Problems of Public Law in Canada: Essays in Honour of Dean F.C. Cronkite* (Saskatoon, 1968), p. 3; and for further references, H.P. Glenn, "Persuasive Authority": (1987) 32 McGill L.J. 261.

[10] J. M. MacIntyre, "The Use of American Cases in Canadian Courts": (1966), 2 U.B.C.L.Rev. 478.

[11] See, for example, P. Maddaugh & J. McCamus, The Law of Restitution (Toronto, 1990)(also noting "intriguing parallels" with civil law of unjust enrichment); R.J. Sharpe, Injunctions and Specific Performance (Toronto,1983); E. Todd, The Law of Expropriation and Compensation in Canada (2nd ed., Toronto, 1992); S.M. Waddams, The Law of Contracts (3rd. ed., Toronto, 1993); *ibid.*, The Law of Damages (2nd ed., Toronto, 1991); M.A. Waldron, The Law of Interest in Canada (Toronto, 1992); D. Waters, The Law of Trusts in Canada (2nd ed., Toronto, 1984)(with separate chapter on trust law in Quebec and relevant civil law principles); B. Welling, Corporate Law in Canada: The Governing Principles (Toronto, 1984).

[12] See, for example, A. Bayefsky, *International Human Rights Law: Use in Canadian Charter of Rights and Freedoms Litigation* (Toronto, 1991); W. Schabas, *International Human Rights Law and the Canadian Charter: A Manual for the Practitioner* (Toronto, 1991); E.R. Alexander, "The Canadian Charter of Rights and Freedoms in the Supreme

Here doctrinal writing clearly is in advance of judicial practice and its influence is only now beginning to have effect. This will be seen in examining judicial practice and methods of judicial comparison.

II. Judicial practice

Comparison in the judicial application of rules of law may take place in common law Canada either because a case presents a foreign element or because, in the resolution of a domestic case, law which may be considered foreign in some respect is recognized as relevant.

A. Cases presenting a foreign element

The most evident instance of comparison in the resolution of cases presenting a foreign element is in the process of characterization in private international law. Judicial practice here appears open to the relevance of foreign law in the characterization process and foreign law is consulted in any case in which the appropriate characterization is open to question. This is the case both for international and inter-provincial cases of conflict of law. Thus in *Tezcan* v. *Tezcan,*[13] Turkish law recognized as governing any implied matrimonial contract of the parties was consulted in characterizing the claim of the wife to immoveable property in British Columbia as being one of matrimonial property or the general law of property. In inter-provincial cases the law of Quebec has been considered in deciding on the nature of claims of spouses or successors to property owned by parties whose matrimonial regime was governed by Quebec law.[14] Resort to the law of both jurisdictions for purposes of characterization is reinforced in inter-provincial cases, moreover, by the role of the Supreme Court of Canada, which acts as the final court of appeal for all provincial courts. In its role as a final court of appeal for all provinces, the Supreme Court cannot take a purely unilateral view of the inter-provincial conflicts cases

---

Court of Canada": (1989), 105 L.Q.R. 561, at p. 577 *et seq.*; A. Bayefsky, "The Impact of the European Convention on Human Rights in the United Kingdom: Implications for Canada": (1981), 13 Ottawa L.Rev. 507; R. Harvie & H. Foster, "Ties that Bind? The Supreme Court of Canada, American Jurisprudence, and the Revision of Canadian Criminal Law under the Charter": (1990), 28 O.H.L.J. 729; *Ibid.*, "Different Drummers, Different Drums: The Supreme Court of Canada, American Jurisprudence and the Continuing Revision of Criminal Law under the *Charter*": (1992), 24 Ottawa L. Rev. 39.

[13] (1992), 87 D.L.R. (4th) 503 (B.C.C.A.), notably at p. 510 ("Turkish characterization").

[14] See *Kerr* v. *Kerr* (1981), 121 D.L.R. (3d) 221 (whether Quebec contract of separation of property encompasses claim to a "division of family assets" in Ontario); *Beaudoin* v. *Trudel*, [1937] 1 D.L.R. 216 (whether Quebec law governing matrimonial regime also extends to claims of surviving spouse as successor).

which come before it.[15] It is entitled, moreover, to take judicial notice of all provincial law.[16] For purposes of characterization of a foreign law as penal, however, it is stated that the determination "is not affected by the view taken by the courts of the foreign country."[17] Even this position would not preclude, however, consideration of foreign sources as a means of ascertaining the true nature and purpose of the foreign law.

Comparison of the implicit territorial reach of domestic rules has also emerged in the choice-of-law process in cases of potential conflicts between the laws of Canadian provinces. Formal choice of law rules are used to resolve most such cases of conflict, but interpretation of domestic rules to determine their appropriate application in space has emerged as a subsidiary choice-of-law method. Since Canadian superior court judges are federally appointed, and since appeals are heard eventually by the Supreme Court of Canada as the final court of appeal for all of the provinces, there is a tendency to avoid purely unilateral interpretation of the laws of the forum. The Supreme Court has used explicitly comparative language in assessing the interest and implicit intent of different provinces to have their law applied to inter-provincial cases.[18]

Cases involving the potential application of aboriginal law may be most appropriately analyzed as cases presenting a foreign element. The foreign element would be the membership of the aboriginal parties in a band, the members of which may be established in more than one province or country. Even where a band occupies land collectively, the land may straddle a political boundary such as that between the U.S.A. and Canada. There is no established principle in Canadian law that the aboriginal population is governed by aboriginal law. A general principle of personality of laws has not been formally articulated. Nevertheless, personalist solutions have emerged through the use of comparative legal reasoning in the context of individual cases. Aboriginal legal solutions must be established by proof of aboriginal law distinct from the solutions of provincial private law. Where aboriginal law is established, it will prevail for aboriginal parties except where it is displaced by provincial laws of "general application."[19] The determination of which provincial laws are of general application involves necessary comparison between aboriginal and non-aboriginal law in order

---

[15] See the remarks of Laskin C.J.C. in *Regina* v. *Thomas Equipment Ltd.* (1979), 96 D.L.R. (3d) 1, at p. 4, on the impropriety of a "one-sided view" in resolving inter-provincial conflicts of laws.

[16] See J.-G. Castel, *Canadian Conflict of Laws* (3rd ed., Toronto, 1994), p. 148, with references.

[17] Castel, *supra*, note 16, at p. 162, with references.

[18] See the language of Laskin, C.J.C. in *Interprovincial Co-operatives Ltd.* v. *The Queen in Right of Manitoba* (1975), 53 D.L.R. (3d) 321 at p. 339 ("Neither Saskatchewan nor Ontario can put forward as strong a claim to have their provincial law apply in the Manitoba action; in other works, the wrong in this case was committed, or the cause of action arose in Manitoba and not in Saskatchewan or Ontario").

[19] *Indian Act*, R.S.C. 1985, c. I-5, s. 88.

to determine their respective territorial scope. Absent formal inter-personal choice-of-law rules, comparative interpretation of the two laws in presence takes place. It has thus been decided that aboriginal marriage,[20] successoral[21] and adoption[22] law will prevail over provincial private law for aboriginal parties. The decisions relating to aboriginal adoption law are the most explicitly comparative in character, the courts deciding that aboriginal adoption law must displace formal, provincial adoption rules because of the need of aboriginal children to benefit from informal, aboriginal adoption in the particular circumstances of northern life. Since provincial adoption rules do not provide the necessary benefits, they are displaced by the aboriginal rules.

The final instance in which comparative law is used with respect to cases presenting a foreign element is in the development of formal choice-of-law rules for such cases. The comparison which takes place is here not of competing rules of substantive law but of available and potentially applicable choice of law rules. Comparison in this instance may be rooted in two underlying circumstances. The first is the jurisprudential or common law character of private international law in Commonwealth jurisdictions. Since the judicial practice towards the common law is one generally of openness to distant, relevant sources (as will be seen, *infra*), the same attitude prevails with respect to rules of private international law. This was demonstrated clearly in recent decisions of the Supreme Court of Canada dealing with recognition of foreign judgments and anti-suit injunctions, in which extensive use was made of Commonwealth and U.S. law in restating Canadian law on these subjects. The second circumstance underlying use of foreign legal models is in interpreting international uniform law to which Canada is a party. Few examples can be given, however, of such a practice. As is usually the case with federal or confederal jurisdictions of divided sovereigny, Canada is a party to few international uniform laws. In recently adhering, however, to the Vienna Convention on Contracts for the International Sale of Goods[23] and the Hague Convention on the Civil Aspects of International Child Abduction[24] it is entirely probable that Canadian courts will take cognizance of foreign case law in the interpretation of these international instruments.[25]

---

[20] *The Queen* v. *Nan-E-Quis-A-Ka* (1889), 2 C.N.L.C. 368, 1 Terr. L.R. 211.

[21] *Re Noah Estate* (1961), 32 D.L.R. (2d) 686, 36 W.W.R. 577.

[22] *Casimel* v. *Insurance Corp. of British Columbia* (1993), 106 D.L.R. (4th) 720.

[23] For implementing legislation in Canada see J.-G. Castel, *supra*, note 16, p. 594.

[24] For implementing legislation see Castel, *supra*, note 16, p. 382.

[25] See *Bagnell* v. *Bagnell* (1991), 108 N.S.R. (2d) 428 (Nova Scotia Family Court judge speaking by telephone with Senior Judge of Orange County, California, Superior Court on state of California law and proceedings in applying Hague Convention on the Civil Aspects of International Child Abduction).

B. Domestic Cases and Law of Foreign Origin

In cases which occur entirely within Canada and which present no relevant foreign element Canadian courts make widespread use of law of foreign origin. The law is of foreign origin at least in political terms. It is derived from institutions which function in foreign, sovereign States. There is a major question, however, as to whether the law itself is best considered foreign. To the extent that it is cited and applied by Canadian courts it functions as local law, while retaining its identity as politically foreign. The two areas in which this occurs are those of maritime law and the common law generally.

In maritime matters, two comparative phenomena should be noted. The first is the widespread and general use of law of diverse origin in the ongoing process of stating contemporary maritime law. The tradition of maritime law being an international corpus of rules "not depending for its validation on any inferred national legislation"[26] is thus continued. In Canada perhaps the best evidence of judicial practice in this regard are the two volumes of Professor Tetley on *Marine Cargo Claims*[27] and *Maritime Liens and Claims*,[28] both of which contain Tables of Cases for Commonwealth and U.S. decisions and for Continental European jurisdictions (listed by country), as well as Tables of Statutes, listed by countries. Canadian judges inevitably read, and cite, trans-national maritime law.[29]

The second comparative phenomena relating to maritime law is more particularly Canadian. For purposes of defining the law over which the Federal Court of Canada may exercise jurisdiction, the Supreme Court of Canada has declared the existence of a Canadian (Federal) maritime law, an exceptional instance of jurisprudential law being declared as attached to or belonging to a particular level of legislative authority.[30] The corpus of this Canadian or Federal maritime law is the "body of law which was administered in England by the High Court on its admiralty side in 1934."[31] The decision to define Federal law in terms of English authority has not

[26] G. Gilmore and C. Black, *The Law of Admiralty* (2nd ed., Mineoloa, N.Y., 1975), p. 45.

[27] 3rd. ed., Montreal, 1988.

[28] Montreal, 1985.

[29] See, for example, the recent decision of the Supreme Court of Canada in *Chartwell Shipping Limited* v. *Q.N.S. Paper Company Limited*, [1989] 2 R.C.S. 683 (over sixty cases cited, approximately 40% Canadian, 40% English, 15% U.S., balance Commonwealth; over 30 doctrinal references, approximately half Canadian including Quebec civilian, balance English, French, U.S. and German).

[30] *ITO-International Terminal Operators Ltd.* v. *Miida Electronics Inc.*, [1986] 1 S.C.R. 360.

[31] *Ibid.*, at p. 771.

been well received by Quebec lawyers.[32] However, the body of law applied by English courts in admiralty matters was essentially civil law (of which the repository was Doctors' Commons). It thus becomes necessary to know what are the best sources of English admiralty practice and of knowing whether, for each question, civilian rules had been replaced by common law ones. Historical, comparative research is necessary to reach any such conclusion.[33]

The largest area of law in which Canadian common law courts make use of authority from a wide number of jurisdictions is that of the common law in general. Since the common law extends to both public and private law it is difficult to establish an area of law which is free from this practice, though its intensity varies from subject area to subject area, in part due to the extent of statutory intervention. Even in cases of statutory interpretation, however, use of foreign decisional law cannot be excluded, since legislation in common law jurisdictions assumes a background of common law rules and is often similar in objective and terminology. To ascertain the extent of reference to local and distant common law sources, an examination was made of ten recent volumes of the largest case reporting series in common law Canada, the Dominion Law Reports.[34] The survey indicated that provincial courts refer to case law of their own province in a proportion ranging from only 4% to 40% of their total citations, with citations to Supreme Court of Canada decisions, representing a law taken to be common and not purely provincial in character, representing another 18% to 28%. Patterns of citation did vary from province to province, however, as the following chart indicates:[35]

---

[32] See, for example, A. Braen, "L'arrêt ITO-International Terminal Operators Ltd. c. Miida Electronics Inc., ou comment écarter l'application du droit civil dans un litige maritime au Québec": (1987), 32 R.D. McGill 386.

[33] See the subsequent, explicitly comparative decision of the Supreme Court of Canada in *Chartwell*, *supra*, note 29 and, as to the survival in admiralty of common law defences long since abolished by provincial legislatures, W. Spicer & W. Laurence, "Not Fade Away: The Re-emergence of Common Law Defences in Canadian Maritime Law": (1992), 71 Can.Bar Rev. 700. Absent proof of reliance on such defences by the English Admiralty court, civilian rules would not be displaced. For the relevance of the 1866 Civil Code of Lower Canada as evidence of English Admiralty Practice, see *Fairway LIfe & Marine Insurance Ltd. & The Fishing Vessel "Susan Darline"* F.C.T.D., Toronto June 17, 1986, No. 196-86, Giles J., cited by Braen, *supra,* note 32, at note 24.

[34] Volumes examined were: 150 D.L.R. (3d) (1984) and, in the 4th series, volumes 11, 24, 30, 40, 51, 63 73, 84 and 96 (1985 through 1993). A total of 644 cases were searched yielding a total number of citations of 4,930.

[35] These citations patterns are broadly consistent with more extensive empirical research undertaken at the level of particular provincial Courts of Appeal. See P. McCormick, "Case-load and Output of the Saskatchewan Court of Appeal: An Analysis of 12 Months of Reported Cases": (1989), 53 Sask.L.Rev. 341; *ibid.*, "Caseload and Output of the Manitoba Court of Appeal, 1990": (1992), 21 Man.L.J.24. *Cf.* considerably higher rates of in-state citation patterns in the United States, as indicated in J.H. Merryman, "Toward a Theory of Citations: An Empirical Study of the Citation Practice of the California Supreme Court in

	Own	SCC	Other Can	Foreign
Alberta	28.7	17.7	34.0	19.6
BC	32.0	19.3	19.6	29.1
Manitoba	19.7	26.3	37.4	16.6
New Brunswick	26.2	27.2	34.0	12.6
Newfoundland	4.3	28.3	43.5	23.9
Nova Scotia	25.8	26.3	32.8	15.2
Ontario	40.4	21.7	15.2	22.7
Pei	15.3	23.5	45.9	15.3
Saskatchewan	25.7	26.9	32.3	15.0
Avg (1)	24.2	24.1	32.7	18.9
Avg (2)	31.9	22.1	24.2	21.8

(1) Average: total of column divided by 9; this calculation treats each province as equal regardless of how many cases were cited by that particular province.
(2) Average: total cases cited to a column divided by the grand total of cases cited; this calculation gives greater weight to provinces that cited more cases.

In terms of fields of law, it is evident that the rate of citation is not dictated by any single variable. The following total citations of foreign, persuasive authority were given in the particular fields of law indicated:

Foreign Citations by Field of Law

Field of Law	Appeal Cts	Trial Cts	Total
Property[1]	69	62	131
Civil Procedure[2]	50	54	104
Constitutional and Int'l[3]	49	48	97
Tort	56	35	91
Contract[4]	46	38	84
Corporations[5]	36	15	51
Labour[6]	29	17	46
Insurance	18	22	40
Criminal	18	11	29
Administrative[7]	10	19	29
Debtor-Creditor	17	10	27
Family	11	7	18
Taxation	0	3	3

1. Property, landlord-tenant, trusts, intellectual property, wills and estates.
2. Civil procedure, conflict of laws, contempt of court, abuse of process, evidence (all except criminal).
3. Constitutional, international law, human rights, admiralty.
4. Contracts, banking, negotiable instruments, guarantee.
5. Corporations, partnerships.
6. Labour, employment, pensions, professions (qualifications, discipline).
7. Administrative, municipal, citizenship, immigration.

1950, 1960, and 1970": (1977), 50 Cal.L.Rev. 381; L.M. Friedman, R.A. Kagan, B. Cartwright & S. Wheeler, "State Supreme Courts: A Century of Style and Citation": (1981), 33 Stan.L.Rev.773.

The traditional common law fields of property, contract and tort – where there has been relatively little statutory intervention – rank high in this list. Legislation or even codification does not preclude resort to persuasive authority, however, as is evident by citation patterns in the field of civil procedure where there has been codification in the form of Rules of Civil Procedure in all of the common law provinces. The existence of taxation legislation, however, appears to have largely driven out any resort to external authority. The rate of citation of foreign authority in the fields of constitutional and international law is of particular interest and is indicative of the increasing internationalization of human rights law. The concept that national public law is or should be impervious to comparative influence[36] is not sustained by these figures.

In recent years the Supreme Court of Canada has maintained and even intensified the use of comparative law in its decision-making. In common law cases the Court has always made liberal use of Commonwealth common law sources and continues to do so. It now also makes frequent, explicit use of U.S. constitutional law in its interpretation of the *Canadian Charter of Rights and Freedoms*.[37] Approximately one-third of its overall citations are now to foreign, persuasive authority of this kind.[38] As well, the Court has always been a meeting place of the civil and common law traditions and its judges have necessarily taken part in decisions from a tradition other than their own.[39]. The Court appears now to be making increased use of civil law authority in its common law decision-making. In

---

[36] See O. Kahn-Freund, "On Uses and Misuses of Comparative Law": (1974), 37 Mod. L. Rev. 1, notably at pp. 12, 13 ("The question is ... who has planted the roots and who cultivates the garden ... how closely [the foreign rule] is linked with the foreign power structure").

[37] See R. Harvie & H. Foster, *supra*, note 12; C. Manfredi, "The Use of United States Decisions by the Supreme Court of Canada Under the Charter of Rights and Freedoms": (1990), 23 Can.J.Pol.Sc. 499; *ibid.* "The Canadian Supreme Court and American Judicial Review: United States Constitutional Jurisprudence and the Canadian Charter of Rights and Freedoms": (1992), 40 Am.J.Comp.L. 213, notably at p. 214 (Canadian Supreme Court citation of U.S. decisional law increasing from 2.9% of its overall citation of authority during the period 1949-1983 to 8.6% in 1989 and 1990).

[38] This figure is drawn from the study of 10 recent volumes of the Dominion Law Reports referred to *supra* in note 34. Earlier studies indicate fluctuations in the Court's citation practice, with a relatively low level of citation to foreign, persuasive authority in mid-century. In the period 1959 to 1979 the number of references to foreign law per judgment increased from .43 to 1.15. D. Casswell, "Doctrine and Foreign Law in the Supreme Court of Canada: A Quantitative Analysis": (1981), 2 Sup. Ct. L. Rev. 435 at 442. This study is noteworthy, however, for not including U.K. decisions in its definition of "foreign" law. References to foreign law were more frequent at a still earlier period, notably in the late nineteenth century when citation of U.S. cases to the Court represented 10 to 25 per cent of cases cited to the Court. MacIntyre, *supra*, note 10, at 486.

[39] There are nine judges of the Court, three of whom are, by statute, necessarily from Quebec. In Quebec private law cases the three Quebec judges will frequently form a majority of a five-judge Bench, though this is a matter of practice and not of law. Quebec judges also regularly participate in common law decisions, whether of public or private law.

a recent tort decision in a case involving pure economic loss occurring in British Columbia, three opinions were given by the members of the Court and in all three there was significant discussion of the significance of civil law decisions, from both Quebec and France, dealing with the extent of liability for such damage.[40] The Supreme Court has also been adamant in its refusal to countenance the general existence of a federal common law and, by implication, common laws of each of the common law provinces.[41]

III. METHODS OF JUDICIAL COMPARISON

The methods of judicial comparison are not scientific, nor are they likely to become so. This unscientific method of comparison is closely related to the judicial function of resolving individual cases. Savigny taught that a multitude of sources is entirely consistent with the judicial function, and it follows that the judiciary will pick and choose, in its own fashion, amongst the multitude of sources which is available to it. Criticism of the methods of judicial comparison should resort to criteria drawn from the adjudicative process itself and not be imposed through resort to external disciplines.

A. Contents and Effects of the Foreign Solution

To the extent that common law courts look to the floating common law of the Commonwealth and Anglo-American world it is perhaps most appropriate to speak of competing or variant common law solutions, as opposed to foreign solutions. Once again the underlying question is whether the common law can be described as foreign simply because non-local courts contribute to its articulation. There is, however, increasing diversification of law within the common law world. This has resulted not so much from adoption of the contents and effects of foreign solutions (those of other common law jurisdictions), as it has resulted from the adoption of particular, local solutions which vary from the common law accepted elsewhere. In the process of reception of the common law throughout the world, exceptions were usually created to displace the metropolitain version of the common law where it was "unsuitable" to local conditions. Local jurisprudence could thus always depart from whatever uniform common law

---

[40] *Canadian National Railway Co.* v. *Norsk Pacific Steamship Co. Ltd.* (1992), 91 D.L.R. (4th) 289. See also, for use of civil law in common law cases, *Sorochan* v. *Sorochan* (1986), 29 D.L.R. (4th) 1, at p. 5 (constructive trust and unjust enrichment); *Central Trust Co.* v. *Rafuse* (1986), 31 D.L.R. (4th) 481 at pp. 520, 521 (alternative claims in tort and contract); *London Drugs Ltd.* v. *Kuehne & Nagel International Ltd.*, [1993] 1 W.W.R. 1, at p. 35 (privity of contract).

[41] *Quebec North Shore Paper Co.* v. *Canadian Pacific Ltd.* (1976), 71 D.L.R. (3d) 111. *Cf.*, however, for maritime law, the discussion *supra*, accompanying note 30.

existed, and this original exception has now blossomed into various forms of national, state or provincial jurisprudence.

The contemporary common law is thus characterized by a range of diverse sources and a corresponding range of commonality and diversity of results. The commonality may be at an abstract level (notions of foreseeability and negligent misrepresentation in the law of torts, consideration in contracts, divisible ownership in property and trusts) but exists to a considerable degree at the level of concrete results. Canadian legal writing evidences the commonality of results across the common law world in announcing general rules or principles with citation to supporting judicial decisions drawn from a number of provinces of Commonwealth jurisdictions. There appears to be no tendency to identify particular jurisdictions as following distinct rules, as does occur in the United States. Departures from commonly held solutions are indicated often simply as "But see..." or "Cf....", with or without an indication of geographic origin. The content and effect of the solutions are thus judged to be entirely compatible with local circumstance, as representative of a range of solutions within the common law world.

There is no institutional device however, in the world of independent common law judges, to ensure uniform results in decision making. The contemporary diversity of the common law in Canada manifests itself in three different ways. Canadian courts, most notably the Supreme Court of Canada, may choose not to follow English or Commonwealth authority. This has occurred, for example, in relation to recovery in tort for economic loss,[42] restitution,[43] the exercise of the *parens patriae* power for purposes of sterilization,[44] hearsay,[45] and confidentiality.[46] Canadian trial and appeal courts may also choose to align themself with more recent Commonwealth authority and abandon prior decisions of the Supreme Court of Canada.[47]

---

[42] See *Norsk Pacific*, *supra*, note 40, notably McLachlin J. at p. 366, using language of shared differences ("The decisions of the House of Lords in *Murphy* and of this court in *Kamloops* illustrate two different approaches to the problem of defining the legal parameters of common law rules").

[43] See generally Maddaugh & McCamus, *supra*, note 11, notably chapters 1 and 2 on tendency of Canadian case law to align itself with U.S. as opposed to Commonwealth authority in matters of restitution.

[44] Compare *Re B (A Minor)*, [1987] 2 W.L.R. 1213 (H.L.)(sterilization granted) and *Re Eve* (1986), 31 D.L.R. (4th) 1 (S.C.C.)(sterilization refused).

[45] *R.* v. *Smith*, [1992] 2 S.C.R. 590, 94 D.L.R. (4th) 590 (reliable hearsay evidence need not be excluded simply because it cannot be tested in cross-examination).

[46] *The Royal Bank of Canada* v. *Lee and Fishman* (1992), 9 C.P.C. (3d) 199, notably at p. 204 ("... privilege and confidentiality have merged in some areas of Canada, but appear distinct in England"), commented by Perell (1993), 72 Can.Bar Rev. 72.

[47] See notably *Batavia Times Publishing Co.* v. *Davis* (1978), 88 D.L.R. (3d) 144; *Salzburger Sparkasse* v. *Total Plastics Service Inc.*, [1988] 6 W.W.R. 408; *Holub* v. *Holub* (1976), 71 D.L.R. (3d) 698; and see S.M. Waddams, *Introduction to the Study of Law* (4th ed., Toronto, 1992), p. 86 (where English case law adopted by Supreme Court of Canada is

Finally, trial and appeal courts within Canada may choose not to follow case law of other provinces, though in doing so may frequently use the language of the declaratory theory and thereby explicitly negate the impression of creating particular provincial common law.[48]

The debate as to the contents and effects of foreign solutions is most vigorous in Canadian jurisdictions with respect to adoption of U.S. constitutional jurisprudence. There is widespread knowledge in Canada of U.S. constitutional law and its merits and demerits have been the object of greater scrutiny since the adoption of the Canadian *Charter of Rights and Freedoms* in 1982. The debate has turned on particular solutions and also on the role of courts in the implementation of constitutional solutions. Most controversial has been the U.S. notion of the structural injunction, by virtue of which U.S. courts have become involved in ongoing decision-making with regard to major institutions such as prisons or electoral systems. Canadian courts have thus far shown considerable reluctance to engage in the use of structural injunction and justices of the Supreme Court of Canada have openly expressed this reluctance in extra-judicial comments.[49]

B. Evaluation and Weight of Foreign Solutions

It is in the evaluation of foreign solutions and the weight accorded to them that the unscientific character of judicial comparison becomes evidence. The methods of comparison are unscientific in the sense of not conforming to contemporary methods of the social sciences because of the general inability of the judiciary to collect or deal with aggregated data. The comparison which takes place is of the evident intrinsic merits of the solutions which are presented and of their compatibility with local law and circumstance, as perceived by the judge. Since the comparison takes place primarily for the limited purpose of resolution of a particular case, the need for aggregated data is less evident than in the case of social science sur-

---

later over-turned in England, lower courts in Canada free to follow earlier or later English decision).

[48]. See, for example, *Spooner* v. *Ridley Terminals* (1991), 62 B.C.L.R. (2d) 132, notably at 140, *per* Macdonald J. ("I do not perceive that to be the law in British Columbia"); *Alex Duff Realty Ltd.* v. *Eagle Crest Holdings Ltd.*, [1983] 5 W.W.R. 61, notably at 75, *per* Kerans J. ("I would not give effect to this approach").

[49] See W. Estey, "The Law of Remedies – an Overview" in Law Society of Upper Canada, *New Developments in the Law of Remedies*, (Toronto,1978) at p. 19 ("This line of remedy is wholly foreign to us, so far, and I would suggest that no amount of prodding by our law schools, professors and commentators will bring this kind of litigation through the doors of our court-rooms"); B. McLachlin, "The Charter: A New Role for the Judiciary": (1991), 29 Alta L. Rev. 540 at p. 552-553 ("The image of a judge making day to day operational decisions in the running of a school – down to what kind of tennis balls to order in one case – is hardly one most Canadian judges would embrace"); both cited in K. Roach, *Constitutional Remedies in Canada* (Toronto, 1994), para. 13.170.

veys. Some differences do exist, however, between traditional, private law adjudication and the contemporary exercise of the judicial power in constitutional matters.

In private law matters the limited scope of the judicial decision, the pervasive character of the common law (drawn from local and distant sources) and the decline in the contemporary concept of *stare decisis*[50] means that common law courts simply engage in whatever form of judicial reasoning they customarily use in order to justify resort to a solution drawn from elsewhere. The foreign character of the solution does not, in general, dictate any particular method of evaluation of it or of determining the weight to be accorded to it.[51] In this regard, judicial practice in the common law world gives considerable credence to the thesis of Professor Watson that "[h]owever historically conditioned their origins might be, rules of private law in their continuing lifetime have no inherent close relationship with a particular people, time or place."[52] Greater sensitivity to problems of evaluation may be shown, however, with respect to non-Commonwealth sources. Resort to U.S. law may thus be justified because of rapid evolution of the law in a field and the "open question" thus presented to the domestic court.[53] However, even resort to the civil law may simply occur with no particular justification or stated methodology, and this is particularly the case at the level of the Supreme Court of Canada.[54]

The evaluation of foreign authority has been the object of more debate in the field of constitutional law, and once again it is the resort to the jurisprudence of the United States Supreme Court which has provoked much of the debate. Discussion has also occurred, however, with respect to the relevancy and weight of international sources of human rights law. A recent study of use of U.S. constitutional law by the Supreme Court of Canada concluded that U.S. law was "...not being systematically consulted and analyzed" and the current use was "selective, almost eccentric..."[55] The same authors concluded two years later that there was "increasing sophistication" being demonstrated by the Court in its use of U.S. law, though it remained the case that " ... some of the justices will cite United States law and others will simply ignore it, so the two sides never debate the impor-

---

[50] See generally H. P. Glenn, "Sur l'impossibilité d'un principe de *stare decisis* ": R.R.J. 1993. 1073.

[51] See, for example, *Canadian Pacific Air Lines, Ltd.* v. *Canadian Imperial Bank of Commerce* (1987), 42 D.L.R. (4th) 375 (Ont. H.C.), notably at p. 379 (whether bankers of travel agents are constructive trustees for airlines of monies derived from sale of airline tickets; no recent Canadian authority dealing with the subject several cases in other jurisdictions (New South Wales, U.S.A.) simply said to be "on point").

[52] A. Watson, "Legal Transplants and Law Reform": (1976), 92 L.Q.R. 79, at p. 81.

[53] See *Suncor Inc.* v. *Canada Wire and Cable Limited*, [1993] 3 W.W.R. 630 (Alta.Q.B.)(liability in tort of successor corporation; only Canadian authority dealing with issue not providing sufficient authority to justify granting of summary judgment).

[54] See the cases referred to *supra*, note 40.

[55] See R. Harvie & H. Foster, *supra*, note 12, "Ties that Bind....," at p. 782.

tant issues that the differences between the jurisdictions reveal.[56] Use of international human rights instruments by the Supreme Court has been less frequent, though the Chief Justice has recently stated that "... Canada's international human rights obligations should inform not only the interpretation of the content of the rights guaranteed by the *Charter* but also the interpretation of what can constitute pressing and substantial s. 1 objectives which may justify restrictions upon those rights."[57] The Court has thus made reference to U.N. and European human rights conventions, in the latter case noting that "...the language [of the European Convention]... bears signifcant resemblance to that of the ... [Canadian] *Charter*."[58] While reference to non-local sources of public law is thus more self-conscious than in the case of private law, it cannot be said that any systematic or scientific means of evaluation have emerged in judicial practice. It is once again the self-evident utility of the foreign source which is paramount, and further analysis is not used to support or rebut its use.

C. Selection of Legal Systems Used for Comparison

The dominant characteristic of the use of distant sources by Canadian common law courts is the pre-established relationship between the local law and the distant sources. Resort to distant common law sources is thus done within the ambit of a transnational common law taken as pre-defined through political, cultural and linguistic history. Resort to the civil law in the Canadian context is facilitated by the commingling of both traditions at the level of the Supreme Court of Canada and this occurs in spite of linguistic diversity. Resort to aboriginal law takes place because of the geographic presence of aboriginal law within the territorial ambit of Canadian law and the impossibility of avoiding resolution of claims for its application. Underlying this entire process is a concept of law which is largely unsystemic, or systemic only in the sense of a large, fluid system largely lacking in precise contours or predictable behaviour.[59] Local law has never been defined with sufficient precision to constitute an autonomous system and resort to distant sources simply continues to occur where it always has, absent national closure.

---

[56] Harvie & Foster, *supra*, note 12, "Different Drummers ...," at p. 110.

[57] *Slaight Communications Inc.* v. *Davidson*, [1989] 1 S.C.R. 1038, at pp. 1056-57.

[58] *R.* v. *Keegstra*, [1990] 3 S.C.R. 697, at p. 753. *Cf.*, however, distinguishing the language of the Canadian Charter from that of the European Convention of Human Rights in another respect, *Andrews* v. *Law Society of British Columbia* (1989), 56 D.L.R. (4th) 1, at p. 20. See also, for reference to the law of the European Economic Community relating to mobility rights, *Black* v. *Law Society of Alberta* (1989), 58 D.L.R. (4th) 317, at p. 345.

[59] For such a modern concept of system, relying on both mathematical and social science developments, see H. P. Glenn, "Law, Revolution and Rights": in A.R.S.P., Beiheft No. 41, *Revolution and Human Rights* (1990), at p. 9.

The use of particular, distant sources is thus largely unexplained and the selection process itself is unarticulated. Since it so evidently occurs, however, there are implications for the possible use of sources beyond the traditional ones. They can be used, since no explicit form of closure prevents their use. This does not happen frequently and its use may therefore appear eccentric in an even startling manner. There will usually, howevever, be specific reasons justifying the citation in the particular case. Thus, in a criminal case the Ontario Court of Appeal recently cited legislation from Germany, Israel and Switzerland, though did so in establishing the practice of other states in determining whether Canadian abortion legislation violated constitutional guarantees of freedom or religion.[60]

D. Sources of Information

Distant sources which are not located within local State structures are not considered as binding ones, though their use obviously puts into question the extent to which local sources can be considered as binding and exclusive. Since the distant sources can be at best persuasive in character, this means that there is no formal ranking of foreign sources, as is often the case in domestic law. In a sense, all that is foreign is doctrine and nothing is to be excluded because of its formal characteristics. Canadian courts make heaviest use of case law drawn from other jurisdictions, as has been explained above. They also make use of foreign doctrinal writing and this has particularly come to be the case in the Supreme Court of Canada, which has in the last decade substantially increased its resort to both local and non-local legal writing. A recent, major decision of the Supreme Court thus contained a section entitled "Doctrine and jurisprudence" and within this section an initial paragraph (citing some thirteen articles) dealt with "international" doctrine, while a second paragraph then set out relevant Canadian authors.[61] Foreign legislation is also, however, a source of information and may be cited as of persuasive authority for a court in reaching

---

[60] *R.* v. *Morgentaler* (1985), 22 D.L.R. (4th) 641, at p. 679.

[61] *Moge* v. *Moge* (1992), 99 D.L.R. (4th) 456, at pp. 485, 486, *per* L'Heureux-Dubé J. The articles referred to were drawn from the U.S.A., the U.K. and Australia. For citation of doctrine in the field of maritime law, see *supra*, note 29. For further citation by the Supreme Court of foreign doctrine, in the field of contractual liability, see *London Drugs*, *supra*, note 40 at p. 34, *per* Iacobucci J. ("Treatment in other jurisdictions"); and for citation of a range of common and civil law doctrine, including the *International Encyclopedia of Comparative Law*, in the field of delictual liability, see *C.N.R.* v. *Norsk Pacific Steamship Co.*, *supra*, note 40, at p.p 323,324 *per* La Forest J. The official case reports of the Supreme Court have listed since 1985, at the beginning of each case, the cases and doctrinal writing referred to by the Court.

its conclusion. This has recently been the case for legislation drawn from common law jurisdictions and for civil law codes.[62]

IV. Limits of judicial comparison

The limits of judicial comparison are not established by any formal rules or universally valid judicial pronouncements. There is considerable diversity, moreover, within the judiciary itself as to the extent to which resort should be made to distant sources. Judicial opposition has thus been expressed to reliance, or at least reliance judged excessive, on both U.K. and U.S. case law, and these statements are closely linked to national concepts of *stare decisis*.[63] In constitutional matters the diversity of national constitutions and constitutional experiences has been explicity cited as a deterrence to judicial comparison.[64] These cautionary statements, however, are of variable effect and rarely constitute an effective bar to recourse to distant sources. Other judges, at other times, will choose to range further afield and will do so, as has been noted, where the distant authority appears to be of self-evident utility. If it is "on point", it may be used.[65] The judicial function, limited to resolution of a particular case, can sift through and use a remarkable range of authority. The authority need not be limited, for instrumental purposes, in order to ensure a particular result. The veritable limits of judicial comparison are thus found in criteria which are difficult to measure, such as linguistic ability, professional training, library and informational resources. These will exist, in adequate form, where the foreign authority exists within a pre-established range of political, cultural and linguistic commonality.[66] This is why the common law can circulate so freely in the contemporary common law world. Even the patterns of book publication and distribution re-inforce and contribute to the broad pattern of citation. Today there are indications that the citation patterns are beginning to move across traditional fields of legal discourse. The best example

---

[62] See, for New Zealand and Australian legislation dealing with the doctrine of privity of contract, *London Drugs*, *supra*, note 40 at p. 351; and for citation of the Civil Code of Lower Canada, *ibid*, p. 351.

[63] See, for judicial opposition to U.K. authorities, *Yepremiam* v. *Scarborough General Hospital* (1980), 28 O.R. (2d) 494 at p. 515 (Ont.C.A.); and for judicial opposition to citation of U.S. law, which was particularly strong in mid-twentieth century, the judgment of Ritchie J. in *R.* v. *Miller* (1976), [1977] 2 S.C.R. 680, at p. 706.

[64] See in particular the statement of La Forest J. in *Rahey* v. *The Queen* [1987] 1 S.C.R. 598, at p. 639: "While it is natural and *even desirable* for Canadian courts to refer to American constitutional jurisprudence in seeking to elucidate the meaning of Charter guarantees that have counterparts in the United States Constitution, they should be wary of drawing too ready a parallel between constitutions born to different countries in different ages and in very different circumstances....")(emphasis added).

[65] *Supra*, note 51.

[66] *Supra*, Part III C.

is the recent tort decision of the Supreme Court of Canada, *Norsk Pacific*, in which, in a British Columbia case, the Supreme Court made extensive reference in its three judgements, to Quebec and French sources of law.[67] There are thus incentives being established by the judiciary for multi-traditional legal training and multi-jurisdictional practice.

V. JUSTIFICATIONS OF JUDICIAL COMPARISON

In the decision of the Supreme Court of Canada in *Norsk Pacific* three members of the Court commented on the utility of comparative law in resorting to civilian authority for resolution of a common law tort case relating to pure economic loss. For Justice La Forest "[t]he legal system of every society faces essentially the same problems and solves these problems by quite different means, though often with similar results ...."[68] It was possible through resort to civil law authority to ascertain that while the concept of "economic loss" was not retained as a limiting factor, claims such as those presented in the instant case were not recognized. For Justice McLachlin, "[a] summary of how different courts in different jurisdictions have dealt with this problem affords us perspective both on the nature of the problem and the possible solutions."[69] In the context of economic loss, "... comparative review suggests that in some cases damages for economic loss should be available where the plaintiff has neither suffered physical damage nor relied in the sense of *Hedley Byrne*."[70] For Justice Stevenson, "[t]he case at bar is a good example of how useful comparative law can be....Because of the experience this court has in the civil law it cannot be frightened by apocalyptic scenarios about life after the rule against the recovery of pure economic loss."[71]

These statements are representative of the immediate utility which comparative law has presented to the Canadian judiciary. At a more abstract level, Justice Gonthier of the Supreme Court has observed that "[Comparative law] allows us to see where the substantive rules and possiby even the conceptual structure of a given legal system hinder the attainment of justice in a particular case. When we see how easily another system or country can deal with a given problem we begin to see the rigidity and inadequacy of our own solutions."[72]

---

[67] *Supra*, note 40.

[68] *Ibid.*, at p. 319, citing K. Zweigert & H. Kötz, *An Introduction to Comparative Law* (2nd ed., Oxford, 1987), vol I, at p. 31.

[69] *Supra.*, note 40, at p. 361

[70] *Ibid.*, at p.365.

[71] *Ibid.*, at p. 384.

[72] Address by the Honorable Charles D. Gonthier presented to the Twenty-Second Annual Workshop on Commercial and Consumer Law, McGill University, Montreal, Quebec, October 16, 1992, pp. 4,5.

List of Abbreviations:

Alta.L.Rev., Alberta Law Review
Alta.Q.B., Alberta Court of Queen's Bench
Am.J.Comp.L., American Journal of Comparative Law
A.R.S.P., Archiv für rechts- und sozial- Philosophie
B.C.L.R, British Columbia Law Reports
Cal.L.R., California Law Review
Can.Bar Rev., Canadian Bar Review
Can.J.Pol.Sc., Canadian Journal of Political Science
C.N.L.C., Case Notes of Lower Canada
D.L.R., Dominion Law Reports
Eur.Rev.Priv.L, European Review of Private Law
F.C.T.D., Federal Court Trial Division
H.L., House of Lords
L.Q.R., Law Quarterly Review
Man.L.J., Manitoba Law Journal
Mod.L.R., Modern Law Review
N.S.R., Nova Scotia Reports
O.H.L.J., Osgoode Hall Law Journal
O.R., Ontario Reports
Ottawa L.R., Ottawa Law Review
McGill L.J., McGill Law Journal
R.R.J., Revue de recherche juridique
R.S.C., Revised Statutes of Canada
Sask.L.R., Saskatchewan Law Review
S.C.C., Supreme Court of Canada
Sup.Ct.L.Rev., Supreme Court Law Review
S.C.R., Supreme Court Reports
Stan.L.R., Stanford Law Review
Terr.L.R., Territories Law Reports
U.B.C.L.Rev, University of British Columbia Law Review
U.T.L.J., University of Toronto Law Journal
W.L.R., Weekly Law Reports
W.W.R., Western Weekly Reports

PIERRE VIAU[*]

Droit comparé et unification du droit L'utilisation du droit comparé par les tribunaux – Rapport canadien

"La vérité est quelque chose qui se fait, et la vérité faite est le produit d'une modification de la réalité qui nous entoure".[1]

Marcel Viau

INTRODUCTION

Vérité et réalité, voilà deux notions apparentées à celle de justice, cette vertu consistant à traiter chacun selon son mérite. Vérité et justice, deux réalités en perpétuelle création pourrait-on dire d'une autre façon. C'est ainsi du moins que le juge est tenu d'aborder ces questions. Placé au centre d'un conflit parfois fort pénible, il cherche dans les faits dont on tente de lui faire la preuve une vérité parfois évanescente. Et il en est généralement réduit à appuyer son jugement sur le vraisemblable plutôt que sur le vrai, comme l'illustre bien l'expression la *prépondérance des probabilités.* Mais forcé de cheminer en terrain miné, le juge doit savoir s'orienter et considérant tantôt un fait, tantôt un autre, il applique à la solution du litige, à la recherche du juste, des principes de droit et des règles dont la limpidité est parfois loin d'être évidente.

Ainsi se modèle la vérité. Ainsi se modifie la réalité et se rend la justice, à mi-chemin entre ce qui peut être et ce qui doit être. Conservant en mémoire ces remarques, nous poserons d'abord quelques repères permettant d'amorcer notre recherche du juste. Nous illusterons ensuite notre démarche en empruntant la voie du droit comparé tel que l'utilisent les tribunaux canadiens.

---

[*] juge à la Cour supérieure du Québec.

[1] Marcel Viau, *La nouvelle théologie pratique;* Editions Pauline, Editions Cerf; Montréal, Paris, 1993; 203.

U. Drobnig and S. van Erp (eds.), The Use of Comparative Law by Courts, 79–95.

I. À LA RECHERCHE DU JUSTE

Tout discours sur le droit, celui du juge plus que tout autre, implique une recherche du juste (*to dikaion*), de la solution juste. Autrement le risque est grand de consacrer trop d'énergies à étudier les choses et les hommes par le mauvais bout de la lorgnette et de ne découvrir, à toutes fins utiles, qu'une infime portion de la vie qui bat. Rater le bon souffle du grand large en naviguant trop près de la côte. Perdre la mesure exacte des êtres et des choses, et en interprétant une règle de droit, se concentrer sur quelques lignes d'un texte en reléguant dans l'ombre l'ensemble, le contexte, les liens entre des monades qui prennent vite l'allure de tout un cosmos, en infiniment petit. Bref, retenir la lettre et négliger l'esprit.

Le juge, confronté à un débat où s'entremêlent les faits et le droit, doit tout d'abord examiner soigneusement les preuves qu'on veut bien lui présenter. Et souvent sa décision sur ce premier élément du litige lui permet de prononcer un jugement. Les faits ont alors dit le droit. Car le droit, malgré les nombreuses définitions proposées, reste un concept traduisant l'état de certaines relations humaines à un moment donné de l'Histoire. Et sa fin se réalise surtout dans la décision du magistrat dont l'office consiste essentiellement à trancher un litige entre deux parties en attribuant à chacun son *jus*. Ce *jus* (*right* en anglais, *droit* en français) prend, au fil des siècles, le sens subjectif de droit individuel que l'on tente, avec plus ou moins de bonheur, de définir en l'opposant à celui d'autrui.

Or, chez les Romains,le *jus* vise autant une relation de devoir qu'une faculté de prétendre. Ainsi, un fond servant est-il affecté d'un *jus* obligeant son propriétaire à y laisser s'écouler les eaux naturelles. Celui du fond dominant peut donc prétendre que son *jus* lui permet d'égoutter son terrain selon le cours normal des choses. Les parties doivent ainsi respecter l'ordre que la nature a inscrit dans le destin du monde.

De ce point de vue du droit naturel, la justice consiste à attribuer à chacun, selon son mérite, sa juste part de biens, d'honneur, voire de peines, le cas échéant. La justice ne distribue pas les lots, elle compense, départage, sanctionne, compte tenu des preuves et du droit en recherchant dans chaque cas la solution juste. Comme le soulignait Michel Villey:

> "Dans son acception spécifique, la justice tend à donner à chacun le sien (*suum cuique tribuere*) ce dont il est digne, ce qu'il mérite par rapport à ce que mérite les autres membres du groupe social."[2]

Ainsi, la nature du débat judiciaire, qu'il soit d'ordre pénal, civil, familial ou administratif, influe sur des notions comme celles de droit individuel, de droit collectif et de bien commun. Il en va de même pour toute autre notion d'ordre juridique d'ailleurs. Non qu'il faille nier la valeur intrinsèque de ces notions, mais parce qu'il faut nécessairement, en établissant la

---

[2] M. Villey, *Leçons d'Histoire de la philosophie du droit*, Dalloz, 1962, 118.

juste part des choses, éviter de s'enferrer dans un dogmatisme rendant impossible ou improbable la découverte d'une solution équitable de conflits affectant la vie de personnes souvent innocentes et bouleversées par les haines agitant leurs semblables.

Bref, il faut éviter de se laisser trop vite emporter vers l'Idée. Un séjour, même prolongé, dans la caverne de la réalité, ne nuit pas à une meilleure compréhension des concepts et des essences. Ainsi, relit-on toujours avec profit cette judicieuse observation de Thomas Merton:

> "Les notions claires que nous trouvons dans les livres nous trompent parfois, nous faisant croire que nous comprenons des choses dont nous n'avons aucune connaissance pratique."[3]

La voie parfois tortueuse du débat judiciaire est souvent un lieu privilégié pour faire valoir ses droits, l'endroit où ils prennent véritablement toute leur signification.

Il est d'ailleurs impossible de déterminer le bien et l'intérêt d'une personne si l'on refuse de croire à l'existence du juste. Juges, avocats et parties doivent s'efforcer de rechercher la solution qu'il convient d'apporter à un litige en examinant les questions qu'il soulève et cela, le plus librement et le plus ouvertement possible car, comme l'affirme Vullierme:

> "Si le juste n'a pas trouvé sa place parmi les hommes, à quelque endroit où il soit reconnaissable comme tel, autant nous résigner, à l'entrée du prétoire comme à celle de l'enfer, à abandonner toute espérance: la force règnera toujours en empruntant les dénominations les plus honnêtes."[4]

Qui dit débat judiciaire dit recherche du juste bien sûr, mais aussi et surtout, analyse de faits et de documents. C'est la quête du vrai qui guide alors nos pas à travers les méandres des preuves. Travail souvent long, fastidieux, sans éclat mais combien essentiel à la tenue d'un procès équitable. Car un justiciable est aussi malheureux d'avoir perdu sa cause sur les faits que sur le droit.

La recherche de la vraie preuve est d'autant plus importante que le processus judicatif comporte une synthèse de plusieurs concepts. Et cette synthèse ne peut s'effectuer qu'à la suite d'une étude méticuleuse de la réalité. L'esprit humain est ainsi fait qu'il lui faut généralement procéder graduellement, à la pièce, après avoir divisé en plusieurs parties le problème qu'il doit résoudre. Expérience toujours renouvelée de la réflexion discursive.

Les preuves étudiées, la règle de droit trouvée et appliquée, nous atteignons la fin du parcours. It faut alors décider, trancher le litige et cela ne

[3] T. Merton, *La nuit privée d'étoiles*, éd. A. Michel, 1951, 157.

[4] J.L. Vullierme in *Archives de philosophie du droit*, t. 26, L'utile et le juste, 1981, Sirey, 17.

va jamais sans douleur, surtout dans des domaines où l'émotivité atteint son paroxysme. Tous les juges savent cela. Ils assument ce fardeau et accomplissent cette charge avec tout le doigté dont ils sont capables, conscients du fait que leurs motifs les plus raisonables et les mieux exprimés ont peu de chance de convaincre toutes les parties présentes devant eux.

Ces quelques remarques permettront, je l'espère, de situer non seulement l'intervention du juge mais aussi sa façon de délibérer et de décider lorsqu'il attribue à un justiciable ce qu'il mérite sans toutefois s'illusionner sur ses moyens d'action ni sur la valeur intrinsèque des preuves présentées au cours d'un procès. Car en poursuivant sa quête du vrai, le juge ne sait que trop bien combien sa recherche est périlleuse, parsemée d'embûches, et à quel point la mauvaise foi d'un justiciable peut réduire à néant le jugement le mieux motivé.

II. UTILISATION DU DROIT COMPARÉ

Et le droit comparé dans tout cela? Il sert au juge canadien de guide et parfois d'autorité. Le Canada, le Québec en particulier, constituent de véritables laboratoires de droit comparé. En vertu de la constitution canadienne, les questions relatives à la propriété et aux droits civils, par exemple, relèvent de la compétence des provinces, non de celle du gouvernement central. Cela affecte une foule de domaines, comme on peut l'imaginer. Ainsi, le gouvernement fédéral n'a-t-il compétence, en matière de biens culturels, que sur ceux qui lui appartiennent en propre ou sur ceux qui sont la propriété d'organismes ou de sociétés qu'il régit comme celles concernant les chemins de fer. Lorsqu'il s'est intéressé à la protection du patrimoine et du bâti, le pouvoir central a principalement fait porter ses efforts sur les lieux et les monuments historiques en adoptant une loi afin, notamment, de commémorer les évènements ou les personnages liés à un lieu historique.

Bien peu de conflits impliquant des individus et l'Etat sont portés devant les tribunaux canadiens sans que, d'une façon ou d'une autre, les justiciables ne parlent de lois ou de règlements fédéraux ou provinciaux. C'est que le Canada est constitué de dix provinces et de "territoires", et que ces "pouvoirs" occupent certains champs de compétences exclusives ou mixtes. Et cela, dans un contexte de traités et d'autres ententes internationales que respectent les tribunaux, référant notamment au principe suivant énoncé par Lord Diplock dans l'arrêt *Salomon*[5] lorsqu'ils doivent interpréter une disposition législative impliquant des engagements pris par le pays en vertu d'un traité:

---

[5] *Salomon v. Commissionner of Customs and Excise* (1967) 2 Q.B.116, 143.

> "(...) if one of the meanings that can reasonably be ascribed to the legislation is consonant with the treaty obligations and another or others are not, the meaning which is so consonant is to be preferred."

Règle simple. Règle de bon sens. Comme on devrait en retrouver plus souvent dans notre droit moderne, particulièrement en droit pénal où l'ignorance de la loi n'est pas un moyen de défense. Cela éviterait de songer parfois comme Montaigne: "qu'il y a plus affaire à interpréter les interprétations qu'à interpréter les choses, et plus de livres sur les livres que sur autre sujet: nous ne faisons que nous entregloser."[6]

Essayons de ne point trop nous entregloser, et voyons un peu ce qui se passe au Québec en matière d'arbitrage international. Cela nous permettra d'illustrer les divers liens existant entre le droit international, le droit civil et l'interprétation de leurs principes et de leurs dispositions par un tribunal québécois.

A. Arbitrage international

Le Québec a un nouveau Code civil. Il est entré en vigueur le ler janvier 1994. On y retrouve plusieurs dispositions nouvelles et d'autres qui datent de quelques années déjà, comme celles concernant les conventions d'arbitrage. Le législateur a repris, au chapitre dix-huitième du Code, des articles qu'il avait adoptés, en 1986, en vertu de la *Loi modifiant le Code civil et le Code de procédure civile en matière d'arbitrage* (L.Q.1986, c.73). L'objet de cette loi était simple: "favoriser la reconnaissance des conventions d'arbitrage, notamment en matière de commerce international."[7]

Grâce à ces dispositions législatives, personnes et sociétés peuvent s'engager, par contrat, à soumettre un différend, né ou éventuel, à la décision d'un ou de plusieurs arbitres et cela à l'exclusion des tribunaux. Toutefois l'article 2639 prévoit que: "Ne peut être soumis à l'arbitrage, le différend portant sur l'état et la capacité des personnes, sur les matières familiales ou sur les autres questions qui intéressent l'ordre public". L'ordre public, voilà une notion assez vaste pour permettre à un plaideur astucieux de se faufiler jusqu'au prétoire et tenter de démontrer, par exemple, qu'une clause de la convention d'arbitrage limitant les parties à la présentation d'une preuve écrite suivie de plaidoiries, violerait le principe de droit naturel *Audi alteram partem*. Proposition habile qui ramène dans un procès civil un principe reconnu par toute société de droit et auquel tant le législateur que les Etats membres des Nations Unies n'ont certes pas voulu déroger, même en droit commercial international. Autre point

---

[6] M. Montaigne, *Essais*, III, c.XIII, 358 dans Folio.

[7] Commentaires du ministre de la Justice, tome II, *Le Code civil du Québec*, les Publications du Québec, 1993, p. 1648.

soulevé: la preuve par simple production de documents permet d'introduire dans le débat judiciaire des éléments de oui-dire inadmissibles devant une cour de justice canadienne. Enfin, un tel procédé élimine à toutes fins utiles une recherche de la vérité dans un forum public, comme la chose doit normalement se faire et devrait en l'espèce se faire, car l'une des parties est une société dont les actions sont transigées sur le Unlisted Securities Market of the London Stock Exchange.

Bref, une des parties serait, par le mécanisme de l'arbitrage, privée de présenter une preuve complète et de contre-interroger des personnes qui ont témoigné de faits par écrit plutôt que verbalement devant une cour de justice. Deux failles importantes dans un système qui, ne permettant pas de rendre justice aux deux parties, mettrait directement en cause l'ordre public. Voilà par quel détour on est passé des Nations Unies à une cour de justice canadienne, en empruntant la voie d'une convention d'arbitrage conclue entre des canadiens, une société commerciale canadienne et sa parente de Grande-Bretagne.

En l'espèce, la loi québécoise même nous permet d'éviter les conflits entre les droits des deux pays concernés et les difficultés d'interprétation que pourrait susciter, par exemple, la Loi type adoptée par la Commission des Nations Unies.

Revenons donc aux principes de droit reconnus par la plupart des nations membres des Nations Unies. Les parties ont ici conclu une convention d'arbitrage librement et volontairement. Elles en connaissaient la portée et elles acceptaient de soustraire à la compétence des tribunaux judiciaires un différend relatif à leur entente concernant l'achat d'actions dont la valeur atteint 12,000,000 $. Il est bien difficile pour un juge de croire qu'un des contractants a contrevenu à l'ordre public en signant un tel contrat suite à d'importants pourparlers et à l'examen d'études et d'opinions préparées par des experts. Au surplus, le contrat étant la loi des parties, celles-ci doivent vivre avec celui-ci et en respecter les dispositions.

En l'espèce, l'un des cocontractants s'adressait au tribunal alors que l'arbitre n'était saisi que de l'exposé de l'autre partie. Il pouvait certainement présenter ses propres propositions et même soulever certaines objections à la compétence de l'arbitre en début d'audition. Mais celui-ci pouvait certainement procéder à entendre les parties et à prendre les décisions appropriées quitte, le cas échéant, à être corrigé par le tribunal s'il commettait quelqu'erreur grave. La loi prévoit en effect que les arbitres peuvent se prononcer sur leur propre compétence mais que le tribunal peut adjuger sur cette question dans les 30 jours de la décision. Au surplus, la sentence arbitrale doit être homologuée par le tribunal afin de devenir exécutoire comme un jugement prononcé par celui-ci.[8]

Voilà pour le monde de la haute finance internationale et ses aléas.

---

[8] *Silverberg et al. c. Clark Hooper plc et al.*, C.S. Montreal 500-05-015310-897, 1990-01-23; C.A. Montréal, 500-09-000133-900, 1990-02-06.

Examinons maintenant une décision concernant une personne atteinte d'une grave maladie et un important quotidien qui en a diffusé la nouvelle.

B. Vie privée et liberté de presse

Le nouveau Code civil du Québec, s'inspirant de la Charte des droits et libertés de la personne (L.R.Q., chap. C.12 a.1,4,5), décrète ce qui suit:

> "Art. 3. Toute personne est titulaire de droits de la personnalité, tels le droit à la vie, à l'inviolabilité et à l'intégrité de sa personne, au respect de son nom, de sa réputation et de sa vie privée. Ces droits sont incessibles."

Cette disposition de droit nouveau codifie des principes déjà bien connus en législation et en jurisprudence canadienne et québécoise. On peut donc étudier une décision antérieure au nouveau Code dans crainte d'en voir les principes généraux écartés par celui-ci.

Un enseignant intente une action en dommages-intérêts suite à la parution d'articles dans un quotidien à fort tirage l'identifiant comme atteint du syndrome d'immunodéficience (sida). Il reproche à la journaliste, à l'éditeur et à la société d'édition d'avoir publié, sans son consentement, deux articles qui, sans l'identifier clairement, ont permis de le reconnaître aisément et d'identifier la grave maladie dont il souffre.

Le défendeurs soutiennent, pour leur part, que les renseignements contenus dans les articles sont véridiques et qu'ils ont été publiés de bonne foi et dans l'intérêt public car il s'agissait d'un cas flagrant de discrimination apparente par une Commission scolaire à l'endroit de l'un de ses enseignants malades. Pour les défendeurs, la discrimination apparente provenait de ce que, selon les informations de la journaliste, la Commission scolaire refusait à son enseignant de reprendre sa tâche, après un long congé de maladie, avant qu'il ne produise un certificat médical le déclarant apte au travail. Pour l'éditeur, cela paraîssait discriminatoire car la décision semblait fondée sur la seule crainte irrationnelle que ce retour pourrait être préjudiciable aux élèves. Mais personne au journal n'avait même demandé à l'enseignant s'il se sentait victime de discrimination, et s'il voulait que l'on étale sur la place publique son état de santé et surtout le type de maladie dont il était atteint qui, à cette époque, faisant d un sidéen un véritable paria.

La rentrée des enseignants s'effectue le 27 août, l'enseignant se voit refuser l'accès à l'école par le directeur qui n'a pas reçu l'autorisation médicale requise. Le 28 août, tout l'espace supérieur de la première page du journal fait état du cas. L'enseignant revient à l'école à la fin de septembre fort ébranlé par ce qu'il qualifie de bombe intérieure. Il décède un an plus tard, détruit par la maladie et par la méchanceté de gens qui en ont fait un " cas public" alors qu'il avait toujours gardé sa maladie secrète et maintenu une attitude stoïque dans l'adversité.

Le tribunal saisi de l'affaire a statué d'abord sur l'atteinte à la vie privée commise par les défendeurs. Toute personne ayant droit au respect de sa vie privée possède celui d'obtenir réparation du préjudice moral ou matériel résultant d'une atteinte illicite à celui-ci. Or, le droit à la vie privée est constitué du droit à l'anonymat et du droit à la solitude, auxquels s'ajoute celui du respect de la santé. C'est ici qu'intervient le droit comparé puisque ces notions ne se retrouvent ni dans la législation, ni dans la jurisprudence canadienne. Il faut, dès le départ, préciser le concept du droit au respect de la vie privée. Le tribunal établit que ce concept comprend celui de vivre de façon retirée, faisant sien la définition qu'en adoptait le Conseil de l'Europe dans une résolution du 23 janvier 1970.

> "Le droit au respect de la vie privée consiste essentiellement à pouvoir mener sa vie comme on l'entend avec un minimum d'ingérences ‹‹..››[9]

Le tribunal réfère ensuite au jugement de la Cour de Paris (9 juillet 1980, D., 1981.72) dans l'affaire du regretté Jacques Brel, où celle-ci avait jugé qu'il y avait eu, en l'espèce, atteinte à la vie privée de l'intéressé "qui, ayant témoigné d'un souci constant de discrétion" sur sa maladie "et s'étant refusé à toute publicité, était en droit de s'opposer à ce que son état de santé soit commenté dans de telles conditions ..."[10]

L'enseignant était loin d'être connu du public et il avait toujours pris soin de protéger sa vie privée. Et même si l'on ne retrouvait pas sa photo dans le journal, comme dans l'affaire Jacques Brel, et qu'il n'était pas identifié par son nom dans les articles, on pouvait aisément le reconnaître, et l'on pouvait identifier sa maladie et spéculer sur son orientation sexuelle. La belle expression du Pr Jacques Robert permettait alors de clore cette partie du jugement:

> "La personne, ineffable dans sa singularité, se caractérise par un être et un avoir l'un et l'autre protégés par un secret. L'être est une histoire personnelle qui dépasse précisément l'individu et dont celui-ci n'est pas totalement responsable. Aussi font partie des secrets de la personne (...) la vie intime et l'état de santé."[11]

Restait à disposer de l'argument soulevé par les défendeurs et portant que l'intérêt public exigeait de dévoiler cette information au risque même d'affecter le droit à l'anonymat. Or, cette question ne se soulevait même pas en l'espèce, les défendeurs désirant de toute évidence parler d'un enseignant souffrant du sida plutôt qu'informer le public sur la nature de cette maladie ou sur les mesures prises par les autorités dans ce cas. Intérêt

---

[9] Rapporté par Raymond Lindon, *Dictionnaire juridique, les droits de la personnalité*, Paris: Dalloz, 1983, p. 259.

[10] *Id*, p. 263.

[11] Jacques Robert, *Libertés publiques et droits de l'homme*, Paris: Montchrestien, 1988, p. 299.

public ne saurait se confondre avec intérêt commercial ou financier d'un puissant moyen d'information.

L'autre volet à examiner dans cette affaire, le droit à la solitude, n'exigeait pas un si large emprunt à des sources extra-canadiennes, les professeurs H. Patrick Glenn et Jean-Louis Baudouin (maintenant juge à la Cour d'appel du Québec) ayant déjà examiné cette notion.

Pour le Pr Glenn, le droit à la solitude signifie:

> "Une sorte d'intégrité mentale ou spirituelle, une condition dans laquelle un individu est libre de toute entrave injustifiable à son état d'esprit."[12]

Quant au Pr Baudouin:

> "Tout citoyen a d'abord le droit d'être laissé tranquille et de ne pas subir de harcèlement de la part des autres".[13]

Sous l'angle de la protection de l'intimité, particulièrement celui relatif au contrôle des informations personnelles, cette protection est aujourd'hui étendue plus largement.

Précisons que, sous l'angle de la protection de l'intimité, particulièrement celui relatif au contrôle des informations personnelles, "(c') est toute diffusion non normalisée d'informations personnelles qui en principe est protégée sous le couvert du droit à l'intimité".[14]

Voilà un exemple de la méthode suivie par un tribunal pour préciser et compléter des notions plus ou moins bien définies par le législateur. En référant à certains principes généraux d'interprétation émanant de la doctrine ou de la jurisprudence étrangère, un juge peut actualiser le droit. La chose s'avérait d'autant plus facile en l'espèce[15] que la Charte des droits et libertés de la personne énonçait clairement un droit qu'il fallait, de toute évidence, protéger.

C. Pouvoirs locaux et responsabilité civile

Nous abordons maintenant un sujet qui peut sembler bien complexe au juriste peu familier avec le régime canadien d'administration locale. Au Canada, nous désignons par "municipalité" ce que les Français nomment "commune". Nous utiliserons aussi le terme "pouvoirs locaux", traduction

---

12 H. Patrick Glenn, *Le droit au respect de la vie privée*, (1979), 39 R du B. 879, 884.

13 J.-L. Baudouin, *La responsabilité civile délictuelle*, 3 éd. Cowansville: Y. Blais, 1990, p. 153, no. 289.

14 *Id*, p. 1081.

15 *Valiquette c. Gazette (The)*, C.S. Montréal 500-05-011148-879, 1191-03-12; jugement confirmé en appel, no: 500-09-000529-917.

de “local government”, qui a l’avantage de bien montrer la nature de l’institution.

La constitution canadienne confère aux provinces une compétence exclusive sur les pouvoirs locaux. Celles-ci peuvent donc, à leur discrétion, établir un système d’administration local plus ou moins centralisé suivant qu’elles exercent elles-mêmes leurs pouvoirs ou qu’elles les délèguent à des organismes politico-administratifs.

Au Québec, deux lois générales encadrent principalement les activités des pouvoirs locaux: le *Code municipal du Québec* (L.R.Q. chap.C-27.1) qui vise surtout les municipalités rurales et la *Loi sur les cités et villes* (L.R.Q.chap. C-19).

Les pouvoirs locaux canadiens sont constitués en corporations publiques et politiques. Il s’agit de véritables gouvernements disposant d’un territoire, d’un conseil élu par le population et de diverses compétences dont celle de lever des impôts. Leurs compétences leur viennent des lois et règlements édictés par la législateur provincial, soit dans des lois générales comme le *Code civil*, le *Code municipal* ou la *Loi sur les cités et villes*, soit dans des lois spéciales, comme les chartes des villes. On peut dire qu’à ce chapitre: Pas de loi, pas de pouvoir.

Tout pouvoir local dispose de certaines compétences d’ordre général lui permettant, par exemple, d’acquérir des biens et d’en disposer, de se lier par contrat, d’ester en justice. Ainsi peut-il acquérir, pour des fins de sa compétence, des biens meubles ou immeubles par achat, donation, legs ou autrement. Comme gouvernement, le pouvoir local peut aussi exercer des pouvoirs d’ordre politique en établissant des normes qui régiront comportements et activités sur son territoire. C’est le cas notamment en matière d’aménagement du territoire et de fiscalité. C’est aussi le cas en matière de services publics comme celui de la mise sur pied et l’exploitation d’un service de lutte contre les incendies afin de protéger adéquatement les personnes et leurs biens. On a tout de même dépassé, au Xxe siècle, les activités des *siphonarii*, les *falciarii* et des *ballistariii* de la Rome impériale qui, armés de sceaux, de siphons, de faux et de ballistes ne réussissaient généralement qu’à sauver les fondations, comme on dit. On ne s’attend plus à ce que la population accourt sur les lieux d’un incendie ou son du tocsin ou au cri d’*Omnes collegiati ...*

Au Québec, les conseil municipaux peuvent adopter des règlements pour “organiser, maintenir et réglementer un département des incendies et une brigade de pompiers et pour les pourvoir de tous les appareils nécessaires, par achat ou louage; pour pourvoir à la construction de postes de pompiers; pour nommer tous les fonctionnaires et employés nécessaires pour éteindre et supprimer les incendies, protéger la propriété contre le feu, et prévenir les accidents par le feu ...”.

Et l’eau! Qui s’en occupe? Le conseil peut promulguer des règlements pour pourvoir à l’établissement, à l’acquisition, à l’entretien, à l’administration et à la réglementation d’aqueducs, de puits publics, citernes ou réservoirs, pour fournir de l'eau à la municipalité, pour installer des bornes-fontaines, des fontaines et des abreuvoirs publics et des appareils pour la filtration et la purification de l'eau. La municipalité n'est pas tenue de garantir la quantité d'eau qui doit être fournie, et nul ne peut refuser, à raison de l'insuffisance de l'eau, de payer la taxe spéciale annuelle et la compensation pour l'usage de l'eau.

Deux observations à ce stade-ci. Un pourvoir local n'est pas tenu par la loi d'organiser un système de protection contre les incendies non plus que de garantir la quantité d'eau qu'il fournit.

Enfin, un article du Code civil se trouve au coeur même du débat judiciaire que nous aborderons maintenant. Il s'agit de l'article 356 (ancien code) divisant les corporations séculières en politiques et en civiles. En voici le libellé.

> "Les corporations séculières se subdivisent encore en politiques et en civiles. Les politiques sont régies par le droit public, et ne tombent sous le contrôle du droit civil que dans leurs rapports, à certains égards, avec les autres membres de la société individuellement
>
> Les corporations civiles étant par le fait de l'incorporation des personnes morales ou fictives, sont comme telles régies par les lois affectant les individus, sauf les privilèges dont elles jouissent et les incapacités dont elles sont frappées."

Les propriétaires d'un complexe hôtelier ont intenté une action en dommages-intérêts contre un de leurs clients et contre la ville dans le territoire de laquelle ce complexe se trouvait.[16] Le client fume au lit. C'est l'incendie. Les pompiers accourent mais l'équipement est défectueux et la bâtisse est une perte totale. Ajoutez à cela les fautes commises par les préposés de la ville, dont le chef de pompiers, et vous vous retrouvez avec une réclamation de l'ordre de deux millions et demi de dollars.

Quel droit faut-il appliquer à la solution de ce litige? Le droit civil québécois soutiennent les appelants, le droit public anglais plaide la ville. Ayant opté pour l'un de ces systèmes, la Cour suprême du Canada devra étudier les conséquences juridiques découlant de l'exercice par une ville de son pouvoir discrétionnaire en matière de responsabilité délictuelle.

L'aspect de l'arrêt portant sur la common law et le droit civil nous intéresse particulièrement ici, l'*Acte de Québec* de 1774 ayant décrété ce qui suit à son article VIII.

> "...et que dans toutes affaires en litige, qui concerneront leurs propriétés et leurs droits de citoïens, ils auront recours aux loix du Canada, comme les maximes sur lesquelles elles doivent être décidées (...) jusqu'à ce

---

[16] *Laurentide Motels c. Beauport (ville)* (1989) 1 R.C.S., 705

> qu'elles soient changées ou altérées par quelques ordonnances qui seront passées à l'avenir dans la dite province ..."[17]

Quant à la propriété et aux droits civils, ils relèvent de la compétence exclusive de chaque province en vertu du paragraphe 13 de l'article 92 de la *Loi constitutionnelle de 1867.*

On voit d'ici le problème: Un pouvoir local érigé en corporation publique, politique, régi par le droit public (de *common law*) susceptible, à certains égards, de l'être par le droit civil dans ses rapports avec certains citoyens. Beau cas de droit comparé, s'il n'en fût jamais un. Après avoir référé aux principes reconnus en la matière, madame le juge l'Heureux-Dubé, qui écrit pour la Cour, met le doigt sur la principale difficulté que soulèvent les textes législatifs.

> "Ce sont là des principes reconnus. Ce n'est pas tout cependant de dire que les corps publics, dont les corporations municipales, sont régis par le droit public, encore faut-il en définir et le contenu et les limites. Dans cette zone grise que constitue le ‹‹silence statutaire››, qui nous occupe ici, face au pouvoir discrétionnaire d'une corporation municipale en matière de lutte contre les incendies, où est la règle et quelle est la règle? J'ai déjà posé les balises relativement aux grandes distinctions qui s'imposent. Je ne traiterai donc ici que de cet aspect restreint qui touche à la question précise à résoudre."[18]

Une revue de la doctrine et de la jurisprudence lui permet ensuite de conclure que "le droit public applicable au Canada comme au Québec veut que les corporations publiques, ce qui englobe les corporations municipales, puissent, dans l'exercice de leurs pouvoirs discrétionnaires résultant de la loi, encourir une responsabilité civile en sus de leurs obligations légales et parallèlement à celles-ci."[19]

Mais cela ne règle pas le problème car le débat judiciaire a porté tant sur les notions de pouvoir et de devoir que sur celles de politique et d'exécution. Pouvoir, parce que la ville n'était pas tenue d'organiser un "service d'incendies" alors qu'elle en avait effectivement mis un sur pied. Politique, parce qu'elle a choisi, dans sa discrétion, d'exercer l'une de ses compétences et qu'au moment de l'incendie, la ville en était venue à mettre en application sa politique, ou si l'on veut elle était passée à l'étape opérationnelle d'une décision prise depuis longtemps déjà.

Donc, responsabilité possible de la ville à l'étape opérationnelle à moins (et là le problème se complique) que "...la loi habilitante, d'une part, ou la ville elle-même, dans l'exercice d'un pouvoir discrétionnaire au niveau de

---

17 The Québec Act of 1774.
18 *Id*, 740.
19 *Id*, 749.

la prise de décision politique, d'autre part, n'ont pas de quelque façon limité les obligations de la corporation publique à cet égard".[20]

La ville soutient alors que la *Loi sur les cités et villes* (art.442) ne l'oblige pas à garantir la quantité d'eau qu'elle doit fournir. Et les juges d'analyser titres, libellé de l'article, ponctuation pour, en Cour d'appel, en venir à la conclusion que cet article conférait une immunité à la ville en matière d'entretien d'aqueduc. Elle ne pouvait être tenue responsible ni des dommages résultant de son défaut d'avoir assuré le déblaiement des bornes-fontaines et leur bon fonctionnement, ni des actes et omissions de ses pompiers.

Madame le juge L'Heureux-Dubé, qui n'a pas été convaincue par ces arguments de texte, croit plutôt qu'ils "doivent céder le pas devant la logique du contexte particulier des villes, ainsi que devant les raisons historiques et factuelles qui permettent de dégager et l'intention du législateur et la véritable portée de cette disposition".[21]

Il faut lire ici son exposé:

> "Si la Loi sur les cités et villes ne confère pas d'immunité aux corporations municipales quant à leur responsabilité extra-contractuelle relative à l'opération de leur service d'aqueduc et d'incendie, il est acquis que cette même loi n'impose pas non plus de responsabilité particulière à cet égard. Par ailleurs, une municipalité ne saurait être dégagée de sa responsabilité civile que si la loi l'en dégageait expressément, ou encore l'autorisait, par une disposition habilitante, à s'en dégager par voie de règlement. Un règlement, source secondaire du droit, portant sur la limitation ou l'exonération de la responsabilité civile d'une municipalité, ne peut valablement modifier le droit commun, source principale du droit, que si une disposition expresse de la loi le permet. Il n'existe pas de telle disposition habilitante dans la *Loi sur les cités et villes*. C'est donc le «silence statutaire» le plus complet, qui, à mon avis, laisse le champ libre à l'application des principes de droit privé, ce qui est conforme aux principes de *common law* applicables au Québec comme au Canada, ainsi qu'on l'a déjà vu".[22]

Restait à examiner les règlements de la ville où l'on voit que les bornes-fontaines font partie du réseau d'aqueduc et que celle-ci accordait la plus haute priorité à l'entretien de ce réseau. En somme, la ville a exercé un pouvoir en assumant explicitement l'obligation de maintenir et d'entretenir ses services d'aqueduc et de lutte contre les incendies. Elle avait donc l'obligation d'agir avec diligence dans l'exécution d'une décision relevant par ailleurs de son pouvoir politique discrétionnaire. Pourquoi? Suivons encore une fois le raisonnement du juge.

---

[20] *Id*, 750.
[21] *Id*, 757.
[22] *Id*, 757.

“Bref, une municipalité engage sa responsabilité civile extra-contractuelle au cas de faute ou négligence de sa part dans l’exécution des obligations qu’elle a ainsi contractées sauf si la loi l’en dégage explicitement ou l’autorise à ce faire par voie réglementaire, et que la municipalité le fait. (Je note en passant qu’évidemment cette obligation en sera une de moyens et non de résultat.) Cette opinion se justifie ici dans les faits mais elle se justifie aussi, même en l’absence de ces faits, par l’expectative qu’elle suscite chez les contribuables qui ont assumé le coût de se doter d’un service d’incendie, et qui, de ce fait, ont tout lieu de croire qu’ils peuvent faire appel à ce service en toute confiance pour combattre l’incendie qui ravage leur propriété. Si aucune expectative n’est créée pour prévenir les incendies, il existe une expectative, soit celle de pouvoir compter sur la municipalité pour combattre le feu le plus efficacement possible. Si aucune responsabilité ne pourra être encourue du fait de l’incendie lui-même, les fautes dans la lutte contre les incendies seront génératrices de responsabilité.

S’il est exact que la municipalité désire s’assurer une protection efficace en cas de conflagration, ce rôle n’est pas unique ni contradictoire avec celui d’assurer une protection efficace aux contribuables en cas d’incendie de leur immeuble. Il ne s’agit pas ici d’une obligation contractuelle envers chacun des contribuables de la ville mais bien plutôt du contenu obligationnel de sa décision discrétionnaire de se doter d’un tel service.

Comment, en effet, pourrait-on justifier l’achat d’équipement dispendieux aux frais des contribuables qui ne servirait qu’en cas de conflagration? Certes, la ville, faute de ressources ou autrement, pourrait restreindre l’étendue de son service, ou même décider ne de ne pas s’en doter, mais, si telle est sa décision, il s’agira d’une décision politique de gestion publique qu’elle devra entériner dans un règlement spécifique. Les contribuables en seraient ainsi informés, ce qui est le but d’un règlement, et ils n’auraient aucune expectative sauf dans le cadre fixé par le règlement. Ils ne sauraient non plus s’en plaindre, sauf par voie électorale. Tel règlement n’existe pas ici.

Je conclus donc qu’en l’espèce les règlements de la ville de Beauport de se doter d’un service d’aqueduc et d’un service des incendies impliquent nécessairement sinon spécifiquement un devoir d’entretien de ce service, devoir ratifié dans les faits. Cette conclusion nous ramène nécessairement au véritable débat qui est de déterminer les règles applicables dans un tel contexte opérationnel à la responsabilité des corporations municipales au Québec en matière de lutte contre les incendies, face au silence statutaire le plus complet à cet égard et compte tenu qui le droit public régit les corps publics au Québec".[23]

Et, passant enfin à l'étude de l'article 356 C.c.B.c., elle pose que:

"La règle générale est que les corporations municipales sont régies par le droit public. Cependent, «à certains égards», elles sont régies par le droit civil, l'expression «droit civil» devant être interprétée dans son sens le plus large. On peut déduire du second alinéa de l'art. 356 C.c.B.c. que le droit civil comprend les «lois affectant les individus». Les règles de la responsabilité civile sont de cette catégorie. Ces règles s'appliqueront aux corporations municipales, à moins qu'elles n'en soient modifiées ou exclues par le droit public".[24]

Mettons ici un terme à notre survol de l'arrêt *Laurentides Motel Ltd. C. Beauport (ville)* tout en soulignant l'intérêt qu'il présente pour le droit comparé. Monsieur le professeur Pierre-Gabriel Jobin a bien illustré la chose dans une chronique sur le droit civil québécois, publiée dans la *Revue trimestrielle de droit civil.*[25] Comme le remarque le Pr Jobin, les tribunaux canadiens, la Cour suprême du Canada notamment, "fait régulièrement appel au droit comparé, spécialement au droit français, dans le but avoué de reconnaître le caractère distinct et autonome du droit québécois".[26] En matière de droit municipal, la mixité du régime québécois est particulièrement intéressante, comme nous venons de le voir. *Common law*, droit civil, intérêt collectif, intérêt individuel, décisions de politique, décision d'exécution, autant de notions qui finissent par s'harmoniser, plutôt bien que mal en l'espèce. D'ailleurs, référant à la thèse de la Cour suprême, le Pr Jobin en souligne le mérite en conclusion de sa chronique. Voici une partie de ses propos.

"La consécration de cette thèse a le mérite d'écarter certaines incidences irritantes, voire socialement inacceptables, de la thèse axée sur la distinction entre les pouvoirs d'intérêt collectif et ceux d'intérêt individuel. Désormais une municipalité qui décide de mettre sur pied et d'opérer un service d'incendie et un réseau de bornes-fontaines ne pourra plus échapper à toute responsabilité au motif que sa loi habilitante ni ses règlements ne lui imposent expressément le devoir d'agir avec prudence. De plus, on ne pourra plus prétendre que, sauf dérogation par le droit québécois lui-même, la *common law* publique en vigueur aujourd'hui au Québec est constituée uniquement des règles reconnues en 1865, année de l'adoption de l'article 356 du code civil, privant ainsi le droit public

---

[23] *Id*, 770.

[24] *Id*, 785.

[25] *Revue trimestrielle de droit civil*, 90(1) janv.-mars 1991, 196.

[26] *Id*, 200.

québécois de l'adaptation du droit public anglais au contexte moderne d'un Etat complexe, omniprésent et très puissant".[27]

Voilà pour la navigation côtière et ses écueils qui, pour nous, se nomment faits, preuves, recherche de la vérité, réalité quoi! Maintenant bordons bien nos voiles, et naviguant au près, poussons une pointe vers le grand large où se trouvent méthode, théorie et principes. Mais là, rien d'exhaustif, un aperçu seulement. L'horizon est trop vaste et le temps trop changeant pour se lancer à l'aventure sur la mer océane des doctrines sophistiquées.

D. Aperçu d'une méthode pour comparer les différentes règles juridiques

Nos tribunaux n'ont jamais hésité à s'inspirer non seulement du droit étranger mais aussi des études menées dans différents domaines des connaissances humaines. Ainsi l'élaboration du syndrome de la femme brutalisée à permis à nos cours de justice de franchir une étape majeure en droit pénal. L'important, selon moi, consiste d'abord à bien circonscrire le débat judiciaire. Voilà un truisme qui ne nous avance pas beaucoup diront certains. Erreur. C'est le fondement même de cette structure parfois baroque qu'on appelle le système judiciaire. Un conflit, un débat, des preuves, un juge impartial cherchant la vérité, une décision souvent lourde de conséquences pour les justiciables.

Une fois la réalité reconnue ou présumée, quelles règles appliquer à la solution du conflit? Celles prévues par le droit positif d'abord. Si une loi est claire, le juge doit l'appliquer, c'est son rôle. Ou, selon Jacques dans *Comme il vous plaira* de Shakespeare:

> "Puis c'est le juge, beau ventre rond fourré de bon chapon, oeil sévère et barbe taillée à la mode plein de sages dictons et d'anecdotes rebattues: tel est son rôle."[28]

Bref, sur le grand théâtre de la vie, le juge doit d'abord suivre la loi du lieu en l'interprétant tout en respectant, autant que faire se peut, les règles du droit international. Mais tout n'est pas toujours limpide dans les écrits et la pensée des hommes. Il faut souvent rechercher les véritables intentions et les principes, comme il a fallu chercher la vérité dans les preuves présentées au tribunal. Or, "le vrai est, d'une chose particulière à tel moment, l'universel de nul moment".[29] Et, tentant de saisir l'insaisissable vie qui poursuit son cours, le juge doit trancher en disant le droit, en rendant la justice. C'est à ce point précis qu'il se tourne, lorsqu'il l'estime nécessaire, vers les sources étrangères. Pourquoi se priverait-il de ce recours

[27] *Id*, 204.

[28] Dans Vito Pandolfi, *Histoire du théâtre*, Marabout unuversité, t. 3, 1964, 85.

[29] Alain*, Les Marchands de sommeil*, cité dans Propos sur les pouvoirs, Gallimard, Folio, 12.

d'ailleurs? Il réfère à ces données en autant qu'elles ne dénaturent pas la règle qu'il doit appliquer. Mais cela ne l'empêche ni d'améliorer, ni de préciser cette règle. Si l'on croit au respect de la loi et en l'existence de la justice, il faut accepter certains dénominateurs communs à tous les hommes, et prendre les mesures pour leur permettre de connaître clairement leurs droits et leurs devoirs.

Cette position heurtera sans doute de plein fouet les tenants de la doctrine positiviste qui ont toujours voulu réduire le juge à un rôle d'automate, appliquant mécaniquement, sinon bêtement, des lois parfois incompréhensibles et d'une utilité douteuse. Vous avez des doutes là-dessus? Lisez n'importe quel article d'une loi d'ordre fiscal, et essayez d'en déchiffrer le sens et surtout la portée à travers l'enchevêtrement de propositions subordonnées qu'elle comporte trop souvent. Puis appliquez ces merveilles de clarté et de précision au cas généralement complexe que l'on vous présente. Enfin, renseignez-vous sur l'opinion du justiciable, une fois votre jugement prononcé. Je parie qu'il songera parfois davantage aux conseils de votre psychiatre qu'à vos talents de juriste.

Donc, émonder, élaguer, retrouver les principes de droit naturel, ou de justice fondamentale comme on préfère le dire aujourd'hui; autant d'activités qui conduisent le juge à utiliser des solutions adoptées dans d'autres pays que le sien. Il hésite d'autant moins à le faire lorsqu'il se rend compte que deux lois ou deux tendances jurisprudentielles provenant de pays différents sont semblables, voire identiques. Combien de lois, d'ailleurs, ne sont-elles que de simples copies de lois étrangères. Il suffit de lire chartes et déclarations des droits et libertés pour s'en convaincre. Quant aux constitutions, on sait, depuis Talleyrand et Napoléon, qu'elles doivent être concises et obscures. Pourquoi alors tirer sur l'interprète? Souhaitons lui plutôt bonne chance.

Quant au poids que tiendra l'autorité étrangère dans un jugement, il sera directement proportionnel à sa valeur, ou mieux, à sa force intrinsèque. Certains concepts ont pris un tel ascendant dans notre monde qu'il ne faut pas hésiter à s'y référer et à s'y ancrer solidement. On en retrouvait de remarquables dans les propos des professeurs et du juge de la Cour suprême du Canada, cités précédemment.

Bref, ne jamais hésiter à voir haut et loin, c'est la seule façon de rendre une justice humaine et fondée sur le droit, ces deux assises de toute société qui se veut libre et démocratique.

CONCLUSION

Notre court périple tire à sa fin. Il faut regagner le port, retourner à nos études, à nos dossiers et surtout à nos justiciables.

Nous avions mis le cap sur la justice, telle que la considère le juge, et j'espère que cette communication aura permis de voir comment il procède pour tenter d'y parvenir.

Juger est un art, une création, une poésie au sens étymologique du mot, un acte posé à mi-chemin entre ce qui peut être et ce qui doit être, comme nous l'écrivions en introduction. Un acte de vie, déterminant ce qui est, maintenant, dans la vérité ou le vraisemblable de l'existence. Jamais absolument certain, jamais définitif, mais toujours tendu vers une croyance et un espoir. La foi en la valeur sacrée de tout être humain et l'espérance en sa bonté, en sa capacité de se relever après l'épreuve et de reprendre sa route vers un monde meilleur et une vision d'éternité.

C.N. KAKOURIS*

L'utilisation de la Methode Comparative par la Cour de Justice des Communautes Europeennes

I. Introduction

A. Recherche comparative. Notion.

1. Eu égard aux points de vue divergents quant à l'objet et à l'utilisation de la méthode comparative[1], il est nécessaire d'exposer, de manière rudimentaire, le point de vue qui détermine la méthode d'aborder la jurisprudence de la Cour dans cet exposé.

2. Le droit est un objet de connaissance pour le juriste. Il est également un objet de connaissance pour le sociologue, le philosophe de l'histoire, le psychologue, l'homme politique, etc. Le juriste constate *ce qui est en vigueur* en tant que droit, si une règle concrète ou un ordre juridique est en vigueur. Le sociologue, et les autres représentants des sciences explicatives cherchent à savoir *pourquoi une règle a été instaurée* ou pourquoi un ordre juridique a pris une forme déterminée plutôt qu'une autre. Ils recherchent les causes.

3. Le droit dit "non écrit" est également objet de connaissance pour le juriste. Il ne devient objet de connaissance pour le sociologue et les autres qu'à partir du moment où il a été transformé en droit écrit par le biais de sa reconnaissance par les tribunaux.

4. Pour des raisons méthodologiques, le chercheur doit toujours clairement distinguer s'il fait oeuvre de juriste ou oeuvre de sociologue. Il sait que, pour avoir une connaissance complète du droit, il doit le connaître sous les deux aspects: il doit savoir *quelle* règle a été instaurée, mais aussi *pourquoi* elle a été instaurée. Il n'est cependant pas toujours nécessaire qu'il en ait une connaissance des deux aspects. Pour l'administration, par

* Court of Justice of the European Communities, Luxembourg

[1] G. Benos, The political debt of Community law to Comparative Law, Revue hellénique de droit international, 1984, pp. 241 ss.

U. Drobnig and S. van Erp (eds.), The Use of Comparative Law by Courts, 97–111.

exemple, il suffit qu'une règle soit en vigueur pour qu'elle l'applique. Il en va de même pour le juge. Pour accomplir leur mission, ils n'ont en principe pas besoin de savoir pourquoi une règle déterminée a été instaurée.

5. Le spécialiste du droit comparé, sous sa forme moderne, ne se borne pas à la constatation du juriste, c'est-à-dire à déterminer ce qui est en vigueur dans chaque ordre juridique sur une certaine "matière"[2] et dans l'établissement, après comparaison, des différences et des similitudes. Il détermine au préalable l'unité des relations socio-politico-économiques qui constituent la "matière". De ce fait, il n'est pas exempt d'éléments d'attitude sociologique[3].

B. Utilisation. Par le législateur. Par les tribunaux.

6. Les constatations de la science du droit comparé sont utilisées tant par le législateur que par le juge, mais chacun de manière différente. Le

---

[2] Nous n'entrerons pas dans la question de la distinction entre la méthode *micro-comparative* et la méthode *macro-comparative*, parce que nous pensons que la méthode micro-comparative (comparaison des solutions données par différents droits à une question concrète) ne doit jamais être considérée en elle-même et indépendamment de la méthode macro-comparative (comparaison entre les différents ordres juridiques considérés globalement). Sur les deux méthodes, voir P. Doris, La recherche micro-comparative et son utilité dans l'interprétation du droit privé hellénique (en grec), NoB, 1983, pp. 609 ss. Cette distinction correspond à la distinction entre les *recherches analytiques* et les *recherches synthétiques* de P. Pescatore, Le recours dans la jurisprudence de la Cour à des normes déduites de la comparaison des droits des Etats membres, Revue internationale de droit comparé, 1980, p. 352.

[3] La notion de "méthode comparative" décrite dans les §§ 2-5 constitue le point de départ du présent exposé. Nous n'entrerons pas dans la problématique relative à la définition de la notion. Toutefois, pour la clarté de l'exposé, il est nécessaire de la délimiter par rapport aux notions connexes suivantes:

a) Les comparaisons entre les institutions et les dispositions d'un seul et même ordre juridique se situent en dehors du domaine du droit comparé. Par exemple, l'argument selon lequel "le fait que le législateur l'a expressément dit dans le cadre d'une autre loi connexe et ne dit rien dans la loi à interpréter signifie qu'il n'a pas voulu le dire dans cette dernière" ne relève pas de la matière comparative.

b) La comparaison de la nouvelle disposition à interpréter avec la disposition précédente remplacée, en vue de déduire un argument *a contrario*, ne relève pas de la méthode comparative.

c) La référence à l'origine historique d'un principe ou d'une disposition, telle qu'elle est faite dans l'arrêt du 25 février 1969 Klomp (23/68, Rec. p. 43, point 13), qui constate que le principe de la continuité des structures juridiques en cas de changement de législation trouve son origine dans le droit romain (voir D.1.3.26 et 28) ne relève pas non plus de la méthode comparative.

d) La référence parfois de la Cour simultanément aux trois traités des Communautés européennes et le recours aux arguments interprétatifs tirés de leur objectif final commun, ne constitue pas non plus une application de la méthode comparative.

e) L'examen du libellé d'un texte législatif de la Communauté dans les différentes langues officielles faisant foi de la Communauté ne constitue pas une application de la méthode comparative.

législateur les utilise comme un élément, parmi d'autres, en vue de se faire une opinion de *lege ferenda*, c'est-à-dire au sujet de la règle qu'il est opportun de mettre en vigueur. Le juge utilise le droit comparé comme méthode d'interprétation du droit qui est en vigueur.

7. Il est vrai que le résultat des décisions judiciaires est souvent similaire à celui du législateur. Cela vaut non seulement pour les ordres juridiques basés sur le principe du *stare decisis*. Le droit "jurisprudentiel" existe aussi dans les autres ordres juridiques. Il y a cependant une différence fondamentale entre l'oeuvre du législateur et celle du juge. Le premier *met en vigueur,* par un travail createur, une règle après avoir fait des appréciations d'opportunité. Le deuxième concrétise les notions vagues ou comble des lacunes du droit écrit en puisant dans le "droit non écrit"[4], *qui est déjà en vigueur*, et qu'il recherche et constate comme étant en vigueur par un travail "cognitif"[5]. La différence d'attitude n'est pas théorique, mais réelle et fondamentale.

8. Dans l'accomplissement de sa mission, la Cour utilise aussi la méthode comparative. L'objectif de cet exposé est de faire quelques observations sur l'utilisation de la méthode comparative par la Cour.

C. Utilisation par la Cour de Justice des C.E. Légitimation.

9. Passons immédiatement à la première observation: la Cour utilise le droit comparé comme méthode d'interprétation. La notion d' "interprétation" comprend aussi le comblement des lacunes du droit écrit, qui consiste, comme il a été dit, en un travail "cognitif", puisqu'il n'ajoute rien au droit en vigueur, mais transpose seulement une règle du droit non-écrit en vigueur dans le droit jurisprudentiel (et donc écrit).

10. Liminairement la question se pose de savoir quelle est la base juridique, qui donne légitimation à la Cour pour utiliser la méthode comparative. Je rappelle tout simplement, de manière succincte, la question.

11. Il n'existe pas de disposition générale[6] expresse. Une règle expresse n'existe que pour une matière concrète (voir plus loin les paragraphes 15 et suivants).

12. Pour le surplus, la légitimation de la Cour est basée sur l'article 164 du

---

[4] En ce qui concerne l'existence d'un droit non écrit, nous ne pouvons ne pas se référer à Antigone de Sophocle, vers 456-457, "άγραπτα κασφαλή θεών νόμιμα...Ου γαρ τι νυν γε καχθές, αλλ'αείποτε ζη ταύτα, κουδείς οίδεν εξ ότου 'φανη" ("lois non écrites et immuables des dieux ... puisque non seulement aujourd'hui ou hier, mais éternellement, ces lois sont vivantes, et personne ne sait quand elles sont apparues").

[5] Voir plus loin les paragraphes 25 et suivants.

[6] Comme il en existe par exemple à l'article 38, paragraphe 1, sous c), du Statut de la Cour Internationale de La Haye.

traité CE[7], en combinaison avec le préambule et l'article 2, qui énonce les buts de la Communauté. Nous reviendrons ultérieurement sur ce point.

13. En ce qui concerne plus particulièrement la Convention de Bruxelles[8],la légitimation de la Cour est fondée sur l'article 5 du Protocole sur l'interprétation de la convention par la Cour, en combinaison toujours avec l'article 164.

II. La methode comparative et la Cour

A. Comparaison imposée par le droit communautaire

14. L'article 215, deuxième alinéa, du traité CEE prévoit que la Communauté doit réparer, "conformément aux principes généraux communs aux droits des Etats membres", les dommages causés par ses institutions ou par ses agents.

15. Ce renvoi explicite n'a pas conduit la Cour à une sorte d'interprétation "mécaniste"[9]. La règle qui constitue le plus grand dénominateur commun est habituellement[10], mais pas nécessairement suivie. La Cour peut choisir la règle la plus appropriée. Selon certains auteurs, elle le peut même lorsque la règle n'existe que dans un seul Etat membre. Par ailleurs, un dénominateur commun n'est pas facile à trouver en raison de la diversité des dispositions nationales[11] ou de l'absence de dispositions en matière de responsabilité civile de l'Etat[12].

16. En effet, dans les Etats membres existe le principe selon lequel il n'y a pas de responsabilité du fait des actes législatifs et une réparation n'est accordée qu'à titre exceptionnel, dans le seul cas où l'acte législatif qui a causé un préjudice le prévoit. Or, la plupart des recours en dommages-intérêts devant la Cour ont invoqué l'illégalité d'actes réglementaires, (qui sont dans la Communauté l'équivalent des actes législatifs dans les Etats membres). De ce fait, les règles que la Cour a reconnues par voie jurisprudentielle sont nouvelles[13].

---

[7] Et sur les articles correspondants du traité CECA: 31, et EURATOM: 136. Pour des raisons de simplification, nous ne nous référerons ci-après qu'au traité CE.

[8] Convention du 27 septembre 1968 concernant la compétence judiciaire et l'exécution de décisions en matière civile et commerciale (voir JO C 189 du 28.7.1990).

[9] "Arithmétique", selon le mot de M. Lagrange (conclusions dans l'arrêt du 12 juillet 1962, Hoogovens, 14/61, Rec. p. 485, conclusions p. 539).

[10] Par exemple, arrêt du 2 juin 1976, Kampffmeyer (56-60/74, , Rec. p. 711, point 6).

[11] Arrêts des 27 février 1980, Just (68/79, Rec. p. 501, points 22 et 23) et 27 mars 1980, Denkavit Italiana (61/79, Rec. p. 1205, point 23). Ces arrêts ne concernaient pas l'article 215, deuxième alinéa.

[12] Voir en tout cas l'arrêt du 1er mars 1983, Deca (250/78, Rec. p. 421, point 15).

[13] Voir à cet égard I. Deligiannis, La science juridique comparative et le droit interna-

17. L'examen comparatif est quelquefois imposé par une disposition du droit dérivé[14].

B. Comparaison imposée par des obligations de droit international public

18. Nous devons observer à titre liminaire que la Cour considère le droit communautaire comme droit interne de la Communauté, et non comme droit international[15].

19. Il en résulte que, selon la jurisprudence de la Cour, les règles générales du droit international ne sont pas appliquées dans les matières régies par le traité et dans les relations entre les Etats membres ou entre la Communauté et les Etats membres[16]. De telles règles sont, par exemple, l'exception *non adimpleti contractus*, la réciprocité, etc[17].

20. On ne peut trouver dans la jurisprudence de la Cour aucun cas d'utilisation de la méthode comparative en exécution d'une obligation internationale de la Communauté.

21. C'est une autre chose le fait que la Cour puise dans le droit international, sans y être obligée, des règles ou des principes susceptibles de faciliter l'interprétation ou le comblement de lacunes du droit communautaire écrit. De tels cas ne sont pas fréquents, mais ils existent[18]. Il est

---

tional (en grec), 1992, p. 30, et les renvois.

[14] Arrêt du 15 juin 1976, Mills (110/75, Rec. p. 955, point 25: "... les principes généraux du droit du travail, auxquels se réfère l'article final du règlement ...").

[15] C'est aussi la raison pour laquelle elle n'utilise pas, pour l'interprétation du traité, les règles des articles 31 à 33 de la convention de Vienne sur le droit des traités de 1969.

[16] Arrêt du 13 novembre 1964, Luxembourg/Belgique (90-91/63, Rec. p. 1217). Voir également, implicitement, l'arrêt du 14 décembre 1971, Commission/France (7/71, Rec. p. 1003, point 23).

[17] Voir A. Bredimas, Comparative Law in the Court of Justice of the European Communities, The Year Book Affairs, 1978, Stevens and Sons, London, p. 322, note 11, avec renvois. Voir aussi, du même auteur: Methods of interpretation and Community Law, European Studies in Law, Vol. 6, Amsterdam, 1978.

[18] L'arrêt du 28 juin 1955, Assider (5/55, Rec. p. 263 et notamment p. 278, point 1.4) se réfère à l'article 60 du Statut de la Cour Internationale de Justice. Voir également l'arrêt du 4 décembre 1974, Van Duyn (41/74, Rec. p. 1337), point 22: "... un principe de droit international, que le traité CEE ne peut pas être censé méconnaître dans les rapports entre les Etats membres ..." (il s'agissait d'un domaine non régi par le traité). L'arrêt du 26 avril 1972, Interfood (92/71, Rec. p. 231), point 6: "... le tarif douanier commun ayant fait l'objet d'accords entre la Communauté et ses partenaires dans le cadre du GATT, les principes sous-jacents à ces accords peuvent constituer un élément utile pour l'application des règles de classification qui lui sont applicables". Voir également, en relation avec le GATT, les arrêts du 16 mars 1983, SIOT (266/81, Rec. p. 731), SPI et SAMI (267 à 269/81, Rec. p. 801) et Singer et Geigy (290-291/81, Rec. p. 847). Voir également l'arrêt du 14.7.1976, Cornelis, ((3, 4 et 6/1976, Rec. p. 1279) et enfin l'arrêt du 27 septembre 1988, Ahlström e.a./Commission (89/85, 104/85, 114/85, 116/85, 117/85, 125 à 129/85, Rec. p. 5193, point 18).

à noter que la Cour se réfère à la Convention européenne des droits de l'homme[19], mais comme une source d'inspiration, parmi d'autres, en précisant que tous les Etats membres de l'époque l'ont conclue ou y ont adhéré. La Cour ne s'est pas référée à la Déclaration universelle des droits de l'homme.

C. Comparaison non expressément prévue. Traité CEE.

a. Fondement juridique

22. L'article 215, deuxième alinéa, ne saurait être interprété comme excluant la méthode comparative en dehors du domaine de la responsabilité non contractuelle[20]. La compétence générale de la Cour pour utiliser la méthode comparative découle de l'article 164, qui lui confère une compétence très large, incluant ainsi cette utilisation. Aux termes de cet article, "La Cour de justice assure le respect du droit dans l'interprétation et l'application du présent traité". Selon cette disposition, le droit écrit du traité, qui se situe au sommet de la pyramide hiérarchique des dispositions du droit communautaire, a au-dessus de lui le Droit avec un D majuscule, le Droit non écrit, l'Idée du Droit, selon la terminologie de Platon. Et la Cour doit assurer le respect de ce Droit. L'Idée du Droit doit guider la Cour comme l'étoile polaire guide les marins, selon la belle image de Stammler.

23. Il est évident que, pour accomplir cette tâche, la Cour peut[21] utiliser la méthode comparative, et cela pour puiser dans les ordres juridiques non seulement des Etats membres, mais également des pays tiers. Elle fait un usage très fréquent de la méthode comparative. A cet égard, il convient de faire les observations suivantes.

b. Interprétation téléologique et méthode comparative

24. La méthode comparative est soumise à l'interprétation téléologique[22].

---

[19] Arrêts: 14 mai 1974, Nold (4/73, Rec. p. 491), 28 octobre 1975, Rutili (36/75, Rec. p. 1219) et dans d'autres arrêts. L'arrêt du 18 octobre 1989, Orkem/Commission (374/87, Rec. p. 3283, points 30 et 31) se réfère à l'article 6 de la Convention européenne des droits de l'homme et à l'article 14 du pacte international de 1966.

[20] Bien au contraire: l'article 215, deuxième alinéa, constitue un signe en faveur de l'utilisation généralisée de la méthode comparative.

[21] Selon M. Hilf, The role of comparative law in the jurisprudence of the C.J.E.C., dans La limitation des droits de l'homme en droit constitutionnel comparé, 1986, Editions Yvon Blais, Québec, p. 549 et suivantes: "The Court has a legal obligation to consider national traditions and concepts". Elle fonde cette obligation sur le principe de la solidarité, énoncé à l'article 5 du traité CEE, et sur le fait que l'intégration européenne ne peut devenir une réalité que dans une "comparative atmosphere".

[22] Voir également, dans un autre cadre, Yokaris, La méthode comparative en droit international public et en droit européen communautaire (en grec), Sakkoulas, Athènes, 1985, p. 26.

La Cour utilise constamment l'interprétation téléologique. Celle-ci cherche à saisir le sens du droit à la lumière de son but, de son "τέλος". Lorsqu'il s'agit d'une disposition concrète, par exemple une disposition qui fait partie d'un règlement, il est assez facile d'en définir le "τέλος" et, partant, le sens spécifique. Mais ce "τέλος" concret de la disposition doit être entendu comme étant greffé sur le "τέλος" plus général de l'ensemble du règlement. Il est plus difficile lorsqu'il s'agit d'une disposition du traité qui s'inscrit dans le "τέλος" plus général du traité (ou même dans le "τέλος" commun des trois traités, comme nous le voyons dans de nombreux arrêts de la Cour).

25. La téléologie est le guide pour l'interprétation des notions vagues ou lorsqu'il s'agit de déterminer s'il existe une lacune dans le droit écrit et de combler cette lacune, notamment en ce qui concerne les principes généraux du droit. La jurisprudence de la Cour aboutit ainsi à opérer une "harmonisation", et même une "substitution" des législations nationales.

26. Dans l'accomplissement de cette tâche, les juges de la Cour doivent, en écartant leurs convictions personnelles, trouver des critères en se référant aux convictions et aux valeurs communes aux peuples de l'Europe. Cette référence se réalise en deux étapes. En premier lieu, la Cour se réfère aux législations des Etats membres, dans lesquelles ces convictions et ces croyances se reflètent, et, si cette méthode n'aboutit pas, elle se réfère directement à ces convictions, croyances et attitudes spirituelles.

27. La première étape constitue précisément la technique juridique de la méthode comparative. On peut clairement déduire de la manière dont la méthode comparative est utilisée par la Cour qu'elle est au service de l'interprétation téléologique. Elle constitue en fait le moyen qui permet à la Cour de puiser dans les convictions, les croyances, l'attitude spirituelle des peuples d'Europe, parce que la concrétisation de ces convictions et croyances dans un certain mode de vie en commun constitue le but poursuivi par les trois Communautés européennes[23]. Cela signifie que si la technique comparative n'est pas fructueuse, c'est-à-dire s'il n'existe pas de règles explicites sur une matière déterminée dans les ordres juridiques des Etats membres, ou si les règles existantes sont incohérentes ou contradictoires, la Cour doit puiser directement dans ces convictions et croyances.

28. La difficulté provient du fait que, du point de vue culturel, si les peuples européens partagent les mêmes conceptions fondamentales sur l'homme, la vie et l'univers, il existe aussi des différences, qui constituent l'identité particulière de chaque région et qui doivent être respectées. Cette orientation pluriculturelle imprègne également l'oeuvre de la Cour: celle-ci doit chaque fois dégager ce qui constitue la résultante des différences, le "τέλος" qui éclairera sa décision. Elle doit agir comme si elle était la

[23] Voir A. Bredimas, Comparative Law etc., op. cit., note 73.

conscience de l'Europe.

29. Le fait que la méthode comparative est au service de l'interprétation téléologique explique pourquoi la Cour écarte parfois la règle qui constitue le dénominateur commun et choisit la règle la plus apte à servir l'objectif final de l'intégration de la Communauté. On a parfois critiqué cette attitude de la Cour comme n'étant qu'une "technique empirique"[24], parce qu'elle n'adopte pas les règles qui sont le plus généralement en vigueur. D'autres répondent que la méthode comparative ne peut pas être "statique" (plutôt "statistique") et qu'elle doit inclure dans la comparaison l'élément téléologique[25]. Je pense que la recherche des règles en vigueur dans les différents Etats membres, ou dans les pays tiers, de la *raison d'être* de ces règles et de leur "τέλος" est d'ordre éminemment scientifique, et non empirique. Le choix de ce qu'il faut reconnaître comme étant du droit en vigueur dans la Communauté comporte un élément créatif.

30. Les deux étapes comportent des difficultés, qui sont de nature différente. La deuxième étape, du choix pour la Communauté, comporte les difficultés qui ont été esquissées plus haut et qui sont généralement reconnues[26]. Les difficultés inhérentes à l'étape précédente, à savoir l'étape "scientifique", c'est-à-dire cognitive, ne sont pas toujours apparentes. Elles existent toutefois, étant donné que la perception des notions et des règles d'un autre ordre juridique dépend dans une large mesure de l'ordre juridique dans lequel se situe le sujet de la perception. A la différence des sciences naturelles, il n'existe pas de terminologie juridique internationale commune, si ce n'est dans la mesure où il existe un droit uniforme. Il faut également être conscient de cette difficulté.

c. Les traces de la méthode comparative dans les arrêts

31. Comment peut-on savoir que la solution, adoptée dans un arrêt, est le résultat d'un examen comparatif préalable? Peut-on déterminer dans quel ordre juridique la Cour a puisé un principe général déterminé?

32. L'examen comparatif préalable i) est mentionné expressément dans certains arrêts, ii) résulte d'un élément évident dans d'autres arrêts et iii) est présumé par l'attitude générale, connue, de la Cour dans une troisième catégorie d'arrêts.

33. i) La Cour ne renvoie généralement pas d'une manière détaillée à

---

[24] L.J. Constantinesco, Traité de Droit Comparé, Tome II, La Méthode Comparative, Librairie Générale, Paris, 1974, p. 355. Voir également P. Pescatore, Le recours dans la jurisprudence de la Cour de justice à des normes déduites de la comparaison des droits des Etats membres, op.cit., p. 353; Sachpekidou, La responsabilité de la CEE du fait des actes réglementaires, 1985, (en grec), pp. 133 ss., 136 ss., notamment n°s 49 et 50.

[25] Deligiannis, op.cit., page 32, note 92.

[26] A. Bredimas, Methods of interpretation and Community Law, North Holland Publishing Company, 1978, p. XV.

l'examen comparatif qui a précédé son arrêt. Une première exception est constituée par l'arrêt du 12 juillet 1957, Algera (7/56, Rec. p. 81, en particulier pp. 114 in fine à 116, conclusions, pp. 133 ss., en particulier pp. 155 et 156), dans lequel on constate une forme classique d'examen comparatif, tant de la part de l'avocat général que de la part de la Cour[27]. Non seulement il n'y a généralement pas de référence détaillée, mais il n'y a même pas du tout de référence. Lorsqu'elle existe, la référence expresse est à son tour généralement succincte[28]. Toutefois, il existe aussi quelques cas de référence plus ample[29].

34. A une époque plus ancienne, les auteurs attribuaient ce silence ou cette litote dans les arrêts à différentes raisons, telles que la difficulté d'indiquer avec précision les règles en vigueur dans les différents ordres juridiques[30], mais il semble que la Cour n'hésite pas, s'il le faut, à exposer ses constatations d'ordre comparatif (voir les arrêts cités dans les notes de bas de page nºs 27 et 28). Dans certains cas, la mention dans l'arrêt n'est pas nécessaire, parce que l'examen comparatif a eu lieu non pas pour choisir entre les solutions comparées, mais pour éclairer la Cour quant aux répercussions qu'aura l'arrêt envisagé dans les ordres juridiques des Etats membres[31], et cela dans le souci de respecter les particularités culturelles.

35. ii) Si l'examen comparatif préalable ne peut pas être déduit habituellement des arrêts, il n'en reste pas moins vrai que cet examen n'est presque jamais absent, comme nous le montrent les éléments suivants.

36. Les conclusions des avocats généraux donnent très souvent différents éléments de comparaison en ce qui concerne les législations nationales, mais également en ce qui concerne la jurisprudence et la doctrine[32]. La

[27] Voir également les exemples de mentions expresses dans les arrêts des 10 juin 1980, Mlle M./Commission (155/78, Rec. p. 1797, point 19); 10 juillet 1980, Ariete (811/79, Rec. p. 2545, points 10 et 11); 10 juillet 1980, MIRECO (826/79, Rec. p. 2559, points 11 et 12); 18 mai 1982, AM&S Europe/Commission (155/79, Rec. p. 1575, points 18 à 21); 11 mai 1983, Klöckner-Werke/Commission (303 à 312/81, Rec. p. 1507, point 45); 21 mai 1983, Ferriere Sant'Anna (168/82, Rec. p. 1681, point 15); 21 septembre 1983, Deutsche Milchkontor (205 à 215/82, Rec. p. 2633, point 30); 18 octobre 1989, Orkem/Commission (374/87, Rec. p. 3283, point 29). Dans l'arrêt du 22 novembre 1977, Industrial Diamond Supplies (43/77, Rec. p. 2175), voir un écart par rapport aux droits nationaux.

[28] Voir par exemple les arrêts des 7 février 1985, Abels (135 83, Rec. p. 469, points 15 à 17) et 21 septembre 1983, Deutsche Milchkontor, précité.

[29] Arrêt du 18 mai 1982, AM&S Europe/Commission, précité, points 18 à 21 et 26; arrêts du 10 juillet 1980, Ariete et MIRECO, 811/79 et 826/79, précités, points 10 à 16.

[30] Deligiannis, op.cit., p. 24, note 60; Pescatore op.cit., p. 346.

[31] Voir à cet égard l'arrêt du 30 novembre 1976, Mines de potasse d'Alsace (21/76, Rec. p. 1735, point 23).

[32] Parmi les premiers cas dans lesquels l'avocat général avait effectué un examen comparatif, alors que l'arrêt n'en avait fait aucune mention expresse, voir les arrêts du 12 juillet 1962, Hoogovens, précité, du 6 avril 1962, Bosch (13/61, Rec. p. 89, conclusions, pp. 111 ss., en particulier pp. 120 à 122), du 16 octobre 1975, Deboeck (90/74, Rec. p. 1123, conclusions pp. 1138 ss., en particulier pp. 1141 et 1142).

Cour charge souvent son service de recherche d'effectuer un examen comparatif sur le problème concret, soulevé dans l'affaire. D'autres fois, elle demande à la Commission[33], en tant que partie ou en tant que *amicus curiae* dans les affaires préjudicielles, des renseignements sur le droit en vigueur dans les Etats membres. Les parties, ou *amici curiae,* exposent aussi quelquefois le droit en vigueur dans les différents ordres juridiques, en particulier sur des questions d'ordre plus général[34]; toutefois, même lorsqu'ils ne présentent pas d'informations, ils exposent leurs thèses et leurs arguments dans le cadre de l'ordre juridique de leur pays[35] et fournissent ainsi indirectement des informations sur cet ordre juridique.

37. iii) Il faut souligner que l'optique comparative est aussi toujours présente du fait que chacun des juges possède une formation juridique, des connaissances et une manière de procéder (par exemple déductive pour les continentaux et les Ecossais, inductive pour les Anglais et les Irlandais) et de raisonner qui porte l'empreinte de l'ordre juridique de son pays. La richesse des délibérés provient de la diversité des apports des juges aux débats. En réalité, un droit comparatif vivant se trouve autour de la table des délibérés.

38. Si on garde ces différents éléments à l'esprit, on peut déceler, même dans les arrêts qui ne contiennent aucune mention expresse, des éléments provenant, parfois peut-être inconsciemment, du droit comparé. Par exemple, le principe de la solidarité est certes inscrit à l'article 5 du traité, mais son élaboration dans la jurisprudence, notamment l'affirmation selon laquelle l'obligation de coopération incombe non seulement aux Etats membres, mais aussi, à l'inverse, aux institutions de la Communauté vis-à-vis des Etats membres, rappelle la "Bundestreue" de l'Etat fédéral allemand[36].

39. Enfin, il y a lieu d'observer que si nous entendons le concept de "comparatif" de manière très large, en y incluant toute influence extérieure, nous pouvons citer différentes influences: par exemple, la présentation des arrêts était à l'origine plus proche du modèle allemand; plus tard, elle a été modifiée en fonction des besoins de la Cour, mais sans jamais atteindre le système des "converging opinions", cher à la House of Lords[37]. L'habitude d'interrompre les plaidoiries par des questions des juges n'est apparue

---

[33] Exemple de mention dans l'arrêt du 10 juin 1980, Mlle M./Commission (155/78, Rec. p. 1797, point 19).

[34] Voir par exemple l'arrêt du 30 septembre 1982, Amylum (108/81, Rec. p. 3107, en particulier pp. 3113 et 3114). Dans l'arrêt du 18 mai 1982, AM & S Europe/Commission (155/79, Rec. p. 1575), la Cour a réouvert la procédure orale afin d'obtenir plus d'éclaircissements sur des questions de droit comparé.

[35] Comparer avec G. Benos, op.cit.

[36] Comme l'observe pertinemment T. Koopmans, The birth of European law on the crossroads of legal traditions, The american journal of Comparative law, 1991, p. 502.

[37] Ce système est beaucoup plus accentué à la U.S. Supreme Court.

qu'après l'adhésion du Royaume-Uni et de l'Irlande[38].

d. Autres observations

40. Ce qui précède fait déjà apparaître certaines particularités de l'utilisation de la méthode comparative par la Cour. Nous ajouterons encore un certain nombre d'observations à cet égard.

41. Une des caractéristiques est que la méthode comparative, qui était généralement une méthode du droit civil et, en tout état de cause, du droit privé, est utilisée par la Cour dans le domaine du droit administratif et du droit constitutionnel[39]. Or, l'examen comparatif ne se fait pas de manière étanche, c'est-à-dire sur des questions administratives: comparaison des droits administratifs des Etats membres, sur des questions civiles: comparaison des droits civils, etc., mais d'une manière ouverte. Ce résultat découle, lui-aussi, du fait que la méthode comparative est au service de la méthode téléologique et que le "τέλος" ultime est déterminé par la résultante de l'ensemble multiculturel de convictions des peuples de l'Europe.

42. C'est aussi la raison pour laquelle l'examen comparatif s'étend également aux règles non écrites qui font partie des différents ordres juridiques. Il est vrai que la recherche au niveau du droit non écrit n'est pas facile lorsque un principe non écrit n'a pas encore été reconnu par la jurisprudence du pays concerné; aussi, l'examen comparatif est-il dans ce cas limité.

43. La Cour a souligné à plusieurs reprises l'autonomie du droit communautaire par rapport aux droits des Etats membres[40]. Il semble à première vue paradoxal que la Cour utilise la méthode comparative en se référant de la sorte aux droits nationaux en vue d'interpréter ensuite le droit communautaire de manière autonome (!) Or, ce recours aux droits nationaux, qui est fait *pour information,* n'équivaut pas à une négation de l'autonomie. Il signifie simplement que la méthode comparative est au service de la méthode d'interprétation téléologique, ainsi qu'il a été signalé ci-dessus.

44. C'est la raison pour laquelle la Cour ne limite pas la méthode comparative aux seuls droits des Etats membres; et même lorsqu'elle ne compare que ces derniers droits, elle ne s'estime pas liée par le résultat de son examen comparatif, même lorsque celui-ci a montré qu'il existe un droit uniforme dans tous les Etats membres[41]. Elle s'informe seulement.

---

38 Avant, on avait qualifié la Cour de "muette".

39 Deligiannis, op. cit. p. 34; Pescatore, op. cit., p. 359.

40 Une des conséquences de cette autonomie se trouve dans la jurisprudence selon laquelle les juridictions nationales, appliquant le droit communautaire, par exemple un règlement, n'ont pas le droit de combler ses lacunes en se référant au droit national. Arrêt du 30 janvier 1974, Hannoversche Zucker (159/73, Rec. p. 121, point 4).

41 Dans un sens contraire, semble-t-il, P. Pescatore, Le recours, op.cit., p. 35.

45. Cela est le corollaire du fait que la Cour n'a jamais admis que ce soit le résultat de la recherche comparative qui constitue *le fondement juridique* de la règle ou du principe non écrit qu'elle reconnaît comme étant en vigueur; leur fondement juridique réside dans le fait qu'ils constituent des principes généraux du droit. Par exemple, elle n'a pas fondé juridiquement le principe de la protection des droits de l'homme sur la protection minimale, commune aux Constitutions des Etats membres. "S'inspirant"[42] seulement des traditions constitutionnelles des Etats membres, elle constate que les règles de protection des droits de l'homme font partie intégrante de l'ordre juridique communautaire.

46. Toujours en application du critère de la recherche de la règle la plus appropriée pour la Communauté, la Cour admet dans certains arrêts le dénominateur commun et préfère dans d'autres arrêts une des solutions basées sur les droits nationaux. D'autres fois, elle n'en tient pas compte[43] ou elle s'éloigne de toutes les solutions nationales. Par exemple, en ce qui concerne la question importante de savoir quelles sont les conséquences de l'annulation d'une disposition violant le principe d'égalité, la méthode comparative a montré que, dans les Etats membres, on estimait que l'annulation créait un vide juridique que seul le législateur était compétent pour combler. Malgré cela, la Cour s'est prononcée dans un sens différent: aussi longtemps que le législateur n'a pas introduit une nouvelle réglementation, la disposition qui est la plus favorable pour une catégorie de personnes est applicable aussi à l'égard des victimes d'un traitement discriminatoire[44].

47. Dans certains cas, le résultat de la recherche comparative est inhabituel. Dans un cas, la Cour a décidé que la protection d'un droit tiré du droit communautaire n'exigeait pas une règle uniforme et commune aux Etats membres et, malgré la divergence de leurs droits, elle a déclaré qu'il incombait aux Etats membres de régler la récupération des taxes nationales, perçues en violation du droit communautaire[45]. Dans un autre cas, la divergence constatée a été un argument décisif pour conclure à l'absence de lacune dans une directive[46].

---

[42] Arrêts du 17 décembre 1970, Internationale Handelsgesellschaft (11/70, Rec. p. 1125, point 4); du 14 mai 1974, Nold (4/73, Rec. p. 491, points 13 et 14); et du 13 décembre 1979, Hauer (44/79, Rec. p. 3727, points 15, 20 et 22).

[43] Arrêt du 18 mars 1975, Acton (44, 46 et 49/74, Rec. p. 383, points 15 et 16).

[44] Par exemple, arrêts des 20 mars 1984, Razzouk et Beydoun (75 et 117/82, Rec. p. 1509); du 4 décembre 1986, F.N.V. (71/85, Rec. p. 3855); du 24 mars 1987, Mc Dermott et Cotter (286/85, Rec. p. 1453); du 17 mai 1990, Barber (C-262/88, Rec. p. I-1889). Voir aussi Y.Galmot, Réflexions sur le recours au droit comparé par la C.J.C.E., Revue française de Droit administratif, 1990, pp. 255 ss.

[45] Arrêt du 10 juillet 1980, MIRECO (811/79, Rec. p. 2545, points 10 et 11).

[46] Arrêt du 7 février 1985, Abels (135/83, Rec. p. 469), point 17: "... permet de conclure que si la directive avait était destinée à s'appliquer également aux transferts d'entreprises intervenus dans le cadre de "faillites ou procédures analogues", une disposition expresse y

D. Comparaison non expressément prévue. Convention de Bruxelles.

48. L'article 5 du protocole, qui prévoit que la Cour est compétente pour interpréter la Convention[47], ne mentionne pas la méthode comparative, mais lorsque la Cour applique la Convention de Bruxelles, elle effectue nécessairement un examen comparatif, parce que la terminologie de la Convention est tirée de celle des droits nationaux, même si cela est fait dans le but de définir une notion de la Convention, en principe autonome par rapport aux sens, souvent divergents, que le même terme a dans les droits nationaux. Tous les arrêts qui interprètent la Convention de Bruxelles utilisent la méthode comparative.

49. Lorsque la Cour dit qu'un terme, utilisé dans une disposition du traité ou du droit dérivé ou de la Convention de Bruxelles, a un sens autonome, elle veut dire que la disposition ne renvoie pas à chacune droit national pour le sens de ce terme, mais qu'elle a un contenu indépendant, qui est le même sur le territoire de tous les Etats membres, mais pas nécessairement différent et totalement distinct de celui de tous les droits nationaux[48].

E. Classifications

50. Le but du présent exposé n'est pas d'énumérer ou de classer par catégories les arrêts de la Cour du point de vue de l'utilisation de la méthode comparative. Toutefois, les observations ci-dessus relatives aux arrêts montrent que plusieurs classifications sont possibles sur la base de différents critères:

– Arrêts qui concernent des principes généraux et arrêts qui concernent l'interprétation de dispositions concrètes.

– Arrêts qui limitent la méthode comparative aux droits des Etats membres et arrêts qui examinent aussi les droits des pays tiers[49] ou le droit inter-

---

aurait été insérée à cette fin".

[47] Voir le paragraphe 13 ci-dessus.

[48] Dans l'arrêt du 14 octobre 1976, Eurocontrol (29/76, Rec. p. 1541, point 3) la Cour affirme que: "Il y a donc lieu de considérer la notion"... (matière civile et commerciale) "comme une notion autonome, qu'il faut interpréter en se référant, d'une part, aux objectifs et au système de la Convention et, d'autre part, aux principes généraux qui se dégagent de l'ensemble des systèmes de droit nationaux". Voir les arrêts des 22 novembre 1977, Industrial Diamond Supplies (43/77, Rec. p. 2175, pp. 22 à 24); 22 février 1979, Gourdain (133/78, Rec. p. 733, points 3 et suivants); 21 juin 1978, Bertrand (150/77, Rec. p. 1431, pp. 19 et 20); et 17 juin 1992, Handte (C-26/91, Rec. p. I-3967, point 20). L'arrêt du 22 mars 1983, Peters (34/82, Rec. p. 987, point 14), tire un argument supplémentaire de la praticabilité de l'interprétation adoptée.

[49] Arrêt du 14 juillet 1972, Imperial Chemical Industries (48 69, Rec. p. 619) qui par le biais des conclusions de l'avocat général, examine la législation américaine; arrêts des 13 juillet 1962, Klöchner-Werke/Haute Autorité (17 et 20/61, Rec. p. 615); 21 février 1973, Europemballage (6/72, Rec. p. 215); 17 mai 1972, Meinhard (24/71, Rec. p. 269, point 6);

national[50].

- Arrêts qui font application du dénominateur commun[51].
- Arrêts qui mentionnent généralement la méthode comparative en termes abstraits, ou bien en termes plus concrets[52], et arrêts, la majorité, qui ne la mentionnent pas.

III. Conclusion

51. L'intégration européenne est réalisée par la législation secondaire (le droit communautaire dérivé), notamment par les règlements et les directives, qui se substituent ou assurent l'harmonisation des législations des Etats membres. L'examen comparatif des législations des Etats membres est une étape préliminaire à l'adoption des règlements, et surtout des directives, où il s'avère plus nécessaire.

52. Outre cette harmonisation au niveau législatif, il existe encore une "quasi harmonisation", qui est réalisée par la jurisprudence de la Cour. L'examen comparatif des législations des Etats membres constitue également une étape préliminaire dans cette "quasi harmonisation". L'examen comparatif a donc une fonction spécifique dans l'oeuvre de la Cour et cette fonction spécifique a déterminé les particularités de l'utilisation de cette méthode, que nous avons essayé de décrire.

53. Qu'il me soit permis de terminer par une observation qui sort un peu de mon sujet: La relation entre la Cour et les droits nationaux n'est pas à sens unique. Non seulement la Cour s'inspire des droits nationaux, mais les droits nationaux sont aussi influencés par le droit communautaire. Les législateurs nationaux tiennent compte du fait que les droits nationaux s'inscrivent dans le système en quelque sorte fédéral du droit de la Communauté; les administrations nationales et les juridictions nationales inter-

---

23 octobre 1974, Transocean Marine Paint Association/Commission (17/74, Rec. p. 1063); 21 janvier 1965, Merlini (108/63, Rec. p. 1: principe de l'estoppel du droit anglais, qui a été reconnu avant l'adhésion du Royaume-Uni à la Communauté. La jurisprudence qui admet l'effet direct, limité, des directives est en fait fondé sur ce principe sans que cela soit expressément dit).

[50] Voir les paragraphes 18 et suivants ci-dessus.

[51] Voir le paragraphe 46 ci-dessus.

[52] Exemples de termes abstraits:
- principes élémentaires de droit (arrêts des 4 juillet 1963, Alvis, 32/62, Rec. p. 101; et 22 mars 1961, SNUPAT/Haute Autorité, 42 et 49/59, Rec. p. 103);
- principes généraux du droit de travail (arrêts des 8 octobre 1974, Syndicat général du personnel des organismes européens, 18/74, Rec. p. 933, point 10; et 8 octobre 1974, Union Syndicale, 175/73, Rec. p. 917, point 14);
- principes généraux même en l'absence de textes (arrêt du 10 mai 1960, Erzbergbau e.a./Haute Autorité, 3 à 18, 25 et 26/58, Rec. p. 459).

prètent le droit national à la lumière du droit communautaire[53]. En outre, les juridictions nationales, qui sont liées par les solutions données par la Cour et qui appliquent ainsi, dans les cas régis par le droit communautaire, des principes qui sont inconnus en droit national, par exemple le principe de proportionnalité, sont familiarisées avec ces principes. Cette familiarisation crée une osmose pour l'application de ces principes, tels que celui de proportionnalité, par le juge national même dans des affaires qui sont régies par le droit national. Il s'agit d'un signe supplémentaire de cette interpénétration qui est à la fois résultat et facteur de la marche vers l'intégration européenne.

[53] Elles ont d'ailleurs l'obligation juridique de le faire, comme la Cour l'a affirmé: arrêts des 22 juin 1989, Fratelli Costanzo (103/88, Rec. p. 1839, points 28 à 33); 10 avril 1984, Von Colson et Kamann (14/83, Rec. p. 1891, point 26); et 13 novembre 1990, Marleasing (C-106/89, Rec. p. I-4135, point 8).

RAYMOND LEGEAIS*

L'utilisation du droit comparé par les tribunaux – Rapport français

Il n'y a pas eu à ce jour, du moins à notre connaissance, d'étude systématique et scientifique du rôle "pratique" du droit comparé dans la vie juridique en France[1]. Mais de nombreux indices permettent de diagnostiquer un contraste, au moins comme hypothèse: autant l'influence du droit comparé paraît avoir pris de l'ampleur dans la procédure législative, autant elle semble rester réduite dans le "travail judiciaire".

C'est vrai le droit comparé a été très présent dans beaucoup des grandes réformes qui ont suivi la fin de la seconde guerre mondiale. En droit pénal, en droit civil, notamment, la rénovation des codes est, à cet égard, une illustration significative, sinon spectaculaire. Même pour des lois séparées, souvent – qu'on pense à la "Loi Badinter", du 5 juillet 1985, relative à l'amélioration de l'indemnisation des victimes d'accidents de la circulation – le législateur a cherché dans certains droits étrangers des modèles ou des raisons lui permettant de mûrir son choix.

A première vue, au contraire, rien d'aussi notable du côté des juges. Et certains de penser qu'autorité de l'Etat dont il a pour mission d'appliquer le droit, le juge n'a sans doute que faire de placer le droit comparé au rang de ses méthodes ou des sciences auxquelles il demanderait d'être ses auxiliaires.

Pourtant, une attention plus durable révèle que le droit comparé est loin d'être absent des débats et de la réflexion dans les prétoires, dans les cabinets ou les "chambres du conseil" où s'élaborent jugements et arrêts.Une étude approfondie pour quantifier, pour apprécier la qualité du travail comparatif et peut-être aussi ses insuffisances, mériterait d'être entreprise. Ce rapport, qui ne peut bien sûr en tenir lieu, réunira quelques premiers éléments, qui, à la lumière des travaux d'Athènes, pourraient justifier les organismes de recherche sur la justice en France de mettre au

* Doyen honoraire de la Faculté de droit, Ancien Président de l'Université de Poitiers

[1] On peut donc se réjouir de l'initiative du Centre français de droit comparé d'avoir organisé le 26 novembre 1993 une journée d'études sur *"Les professions juridiques et le droit comparé"*, Revue internationale de droit comparé, numéro spécial, 1994.

U. Drobnig and S. van Erp (eds.), The Use of Comparative Law by Courts, 113–125.

rang de leurs thèmes d'études: "L'utilisation du droit comparé par les Cours et tribunaux".

Dans une première approche, il nous a semblé utile de distinguer deux perspectives dans les rapports de l'activité judiciaire avec le droit comparé. Assez souvent aujourd'hui, en raison de conventions internationales, mais aussi de par les règles françaises de droit international privé, le juge doit appliquer ou tout au moins consulter la loi étrangère. Quelquefois, c'est librement que, pour ses raisonnements, il prend appui sur les solutions définies dans un autre système de droit. Que représente, dans notre pays, l'utilisation obligée du droit comparé par les Cours et tribunaux et dans quelle mesure se double-t-elle d'une utilisation plus libre?

I. L'UTILISATION OBLIGÉE DU DROIT COMPARÉ

Dans beaucoup d'affaires venant devant la juridiction civile ou devant la juridiction pénale, un "aspect international" est souvent essentiel et, s'il n'en est qu'exceptionnellement ainsi devant les juridictions administratives, des exemples peuvent néanmoins en être trouvés. Les sources qui s'imposent au juge français – conventions internationales, dispositions légales, principes consacrés par les plus hautes juridictions – ont peu à peu "valorisé" le droit étranger. Le juge français doit ainsi "consulter" souvent la "loi étrangère" puis, dans une part des affaires présentant un aspect international, fonder sur elle la solution qu'il retiendra. Sans prétendre à l'exhaustivité, nous allons chercher à inventorier les situations les plus répétitives pour lesquelles joue l'obligation du juge, puis nous nous demanderons s'il est possible de rendre compte de la manière dont les juridictions s'acquittent de leur obligation.

A. Les principales situations qui impliquent un recours obligatoire au droit comparé

Relativement fréquentes sont les situations qui relèvent du droit privé; mais dans des cas qui progressent quantitativement, où c'est le droit pénal ou le droit administratif qui se trouve concerné, on a aussi une obligation pour le juge de tenir compte du droit étranger de manière telle que le recours au droit comparé s'impose à lui.

1. Les juridictions françaises de l'ordre judiciaire sont saisies d'affaires variées, dont les questions de droit privé qui s'y trouvent impliquées ne peuvent recevoir de solution que par un recours obligé à la loi étrangère[2].

---

[2] Un nombre d'affaires appréciable qui ressortent à l'évidence d'une loi étrangère sont néanmoins soumises aux juridictions françaises qui peuvent en connaître, en raison des articles 14 et 15 du code civil (V.L. Cadiet, *Droit judiciaire privé*, n°s 512 et s.).

L'accroissement du nombre de ces cas ne provient pas seulement de "l'internationalisation" de la vie des personnes ou des rapports d'affaires, il est dû aussi à notre jurisprudence qui a évolué de telle manière que les juridictions du fond ne peuvent plus comme naguère trancher presque systématiquement selon la loi française les situations présentant un aspect international.

Au prix d'un revirement de jurisprudence remarqué, la Cour de cassation a décidé que, même lorsque les parties n'ont pas formulé d'allégation relative au droit qu'il y a lieu d'appliquer, *la juridiction saisie a l'obligation d'appliquer d'office la règle de conflit française, lorsque pour trancher le type de conflit qui apparaît dans l'affaire le droit international privé français désigne une loi étrangère*[3]. Avant les arrêts du 11 et 18 octobre 1988, la juridiction avait la possibilité d'appliquer d'office la loi française de conflit désignant une loi étrangère, mais il ne s'agissait pas d'un impératif pour elle[4].

Par ailleurs – mais sur ce point l'évolution jurisprudentielle a commencé plus tôt[5] – si la loi étrangère est applicable, elle ne peut être écartée qu'exceptionnellement au nom de l'ordre public, pour faire retour à la loi française, même si les différences sont significatives entre notre loi et la loi étrangère normalement applicable[6].

Ces positions permettent aux principes du droit international privé d'être pleinement efficaces dans toutes celles de leurs implications qui valorisent la loi étrangère, de sorte que le recours obligatoire au droit comparé par le juge a dans notre pays une réelle actualité[7].

Si un inventaire exhaustif des affaires n'a pu être réalisé à ce jour, l'actualité montre que le juge a l'obligation de recourir au droit comparé pour des questions qui se rattachent principalement au droit des personnes, tout autant que pour des questions relevant plutôt du droit des affaires.

Dans le droit des personnes les questions relevant de la vie des couples (mariage-divorce) ont toujours alimenté substantiellemnt les recueils de jurisprudence. Très souvent le juge a l'obligation de recourir au droit comparé, pour choisir la loi applicable, puis pour la mettre en oeuvre[8].

---

[3] Cass. 1ère civ., 11 oct. 1988, Cass. 1ère civ. 18 oct. 1988, Rev.crit. de dr. internation. priv., 1990, p.367.

[4] Y. Lequette, *L'abandon de la jurisprudence Bisbal (à propos des arrêts de la Première chambre civile des 11 et 18 octobre 1988)*, Rev. crit. dr. international privé, 1990, 277 et s.

[5] V.déjà Cass.1ère, Ch.civ.30 mai 1967 (Kieger c.Consorts Amigues), D.1967, P.629, note Ph. Malaurie.

[6] V., parmi les décisions récentes, Cass.1ère Ch.civ. 6 juin 1990, D.1990, sommaires commentés, p.265.

[7] V.Y. Loussouarn, *Le rôle de la méthode comparative en droit international privé*, Rev. crit. dr. international privé, 1979, 3077 et s.

[8] Colmar 19 janvier 1993, Rép.Defrénois 35542, note Mariel Révillard (référence à la loi allemande pour apprécier si des époux allemands pouvaient changer de régime matrimonial. Au vu des textes la Cour admet que les époux ont pu valablement opter pour la législation française concernant les régimes matrimoniaux). Problèmes de divorce; prestations compen-

Les rapports de filiation donnent aussi aux tribunaux depuis quelques années des occasions fréquentes d'intervenir[9]. Il en est ainsi tout particulièrement d'une forme d'adoption "en euphorie", pour reprendre une expression du Doyen René Savatier, l'adoption plénière, qui ne peut se réaliser qu'en vertu d'une décision judiciaire. S'agit-il pour un couple français d'adopter selon cette forme d'adoption un enfant de nationalité étrangère, la juridiction saisie doit non seulement bien connaître la loi nationale de l'enfant, qui va régir certaines conditions de celle-ci, mais procéder à une comparaison délicate pour apprécier si l'adoption plénière sera ou non réalisable[10]. La Cour de cassation a dû intervenir plusieurs fois pour exiger la justesse de cette comparaison[11].

Pour le droit des obligations et le droit des affaires, la diversité des questions est extrême et c'est sans doute dans ce domaine qu'une étude systématique, portant non seulement sur les décisions publiées, mais aussi sur celles qui peuvent être connues par les banques de données, mériterait d'être entreprise. Un contentieux relativement important est lié aux aspects internationaux de la responsabilité civile[12] et il conduit les juridictions à recourir souvent au droit comparé. Il en est de même pour beaucoup de questions concernant les contrats, dès lors qu'un problème de droit international privé se revèle, car si le principe de la compétence de la loi d'autonomie généralement admis semble permettre de connaître facilement la solution applicable, la mise en oeuvre de ce principe est en réalité très délicate[13].Certaines matières spéciales, comme celles relevant du droit maritime, obligent aussi fréquemment les juridictions à pratiquer la com-

---

satoires (la loi marocaine, ne la permettant pas est contraire à l'ordre public, Cass.1ère civ. 16 juil.1992, JCP, 1993, II, 22138, obs. Déprez).

[9] L'important arrêt du 11 oct.1988, précit., supra note 3, concerne précisément la détermination de la loi applicable à une action en recherche de paternité (v.aussi sur cet arrêt les observ. de P. Courbe, JCP , 1989, II, 21327).

[10] V.Dijon 25 fév.1992 (JCP, 1993, IV , n°127) qui pour l'adoption d'un enfant bengalais dont la loi personnelle prohibe ou ignore l'adoption, retient un raisonnement "audacieux"; Versailles 24 sept. 1992 (JCP, 1992, II, 22049, obs. Horatia Muir Watt): la loi nationale de l'enfant détermine les conditions de consentement ou de représentation de l'adopté, de sorte qu'un enfant de nationalité algérienne ne peut être adopté, la loi algérienne ne permettant pas l'adoption (la "kafala" qui s'en rapproche est différente, car elle ne crée pas un lien de filiation).

[11] Civ. 1, 18 nov.1992, Benali c. Mme Makhlouf, JCP, 1993, IV, p.237, D. 1993, J. 213, note P. Courbe: nécessité d'appliquer loi de la mère pour action en recherche de paternité naturelle: en l'espèce loi algérienne: juridiction devait rechercher d'office contenu de la loi algérienne: cassation.

[12] A titre d'exemples, parmi de nombreuses décisions, Cass. lére Ch.civ. 6 juin 1990, D.1990, Sommaires commentés, Droit intern.priv. par B. Audit, p.265; Cass.1ère Ch.civ., 19 avr. 1988, D.1988, Sommaires commentés, Droit intern.priv.par B. Audit; Cass.1ère, Ch.civ.2 oct.1984, JCP, 1984, Actualit. n°45; Cass.1ère Ch.civ., 20 mars 1978, JCP, 1980, II, 19311.

[13] Versailles 6 Fév. 1991, JCP, 1992, II, 21972, obs. F.Osman: la Cour fait application de la loi italienne, en se référant à la Convention de Rome, pour déterminer la loi applicable à un cautionnement.

paraison[14].

2. L'obligation pour le juge de recourir à la méthode comparative, même si elle demeure encore plus exceptionnelle que pour les questions de droit privé, est néanmoins aujourd'hui reconnue dans certains cas pour la mise en oeuvre des règles pénales ou des solutions du droit administratif.

a) Les juridictions pénales françaises doivent connaître des lois pénales étrangères et recourir ainsi au droit comparé dans plusieurs variétés de situations.

D'abord lorsqu'un français commet à l'étranger certaines infractions. Si l'infraction est un "délit" (au sens technique précis donné à ce mot en droit français) , une poursuite ne pourra intervenir en France (dès lors qu'il n'y aura pas eu à l'étranger de jugement définitif) que dans la mesure où ce délit est également réprimé par la loi du pays où il a été commis (art.689, alinéa 2, du code de procédure pénale et art.L.113-6 du nouveau code pénal). Ce n'est que pour les délits attentatoires à la sûreté de l'Etat, ou pour les délits connexes à des délits commis en France, qu'une solution plus sévère est donnée reprenant la règle retenue pour les crimes qui peuvent être poursuivis en France sans qu'il y ait lieu à consulter la loi du pays où se sont réalisés les faits[15]. En ce qui concerne les contraventions, les juridictions françaises n'ont de compétence que très exceptionnellement[16] et, pour que des poursuites soient possibles, il est nécessaire que l'Etat où a été commise la contravention puisse poursuivre de son côté ses nationaux qui commettraient en France des contraventions de même nature:une comparaison des lois est donc alors aussi nécessaire. La pratique montre que, tout au moins pour les délits, les textes permettant la poursuite d'infractions commises par les français à l'étranger ne restent pas lettre morte[17].

Lorsque une extradition est demandée à l'Etat français, la Chambre d'accusation, qui doit formuler un avis, a l'obligation de consulter la loi du pays demandeur, d'une part pour connaître les peines qu'elle retient, d'autre part pour apprécier si l'action publique a pu être éteinte par l'une des causes auxquelles cette loi attache un tel pouvoir.

[14] Com.2 mars 1993, JCP, IV, 1149 (En cas de lacune dans le code de commerce du pays dont la loi est applicable, le juge français peut y suppléer en appliquant une règle tirée du droit français de portée générale, alors que par ailleurs il n'est fait état d'aucun usage local).

[15] Stéfani, Levasseur et Bouloc, *Procédure pénale*, 15ème édit., n°s 398 et s; J. Pradel, *Le nouveau code pénal (partie générale)*, n° 20 et s..

[16] Il en est ainsi pour les contraventions commises par un français dans un Etat limitrophe de notre pays, en matière de contribution directes ou de douane, de même que pour les contraventions forestières, rurales ou relatives à la pêche.

[17] Différents arrêts de la Cour de cassation en témoignent: Crim.19 mai 1971, JCP, 1972, II, 16947, obs. VITU; Crim. 6 mars 1984, Bull. Cass. Ch.crim 1984, n°90; Crim. 27 juin 1984, Bull.Cass. Ch.crim. 1984, n°284; Crim.10 oct.1988, Bull. Cass. Ch.crim.1988, n°331; Crim.9 nov.1988, Bull.Cass. Ch.crim. 1988, n°385.

Si lors du procès pénal doit être tranchée une question d'ordre civil, la juridiction civile doit appliquer la loi étrangère à la compétence de laquelle ressortit cette question. Il en est ainsi pour certaines "questions préjudicielles"[18]. Il en est ainsi surtout pour l'action civile en réparation du dommage causé par l'infraction, qui, en France, peut être portée devant la juridiction répressive et qui l'est effectivement presque toujours: la réparation du dommage est en principe assurée selon la loi du pays où les faits se sont produits[19].

b) Juridictions administratives

On pourrait penser que le droit public, nécessairement marqué par une "territorialité" rigide, ne suscite jamais de situations obligeant le juge administratif à recourir au droit comparé. Pourtant il est des exemples de la reconnaissance par le Conseil d'Etat d'une telle obligation.

C'est pour les contrats de travail conclus à l'étranger par les Ambassades ou Consulats que plusieurs arrêts illustrent à cet égard la jurisprudence de la Haute juridiction administrative: celle-ci considère qu'un contrat de travail tout en étant un contrat administratif au regard des critères jurisprudentiels français n'en doit pas moins être soumis à la législation sociale du pays où il a été conclu et où il s'exécute[20].

Des arrêts relatifs à d'autres situations[21] témoignent de la même démarche respectueuse de la loi étrangère. Toutefois le Conseil d'Etat peut parfois régler un problème dont les éléments sont apparus à l'étranger par un principe qui fait l'économie du recours à la loi étrangère[22]. Mais ce n'est pas l'esprit du Conseil d'Etat de chercher à écarter systématiquement la loi étrangère. Aujourd'hui, les hautes juridictions françaises paraissent bien, chacune au sommet de l'ordre juridictionnel qui est le sien, chercher à valoriser la pratique du droit comparé.

B. La réalité de la pratique du droit comparé

Lorsqu'une juridiction doit recourir au droit comparé, est-il possible

[18] V.ainsi en matière de bigamie ou d'adultère, Crim. 14 fév.1929, S. 1930. I. 280; en matière de chèque, Crim.20 octobre 1959, D. 1960, p.300, note P. Lagarde.

[19] J.P. Doucet, *La loi applicable à l'action civile*, Mélanges Levasseur, 1992, p.89 et s.

[20] C.E. 7 janvier1989, (arrêt Félicien), Recueil Lebon, 1989, p.521. Et déjà, C.E. 8 mai 1968 (arrêt Fourny), Recueil Lebon 1968, p.269.

[21] V. pour l'application par le Conseil d'Etat de la loi Cambodgienne à un appel d'offres régi par cette loi, C.E., 3 juillet 1968, (arrêt Lavigne et Le Mée), Recueil Lebon 1968, p.884.

[22] C.E.13 janvier 1993 (Mme Galtié): la Haute juridiction administrative considère comme "collaborateur occasionnel du service public" la victime d'un accident de la circulation, survenu alors qu'elle encadrait pour une sortie à Delphes des élèves du lycée franco-hellénique d'Athènes, et décide que l'indemnisation doit ainsi intervenir selon les règles du droit administratif français, l'Etat français étant subrogé dans les droits que cette victime pouvait faire valoir à l'encontre des responsables de l'accident.

d'apprécier la qualité de la démarche comparative qui est la sienne? Sans doute, là encore, les indices qui peuvent être réunis ne conduisent qu'à formuler des vraisemblances, sinon de simples hypothèses.

1. Le juge connaît-il la loi étrangère?

La condition "sine qua non" pour que le recours au droit comparé puisse se faire avec justesse et utilité, c'est évidemment que la loi étrangère, qui doit être consultée et éventuellement appliquée, soit accessible au juge, selon des modalités suffisamment économiques et rapides tout en lui permettant une connaissance sûre de cette loi.

Le principe "jura novit curia", qui dispense normalement les parties au procès d'avoir à établir l'existence et le contenu de la loi, ne concerne que les lois françaises (et les conventions ou traités qui lient la France). C'est le plaideur qui invoque le droit étranger qui doit en principe faire la preuve du contenu de ce droit et il satisfera à cette obligation de preuve en produisant "un certificat de coutume"[23]. Le juge n'est cependant pas tenu de se fier au contenu d'un tel certificat, il peut ordonner une expertise[24] ou se fonder sur des informations personnelles.

L'amélioration du système traditionnel a été souhaitée et des progrès se réalisent peu à peu. En 1968 a été signée à Londres, le 7 juin, la Convention européenne relative à "l'information sur le droit étranger"[25]. Mais dans la pratique peu de demandes sont faites pour utiliser les possibilités qu'elle offre. Le Ministère de la justice disposait depuis le XIXème siècle d'un Service de législation étrangère, insuffisamment connu, qui a progressivement perdu son effectivité. La mise en place d'un centre d'information moderne sur le droit étranger était demandée depuis longtemps[26] et elle apparaissait d'autant plus indispensable que le juge doit maintenant appliquer d'office la loi étrangère dans beaucoup de cas (v.supra, A). Un tel centre a été créé récemment[27], le Ministère de la Justice participant à sa gestion, de sorte que les meilleures possibilités maintenant offertes aux juges français de connaître le droit étranger ne pourront que renforcer le courant d'ouverture qui se manifeste en France, valorisant le recours au droit comparé.

2. Le juge compare-t-il vraiment avec les solutions françaises?

On peut enregistrer différents signes d'un plus grand respect de la loi

---

[23] Cass. Civ., 26 avr.1950, D.1950, 361, note Lenoan. Cyrille David, *La loi étrangère devant le juge du fond*, 1965, p.224 et s.

[24] Cass.1ère Ch.Civ., 19 oct. 1971 (2ème espèce), D. 1972, p.633, note Ph. Malaurie.

[25] Publiée par décret du 11 octobre 1972 (J.O. du 20 oct.1972), la convention est entrée en vigueur pour la France le 10 juillet 1972.

[26] Marc Ancel, *La création d'un Centre international de documentation juridique*, Etudes de droit contemporain, Paris 1959, T.1, p.259 et s.

[27] Centre d'information et de renseignements juridiques internationaux, Téléport 2, Boulevard 3, Chasseneuil du Poitou, 86960 Futuroscope cedex.

étrangère et de la recherche d'une "véritable" comparaison avec la loi française, lorsque cette comparaison s'impose.

Dans le passé le juge civil éludait souvent son obligation de consulter et d'appliquer la loi étrangère en admettant qu'était caractérisée l'une des causes qui, selon la Cour de cassation, permettaient de revenir à la "lex fori", c'est à dire à la loi française. Cette cause pouvait être l'impossibilité de connaître la loi étrangère. C'était surtout l'incompatibilité de la loi étrangère avec l'ordre public français, ce qui permettait de revenir à la loi française, dès qu'une différence notable entre celle-ci et la loi étrangère normalement applicable pouvait être décelée. La Cour de cassation a infléchi sa jurisprudence de manière à rendre le jeu de l'ordre public exceptionnel[28]. Il y a ainsi pour le juge du fond l'obligation de procéder à une véritable comparaison entre la loi étrangère et la loi française.

La Cour de cassation se refuse sans doute toujours à exercer de manière systématique un contrôle sur l'interprétation donnée par les juges du fond à la loi étrangère, mais elle censure la dénaturation, tout au moins la dénaturation d'un "document législatif"[29].

Le juge administratif, obligé moins souvent que le juge judiciaire, de consulter une loi étrangère pour éventuellemnt l'appliquer, semble en tout cas soucieux, lorsqu'il en est ainsi, d'en respecter la teneur[30].

Cour de cassation et Conseil d'Etat ont ainsi peu à peu accentué l'ouverture vers le droit étranger, avec les exigences du droit comparé, dans les cas où il y avait lieu de préciser une obligation de recourir à la loi étrangère. Ce "climat" ne pouvait que favoriser aussi dans les juridictions le développement d'un recours plus spontané au droit comparé, le juge y cherchant un appui pour mieux remplir sa mission, toujours à parfaire, d'interpréter les lois pour les besoins d'une société qui change.

II. L'UTILISATION LIBRE DU DROIT COMPARÉ

Il n'est pas possible à notre connaissance de trouver dans les décisions des plus hautes juridictions françaises une invitation au juge à recourir à la méthode comparative pour interpréter le droit ou en combler les lacunes, aussi précisément formulée qu'on la trouve dans un arrêt de la Cour Con-

---

[28] V.pour un éclairage récent de cette évolution, F.Boulanger, note sous Paris 5 décembre 1991, D.1992, J. p. 290, B. Audit obs. sous la même décision, D. 1992, Sommaires, p.170.

[29] Cass. Civ. I, 21 nov.1961, D.1963, 37, note Ph.F., JCP, 1962, II, 12521, obs. Louis-Lucas.

[30] V.notam.C.E.28 janv.1983 (arrêt Johnston), Recueil Lebon, p.28: statuant à propos d'un contrat de travail conclu en Grande Bretagne entre les Services français d'expansion économique et une anglaise, le Conseil d'Etat, appliquant la loi anglaise recherche si, à la suite du licenciement de celle-ci, l'Etat français, son employeur, lui a offert en Grande-Bretagne un nouvel emploi "convenable" au sens du droit anglais, justifiant qu'il ne lui soit pas versé d'indemnité de licenciement pour l'éviction de son premier emploi.

stitutionnelle allemande[31], mais il y a tout de même beaucoup d'indices que, pour certaines juridictions, le droit comparé entre peu à peu au rang des méthodes de travail. Pourtant il est très difficile à ce jour pour l'observateur de pouvoir apprécier quantitativement et qualitativement ce qu'est réellement l'utilisation libre du droit comparé par les tribunaux français.

A. La multiplication des indices d'un recours délibéré au droit comparé

Que le droit comparé, en dehors de toute obligation pour le juge de consulter et d'appliquer la loi étrangère, intervienne dans le travail de celui-ci, il est difficile d'en douter aujourd'hui tant se multiplient les signes d'un recours à la méthode comparative.

1. Juridictions de l'ordre judiciaire

Il convient de rappeler qu'un certain nombre de ceux qui, dans la seconde moitié du XXème siècle, ont contribué au rayonnement du droit comparé ont été des magistrats[32]. Il est probable qu'ils ont ainsi eu recours à "la méthode comparative" lors de l'élaboration de certaines décisions. Quelques uns d'entre eux l'ont d'ailleurs confié[33] et, grâce à leur témoignage, on peut se rendre compte que certaines solutions données récemment à des questions à la fois importantes et très débattues ont évolué chez nous à la lumière du droit comparé.

On doit aussi mettre en relief que le droit comparé a maintenant une place dans la formation initiale des magistrats ainsi que dans leur formation continue. Nombreux sont les évènements qui démontrent que l'attention au droit comparé devient plus systématique, plus collective. Ainsi en est-il des journées organisées à la Cour d appel de Paris, les 12, 13 et 14 novembre 1992, qui ont permis de traiter un cas civil et un cas pénal, avec les procédures et rituels respectifs, pour l'Allemagne, l'Espagne, la Grande Bretagne, l'Italie, les Pays-Bas, le Portugal et la France (La Vie Judiciaire en a rendu compte, dans son n° 2431, du 9 au 15 novembre 1992). Pareillement les jumelages de juridictions, de barreaux, qui sont intervenus depuis quelques mois et qui se multiplient, contribuent à modifier l'esprit, à sensibiliser aux difficultés du droit comparé, à mettre sur la voie des méthodes qui permettent de les résoudre.

En plus de l'utilisation du droit comparé par les juridictions proprement

---

[31] "Im übrigen haben die Gerichte sich der erprobten Hilfsmittel, nämlich der Interpretation und Lückenfüllung, unter Verwertung auch der rechtsvergleichenden Methode bedient" (BVerfGE 3, 208, 244).

[32] Le rôle du Président Marc Ancel comme animateur de la vie scientifique, son oeuvre de juriste où le droit comparé a tant de place, sont à cet égard exemplaires. Mais beaucoup de magistrats ont contribué a éveiller l'attention des praticiens pour le droit comparé.

[33] V.l'exposé du Président Bézard, n° spécial de la Revue intern. de dr. comp., cité en note 1.

dites, il importe de rappeler que d'autres autorités, dont les missions se rattachent à l'activité judiciaire ou apparaissent bien proches de celle-ci, n'hésitent pas à recourir à la méthode comparative.

Les arbitres, libres de prendre du champ par rapport à un ordre juridique national, paraissent trouver souvent leur inspiration dans des législations différentes[34]. Et, pour un éminent spécialiste français du droit international privé et de la pratique arbitrale "une telle synthèse qui procède typiquement d'une démarche comparative est la seule voie praticable dans la formation de la "lex mercatoria" et représente l'avenir du droit du commerce international"[35].

Il arrive que les autorités du Parquet, confrontés à une affaire présentant des aspects internationaux, s'informent très complètement de la manière dont serait abordée et développée la procédure dans l'Etat avec lequel cette affaire présente des liens[36].

2. En dehors des juridictions de l'ordre judiciaire

De remarquables exemples d'un recours au droit comparé dans le travail des juridictions, libre d'obligation mais délibéré, sont à rechercher près du Conseil d'Etat et près du Conseil Constitutionnel.

Le Conseil d'Etat a fait place, de plus en plus, dans ses raisonnements à des "standards", c'est à dire à des notions qui supposent une appréciation en rapport avec les moeurs, avec le "temps": c'est la notion de "délai raisonnable", de "risque anormal", "d'inconvénient excessif", de bien d'autres notions encore. Dans la minutieuse étude que le Professeur Rials a consacrée à cet aspect de l'oeuvre du Conseil d'Etat[37], il met en lumière la démarche comparative de la Haute juridiction. Celle-ci, en retenant à partir des années 60 la notion "d'erreur manifeste", pour apprécier la validité de beaucoup de décisions administratives, paraît bien l'avoir transposée de la jurisprudence du Tribunal fédéral suisse. Il semble que la jurisprudence de l'Organisation internationale du travail, bien que concernant un domaine tout autre (le droit disciplinaire) ait inspiré les notions que le Conseil d'Etat conjuguent dans le contrôle de proportionalité qu'il opère en matière d'expropriation[38].

Le droit comparé pourrait bien déjà compter beaucoup aussi pour le développement en France de la jurisprudence du Conseil constitutionnel. La Constitution de 1958 a confié au Conseil une mission importante de contrôle "a-priori" de la constitutionnalité de l'activité législative. Mais le rôle du Conseil constitutionnel paraissait devoir rester exceptionnel. Une dynamique a joué pour l'extension des possibilités de ses interventions et

[34] Y. Derains, Rev.crit.dr.internation.priv., 1973, p.357 et s.
[35] Y. Loussouarn, art.précit., p.339.
[36] Ce fut le cas à Lyon, à l'occasion de "l'affaire Barbie".
[37] S. Rials, *Le juge administratif français et la technique du standard*, 1980.
[38] V.sur la probabilité de ces influences, S. Rials, notam. p.207.

le Conseil a montré lui-même de plus en plus d'audace dans ses décisions. Il est sûr que les exemples venant des Etats-Unis, de l'Allemagne, de l'Italie, de l'Espagne, ont compté. Tout récemment le Président du Conseil constitutionnel français, le Président Robert Badinter, ouvrant la IXème Conférence des Cours constitutionnelles européennes, qui avait comme thème de ses travaux "La coexistence sur le continent européen de deux ordres juridiques – l'un national, l'autre international régi notamment par la Convention européenne des droits de l'homme et les traités des Communautés européennes", a pu ainsi faire une synthèse très suggestive à cet égard: "Cette dualité est en effet de nature à susciter des interprétations diverses, parfois – mais heureusement très rarement – divergentes, du contenu et de la portée des libertés publiques et des droits fondamentaux des citoyens. Certes, la Cour de Justice des Communautés européennes dont je salue l'oeuvre, en même temps que ses représentants, a intégré dans sa jurisprudence les principes fondamentaux qui sont reconnus par la législation des Etats membres. Elle s'inspire aussi de ceux de la Convention européenne des droits de l'Homme et de ses protocoles annexes, tels qu'ils sont interprétés par la Commission et la Cour européenne des Droits de l'Homme dont les Présidents et les membres sont également parmi nous. Celles-ci prêtent intérêt aux décisions de nos Cours tout comme, nous-mêmes, juridictions constitutionnelles, sommes très attentifs aux décisions rendues par la Cour de Justice des Communautés européennes et aussi – et parfois particulièrement – à la jurisprudence de la Cour de Strasbourg. De même encore, chacune de nos Cours s'informe des décisions rendues par les autres juridictions constitutionnelles en Europe à propos des sujets dont nos Cours ont à traiter et nous y trouvons toujours matière à réflexion, parfois même à inspiration. J'ajouterai enfin que les relations cordiales et souvent amicales – j'en porte témoignage – qui se nouent entre les membres des Hautes juridictions – et notamment entre leurs présidents – sont de nature à renforcer ce phénomène si remarquable – je n'irai pas dire d'osmose – mais d'influence réciproque entre les jurisprudences des Cours constitutionnelles et celles des Cours internationales européennes. Il semble toutefois que cette harmonisation pourrait être confortée si – je fais à cet égard une suggestion – nous nous donnions les moyens d'une information régulière et complète sur l'évolution de nos jurisprudences".[39]

Les propos du Président Badinter reflètent excellemment la dynamique de l'attention comparative dans le monde judiciaire de la France aujourd'hui. Mais s'il convient de mettre celle-ci en évidence, il serait souhaitable de pouvoir mieux cerner la manière dont se fait le cheminement des idées et des influences, en d'autres termes, de parvenir à une mesure de l'ampleur exacte de ce que représente dans l'activité juridictionnelle le

[39] L'intégralité de l'allocution du Président Badinter, ainsi que l'ensemble des rapports et interventions à la IXème Conférence des Cours constitutionnelles européennes, qui s'est tenu à l'UNESCO en 1993 sont en cours de publication.

recours volontaire au droit comparé.

B. Les difficultés de discerner l'ampleur exacte de ce que représente dans l'activité juridictionnelle le recours volontaire au droit comparé.

Il est sans doute possible de parvenir à une appréhension plus fine de l'utilisation libre du droit comparé par les tribunaux, mais de toute manière il faudra compter avec certaines réalités qui rendent cette appréhension difficile.

D'abord il convient de mettre en relief que les hautes juridictions françaises motivent leurs décisions de manière beaucoup moins développée que ne le font leurs homologues hors de France. A la Chambre des Lords, à la Cour Suprême du Canada, des références explicites à de solutions retenues dans d'autres pays, sont parfois données et exploitées. En France à la Cour de cassation ou au Conseil d'Etat la consultation des droits étrangers précède quelquefois la prise de décision; ce n'est pas pour autant qu'un signe de l'influence de la loi étrangère apparaîtra dans la motivation de l'arrêt [40].Pour éclairer certaines décisions de la Cour de cassation, la connaissance des conclusions de l'avocat général, celle du rapport du Conseiller rapporteur serait précieuse. Pareillement au Conseil d'Etat, les conclusions du Commissaire du Gouvernement peuvent souvent permettre de discerner quelles influences ont compté pour la Haute juridiction. Mais de tels documents ne sont publiés que de manière exceptionnelle dans les recueils de jurisprudence.

Par ailleurs, il faut compter avec le secret, l'imprévu du cheminement des idées. Lorsque l'Assemblée plénière de la Cour de cassation, changeant la jurisprudence antérieure a admis le 29 mars 1991 que l'article 1384, alinéa 1, du code civil consacrait non seulement un principe de responsabilité du fait des choses, mais aussi un principe général de responsabilité civile du fait d'autrui[41], elle ne fait que reprendre un raisonnement qui avait retenu en 1922 au "Privy Council" de Londres[42]. Il n'est pas impossible que ce raisonnement ait compté pour un courant de la doctrine française, courant auquel le Premier Avocat général Dontenwille ne semble pas avoir été indifférent, les conclusions de l'avocat général ayant ensuite été suivies par l'Assemblée plénière.

Enfin il est très difficile de déterminer ce que le juge a demandé exacte-

---

[40] Le droit comparé a sans doute joué un rôle dans le revirement de la Cour de cassation relativement à la nullité des clauses d'échelle mobile (Cass.1ère Ch.civ. 27 juin 1957, D.1957, p.649, note G. Ripert, JCP, 1957, II, 10093, concl. Proc. Gén. Besson). Mais c'est en vain qu'on en chercherait une trace dans la motivation de l'arrêt.

[41] Cass. Ass.plén. 29 mars 1991, JCP, 1991, II, 21673, concl. Premier Avocat Général Dontenwille, obs. J.Ghestin, D.1991, J, 324, note C. Larroumet.

[42] V.l'opinion de Lord Summer in "Québec Railway, Light, Heat and Power Co. v. Vandry", Privy Council 1920, A. C., 662, interprétant l'article 1054, alin.1 du code civil de la Province de Québec, équivalent alors à l'article 1384, alinéa 1, du code civil français.

ment au droit comparé. Dans les pays de common law, il n'est pas rare que les cours se réfèrent à des solutions données dans un autre Etat dont le système de droit appartient à la même famille, pour argumenter en faveur d'une solution. Mais il y a sans doute cette explication particulière que l'on considère le droit comme ayant une certaine unité, pour tous les pays qui se sont inspirés de la technique anglaise et dont certains ont coexisté avec le Royaume uni, dans un même ensemble politique. En France une telle démarche était concevable lorsque le code civil n'avait pas été modifié ou interprété avec trop de liberté, de sorte qu'à la fin du XIXème siècle et au début du XXème siècle notamment les juridictions françaises ont pu être attentives aux décisions rendues en Belgique, notamment pour interpréter les textes concernant la responsabilité civile[43]. Mais au fur et à mesure que les droits ont divergé, il semble bien que se soient arrêtées ces références, qui étaient restées d'ailleurs exceptionnelles. Ce sont donc d'autres types d'inspiration qui paraissent compter maintenant.

---

[43] Même en ces temps où l'attention à la jurisprudence belge eut été normale, elle était restée très limitée: v.Paul DURAND, *Le droit des obligations dans les jurisprudences française et belge*, Paris, Sirey, 1933.

ULRICH DROBNIG*

The Use of Foreign Law by German Courts**

The comparative law method is fruitful for all branches of the law, not only for academic research and for legislation[1] but also for court practice. In this report, I will examine the practical significance of recourse to foreign law in German court practice, especially the areas, methods and results of its application.

To clarify the ambit of the study, two preliminary remarks are appropriate. First, the use of foreign law by the courts is not necessarily an instance of comparison of laws, i.e. the juxtaposition of one or more foreign rules with a rule of the home country. In practice, courts are often, if not almost always, only describing one or more foreign rules in a more or less comprehensive way without really comparing them, in the strict sense, with other rules. Secondly, recourse to foreign law does not embrace, in the present context, the application of foreign law by virtue of the German conflict of laws rules because, in this case, the application of foreign law is obligatory. By contrast, this study is interested in those cases in which there is a more or less voluntary recourse to foreign law because this is a criterion indicating the openness of the legal system to its international environment.

I. Opinions in the Literature

Which theoretical justifications can be given to support the application of foreign law by national judges? And, further, how have legal writers dealt with and evaluated this court practice?

Surprisingly, there is a remarkable deficit of answers to these two ques-

* Max-Planck-Institut für ausländisches und internationales Privatrecht, Hamburg.

** I am indebted to my assistant C. Seibt for effective assistance in the collection of recent material and in the translation of this report.

For abbreviations see end of chapter.

[1] Cf. Drobnig/Dopffel, Die Nutzung der Rechtsvergleichung durch den deutschen Gesetzgeber: RabelsZ 46 (1982) 253-307.

U. Drobnig and S. van Erp (eds.), The Use of Comparative Law by Courts, 127–147.

tions, which is exacerbated by conflicting views among writers. The small group of German comparatists proposes, vigorously and constantly, the use of the comparative law method as a means to interpret German legal rules, particularly in cases where the interpretation of a norm is disputed or where there is a *lacuna* in the legal system. The following justification for the use of this method, given by *Zweigert/Kötz,* is generally acknowledged: the criteria for filling a legal *lacuna* are the ones which can be found in the famous art. 1 of the Swiss Civil Code, according to which the judge has to proceed as follows:

> "If no rule can be found in the statute, the judge shall follow the customary law, and in the case where no customary rule exists he has to decide according to the rule he would enact as a legislator." (§ 2) – "In this regard he follows established doctrine and tradition." (§ 3).

Since the modern legislator takes the solutions of foreign legal systems into consideration when preparing new statutes, the judge, so the argument goes, should act in the same way.[2]

Two objections may be raised against this reasoning. First, it is not very convincing to justify the recourse to foreign law by referring to a foreign legal rule. Moreover, this Swiss view of the judge as a substitute for the legislator, while certainly realistic in many respects, is generally not highly regarded among German jurists, especially not among German judges.[3] Therefore, it would be more convincing if the judicial recourse to foreign law as a means for interpreting German law were based on an extension of the traditional canon of the methods of interpretation and this extension were justified accordingly.

This deficit in the justification for the comparative law method may be the reason why the second, more numerous and influential, group of academics are silent about the importance of this method in court practice. Books on jurisprudence and the methodology of law, as well as studies on the General Part of the German Civil Code, do not even mention the comparative law method in connection with the interpretation of legal norms, and these are the books that are read and studied by students, practitioners and academics alike.

In view of this dissent among academic writers, only a concise and comprehensive analysis of court practice will shed some light on the real significance of recourse to foreign law in German court practice.

---

[2] Zweigert/Kötz, Einführung in die Rechtsvergleichung I (ed. 2 1984) 20. More extensively already Zweigert, Rechtsvergleichung als universale Interpretationsmethode: RabelsZ 15 (1949/50) 5-21 (esp. 9). For a judicial confirmation of this argument, cf. *infra* II 2 c, at n. 34.

[3] Kropholler, Gleichberechtigung durch Richterrecht (1975) 68 confirms, based upon a wealth of case law, that the judges prefer to regard themselves as applying rather than improving the law.

II. Court Practice

A comprehensive analysis of the significance of comparative law for German courts has been missing up to now. However, there are some studies concerning the practice of specific Federal High Courts;[4] these works have been supplemented by my own research.[5] The following analysis refers mainly to the court practice of the Federal High Courts in the years 1950 to 1990. About 70 of the reported cases were handed down by the Federal Supreme Court (*Bundesgerichtshof*); another 25 cases originate from the Federal Constitutional Court (*Bundesverfassungsgericht*). In contrast, the other Federal High Courts have used comparative law in only a few instances. The practice of the first-instance courts and the appellate courts has not yet been analyzed and was therefore only considered briefly for this study. Generally speaking, it appears that their recourse to foreign law is only of very little importance.

I have classified court practice into three groups, depending on the motivation for the use of foreign law.[6] The first group includes cases involving rules of German law that can only be applied with the help of foreign law; in these cases, comparison is necessary (*infra* 1). In the two other groups, by contrast, recourse to foreign law is voluntary. These two groups may be distinguished from each other by the fact that, in one group, the only legal provisions at issue are those that are related in some sense to foreign countries or international legal developments (*infra* 2), whereas, in the other group, there is no such link (*infra* 3). Therefore, in the second group, comparison with foreign law is more likely than in the third group.

1. Necessary comparison

This group of cases has to be mentioned only briefly because recourse to foreign law by the courts is inevitable. The methods of comparison used by

---

[4] Reinhart, Rechtsvergleichung und richterliche Rechtsfortbildung auf dem Gebiet des Privatrechts: Richterliche Rechtsfortbildung (1986) 599–617; Kropholler, Die vergleichende Methode und das Internationale Privatrecht: ZVergl.RW 77 (1978) 1–17; Aubin, Die rechtsvergleichende Konkretisierung von Kontrollmaßstäben des Verfassungsrechts und des Kollisionsrechts in der deutschen Rechtsprechung, in: Deutsche Landesreferate zum VII. Internationalen Kongreß für Rechtsvergleichung in Uppsala 1966 (1967) 99–125; *idem*, Die rechtsvergleichende Interpretation autonom-internen Rechts in der deutschen Rechtsprechung: RabelsZ 34 (1970) 458–480; Dölle, Der Beitrag der Rechtsvergleichung zum deutschen Recht, in: Hundert Jahre deutsches Rechtsleben. Festschrift zum 100jährigen Bestehens des Deutschen Juristentages (1960) II 19–47 (33–37); Mössner, Rechtsvergleichung und Verfassungsrechtsprechung: ArchÖffR 99 (1974) 193–242.

[5] An earlier analysis is to be found at Drobnig, Rechtsvergleichung in der deutschen Rechtsprechung: RabelsZ 50 (1986) 610–630.

[6] Aubin (*supra* n. 4) distinguishes between merely two types of German provisions, i.e. those with an international or foreign connection for which comparison is necessary, and autonomous domestic provisions where comparison is merely useful.

the courts will be described later.

a) The *generally recognized rules of public international law* are according to art. 25 of the German Constitution (*Grundgesetz*) part of federal law, and they have priority over national laws. In disputed cases, the Federal Constitutional Court is exclusively competent to determine and to interpret these rules. According to the case law of the Court, rules of public international law are generally recognized if they are acknowledged by the majority of countries.[7] This formula obliges the Court to undertake a comprehensive inquiry and comparison of the views held in foreign countries on the relevant rules of public international law. The Federal Constitutional Court has fulfilled this self-imposed obligation in an exemplary fashion. This is evidenced by its decisions concerning the immunity of foreign states[8] and on the question of whether the criminal procedural prohibition of *ne bis in idem* also applies if the earlier criminal sentence has been pronounced by a foreign court.[9]

b) *Private international law* furnishes two other examples of necessary comparison.

The first instance is the famous problem of qualification: which foreign legal institutions and which rules are covered by a specific German choice of law rule? *Rabel*'s postulate of comparative qualification[10] has been rarely put into effect; it requires too much from an average judge. However, even according to the traditional view of a qualification *lege fori,* a comparison of the legal rules and institutions is necessary. According to the case-law of the Federal Supreme Court, the foreign legal institution has to be characterized and evaluated primarily according to its meaning and purpose. Thereafter, the foreign institution "must be compared with legal institutions of German law." Based on this two-step procedure, finally the foreign legal institution has to be attributed to the criteria of a German choice of law rule; these criteria are derived from notions of German law.[11] Of the many examples, only the qualification of a marriage where one spouse is duly represented by a third person as a question of form[12] and the equation of judicial separation with divorce[13] will be mentioned here.

---

[7] BVerfG: 30 Oct. 1962, BVerfGE 15, 25 (34); – 30 April 1963, BVerfGE 16, 27 (33).

[8] BVerfG: 30 Oct. 1962, BVerfGE 15, 25 (36 ss.); – 30 April 1963, BVerfGE 16, 27 (33 ss.); – 13 Dec. 1977, BVerfGE 46, 342 (364 ss.).

[9] BVerfG 31 March 1987, BVerfGE 75, 1 (21 ss.).

[10] Rabel, Das Problem der Qualifikation: RabelsZ 5 (1931) 241–288 = Gesammelte Aufsätze II (1965) 189-241.

[11] BGH 22 March 1967, BGHZ 47, 324 (332), IPRspr. 1966–1967 no. 90 (p. 295). Cf. also BGH: 12 Jan. 1967, IPRspr. 1966-1967 no. 19 (p. 66); – 19 Dec. 1958, BGHZ 29, 137 (139), IPRspr. 1958–1959 no. 112 (p. 390 s.).

[12] BGH 19 Dec. 1958 (preceding n.).

[13] BGH 22 March 1967 (*supra* n. 11).

Even more obvious is the necessity for a comparison of foreign rules if such a comparison is expressly required by a choice of law rule. The specific public policy clause of art. 38 of the Introductory Law to the German Civil Code protects a German defendant by disallowing any more far-reaching claim based on the applicable foreign tort law than would be justified under German law. Also the doctrine of the alternative connecting points for border-crossing torts which was developed by the Federal Supreme Court requires the judge to compare the rules on torts existing in the legal systems at the place of commission of the tort and at the place where the injury occurred.[14] Rules on reciprocity, which still appear in some statutes, may also be mentioned here; thus, according to § 110 of the Code of Civil Procedure, a foreign plaintiff exceptionally need not furnish security for costs (*cautio judicati solvi*) if a German plaintiff in a corresponding case in the plaintiff's home country would not have to furnish security.

All of the aforementioned German choice of law rules can only be correctly applied if the respective substantive rules of foreign law are compared with the corresponding rules of German law.

2. *Voluntary comparison as to norms related to foreign countries*

In the second class of cases, comparison is not necessary for an accurate application of the relevant German rule. But various international links and relationships with foreign countries make it appropriate and reasonable to use the comparative method. The following six subclasses are arranged according to the extent of relationships with foreign countries, in descending order.

a) *Uniform international rules* – A particularly strong international link is inherent in those rules of the national law that are based on international conventions providing uniform rules of substantive law or of the conflict of laws, or that are found in such international rules themselves (depending on the method of transformation). In many cases, also, the decisions of various national courts regarding these international treaties are easily accessible.[15] But, have courts accepted this invitation to look across the borders of their own country – an invitation that the legal literature has rightly regarded as an obligation?[16]

The Federal Supreme Court has ruled that the interpretation of uniform international rules has to pursue, beyond the traditional methods of inter-

---

[14] BGH 23 June 1964, IPRspr. 1964–1965 no. 51 (p. 181, 182).

[15] See especially the collections of cases edited by UNIDROIT: Jurisprudence de droit uniforme (1959–1971); Unidroit, Revue de droit uniforme (since 1972). Further von Caemmerer (ed.), Internationale Rechtsprechung zum Genfer Einheitlichen Wechsel- und Scheckrecht, 3 vol. (1954, 1967, 1976).

[16] Cf., e.g., Beitzke, Bemerkungen zur Kollisionsrechtsvergleichung in der Praxis: RabelsZ 48 (1984) 623–648 (636); Kropholler (*supra* n. 4) 6.

pretation, a further purpose, to guarantee to the fullest extent possible a uniform interpretation in all contracting states. Consequently, the interpretation of the rules should be autonomous because recourse to the meaning of the corresponding national legal notions would endanger the uniformity of the rules, i.e. the primary aim of the international treaties.[17] In a case of doubt, however, a rule of uniform law retains the meaning attached to the same rule in its home country from which the uniform rule was derived.[18] Furthermore, the need for uniform interpretation would speak in favor of giving the wording of the uniform provisions more weight than usual in the process of interpretation.[19]

Which practical consequences did these admonitions have on the case-law of the Federal Supreme Court itself and the higher appellate courts? A survey of the court practice on seven international conventions establishing uniform law may be summarized as follows: In the years between 1950 and 1990, less than 30 published decisions of the Federal Supreme Court and about 20 decisions of the higher appellate courts applying those international conventions refer to foreign law.

Two decisions merit special attention because they shed some light on the need for as well as the limits of the comparative method in interpreting uniform international laws. In November 1956, the Federal Supreme Court had to decide whether a signature on a bill of exchange placed beneath the drawer's signature means a guarantee of the bill of exchange for the drawer. Article 31 par. 4 of the Geneva Uniform Bill of Exchange Law of 1930 as well as art. 31 par. 4 of the German Bill of Exchange Act provide:

> "An 'aval' must specify for whose account it is given. In default of this, it is deemed to be given for the drawer."

Whether this presumption is refutable is, not only in Germany but also in other contracting states, strongly disputed. The court cited contradictory decisions from six countries, both views balancing each other in numbers. Among the cited decisions, three originated from French appellate courts; the Federal Supreme Court adopted their view that the presumption established by the provision is refutable.[20] However, ten months earlier the French Court of Cassation had overruled those French cases; and four years later a plenary decision of the French Court of Cassation confirmed that

---

[17] BGH 19 March 1976, ZLuftR 1977, 79, Rev.dr.unif. 1977 I 282 (286 s.). In the same sense BGH: 16 June 1982, BGHZ 84, 339 (343); – 14 July 1983, BGHZ 88, 157 (161, 164), NJW 1984, 565 (566, 567), Eur.Transp.L. 1985, 95 (100, 102), TranspR 1984, 68 with critical note Heuer; – 23 March 1976 – VI ZR 150/74, IPRspr. 1976 no. 123c (p. 359 ss.), ZLuftR 1976, 258, Rev.dr.unif. 1976 II 324 (327); – 23 March 1976 – VI ZR 92/75, IPRspr. 1976 no. 123 b (p. 357), ZLuftR 1976, 255; OLG Düsseldorf 27 March 1980, RIW 1981, 558, Rev.dr.unif. 1981 I 256 (257, 259).

[18] BGH 27 Oct. 1986, JZ 1986, 310 (311), Rev.dr.unif. 1988, 801 (803).

[19] BGH 16 June 1982 (*supra* n. 17) and 14 July 1983 (*supra* n. 17).

[20] BGH 15 Nov. 1956, BGHZ 22, 148 (152).

decision, most probably also without any knowledge of the contrary German ruling.[21] Another ten months later, the German Federal Supreme Court confirmed its decision of 1956, apparently still in ignorance of the latest French decisions.[22]

This case study illustrates the need for an interpretation of uniform international rules using foreign law as well as the technical problem of a rapid exchange of information. The printed sources of information are more or less comprehensive; the still lacking topicality may be gained in the near future by the use of cross-border electronic computer-based collections of court decisions.

As to another aspect of the application of uniform international rules, i.e. the anticipatory application of international treaties in maritime law, see under d).

b) *European Community law* – Primary as well as secondary European Community law is – as supranational law – uniform law of a specific quality. The rules of interpretation for general uniform law must be valid for this specific uniform law *a fortiori*. Regarding the interpretation of EC directives, on the basis of which the national laws of the member states were harmonized, *Lutter* has only recently in a comprehensive study demanded that national judges should take into account the judicial and academic interpretation of the harmonized norms of all the other EC member states.[23] This ideal postulate is, however, hard to realize in the real world of national courts – but the basic idea is correct.

To what extent have German courts lived up to this ideal, considering the *whole* of primary and secondary Community law? An exhaustive answer would require a comprehensive study that cannot be performed now and in this context. Therefore, only a few examples of the interpretation of the EEC Treaty, which were chosen more or less randomly, are presented here.

In its well-known controversy with the Federal Finance Court (*Bundesfinanzhof*) about the ranking of European Community law in the German legal system, the Federal Constitutional Court has referred several times to academic writings in other member countries.[24] In countering the objections to the progressive and law-making function of the European Court of Justice, the Constitutional Court underlined: "The Treaties constituting the European Communities have to be interpreted in the light of common

[21] See the broad discussion by Hirsch, Einheitliches Wechselgesetz oder einheitliches Wechselrecht?: NJW 1961, 1089–1094.

[22] BGH 12 Jan. 1961, NJW 1961, 671. One year later, however, an appellate court took judicial notice of the differing French interpretation of the provision and applied it in a case which, it held, was governed by French law: OLG Saarbrücken 10 Jan. 1962, JBl. Saar 1962, 54. Cf. on this issue at the borderline between uniform law and conflict of laws generally Kropholler, Internationales Einheitsrecht (1975) 204–212.

[23] Lutter, Die Auslegung angeglichenen Rechts: JZ 1992, 593 ss. (604).

[24] BVerfG 8 April 1987, BVerfGE 75, 223 (239 s.).

European legal tradition and legal culture, too."[25] Referring to Roman law, to the English common law, the Continental *jus commune* and French administrative law, the German court justified the law-creating role of the European Court.[26] In an earlier decision, the Constitutional Court had, however, pointed out certain limits to the transfer of sovereign rights to the European Communities according to art. 24 of the German Constitution, and it had based its ruling, *inter alia*, on the legal situation existing in Italy.[27]

Finally, a decision by the Regional Court of Bonn dealt with an action asking for the invalidation of an execution clause which had been affixed by the Federal Minister of Justice to a judgment of the European Court of Justice. The extent of review of the decision by the Minister of Justice to grant the clause was in dispute. The court decided that there is no right to examine the merits of the European Court's decision, and it referred, *inter alia*, to Belgian and British literature concerning the interpretation of art. 192 of the EEC Treaty to justify its ruling.[28]

c) In the interpretation of provisions *adopted from a foreign country* or *inspired by foreign rules*, German courts have occasionally looked into the legal system of the country from which the rule originated. In two decisions, the Federal Supreme Court referred to provisions of Swiss law which had served as models for the German legislator and which contained in their wording the answer to the issue which had to be decided by the court.[29] In two other decisions, the Federal Supreme Court based its result upon references to Austrian provisions which had served as models for the relevant German rules.[30] Similarly, in a set of two further cases, the courts based their decision on the case-law of the country from which the provisions originated.[31] In a seventh case, however, foreign court practice was declared irrelevant, because it was incompatible with the clear content and purpose of the derived German provision.[32]

One of the six "positive" decisions justifies the recourse to the foreign law with the plausible idea that the legislator has used this source for the preparation of the relevant German provision.[33] Curiously enough, this appears to be the only attempt at judicial justification; because of its plausi-

---

[25] *Ibidem* p. 244; s. also p. 243.

[26] *Ibidem* p. 243.

[27] BVerfG 22 Oct. 1986, BVerfGE 73, 339 (376), NJW 1987, 577 (580) ("Solange II").

[28] LG Bonn 16 Oct. 1985, IPRspr. 1985 no. 181 p. 483; s. also p. 484.

[29] BGH (Great Senate in Criminal Matters) 22 Sept. 1956, BGHSt 9, 385 (387, 389); BGH 13 May 1957, BGHZ 24, 214 (219).

[30] BGH 31 Jan. 1952, BGHZ 4, 369 (375 s.); – 26 April 1960, BGHZ 32, 218 (220).

[31] BGH 22 June 1956, BGHZ 21, 112 (119); cf. also RG 7 April 1902, RGZ 51, 166 (169).

[32] BVerwG 8 Feb. 1961, BVerwGE 12, 42 (44).

[33] BGH 13 May 1957 (*supra* n. 29) 218.

ble character,[34] however, this reasoning may also be implied for the other decisions.

d) *Maritime law* is a field of law which derives its international character from numerous international conventions, and, moreover, it is strongly influenced by English law.

This strong link with the international legal environment explains an apparently unique (at least in Germany[35]) phenomenon, i.e. the anticipatory application of international conventions even before these have come into force in Germany.

An instructive example is a decision of the Federal Supreme Court of 1971 in which the Court had to decide whether the time-charterer of a ship may invoke the same limitations of liability as the shipowner. In German law, there was no provision on the point. To fill this gap, the Court referred to the International Conventions on Limitation of the Shipowners' Liability of 1924 and 1957,[36] which are applicable also to time-charterers.[37] The first Convention, however, was not in force for the Federal Republic. The Convention of 1957 had been signed by the Federal Republic at the time of the decision; the procedure for ratification had already started, but, in contrast to many other countries, was not yet completed by the Federal Republic. The court held on this point:

> "In the law in force one can find, if the facts of the case are evaluated according to the criteria that were clearly developed in international maritime law, sufficient grounds to fill the gap as to the limitation of liability for the time-charterer without inadmissible recourse to the free-law creation of 'judge-made law'."[38]

In later decisions, the court used an interesting, but also doubtful, distinction with regard to the anticipatory application of international conventions. One case dealt with the famous question of whether a container is a package or whether it contains several packages; the answer to this question determines the maximum amount of liability for the shipowner. The appellate court had decided in favor of the second alternative making reference to two international conventions not binding upon the Federal Republic; the

---

[34] The reasoning is in conformity with an academic opinion, cf. *supra* I at n. 2.

[35] Contrast for the Netherlands Jessurun d'Oliveira, Die Freiheit des niederländischen Richters bei der Entwicklung des IPR. Zur antizipierenden Anwendung des Benelux-Einheitsgesetzes über das IPR – ein Requiem: RabelsZ 39 (1975) 224–252.

[36] International Convention for the Unification of Certain Rules Relating to the Limitation of the Liability of Owners of Sea-Going Vessels of 25 Aug. 1924; International Convention Relating to the Limitation of the Liability of Owners of Sea-Going Ships of 10 Oct. 1957.

[37] Article 10 of the Convention of 1924 extends this only to the bare-boat charterer, whereas art. 6 par. 2 of the Convention of 1957 covers charterers in general.

[38] BGH 28 June 1971, NJW 1971, 2223 (2225), Jur.dr.unif. 1971, 191 (195).

Federal Supreme Court reversed this decision on the grounds that the ratification of both conventions was disputed in the Federal Republic.[39] Two years later the Federal Supreme Court itself based a decision on the same conventions, although the Federal Republic had still not yet ratified them. This case dealt with the question of whether the limitation of shipowners' liability as to contractual claims applies also with regard to claims based on torts. The court stated that the interpretation of a German provision that is based on an ambiguous norm of an international convention may take into consideration the subsequent development of this international rule. Such a recourse to a non-ratified international convention is, in the opinion of the court, distinguishable from the earlier case because, in that case, the problem before the court had arisen from technical developments in the shipping field.[40] The alleged significance of this distinction is, however, more than doubtful.[41]

Apart from international conventions German maritime law is strongly influenced by English law. This is especially obvious with regard to the interpretation of "English" clauses, e.g. "shipper's declared weight" or "weight unknown" [42], the "indemnity" clause [43] and the loading-clause "on deck at shipper's risk".[44] The Federal Supreme Court has also solved the disputed question of invalidity of a written undertaking in the context of a fraudulently issued bill of landing by making reference to English case practice and to the French Maritime Act.[45] English maritime law is used sometimes even for the interpretation of provisions of the German Inland Navigation Act (*Binnenschiffahrtsgesetz*).[46]

e) *Conflict of laws* – Apart from those rules of the conflict of laws which are not at all applicable without recourse to foreign law (see *supra* 1), the "normal" choice of law rules have, of course, also an obvious relationship to foreign countries. Various counts show that about 10 per cent of all the published decisions of the Federal Supreme Court in this field refer to foreign choice of law provisions.[47]

In creating new conflict-of-laws rules, the Federal Supreme Court has often referred to foreign conflict rules.[48] One of the reasons for this open-

---

[39] BGH 22 Sept. 1980, BGHZ 78, 121 (125–126), NJW 1981, 1159 (1160).

[40] BGH 17 Jan. 1983, BGHZ 86, 234 (239), NJW 1983, 1263 (1264), TranspR 1983, 100 (102) with approving note by Herber at p. 103 s., IPRspr. 1983 no. 43 (p. 112 s.).

[41] Critical also Herber (preceding n.) 103.

[42] BGH 26 Sept. 1957, BGHZ 25, 250 (263 s.), Jur.dr.unif. 1959/1960 I 3 (11).

[43] BGH 2 Dec. 1991, TranspR 1992, 103 (105 s.).

[44] In extenso BGH 20 May 1952, BGHZ 6, 127 (131 ss.).

[45] BGH 25 Jan. 1973, BGHZ 60, 102 (105), NJW 1973, 465 (466).

[46] BGH 20 June 1952, BGHZ 6, 324 (329).

[47] For the period from 1951 to 1969 cf. Müller-Gindullis, Das Internationale Privatrecht in der Rechtsprechung des Bundesgerichtshofes (1971) 153–154, 165–181; and for the period from 1970 to 1975 cf. Kropholler (*supra* n. 4) 16.

[48] Cf. Müller-Gindullis (preceding n.) 153 s.

ness towards foreign legal systems is obviously that the German statutory rules of conflict of laws contain many gaps. One example for such judicial recourse to foreign ideas is the development of a choice-of-laws rule concerning collisions of ships in territorial sea. The Federal Supreme Court ruled that the law of the place of collision is to be applied, and it justified its position, *inter alia*, by stating that this rule is also accepted in various foreign countries and that therefore the decision in favor of this rule promotes the international conformity of judicial practice in this field.[49] The same reason is to be found in the decision of the Federal Supreme Court in which it ruled that certain traffic accidents occurring abroad are subject to the law of the common residence of the tortfeasor and the injured driver.[50]

Two other illustrations are also furnished by the law on international civil procedure. The Federal Supreme Court has based its decision restricting the scope of the "exorbitant" head of competence contained in § 23 of the Code of Civil Procedure *inter alia* on various international conventions.[51] An appellate court relied on a "general principle prevailing in international legal orders that support orders are subject to alteration".[52]

Another application of the comparative method is worth underlining, i.e. to specify the German public policy clause. In examining the question of whether the German public policy clause should be used against the application of foreign law, the Federal Supreme Court has, in numerous cases, given a broad comparative overview of the legal rules applied in different countries. The Court tried to determine whether the foreign rule at issue represented one of the "typical" solutions used on the international scene, even if this idea was unknown in Germany. In most cases, such a comparative survey saved the foreign rule from being disregarded as being contrary to German public policy. This procedure was used, for instance, to evaluate contracts with American attorneys stipulating contingent fees,[53] in a case of unfair competition[54], in evaluating a one-year period for avoiding the legitimacy of a child,[55] and regarding the rule of Islamic law concerning paternal custody over minors.[56]

We will explore some other examples for this specific application of the comparative method.

f) In the *law of extradition*, courts have similarly used the method for the same purpose, i.e. to determine an international standard with the help of comparative law.

---

49 BGH 29 Jan. 1959, BGHZ 29, 237 (243), IPRspr. 1958–1959 no. 73 (p. 289 s.).

50 BGH 8 Jan. 1985, BGHZ 93, 214 (219), IPRspr. 1985 no. 37 p. 98 s.

51 BGH 2 July 1991, BGHZ 115, 90 (95 ss.).

52 OLG Karlsruhe 20 April 1989, IPRspr. 1989 no. 204 (p. 4[illegible]3).

53 BGH 15 Nov. 1956, BGHZ 22, 162 (163 s.), IPRspr. 1956–1957 no. 3 (p. 7 s.).

54 BGH 30 June 1961, BGHZ 35, 329 (337), IPRspr. 1960–1961 no. 155 (p. 515).

55 OLG Karlsruhe 3 April 1986, IPRspr. 1986 no. 72 (p. 169 s.).

56 BGH 18 June 1970, BGHZ 54, 132 (140 s.), IPRspr. 1970 no. 61b (p. 195).

In one case, an arrested person objected to his extradition to a country that still had the death penalty whereas the German constitution had abolished it. The Federal Constitutional Court, in a decision in 1964, refused to follow this argument as numerous "civilized countries, and among them the leading democracies of the Western world" had retained the death penalty. A country like the Federal Republic of Germany could not enforce its own legal solution without regard to these facts.[57]

Two other cases dealt with foreign criminal trials which had been conducted in the absence of the accused. Such procedure is contrary to German law. In the first case, the Federal Supreme Court stated that the sentence of the foreign court was valid according to the law of the country requesting the extradition. German public policy would only be affected if trial in the absence of the accused would violate "high-ranking principles, that are recognized by all countries in which the rule of law prevails". In the given circumstances, however, this was not the case.[58]

In 1982, the Federal Constitutional Court added a further criterion for the examination of cases in which an accused is sentenced in his absence, i.e. the procedural minimum standard of public international law which has to be taken into consideration according to art. 25 of the German Constitution. The Court referred to the decisions of three European countries to show that the application of such standards is justified in extradition cases.[59]

This court practice concerning extradition applies the same method as the decisions regarding German public policy in the conflict of laws. Also in extradition cases, international standards are used to specify the public policy clause. Rules of foreign countries differing from or even contrary to German law are measured against these international standards. If the court comes to the conclusion that the foreign rule corresponds to a typical solution which is used in a number of foreign countries that share the same political ideas as the Federal Republic, the foreign provision will be saved from being disregarded as contravening German public policy. This comparative interpretation of the public policy clause is welcome because it takes the parochial character away from the clause and broadens and internationalizes its application. Already 20 years ago, *Aubin* had drawn attention to this important function of the comparative method, to give precision to the public policy clauses of German constitutional law and conflict of laws.[60]

---

57 BVerfG 30 June 1964, BVerfGE 18, 112 (117 s.).

58 BGH 31 March 1965, NJW 1965, 1146 (1147).

59 BVerfG 26 Jan. 1982, BVerfGE 59, 280 (283; cf. also p. 286).

60 Aubin, Rechtsvergleichende Konkretisierung (*supra* n. 4); cf. also Mössner (*supra* n. 4).

3. Voluntary comparison of norms unrelated to foreign countries

The vast majority of German legal provisions may be put into this third group. Here, the influence of the comparative method is much less important; actually, it is only seldom used as a method of interpretation. There are, however, some remarkable exceptions. In this context, it is useful to distinguish between the three main branches of the law.

a) The vast field of *private law* furnishes only a few examples worth citing.

In three decisions, the comparative method was used to justify a deviation from the clear statutory wording of § 253 of the German Civil Code, which generally excludes the compensation of moral damages. In one of the first decisions of the Federal Supreme Court, in which the Court disregarded this rule in a case of an invasion of personal privacy, it justified its conclusion by referring briefly to Swiss law.[61] Shortly afterwards, the Court gave a more comprehensive justification for its recourse to foreign law in a case in which the defendant, a newspaper publisher, argued that the previous decision endangered the freedom of the press:

> "In recognition of this, in almost all legal systems in which the value of the individual has the central position in the legal system as in ours, the compensation of moral damage is recognized as the adequate private law sanction for invasions of privacy."

Nor does this remedy limit the freedom of the press in these countries.[62] Finally, redress was sought against this "judge-made" law from the Federal Constitutional Court. This Court based its confirming decision on the corresponding "development of the law in other countries of the Western world" and on the fact that the case-law of the German courts regarding this question had succeeded in establishing a legal situation "that is in broad conformity with this international development of the law".[63]

Three other decisions are worth mentioning. One of them dealt with the issue of the constitutionality of a provision of the German Marriage Act which prevented marriages in cases in which one of the persons had had sexual intercourse with a parent or a descendant of the other person (*Eheverbot der Geschlechtsgemeinschaft*). The Federal Constitutional Court declared this impediment of marriage unconstitutional and referred, in its reasons, to studies of German comparatists who had found that this impediment is practically unknown outside Germany.[64]

In another case, a child claimed a new head of damages, namely for its "wrongful life". The Federal Supreme Court not only used this American

61 BGH 19 Sept. 1961, BGHZ 35, 363 (369).
62 BGH 5 March 1963, BGHZ 39, 124 (132).
63 BVerfG 14 Feb. 1973, BVerfGE 34, 269 (289, 291).
64 BVerfG 14 Nov. 1973, BVerfGE 36, 146 (165).

legal term, but also discussed English and American decisions on this topic, most of them refusing such a claim. The Federal Supreme Court reached the same result,[65] obviously under the influence of the foreign case-law.

In a third case, the family name of a child of a "mixed marriage" was at issue; the parents, with different nationalities, had not chosen a common family name but had given their child a double name combining their two family names. Basing its arguments upon copious references to foreign laws, the appellate court held that the parents' creation of the double name was not admissible.[66]

Surprisingly, the civil courts have not taken the opportunity to fill in the legal vacuum which arose after 1953 when legal provisions discriminating between women and men ceased to have effect, with comparative law. The Federal Supreme Court itself had, in an opinion submitted to the Federal Constitutional Court, referred to "comparison with the experiences of family laws of other countries" as the cornerstones of a creative law-finding process.[67] But this Court of last resort itself has not used this method at all and the higher and appellate court have referred to it only rarely.[68]

On the whole, the use of foreign law is extremely poor. The only comforting observation is that the judicial use of foreign law was not limited to the areas of contract and commercial law, which had been described by *Zweigert* as international ("*weltläufig*")[69], but found its application also, and even more so, in fields of law which are known to be more parochial, as in family law and in the law of persons.

b) In the area of *criminal law* comparative efforts are even sparser. Only one early decision of the Federal Supreme Court is worth stressing. The Court justified its narrow reading of a criminal code provision concerning homosexual activities by a short overview of the legal development in Europe since the beginning of this century. The extension of the penalization of homosexuality, which was introduced to Germany in 1935, was contrary to the general tendency to restrict its penalization. The Court concluded that the effect of its narrow reading of the penal provision would be that "the German legal development is placed again in the framework of the European legal development".[70]

c) In the field of *public law* comparative law is employed almost only at the

---

65 BGH 18 Jan. 1983, BGHZ 86, 240 (250 f.), NJW 1983, 1371 (1373).

66 OLG Hamburg 17 Feb. 1987, IPRspr. 1987 no. 4 (p. 21 ss.).

67 BGH 6 Sept. 1953, BGHZ 11, appendix p. 34* (70*).

68 Cf. Kropholler (*supra* n. 3) 76 s. with references. The view expressed by the Federal Constitutional Court (18 Dec. 1953, BVerfGE 3, 225 [244]) that the courts had made recourse to foreign law in order to remedy the uncertainty of the German law, unfortunately is not correct.

69 Zweigert (*supra* n. 2) 12 s.

70 BGH 3 July 1951, BGHSt 1, 293 (297).

top, i.e. regarding constitutional law issues and, in particular, by the Federal Constitutional Court.[71] Important as some of these decisions are, their share of all the published decisions amounts to hardly more than about one per cent.

Apart from the decisions which have been mentioned already in other parts of this paper, five decisions will be analyzed which demonstrate two different reasons for recourse to foreign law. In the first group of three decisions, the comparative approach was used for the traditional purpose of interpreting a German provision or legal concept. In one case regarding the interpretation of art. 4 § 3 of the German Constitution, which deals with the right of conscientious objection to military service, the court was looking for help from foreign legal systems. But, neither on the international level nor in the Western democracies was a common ground concerning this legal institution found.[72] Another case concerned the interpretation of the notion "political treaty" in art. 59 § 2 of the Constitution. The Court found, in the laws of several Central European countries, a uniform understanding of that concept and used this as a basis for its decisions.[73] The Court came to a similar result in the interpretation of the concept of "home" which art. 13 § 1 of the Constitution declares to be inviolable. Looking across the German borders, the Court found decisions in four countries which interpreted this or a similar notion broadly;[74] in the end, the Court joined in this solution.

Two other decisions have looked to foreign countries in order to obtain criteria for the question of the constitutionality of provisions of the German Constitution. In the first case, the legitimacy of the law-creating role of the judge was at issue. After a four-year transitional period, the constitutional principle of non-discrimination between men and women became effective in 1953. Since the legislator had not amended the provisions of the German Civil Code which were contrary to this constitutional rule, the courts were forced in many cases to enforce creatively the constitutional non-discrimination rule.[75] Against this novel task of the courts, the objection was raised that such "judge-made law" was unconstitutional as violating the principle of separation of powers. The Federal Supreme Court referred in one decision, as well as in an opinion submitted to the Federal Constitutional Court, to the fact that the practical realization of this constitutional principle was varied in modern constitutions,[76] and that even countries which had enshrined this principle in their constitution nevertheless allowed a law-creating function of the courts, e.g. in the United States.[77] The

---

[71] Cf. on this Mössner (*supra* n. 4).
[72] BVerfG 26 May 1970, BVerfGE 28, 243 (258).
[73] BVerfG 29 July 1952, BVerfGE 1, 372 (382 s.).
[74] BVerfG 13 Oct. 1971, BVerfGE 32, 54 (70).
[75] Comprehensive analysis by Kropholler (*supra* n. 3).
[76] BGH 14 July 1953, BGHZ 10, 266 (275).
[77] BGH 6 Sept. 1953 (*supra* n. 67) 54*.

Federal Constitutional Court took up and stressed this last argument by generally stating that "even in constitutional systems recognizing this principle, ... there are certain overlaps of functions and influences from one power into another".[78]

Of general importance is the decision of the Federal Constitutional Court concerning the prohibition of the German Communist Party in 1956. In this case, doubts had been raised against the constitutionality of art. 21 § 2 of the German Constitution, which provides a constitutional procedure for the prohibition of parties. The Court pointed out that, on one hand, the constitutions of the liberal Western democracies did not contain rules on the prohibition of parties, but, on the other hand, that all of these countries had to deal with this problem in practice and were employing various methods to achieve this purpose.[79] On the strength of this argument as well as others the Court affirmed the constitutionality of the aforementioned constitutional provision.

III. Methods of Comparison Used by Courts

The practical ways used by the courts in making recourse to foreign law are an important aspect that should not be neglected.

1. Contents or effect of rules

One important initial question is, whether the courts direct their attention solely to the contents of a foreign rule or whether they regard also, or even exclusively, its effects. Apparently, the courts are directing their attention mainly – in contrast to the modern legislator[80] – to the contents of the foreign rule.

A few exceptions to this general attitude may, however, be found in decisions of the Federal Constitutional Court. In two cases, the effects of a foreign legal provision were taken into account, in both cases exclusively.[81] Both cases were concerned with the constitutionality of German statutes. The Court endeavored to assess the consequences of a decision declaring a German law unconstitutional by examining the legal situation in those countries which had incorporated a different legal solution in their laws.[82] Also, a recent ruling (dealing with a new legal regime for abortions) made a general reference to experiences with different legal solutions abroad;

---

[78] BVerfG 18 Dec. 1953 (*supra* n. 68) 247.

[79] BVerfG 17 Aug. 1956, BVerfGE 5, 85 (135 f.).

[80] Drobnig/Dopffel (*supra* n. 1) 268.

[81] On this cf. Mössner (*supra* n. 4) 223 ss.

[82] BVerfG 11 June 1958, BVerfGE 7, 375 (386, 415 s.) on the freedom of establishment of pharmacists; BVerfG 25 Feb. 1975, BVerfGE 39, 1 (60, 64) on abortion.

however, the Court expressed some reservations "because the uncertain degree of comparability of the circumstances" qualifies the relevance of such experiences.[83]

For practical reasons it is, however, difficult to generalize such an approach for other courts, desirable as it is.[84]

2. Weight of comparative arguments

The weight of foreign solutions is always limited. No court bases its judgment solely on rules of foreign law. The recourse to foreign law furnishes but a supplementary element for the court's reasoning.

Even within these limits, it is difficult to draw general conclusions about the relative weight of foreign law. The references to foreign legal materials are sometimes extremely short, rarely more comprehensive. If courts cite foreign decisions, in most cases they describe only their results, and rarely also their reasoning. Courts are, apparently, proceeding pragmatically and largely disregard the state of the art of the academic comparison of law.

3. Countries used for comparison

The group of countries used for comparison differs widely and appears sometimes to be rather accidental. Often only one foreign legal solution is described by the court, without indicating the criterion used for the choice of legal system, much less justifying it. Occasionally, an overview of more than one foreign legal solution is given. Very seldom can one find descriptions of the legal situation in geographical or political units, which are then often oversimplistic.

It is plausible that geographically broader findings have a stronger persuasive value than others. This may be one reason why the Federal Constitutional Court prefers to refer to general principles or standards; however, the Court understandably limits its statements to particular groups of countries, e.g. to the liberal or Western democracies, to peoples with a common cultural heritage or to the Western European countries.[85]

Whether and to what extent the choice of countries used for comparison is determined or limited by practical problems of access to information can unfortunately not be said. The courts themselves are silent on this point.

However, it is possible to say that the laws of certain countries are preferred for comparisons. In this regard, the first place is taken by Switzer-

---

[83] BVerfG 28 May 1993, JZ 1993 special issue of 7 June, p. 20. At p. 30 there is a reference to experience in France.

[84] But the German legislator uses this method, cf. Drobnig/Dopffel (*supra* n. 1) 270, 274, 298.

[85] See text *supra*, at n. 56, 57, 62, 69, 71 and 78.

land.[86] This top position appears to be based on two grounds: This country has, within the group of Germanic legal systems, a slightly more modern codification of private law than Germany, and it also has, in places, some more modern amendments. Moreover, the German language used in most publications of the country facilitates access to Swiss law. Austria, which in part shares the same characteristics, and which was previously referred to as the "number one" source of inspiration,[87] has dropped back today. The reason for this seems to be that there is less modern legislation. The lack of references to the law of the former German Democratic Republic can be explained by the great ideological differences between the two states and by the big discrepancy in living standards.

4. Sources of information

Looking at the decisions of the German courts, it is apparent that their most important source of information on foreign law is the German comparative literature. And in fact, comparative interest and learning is well developed in Germany, so that a rich source of information is available to attorneys and judges. Recourse to German comparative literature has the additional advantage that one may expect, at least in general, a balanced account of the foreign law in question; this helps the courts to guard against prejudiced one-sided information.[88]

In one case, international conventions were taken as an expression of the legal situations in foreign countries.[89] This is a doubtful makeshift solution. By contrast, international conventions may be employed in some cases as specific expressions of generally accepted and recognized rules.

How do the courts obtain access to foreign legal material? The practice of the Federal Constitutional Court – which cannot, however, be generalized for courts in general – has furnished some interesting examples. In one case, the Court asked the Ministry of Foreign Affairs for reports about the legal situation in 16 countries. The reports were delivered by German diplomatic representations, most probably from local attorneys, who regularly advise the representations.[90] In another case, foreign legal experts were heard in court, and the court asked for a statement by a private international association.[91]

It is difficult to establish the role of the attorneys of the parties in ob-

---

[86] Aubin, Rechtsvergleichende Interpretation (*supra* n. 4) 470 has reached the same result.

[87] *Idem* 463.

[88] Cf. Reinhart (*supra* n. 4) 617.

[89] BGH 28 June 1971 (*supra* n. 38).

[90] BVerfG 11 Oct. 1978, BVerfGE 49, 286. The reports, however, were neither integrated into nor even mentioned in the reasons for the decision. But they were used in and integrated into the subsequent bill for an Act on Transsexuals (Bundestags-Drucksache 8/2947 p. 13).

[91] BVerfG 11 June 1958 (*supra* n. 82) 415 s.

taining foreign legal materials. There is, however, some basis for the assertion that this source of information is important in cases where high amounts are involved. Because, generally, attorneys do not have libraries containing foreign literature at their disposal, except on some very specific subjects, they frequently receive the necessary information from foreign lawyers who are normally acting as agents or correspondents for them, and occasionally also from German academic experts on foreign law. The openness of the courts to regard arguments based upon foreign law as relevant varies, most probably depending on the scale which was developed in part II of this paper.

IV. THE LIMITS OF RECOURSE TO FOREIGN LAW

Among the published decisions, there is no basis for the assertion that German courts are refusing foreign law arguments generally. It is said, however, that this has happened in a few isolated cases.

Occasionally, courts have refused to deal with foreign law arguments for substantive reasons, especially if the unequivocal wording and purpose of a German provision was to be interpreted (even if this norm was adopted from a foreign country).[92] Indeed, at first sight, it would appear that there is no scope for application of the comparative method when the applicable German provision is clear and unambiguous.[93] The creative interpretation of § 253 of the Civil Code, which was based on comparative law arguments and was confirmed by the Federal Constitutional Court, shows, however, that the Federal Supreme Court has used foreign law arguments in exceptional cases even to circumvent a German statutory norm.[94]

One may say, therefore, that there are no absolute limits on recourse to foreign law before German courts.

V. JUSTIFICATIONS FOR THE USE OF FOREIGN LAW

A general postulate, such as *Zweigert*'s characterization of comparative law as a "universal method of interpretation",[95] would appear to be insufficiently differentiated.

It is preferable to differentiate according to the extent to which a German provision is related to provisions of international, European or foreign law. This helps to ascertain the different justifications for recourse to foreign law.

---

[92] BVerwG 8 Feb. 1961 (*supra* n. 32) 44.

[93] In this sense apparently Zweigert/Kötz (*supra* n. 2) I 20.

[94] Cf. *supra* II 3 a), at n. 61–63.

[95] Zweigert (*supra* n. 2).

1. Cases of necessary comparison (see *supra* II 1) do not require any analysis or justification.

2. Voluntary comparison of norms related to foreign countries (see *supra* II 2) comprises quite different situations that should be analyzed with regard to the kind of foreign linkage which the relevant German provision has.

a) For German provisions which are based on international uniform rules (see *supra* II 2 a), comparison with the laws of the other contracting parties should be thought of as necessary in order to preserve the uniformity achieved by unified rules. Therefore, the task of comparison is, basically, the performance of a duty derived from public international law.

b) For European law (*supra* II 2 b), the preceding argument for preserving uniformity is even more compelling.

c) The linkages of maritime law, conflict of laws and the law of extradition (see *supra* II 2 d-f) with foreign countries and international situations suggest a two-fold view of foreign countries: firstly to reach, especially in the fields of maritime law and conflict of laws, uniformity of judicial decisions, and thereby implicit harmonization of laws. Secondly, notably in the conflict of laws and the law of extradition, to internationalize the interpretation and application of public policy clauses; in these cases, rules of foreign laws should only be disregarded when the rules violate international standards.

d) Where German provisions were adopted from or inspired by foreign legal systems (see *supra* II 2 c), comparison with the state of origin can be understood and justified as a resort to the legislative history of the German provision.

3. Matters are quite different with regard to norms not related to foreign countries (see *supra* II 3). In these cases, recourse to foreign law is exceptional, and here it is more difficult to explain its necessity or to justify its application. A survey of German case law, with respect to these genuinely "domestic" provisions of German law, suggests a classification according to the three functions which may be fulfilled by comparative law. First, legal comparison helps to fill gaps in German law, especially if novel problems are arising in more than one country. Secondly, a similar but independent function of comparative law is to help develop German law, if need be, even against the clear wording of the relevant statutory provision. Both are cases of creative development of law by judges, on the one hand by filling legal gaps, and on the other by overcoming a positive rule. Thirdly, the Federal Constitutional Court has employed recourse to foreign

law to control the constitutionality of constitutional norms with the help of generally accepted constitutional standards or principles which were gained through comparative inquiry.

List of Abbreviations:

BGH	Bundesgerichtshof (Federal Supreme Court)
BGHSt	Entscheidungen des Bundesgerichtshofes in Strafsachen (Decisions of the Federal Supreme Court in Criminal Matters)
BGHZ	Entscheidungen des Bundesgerichtshofes in Zivilsachen (Decisions of the Federal Supreme Court in Civil Matters)
BVerfG	Bundesverfassungsgericht (Federal Constitutional Court)
BVerfGE	Entscheidungen des Bundesverfassungsgerichts (Decisions of the Federal Constitutional Court)
BVerwG	Bundesverwaltungsgericht (Federal Administrative Court)
BVerwGE	Entscheidungen des Bundesverwaltungsgerichts (Decisions of the Federal Administrative Court)
Eur.Transp.L.	European Transport Law
IPRspr.	Die deutsche Rechtsprechung auf dem Gebiete des internationalen Privatrechts im Jahre ......
Jur.dr.unif.	Jurisprudence de droit uniforme
JZ	Juristen-Zeitung
NJW	Neue Juristische Wochenschrift
OLG	Oberlandesgericht (Higher Appellate Court)
RabelsZ	Rabels Zeitschrift für ausländisches und internationales Privatrecht
Rev.dr.unif.	Revue de droit uniforme
RG	Reichsgericht (Supreme Court)
RIW	Recht der Internationalen Wirtschaft
TranspR	Transportrecht
ZLuftR	Zeitschrift für Luftrecht

PÉNÉLOPE AGALLOPOULOU[*], CHRISTINA DELIYANNI-DIMITRAKOU[**]

L'utilisation du droit comparé par les tribunaux helléniques[***]

I. INTRODUCTION

Si on parcourt la jurisprudence hellénique on aperçoit souvent des jugements qui se réfèrent aux ouvrages réputés de la doctrine des pays étrangers, et parfois même à la législation et à la jurisprudence de ces derniers[1]. Quelles sont les causes de ce recours jurisprudentiel au droit étranger? et

[*] Professeur, Université du Pirée

[**] Maître de Conférences, Université Aristote de Thessaloniki

[***] *Principales abréviations*

AED	Anotato Eidiko Dikastirio (= Cour Suprême Speciale)
AJCL	The American Journal of Compative Law
Arch. Nom.	Αρχείο Νομολογίας (= Archeio Nomologias)
DPFN	Διαρκής Πανδέκτης Φορολογικής Νομοθεσίας (= Diarkis Pandektis Forologikis Nomothessias)
EEN	Εφημερίς Ελλήνων Νομικών (= Efimeris Ellinon Nomikon)
END	Επιθεώρησις Ναυτιλιακού Δικαίου (= Epitheorissis Nautiliakou Dikaiou)
Hell. Dni	Ελληνική Δικαιοσύνη (= Elliniki Dikaiossyni)
ICLQ	International and Comparative Law Quarterly,
ND	Νεον Δίκαιον (Neon Dikaion)
NoB	Νομικόν Βήμα (Nomikon Vima)
RabelsZ	Rabels Zetschrift für ausländisches und internationales Privatrecht
RHDEur.	Revue Hellénique de Droit Européen
RHDI	Revue Hellénique de Droit International
RIDC	Revue Internationale de Droit Comparé
Rev. Trim. Dr. Civ.	Revue Trimestrielle de Droit Civil
ToS	Το Σύνταγμα (= To Syntagma)

[1] V. sur la question de l'application, par le juge, du droit comparé, Klein, *L'application de la méthode comparative dans la jurisprudence du TF*, RIDC, 1959, p. 321 et s; Constantinesco, *Traité de droit comparé,* t. II*, La méthode comparative*, (Paris 1974), p. 332 et s.; Aubin, *Die rechtsvergleichende Interpretation autonom-internen Rechts in der deutschen Rechtsprechung*, RabelsZ, 1970, p. 458 et s.; Drobnig, *Rechtsvergleichung in der deutschen Rechtsprechung*, RabelsZ, 1986, p. 610 et s.; Gerber, *Der Einfluss des ausländischen Rechts in der Rechtsprechung des Bundesgericht* in Institut suisse de droit comparé, *Perméabilité des ordres juridiques*, (Zürich 1992), p. 141, et s.; Werro, *La jurisprudence et le droit comparé. La réception des concepts juridiques étrangers*, in Institut suisse de droit comparé, *Perméabilité des ordres juridiques*, (Zürich 1992), p. 165 et. s. V. en ce qui concerne l'application du droit comparé par les juridictions helléniques, Frangistas, *L'usage qui est fait par la jurisprudence du droit comparé*, RHDI, 1965, p. 301 et s.

U. Drobnig and S. van Erp (eds.), The Use of Comparative Law by Courts, 149–188.

quelles sont les utilisations que les juridictions helléniques font de la méthode comparative? La présente étude vise à répondre à ces questions. Pour ce but nous nous proposons d'examiner l'utilisation jurisprudentielle du droit comparé à la lumière de certaines caractéristiques essentielles du système juridique hellénique. Il s'agit, en particulier: d'une part, de l'évolution historique de ce système et de l'origine étrangère des éléments qui ont empreint sa formation, et d'autre part, du rôle de la jurisprudence par rapport aux autres sources de droit, et de l'impact de ce rôle sur le style des décisions judiciaires.

Mais, parallèlement aux facteurs précités, la nature spécifique des règles qui régissent le litige en cause détermine également l'intensité, la fréquence et la façon avec laquelle la méthode comparative est utilisée par les tribunaux. Le recours au droit comparé est ainsi indispensable pour le juge qui est saisi d'un litige à caractère international. L'application des règles qui régissent un tel litige nécessitent dans la plus part des cas une connaissance plus ou moins profonde du droit étranger ainsi que la confrontation éventuelle de celui-ci avec l'ordre juridique interne. Dans les litiges à caractère interne, au contraire, le recours au droit comparé est facultatif. Il dépend de la formation et des prédilections du juge et elle vise à servir à la meilleure connaissance du droit national et à la meilleure application de celui-ci.

Ainsi, après l'examen de l'utilisation jurisprudentielle du droit comparé à la lumière des caractéristiques du système juridique hellénique (II), nous essaierons de montrer à la suite, l'apport du droit comparé dans les domaines spécifiques de la jurisprudence hellénique (III), et notamment lors de l'interprétation par le juge des règles à caractère international, d'une part (A), et des règles du droit interne, d'autre part (B).

La rédaction des deux premières parties de ce rapport concernant, d'une part, "l'utilisation jurisprudentielle du droit comparé à la lumière des caractéristiques du système juridique hellénique" et, d'autre part, "l'utilisation du droit comparé lors de l'interprétation par le juge des règles à caractère international", a été effectuée par *Mme Christina Deliyanni-Dimitrakou.* La troisième partie du rapport concernant "L'utilisation du droit comparé lors de l'interprétation par le juge des règles du droit interne" a été rédigée par *Mme Pénélope Agallopoulou.*

II. L'APPLICATION JURISPRUDENTIELLE DU DROIT COMPARÉ VUE SOUS L'ANGLE DES CARACTÉRISTIQUES DU SYSTÈME HELLÉNIQUE.

par Christina Deliyanni-Dimitrakou

A. L'utilisation jurisprudentielle du droit comparé en tant que conséquence de la perméabilité du système aux influences juridiques étrangères.

Une des causes principales expliquant le recours des juges au droit étranger est la perméabilité du système juridique national aux influences étrangères. Le droit hellénique constitue un exemple typique d'une telle perméabilité. Les modèles juridiques étrangers ont influencé de façon profonde sa physionomie tout au long de son histoire et notamment pendant la période contemporaine de son évolution.

1. Les influences étrangères du système, dès la période de l'antiquité jusqu'à la veille de la révolution contre l'empire ottoman en 1821[2].

Le recours du législateur et des tribunaux à l'utilisation du droit comparé constitue un processus, connu en Grèce, dès la période de l'antiquité[3]. Après la conquête romaine on aperçoit, en effet, l'interpénétration du droit grec ancien et du droit romain[4]. Néanmoins, le droit greco-romain qui résulta de cette interpénétration connut par la suite, grâce à sa codification par Justinien et par les empereurs byjantins postérieurs, une évolution autonome, exempte de toute influence étrangère, qui dura aussi bien pendant la période byzantine qu'après la fin de celle-ci[5].

---

[2] V. pour cette période de l'évolution historique du droit hellénique, entre autres, Pantazopoulos, *Introduction historique aux sources du droit hellénique*, t. 1, (Thessaloniki 1973) (en grec); Idem, *Histoire du droit hellénique; de la tradition savante au code civil*, (Thessaloniki), (en grec);, Petropoulos, *Histoire et Institutions du Droit Romain*, (Athènes 1963), (en grec); Papachristos, *La réception des droits ètrangers comme phénomène de sociologie juridique*, (Paris 1975); Vrellis, *Influences juridiques étrangères et droit comparé dans la Grèce du XIXe siècle* in Institut suisse de droit comparé, *Perméabilité des ordres juridiques*, *op. cit.*, p. 197 et s.; Francescakis, Evrigenis, Symeonides, *Droit comparé*, (Thessaloniki 1978), (en grec), p. 76 et s.; Yiannopoulos, *Historical Development, in* Kerameus, Kozyris (éd), *Introduction to Greek Law*, (Athens 1988), p. 1 et s.; Hamza, *Comparative law and antiquity*, (Budapest 1991).

[3] On aperçoit, pendant cette période, des réflexions comapratives, non seulement dans l'oeuvre du législateur et des philosophes, mais également dans la pratique judiciaire. Les orateurs de l'antiquité hellénique invoquaient ainsi, pour fonder leurs allégations, non seulement les lois de la Cité du juge saisi, mais également les lois d'autres Cités helléniques qui presentaient un lien avec le litige en cause. V. Francescakis, Evrigenis, Symeonides, *op. cit*, p. 76 et s.

[4] V. Pantazopoulos, *Le droit romain en correlation dialectique avec le droit hellénique*, (Thessaloniki 1974), (en grec); idem, *Aspect général de l'évolution historique du droit grec*, *op. cit.*, pp. 178-179; Petropoulos, *Histoire et Institutions du droit romain, op. cit.*, 158 et s., 166, no. 15.

[5] Maridakis, *Le caractère national du droit civile en vigueur en Grèce*, *op. cit.*, p. 267 et s.

Il est intéressant de signaler que la soumission de la nation hellénique à la domination de l'empire ottoman, qui dura près de quatre siècles, (1453-1830), n'affecta pas l'évolution autonome de ce droit et n'altéra pas sa physionomie. C'est, notamment, la contribution de deux facteurs principaux qui provoqua ce phénomène[6]: d'une part, le caractère religieux du droit ottoman qui imposait l'application exclusive de celui-ci aux rapports entre musulmans, et, d'autre part, la pratique des Grecs de soumettre leurs différends non pas au juge turc (le kadi), mais à leurs notables locaux ou aux évêques. Munis du privilège de l'administration de la justice, discerné par la Porte, les autorités précitées se prononçaient en matière de différends entre Grecs en appliquant le droit byzantin[7] et les coutumes locales.

Toutefois, cet isolement de l'ordre juridique hellénique se vit fléchir progressivement pendant les dernières décennies de la domination ottomane[8]. La formation d'un certain nombre d'intellectuels grecs aux grandes universités européennes et l'écho favorable en Grèce des idées de la Révolution française, incitèrent le peuple grec de nouer des liens culturels avec l'Occident et notamment avec la France. Ces liens, qui se traduisent sur le plan juridique, avec l'application, durant l'occupation turque, sous forme coutumière, du code de commerce français de 1807 aux rapports entre commerçants Grecs[9], se virent renforcer après l'éclatement de la Révolution pour l'indépendance de 1821.

---

[6] V. Pantazopoulos, *Histoire du Droit hellénique*, *op. cit*, p. 111 et s.; idem, *Aspect général*, *op. et loc. cit*, p. p. 183-187; Von Mauer, *Das griechische Volk*, *op. cit.*, p. 54 et s.

[7] Il est nécessaire d'être mentonné ici que, pendant la dérnière période de l'Empire hellénique de Byzance, le droit byzantin ne s'appliquait pas dans son état pure, c'est à dire sur la base des codifications des Empéreurs byzantins, mais sur la base des *novelles* de ces Empereurs ainsi que sur la base de différentes *bréviaires*, dont la bréviaire "Hexabiblos" rédigée en 1345, par le juge de Théssaloniki Constantin Armenopoulos, avait une place prépondérante. C'est notamment cette dérnière brévière qui fut appliquée, par les notables locaux et les évêques, pendant l'occupation de la nation hellénique par l'Empire ottoman. V. Von Maurer, *loc et op. cit*, p. p. 90-91; Maridakis, *op. et loc. cit.*, p. 269; Vrellis, *op. et loc. cit.*, p. 198.

[8] Les relations intellectuelles réciproques du peuple grec avec l'Occident datent du XV siècle. A partir de cette époque un nombre important d'intellectuels grecs, ne pouvant pas supporter l'esclavage, se sont éxilés en Europe, y amennant leur culture et leur civilisation. Toutefois, c'est à partir du XVII que ces relations se sont intensifiées, non seulement, en raison de l'épanouissement du commerce des régions helléniques avec l'Occident, mais également, à cause de l'activité des intellectuels grecs de la *Diaspora* qui tant avec leur enseignement qu'avec leur oeuvre d'interprétation portant sur un grand nombre d'ouvrages de philosophie et de litterature étrangers, mirent en contact la population hellénique avec la pensée occidentale. V. Von Maurer, *op. et loc cit.*, p. 39 et p. 290; Vrellis, *op. et loc. cit*, p. p. 199-200.

[9] Triantaphylopoulos, *La prémière traduction en grec du code de commerce français*, AID, 1943, 361 et s.

2. Influences françaises et allemandes sur le droit hellénique du 19ème siècle.

La création de l'Etat hellénique qui suivit cette Révolution posa avec acuité le problème de la formation nouveau système juridique[10]. Face aux tendances traditionalistes optant pour la réception du droit romano-byzantin ou bien pour l'application du droit coutumier, une troisième solution fut soutenue avec ardeur. Il s'agit, en particulier, de la réception d'un droit étranger et notamment du droit français[11]. Préconisée par les éléments les plus progressistes de la société hellénique, nourris par l'esprit démocratique et les idées de la Révolution française, cette solution ne favorisa pas seulement l'étude systématique en Grèce du droit français ainsi que l'enseignement de celui-ci dans la Faculté de droit d'Athènes[12], mais elle fut également exprimée de façon explicite dans l'oeuvre du législateur.

Or, tout en optant pour l'application provisoire du droit romano-byzantin, les Constitutions adoptées en Grèce pendant la période révolutionnaire[13] exprimaient en même temps la volonté du peuple d'obtenir des codes modernes. La Constitution de Trézène de (1827) alla plus loin dans cette direction en précisant dans son article 99 que "les futurs codes (civil, pénal, militaire) devraient avoir particulièrement comme base la législation française".

La suspension de cette Constitution par le premier gouverneur de l'Etat hellénique Jean Kapodistrias, venu au pouvoir en 1827, n'empêcha pas l'influence française sur la législation hellénique[14]. Le code pénal ainsi que le code de procédure pénale, adoptés pendant cette période (1827-1831),

---

[10] V. sur les solutions soutenues quant aux sources du nouveau système juridique hellénique en formation et la correlation entre ces solutions et les classses sociales de la société hellénique, Papachristos, *op. cit.* p. 15 et s.; Idem, *Le code civil français en Grèce, in "Haristia" Jean Deliyannis (Récueil d'études offertes en l'honneur de Jean Deliyannis)*, Deuxième partie, (Thessaloniki 1991), p. 133 et s., (en grec); Papantoniou, *Le droit privé des grecs pendant la Révolution de 1821*, Armenopoulos, 1976, p. 258 et s., (en grec).

[11] V. en ce qui concerne l'influence de la Révolution francaise et du droit français sur la formation du droit grec moderne Vlachos, *La portée de la Révolution française sur la formation du droit grec moderne in "Haristia" Jean Deliyannis (Récueil d'études offertes en l'honneur de Jean Deliyannis)*, Prémière partie, (Thessaloniki 1991), p. 81 et s.; Papachristou, *Le code civil français en Grèce*, *op. cit.*, p. 133 et s.; Francescakis, Evrigenis, Syméonides, *op. cit.*, p. p. 100-107; Vrellis, *op. et loc. cit.*, p. p. 199-120.

[12] Parallèlement à l'enseignement du droit français à la Faculté des droit d'Athènes, pendant les années 1837-1884, on aperçoit la publication, dans les Revues juridiques helléniques, des articles de la doctrine et des arrêts de la jurisprudence françaises et étrangères. Une revue spéciale, à savoir la Revue de la jurisprudence française et étrangère, se vit, d'autre part, fonder en 1881 avec l'initiative de S. Balanos. Cette dernière Revue continua à parraître, sous la direction de P. Valindas, jusqu'en 1942. V. Evrigenis, Francescakis, Siméonides, *op. cit.* p. 100 et s.; Vrellis, *op. et loc. cit.*, p. p. 208-209.

[13] Papantoniou, *op. cit.*, p. 258 et s.

[14] Von Maurer, *op. et loc. cit.*, p. p. 359, 379, 388; Vrellis, *op. et loc. cit.*, p. 203.

eurent comme source d'inspiration les codes respectifs français[15], tandis que le code de commerce, introduit également pendant cette même période, ne constituait qu'une traduction nouvelle du code de commerce français de 1807[16].

Toutefois, le Conseil de Régence, qui assuma en 1831 le gouvernement provisoire de l'Etat jusqu'à la majorité du roi Othon I, prince de Bavière, mit fin à cette emprise exclusive française sur la législation hellénique. La grande oeuvre législative, accomplie pendant cette période sous la direction du juriste Georg Ludwig von Maurer, membre du Conseil précité, eut comme source d'inspiration, parallèlement à la législation française, le droit allemand[17].

Von Maurer ne voulait pas, certes, s'éloigner du modèle juridique français, qui avait développé des profondes racines dans l'ordre juridique grec[18]. Mais, disciple lui même de Savigny et de l'école historique du droit, il estimait que la législation française n'était pas toujours compatible avec la réalité sociale de la Grèce. Les anciennes coutumes germaniques qui ressemblaient aux coutumes grecs lui paraissaient, au contraire, plus conformes à cette réalité. Les quatre codes qui composent son oeuvre législative -le code pénal, le code de procédure pénale, le code de procédure civile et le code sur l'administration des tribunaux sont ainsi les résultats d'un effort d'adaptation des traditions juridiques françaises et allemandes aux conditions économiques et sociales helléniques. [19]

Dans le domaine de droit privé von Maurer voulait élaborer un code civil d'origine coutumière[20]. Il s'agissait d'un projet qui visa à freiner le

---

[15] Vrellis, ibidem

[16] Étant donné que le Code de commerce précité renvoyait souvent au Code civil français, certaines décisions judiciaires étaient dictées sur la base de ce dernier Code et non sur la base du droit romano-byzantin qui était le droit civil en vigueur en Grèce. Les tribunaux helléniques donnaient ainsi l'impression qu'ils considéraient le Code Napoléon comme le droit civil de la Grèce. V. Triantaphyllopoulos, *op. et loc. cit.*, p. 376 et s.; Papachristou, *La réception*, *op. cit.* p. 20.

[17] V. Pantazopoulos, *Le tournant de la législation hellénique vers les modèles européens: Georg Ludwig von Maurer, Reccueil d'études en Hommage H. Kyriakopoulos*, Annalles de la Faculté de Droit et des Sciences Économiques de l'Université Aristote de Thessaloniki, t. 1 Γ' -B', (Thessaloniki 1966-1969), (en grec), réproduit in "*Anti-charisma*", loc. cit., Fasc. Δ', p. 285 et s.; Stathopoulos, *Les coutumes, Maurer et la politique législative dans le domaine du droit civil pendant le 19me siecle*, Armenopoulos, 1992, p. 465 et s. (en grec); Vrellis, *op. et loc. cit.*, p. 204.

[18] Il est à noter que von Maurer avait fait des études en France et avait subi l'influence des idées de la Révolution française. V. Vlachos, *op. cit.*, p. 93.

[19] Panatzopoulos, *Le tournant de la législation hellénique vers les modèles européens*, *op. cit.* p. p. 304-322; Vrellis, *op. et loc. cit.*, p. p. 203-204.

[20] C'est donc pour atteindre ce but que von Maurer commença à collectionner les coutumes qui serviraient de base à la future codification du droit civil hellénique. Cette collection qui se trouve incorporée dans son ouvrage "*Das griechische Volk*", *op. cit.*, p. p. 146-261, a servi, ensuite, de source d'information aux collections de coutumes efféctuées ultérieurement en Grèce. V. Stathopoulos, *op. et loc. cit.*, p. 470, n. 22; Vrellis, op. et loc. cit, p. 204.

mouvement en faveur de la réception du code Napoléon, et qui resta, tout de même, inachevé à cause du départ prématuré de von Maurer en 1834. Se trouvant dans une impasse, le gouvernement royal envisagea de nouveau l'idée de l'introduction du Code civil français. Mais le décret du 23 Février 1835 introduisit pour une nouvelle fois provisoirement comme droit civil le droit romano-byzantin. D'après les termes de ce décret "les lois civiles des Empereurs Byzantins, contenues dans l'Hexabible de Constantin Armenopoulos, seront en vigueur jusqu'à la rédaction d'un nouveau code civil". Mais les lois en question ne répondaient plus aux besoins de la société hellénique. La seule solution pour sortir de l'embarras fut l'utilisation de l'oeuvre systématisée des Pandectistes allemands. Pour arriver à cette solution, la doctrine et la jurisprudence grecques[21] ont considéré comme lois byzantines introduites dans le nouvel Etat, non seulement le droit contenu dans l'Hexabible de C. Harmenopoulos, mais aussi les Basiliques et au delà d'elles le Corpus Juris Civilis tel qu'il était interprété à l'époque par les jurisconsultes allemands. C'est donc cette interprétation erronée du décret 1835 qui imposa en Grèce le droit des pendectistes[22]. Car il paraissait raisonnable de se servir des travaux des juristes allemands pour acquérir un droit plus évolué et plus systématique que celui du Corpus juris à l'état pur. On arriva, ainsi, au paradoxe, d'avoir pendant cette période des décisions des tribunaux, même de la Cour de Cassation, qui se référaient directement aux ouvrages des pandectistes, et principalement à celle de Windscheid; l'oeuvre des pandectisres fut ainsi pendant longtemps le véritable droit en vigueur en Grèce. [23]

3. Le recours éclectique aux modèles juridiques étrangers: la tendance actuelle du législateur grec.

Néanmoins, on aperçoit pendant la deuxième moitié du 19me siècle la tendance du législateur grec de s'émanciper progressivement de l'emprise exclusive d'un seul système juridique[24]. Cette tendance trouve sa manifestation timide dans les codes qui furent adoptés pendant cette époque dans d'autres régions du monde hellénique telles que les îles Ioniennes, l'île de Samos et l'île de la Crète. Ces codes qui sont restés en vigueur même après le rattachement de ces régions en Grèce, avaient leurs sources d'inspiration dans les législations française et italienne. Il faut, tout de même, remarquer que c'est plutôt la rédaction du code civil hellénique qui donna à la tendance précitée sa manifestation la plus complète. Le code civil hellénique de 1940, entré en vigueur le 23. 2. 1946[25], qui est composé de 2035 arti-

---

[21] Pantazopoulos, *Aspect général*, *op. cit.*, p. p. 190-193.

[22] Papachristos, *La réception des droits privés étrangers*, *op. cit.* p. p. 18-20, 50-51.

[23] Papachristos, *loc. et op. cit,* p. 45 et s.; Petropoulos, *Histoire du droit romain*, *op. cit.*, p. 382.

[24] Vrellis, *op. et loc. cit.*, p. 206.

[25] V. pour les caractérisriques de ce code, entre autres, Michaélidès-Nouaros, *Les systèmes juridiques des peuples européens*, (Athènes 1958), p. 74; Zepos, *Greek Law*,

cles, constitue une codification du droit romano-byzantin, comme il avait été élaboré par la doctrine et appliqué par la jurisprudence pendant une longue période qui dépasse un siècle (1830-1946).

Le droit comparé a, d'autre part, largement alimenté l'oeuvre de ses rédacteurs. Certes, la division de ce code en cinq livres, selon le plan des ouvrages des pandectistes ainsi que celui du code civil allemand, à savoir: partie générale, droit des obligations, droit des biens, droit de la famille, droit des successions, ainsi que quelques ressemblances extérieures à la forme et à la technique du code civil allemand, ont permis à une partie de la doctrine de considérer décisive l'influence allemande à sa formation[26]. Mais cette conception ne correspond pas à la réalité. Si on étudie les travaux préparatoires de ce code on constate que, tant les membres de la Commission qui fut chargée de la rédaction de son projet initial, que le professeur G. Balis qui élabora son texte définitif, se fondèrent sur les règles du droit romano-byzantin, aussi bien que sur les principaux codes et projets de codification de l'époque, y compris, certainement le code civil allemand de 1896, le code civil suisse, le code suisse des obligations de 1907, le code civil français et le projet franco-italien du code des obligations de 1927[27].

Ce recours éclectique du législateur grec aux enseignements du droit comparé ne se manifesta pas exclusivement à l'occasion de la rédaction du code civil, mais il caractérise également toute oeuvre législative de grande envergure, opérée soit avant soit après la période qui suivit la deuxième guerre mondiale. Il mérite de mentionner à titre d'exemple pour ce qui est, plus particulièrement, la période d'après guerre: les réformes constitutionnelles, réalisées par les deux constitutions démocratiques, à savoir celle de 1952[28] et celle de 1975[29]; la réforme du droit civil et notamment du droit de la famille des années 80, effectuée, d'une part, par la loi no 1250/1982, ayant introduit le mariage civil, et d'autre part, par la loi no 1329/1983, ayant adapté les dispositions du code civil et notamment du droit de la famille au principe constitutionnel de l'égalité des sexes[30]; la réforme dans

---

(Athens 1949) p. 76 et. s.; Idem, *Twenty years of the Greek Civil Code*: *Achievements-objectivs*, Balkan Studies, 8, 2, (1967), p. p. 395-396, reproduit in *Recueil d' ouvrages de P. Zepos (Réédités), offerts à sa mémoire par la Faculté de Droit et des Sciences Économiques de l'Université Aristote de Thessaloniki*, (Thessaloniki 1988), Fasc. 2, p. 923 et s.; Valticos, *Le nouveau Code civil hellénique,* Bull. Trim. de la Société de Legisl. Comparée, 1947, p. 54 et s.; Zweigert, Kötz, *Introduction to Comparative Law*, (traduit de l'allemand par Weir), T 1, (Oxford 1987), p. p. 160-162.

26 V. par exemple Zweigert, Kötz, *op. et loc. cit.*, p. p. 160-162, qui classifient le Code civil hellénique dans la famille du Code civil allemand.

27 Michaélidès-Nouaros, *op. cit.*, p. 74; Zepos, *Greek Law*, *op. cit.*, p. 76 et s.

28 Svolos, Vlachos, *La Constitution de la Grèce*, (Athènes 1955), (en grec).

29 Vlachos, La Constitution de la Grèce, (Athènes, Komotini 1979), (en grec),.

30 V. en ce qui concerne les influences étrangères de cette dernière loi, Gazis, *Avant-projet et exposé des motifs de la loi concernant l'adaptation des dispositions du Code civil et spécialement du droit de la famille au principe constitutionnel de l'égalité entre hommes*

le domaine des rapports collectifs du travail, réalisée pendant cette même période, en vertu de la loi no 1264/1982 concernant la liberté syndicale et l'exercice libre du droit syndical ainsi qu'en vertu des lois nos 1767/1988 et 1876/1990 qui concernent respectivement, les conseils des travailleurs, d'une part, et les négociations collectives libres, d'autre part[31].

B. Le droit comparé vu sous l'angle de l'accomplissement des fonctions du juge.

1. Remarques préliminaires.

Toutefois, si cette utilisation éclectique, par le législateur grec, des modèles juridiques étrangers a influencé l'oeuvre des tribunaux en les orientant vers l'étude du droit étranger, elle n'a pas réussi, au contraire, de convaincre ceux-ci des mérites de la méthode comparative et des avantages qu'ils peuvent tirer de son application scientifique.

Les juridictions helléniques se contentent plutôt d utiliser les institutions et les réglementations juridiques étrangères, que de faire du droit comparé à proprement parler. Si elles acceptent de prendre en considération une solution consacrée ailleurs qu'en Grèce, elles ne le font qu'à titre d'appoint, sans recourir à une analyse scientifique du contenu des plusieurs droits étrangers comme une méthode de recherche leur permettant de connaître mieux leur propre droit.

2. Le mode aberrant de l'utilisation du droit comparé comme moyen permettant au juge d'interpréter le droit national.

Le rôle que l'ordre juridique hellénique reconnaît à la jurisprudence[32] constitue la cause principale de l'attitude précitée. Le droit grec est, comme celui des autres pays de l'Europe continentale, un droit par excellence législatif et non jurisprudentiel. La jurisprudence a par conséquent un rôle créateur limité[33]. Sa fonction principale est d'interpréter le droit écrit

---

et femmes, Ministère de la justice hellénique, *Introduction de l'egalité des droits et des devoirs entre hommes et femmes*, (Athènes 1979).

[31] V. en ce qui concerne les influences étrangères de ces lois. Kravaritou, *Introduction à le réglementation des conditions du travail*, (Thessaloniki 1991), (en grec); Deliyanni-Dimitrakou, *Les systèmes de négociation collective en Allemagne Fédérale et en Grèce façe au phénomène de l'internationalisation de l'institution*, (Thessaloniki 1990), p. 263 et s.

[32] V. Simantiras, *Principes généraux du droit civil*, (Thessaloniki 1973), p. 48 et s. (en grec); Ligeropoulos, *Rapport grec* in Travaux de l'Association Henri Capitant, (journées italiennes), *Les réactions de la doctrine à la création du droit par le juges*, (Paris 1980), p. 105 et s.

[33] Il faut tout de même signaler qu' avant l' entrée en vigueur du Code civil hellénique, les tribunaux développèrent en Grèce un rôle créateur important afin d'adapter le droit romano-byzantin aux besoins et aux idées de la vie moderne. V. Ligeropoulos, *op. et loc. cit.* p. 106, n. 1. En droit administratif, d'autre part, l'absence d'un code hellénique édictant les principes généraux de ce droit, obligea les tribunaux et notamment le Conseil d'État de déployer une activité créatrice importante. V. pour cette activité, Arnaoutoglou, *Rapport*

et non de créer des nouvelles règles de droit. C'est donc dans le cadre de cette interprétation qu'elle s'intéresse des droits étrangers. Mais, pour des raisons qui seront expliquées à la suite[34], les juridictions helléniques renvoient de préférence au droit allemand et non pas à l'ensemble des ordres juridiques étrangers qui ont servi de modèle, lors de l'élaboration, par le législateur de la disposition concrète faisant l'objet de leur interprétation. C'est, d'autre part, à la doctrine allemande que se réfèrent de préférence ces juridictions. La disposition législative, sur laquelle porte l'interprétation doctrinale allemande, le rapport de cette disposition avec la disposition respective faisant l'objet de l'interprétation judiciaire, la correspondance des cadres juridiques et extra-juridiques dans lesquels ces dispositions déploient leurs fonctions, constituent des facteurs qui, même dans les cas où ils sont pris en considération par le juge grec, ils ne figurent jamais dans le libellé de ses décisions. Présumant l'identité du droit étranger avec son propre droit, celui-ci se borne de citer les auteurs de la doctrine étrangère en les traitant parfois comme s'il s'agissait d'auteurs grecs[35].

3. Le rôle du droit comparé lors de la création par le juge de nouvelles règles de droit.

Toutefois, ce n'est pas seulement lorsqu'il interprète le droit écrit, mais également quand il crée des nouvelles règles de droit, que le juge grec s'abstient d'appliquer systématiquement la méthode comparative. Certes, il n'existe pas en Grèce une disposition, similaire à l'article 1 du code civile suisse, permettant explicitement au juge de faire oeuvre de législateur, lorsqu'il envisage un vide législatif. L'ordre juridique hellénique confère, cependant, de façon implicite, au juge un rôle créateur important, non seulement pour remplir les vides législatifs, mais également pour concrétiser les principes généraux du droit[36]. Il s'agit, plus particulièrement, des clauses générales et abstraites, comme par exemple celles de l'abus du droit, de la bonne fois, du changement impératif des circonstances, de la

---

grec, Travaux de l'Association Henri Capitant, (journées italiennes), *op. cit.*, p. 576 et s.; Stassinopoulos, Préface, *Reccueil d'études offertes en l'honneur du Conseil d'État*, (Athènes 1979), (en grec); Vegleris, *Caractéristiques du Conseil d' État*, ibid, p. 25 et s.

[34] V. infra p. p. 13 et s, 15 et s.

[35] V. pour une attitude similaire des tribunaux suisses, Gerber, *op. et loc. cit.* p. 142.

[36] V. sur le rôle créateur de la jurisprudence hellénique, Ligeropoulos, *La jurisprudence, facteur de formation du droit privé*, (1932-1934), (en grec); idem, *Rapport grec*, Travaux de l'Association Henri Capitant, *op. et loc. cit.*, p. 106; Michaélidès-Nouaros, *L'oeuvre créatrice de la jurisprudence grecque en cas de silence de la loi*, RHDI, 1951, p. 163 et s; v. en ce qui concerne le rôle du juge lors de la concrétisation des principes généraux du droit public, Arnaoutoglou, *loc. et op. cit.* p. 576 et s.; Stassinopoulos, *loc. et op. cit.*, p. 1 et s.; Vegleris, *loc. et op. cit.*, p. 25 et s.; Koutoupa-Regakou, *Le rôle des notions abstraites du droit et l'État de Droit contemporain* in Manitakis, Paparrigopoulos, Stamatis, Sourlas, Voutsakis, Koutoupa-Regakou (éds), *Aspects de L'État de Droit*, (Thessaloniki 1990), p. 257 et s (en grec).)

proportionnalité, de la protection de la vie privée, de la protection de l'enfant etc., qui expriment les principes fondamentaux de l'ordre juridique hellénique et qui nécessitent, pour produire leurs effets, une concrétisation de la part du juge. C'est donc cette oeuvre de concrétisation qui offre au juge grec l'occasion de développer une importante activité créatrice de droit et d'alimenter ses jugements des enseignements du droit comparé. Pourtant, celui-ci ne se voit pas pour l'instant prêt à saisir cette occasion. Qu'il se mette à combler les vides de la loi ou bien à concrétiser les notions générales et abstraites, le juge se borne en Grèce d'introduire des concepts et des constructions juridiques étrangères sans examiner ouvertement leur conformité avec la réalité juridique et sociale de son pays.

4. Le droit comparé et le style des décision judiciaires.

C'est entre autres le style des décisions judiciaires helléniques[37] et leur propre mode de motivation qui laisse peu de place à l'élaboration par le juge d'analyses comparatives étendues. En effet, contrairement aux décisions judiciaires des pays de common law qui ont un style discursif permettant au juge d'exprimer ouvertement ses avis personnels et de fonder ses jugements, tant sur des arguments juridiques que sur des appréciations extra-juridiques[38], les décisions judiciaires helléniques, tout comme celles de la majorité des systèmes qui ont reçu l'influence du droit français[39], ont une formulation brève et lapidaire. Fidèles à un style déductif et austère, elles se fondent sur des raisonnements par excellence formalistes et n'expriment jamais ouvertement les appréciations téléologiques du juge ou bien les estimations d'ordre socio-économique de celui-ci[40]. Le poids de la doctrine officielle qui nie à la jurisprudence un rôle de source de droit, le principe procédural qui nie l'éfficacité contraignante du précédent jurisprudentiel, le poids enfin de la tradition historique hostile à une jurispru-

---

[37] V. sur le style de décisions judiciaires en droit comparé Kötz, *Uber den Stil von höchstrichterlicher Entscheidungen*, RabelsZ, 1973, p. 245 et s.; idem, *Die Zitierpraxis der Gerichte*, RabelsZ, 1988, p. 643 et s.; idem, *Scholarship and the Courts: A Comparative Survey*, in Festschrift Merryman, (Berlin 1990), p. 183 et s.; Rudden, *Courts and Codes in England, France and Soviet Russia*, Tulane Law Review, 1974, p. 1010 et s.; Goutal, *Characteristics of Judicial Style in France, Britain and U.S.A.*, AJCL., 1976, p. 43 et s.; Lawson, *Comparative Judicial Style*, AJCL, 1977, p. 364 et s.; Markesinis, *Conceptualism, Pragmatism and Courage. A Common Lawyer Looks at Some Judgements of the German Federal Court*, AJCL, 1986, p. 349 et. s. V., en ce qui concerne le style et le mode de motivation des décisions judiciaires grecques, Kerameus, *La motivation des décisions judiciaires* in Société des juristes de la Grèce du Nord (éd), *La motivation des décisions judiciaires - L'opinion minoritaire - Les commentaires de la jurisprudence*, (Thessaloniki 1992), p. 26 et s. (en grec).

[38] V., entre autres. Goutal, *op. et loc. cit.* p. 43 et s.

[39] V. notamment sur la motivation des décisions de justice en France, Touffait, Tunc, *Pour une motivation plus explicite des decisions de justice et notamment celles de la Cour de Cassation*, Rev. Trim. Dr, Civ., 1974, p. 487 et s.

[40] Kerameus, *op. et loc. cit.* p. 26 et s.

dence libre, voici quelques facteurs décisifs qui expliquent le style jurisprudentiel précité[41]. Compte tenu de ce dernier, des réflexions comparatives concernant la nécessite de la réception de concepts juridiques étrangers ou bien l'adaptabilité de ceux-ci à l'ordre juridique interne, ne trouvent jamais une expression explicite dans le texte des décisions judiciaires. Or, la question se pose maintenant de savoir s'il appartient vraîment à la compétance du juge de mettre en place des analyses précitées, ou bien si celles-ci relèvent plutôt de la compétence de la doctrine.

5. La conception étroite et unilatérale de la doctrine en matière du droit comparé et son impact négatif sur l'oeuvre de la jurisprudence.

a) Position du problème.

Le droit hellénique fait partie des systèmes juridiques de la famille romano-germanique, qui se caractérisent par le rôle dominant de la doctrine dans la création des concepts juridiques et l'élaboration des constructions théoriques. [42] L'oeuvre doctrinale influence ainsi de façon décisive, dans les pays des systèmes juridiques en question, la jurisprudence des tribunaux. Qu'il se mette à élucider les obscurités de la loi, ou bien à combler les lacunes législatives, le juge grec n'invente pas à proprement parler les solutions données, mais il les trouve le plus souvent toutes prêtes dans la doctrine, qui oriente ainsi de façon décisive ses décisions[43]. Or, si la doctrine a un rôle prépondérant en Grèce dans le domaine de l'élucidation et du comblement des lacunes du droit écrit, c'est à elle qu'incombe également l'initiative de la réception des solutions juridiques étrangères ainsi que la mise en valeur de celles-ci par le biais des analyses comparatives.

Est ce que la doctrine juridique hellénique remplit avec succès cette fonction? Est ce qu'elle aide réellement les juges de mieux comprendre et d'améliorer leur droit en les informant de l'éxistance d'autres modes de raisonnement et d'autres façons de résoudre les mêmes problèmes juridiques? Une réponse à cette question parait certes prématurée. Nous jugeons tout de même nécéssaire de faire ici quelques remarques préliminaires.

b) Conception étroite et unilatérale de la doctrine en matière du droit comparé.

La perméabilité de la législation hellénique aux influences juridiques étrangères et la formation traditionnelle des juristes grecs aux facultés de

---

[41] V. Scalfi, Romagnoli, *Rapport général*, Travaux de l' Association Henri Capitant, loc. et *op. cit.*, p. 16 et s. (18).

[42] Litzeropoulos, *Rapport grec*, Travaux de l' Association Henri Capitant, *op. et loc. cit.*, p. 106. Le système allemand et le système suisse se caractérisent également du rôle dominant de la doctrine à la formation de concepts du droit. V. respéctivement, Kötz, *Scholarship and the Courts, A Comparative Survey*, *op. cit.*, p. 183 ets. (193). Werro, op. et loc cit., p. 169.

[43] Litzeropoulos, ibidem

droit des grandes universités européennes[44] ont familiarisé la doctrine juridique hellénique avec l'étude des droits étrangers. Mais le fait que celle-ci étudie et renvoie très souvent au droit étranger, ne signifie pas qu'elle suit toujours les principes méthodologiques du droit comparé[45] ni qu'elle tire pleinement profit des apports de celui-ci [46]
Les auteurs grecs n'utilisent qu'à titre exceptionnel la comparaison fonctionnelle[47]. Leurs études ne partent pas ainsi de la situation de fait pour voir comment les normes des divers systèmes juridiques nationaux régissent celle-ci et pour comparer ensuite ce résultat avec celui qu'on obtient en droit hellénique. Se mettant le plus souvent d étudier une institution juridique à la lumière du droit national, ils cherchent à appuyer leurs approches théoriques sur la doctrine et la législation étrangères sans faire du droit comparé à proprement parler. On aperçoit, certes, souvent dans les monographies des juristes grecs une présentation préliminaire du cadre juridique que les divers ordres juridiques étrangers confèrent à l'institution concrète qui fait l'objet de leur recherche. Mais cette présentation préliminaire n'est pas dans la plus part de cas suivie d'une analyse comparative approfondie[48]. Les auteurs grecs abandonnent, d'autre part, toute analyse comparative dès qu'ils commencent à aborder théoriquement en question[49]. A partir de ce stade ils se bornent à développer leurs propres constructions théoriques. Biens qu'ils se réfèrent constamment à la doctrine étrangère, ils n'examinent presque jamais le fonctionnement de l'institution en cause dans le cadre juridique et social étranger, ni l'impact de la jurisprudence étrangère sur sa formation[50].

Une conception unilatérale prévaut, d'autre part, dans la doctrine en ce qui concerne les droits étrangers qui peuvent faire l'objet de la recherche scientifique[51]. La majorité des auteurs grecs s'intéressent surtout des droits étrangers qu'ils estiment proches au droit hellénique. C'est donc pour cette raison qu'ils se réfèrent dans la plus part de cas au droit allemand. Cette

---

[44] V. supra, p. 4 et p. 9.

[45] V. sur les principes méthodologiques du droit comparé, entre autres, Zweiget, Kötz, *op. cit.* t 1 p. 29 et s.; Kokkini-Iatridou, *Some Methodological Aspects of Comparative Law, The third part of a (pre-)paradigma*, Netherlands International Law Review, 1986, p. 144 et s.; Evrigenis, Francescakis, Simeonides, *op. cit.*, p. p. 119-169.

[46] V. sur l' utilisation du droit comparé par la doctrine hellénique, les observations critiques de Kerameus, *Dimitrios Evrigenis et le droit comparé* (en grec), in *Études offertes à la mémoire de D. Evrigenis*, RHDEur, 1986, p. 264 et s.

[47] V. sur la notion de la comparaison fonctionnelle, Zweigert, Kötz, *op. cit.*, p. 29 et. s.; Zweigert, *Des solutions identiques par des voies differentes*, RIDC, 1966, p. 16 et s.; Ancel, *Le problème de la comparabilité et la méthode fonctionnelle de droit comparé*, Festschrift für I. Jastay, (Tübingen 1982), p. 1 et s.

[48] V. Kerameus, op. cit, p. p., 275-276

[49] Ibidem

[50] Ibidem

[51] V. les commentaires critiques de Werro sur l'attitude similaire des juridictions suisses, *op. et loc. cit.*, p. 165 et s.

attitude, bien que compréhensible, est, tout de même, regrettable. L'étude du droit étranger et le droit comparé en général sont utiles, non seulement parce qu'ils nous mettent en contact avec d'ordres juridiques qui ressemblent à la nôtre, mais également parce qu'ils nous permettent de connaître les solutions que de droits tout à fait différents donnent aux problèmes sociaux et aux situations de fait envisagés par notre droit[52].

Reproduite par la jurisprudence, cette conception étroite et unilatérale du droit comparé eut souvent des effets négatifs sur l'ordre juridique hellénique. Il a été ainsi constaté, qu'elle constitue la cause, non seulement de certaines interprétations erronées du droit écrit, mais également de l'introduction arbitraire, dans notre système juridique, de concepts et de constructions théoriques étrangères, qui se concilient mal avec la réalité juridique et sociale de celui-ci.

c) Exemples d'une application doctrinale et jurisprudentielle erroné de la méthode comparative.

Une partie de la doctrine et la jurisprudence majoritaire ont interprété ainsi l'article 914 du C. civ hell., portant formule générale de la responsabilité délictuelle pour faute (acte illicite et coupable) et, notamment, la notion d'illicéité, en se fondant exclusivement sur les enseignements de la doctrine et de la jurisprudence allemandes, bien que la disposition précitée n'eût pas sa sourçe d'inspiration dans les dispositions respectives du Code civile allemand (par. 823 et 826), mais plutôt dans l'article 41 par. 1 du code suisse des obligations[53].

Ce dernier article, ainsi que l'article 914 C. civ. hell., se bornent à consacrer la restitution de tout dommage provoqué à une personne, par un acte illicite coupable, sans préciser le contenu de la notion d'illicéité. Elles se différencient ainsi considérablement du par. 823 C. civ. all. qui concrétise de façon expresse cette notion, en déclarant illicites deux catégories spécifiques d'actes dommageables, à savoir: d'une part, les actes qui portent atteinte à un droit subjectif absolu, tel que l'intégrité physique, la santé, la liberté, la propriété, etc, (par. 823 al. 1) et, d'autre part, les actes qui enfreignent une disposition expresse d'une loi protectrice (par. 823 al. 2)[54].

Profondément influencée, par le contenu de la disposition allemande précitée, la doctrine et la jurisprudence helléniques ne se contentèrent pas à ce que l'acte dommageable soit contraire à une norme du droit positif, pour qualifier celui-ci d'illicite, mais elles exigèrent en plus qu'il portât atteinte à un droit subjectif absolu. A la suite de cette interprétation elles rétrécirent considérablement la portée de l'article 914 C. civ. hell., en excluant de son

---

[52] V. Evrigenis, Francescakis, Simeonides, *op. cit.*, p. 130.

[53] V. pour ce phenomène le critiques de Deliyannis, *L'illicéité comme élément de la responsabilité civile délictuelle*, Rev. int. dr. comp.-Journées 1984, p. 177 et s., Deliyannis, Kornilakis, *Droit des obligations,* t. 3, (Thessaloniki 1992), § § 346-347, p. 129 et s

[54] V. sur le contenu de l'article 823 Code civ. all., entre autres, Markesinis, *The German Law of Torts, A Comparative Introduction,* (2ème ed.), (Oxford 1990), p. 10 et s.

champ d'application les comportements dommageables qui provoquent un préjudice purement économique. [55, 56]

Le droit du travail offre, d'autre part, un nombre important d'exemples de réception des concepts et des constructions juridiques étrangères qui s'adaptent mal à la réalité juridique et au contexte socio-politique de la Grèce[57]. Ce sont par exemple les obligations "de fidélité du travailleur" (*Treupflicht*) et "d'assistance de l'employeur" (*Fürsorgepflicht*) qui firent l'objet d'une telle réception[58]. Développés en Allemagne vers la fin du siècle passé, ces principes, qui ont leur origine dans le "Treudienstvertrag" médiéval, ont réussi de survivre dans l'ordre juridique de ce pays, non seulement à cause de l'impact profond que le contrat de travail susmentionné eut sur la formation idéologique des rapports du travail allemands, mais également en raison de l'enseignement de Otto von Gierke. Ce dernier auteur donna à ces principes un fondement dogmatique solide[59], avant la confirmation de l'idéologie libérale dans l'ordre constitutionnel allemand en vertu de la Constitution de Weimar de 1919,

Toutefois, si les facteurs socio-historiques et juridiques précités expli-

---

[55] V. sur les resultats similaires de l'interprétation jurisprudentielle de l'art. 823 C. civ. all., Markesinis, *op. et loc. cit.*, p. 37 et s. p. p. 148-238. Le dommages économiques sont, en revenche, restitués, par l'ordre juridique français, v., entre autres, sur ce sujet, les refléxions comparatives des Zweigert, Kötz, *op. cit.*, t. 2 p. 291 et s. (310)

[56] V. pour les réactions d' une partie de la doctrine hellénique façe à cette restriction du champ d'application de l'article 914 C. civ. hell., Deliyannis *op. et loc. cit.*, p. 83 Cet auteur à soutenu que la restitution, en vertu de l'article 914 C. civ. hell., des domages économiques est possible si on admet une conception objective en matière de notion de négligeance ainsi qu'une conception large en matière de notion d'illicéité. D'après cet auteur, cette dernière notion comprend dans son contenu tout comportement contraire à une règle de droit positif et par conséquent même les comportements qui se heurtent à la règle de l'art. 281 cod civ. hell qui intedit, d'après l'interpétation de la doctrine dominante, l'exercice abusif non seulement des droits strictement définis par le droit positif mais encore des prérogatives et des facultés appartenant à la liberté générale de la personne humaine. Il faut tout de même mentionner que la jurisprudence hellénique n'a pas pu se familiariser, à l'exéption d'un seul cas (V. Aréopage, (Cour de Cassation hellénique), 717/1985, NoB, 34/1986, 560 ainsi que Stathopoulos in *"Haristia" Jean Deliyannis*, *op. cit.* 2ème Partie, p. 603, 606-7), avec l'idée de l'application de l'article 281 cod. civ. hell. aux cas d'exercice abusive de la liberté générale de la personne. V. notamment sur ce sujet les arrêts récents de l'Aréopage, 33/1987 (Chambres réunies), EEN 1987. 853, NoB 1988. 324, 48/1987, EEN 1987, 867 ainsi que 404/1987 NoB 1988. 907 qui ont renversé la jurisprudence établie par l'arrêt 717/1985.

[57] V. sur ce sujet Aliprantis, *Influences étrangères problématiques sur la théorie du droit du travail hellénique, Etudes offertes à G. Michaélidès-Nouaros*, t. A', (Athènes 1987), p. 43 et s., Koukiadis, *Droit du travail - Rapports collectifs du travail*, (Thessaloniki 1981), p. 489.

[58] V. sur cette réception, les pertinentes analyses de Aliprantis, *op. et loc. cit.*, p. p. 48-55. Cet. auteur fait également une analyses socio-juridique très approfondie, pour prouver le caractère eronné de l'introduction, dans le cadre juridique des rapports collectifs du travail grecs, du principe allemand "de l'obligation de paix". V., notamment, p. p. 55-62, idem, *La place de la convention collective,* (Paris 1980), p. 135 et s.

[59] V. Aliprantis, *Influences étrangères, op. cit.,* p. 48

quent le maintient des obligations "de fidélité du travailleur" (*Treupflicht*) et "d'assistance de l'employeur" (*Fürsorgepflicht*) dans l'ordre juridique allemand contemporain, ils ne justifient pas, au contraire, la reconnaissance de ces obligations dans l'ordre juridique hellénique. Réalisée, par la doctrine[60] et la jurisprudence, pendant la période qui suivit la deuxième guerre mondiale, cette reconnaissance se présente incompatible avec la réalité sociale et juridique de la Grèce, pour deux raisons principales[61]: d'une part, parce qu'elle méconnaît la portée limitée, qu'elles eurent dans l'ordre social et juridique de ce pays, les rapports de travail comportant, entre leurs acteurs, des liens personnels similaires à ceux du "Treudienstvertrag" allemand; d'autre part, parce qu'elle se heurte à l'esprit libéral et démocratique de l'ordre constitutionnel hellénique qui, grâce aux Constitutions de la période révolutionnaire (1821-1830)[62], reconnût, avec un siècle d'avance, par rapport à l'ordre constitutionnel allemand, le principe fondamental de l'égalité des citoyens devant la loi.

8. Droit comparé et mode de citation des tribunaux.

Mais, qu'il soit positif ou négatif cet'impact de la doctrine hellénique sur la recéption jurisprudentielle des concepts et des solutions juridiques étrengèrs, ne resulte pourtant pas toujours clairement du texte des décisions judiciaires. C'est, notamment, dans le mode des citations opérés dans les jugements qu'il faut chercher les causes de ce phénomène[63]. Les juridictions du fond renvoient souvent, en Grèce, à la doctrine ainsi qu'à la jurisprudence constante des juridictions supérieures en suivant ainsi la pratique jurisprudentielle allemande[64]. L'attitude précitée n'est pas suivie, en revenche, par les juridictions supérieures. Tant le Conseil d'Etat[65] que la Cour de Cassation suivent en Grèce le style extrêmement austère et fragmentaire des juridictions françaises en se dispensant ainsi de toute référence à la doctrine et à leurs propres précédents. La pratique précitée n'exclut pas, tout de même, l'influence indirecte sur les juridictions précitées des enseignements de la doctrine[66]. Il résulte ainsi des conclusions des procureurs généraux que ces juridictions adoptent souvent des solutions juridiques consacrées ailleurs qu'en Grèce sans présenter, dans le texte de leurs arrêts, le droit et la pratique étrangers qui constituent les sources d'inspiration de ces solutions.

---

[60] V. Kapodistrias, *La bonne fois dans le droit grec du travail*, AID, 1943, p. 703 et s.

[61] V. Aliprantis, *Influences étrangères*, *op. cit.*, p. 50

[62] V. supra p. 153-154

[63] V. sur ce sujet Kötz, *Die Zitierpraxis der Gerichte*, *op. cit.*, p. 245 et s.

[64] V. Kötz, *op. et loc. cit.*, p. 193

[65] V. Arnaoutoglou, *op. et loc. cit.*, p. 577, et s.; Litzeropoulos, *op. et loc. cit.*, p. 105 et s.

[66] La jurisprudece du Conseil d'Etat hellénique a subi ainsi une forte influence des créations de la jurisprudence du Conseil d'Etat et du Tribunal des Conflits français, sans que cette influence resulte clairement du libellé de ses arrêts. V. notamment Arnaoutoglou, *op. et loc. cit.*, p. 582.

III. LE RECOURS JURISPRUDENTIEL AU DROIT COMPARÉ VU SOUS L'ANGLE DE LA NATURE DES RÈGLES QUI FONT L'OBJET D'UNE APPLICATION ET D'UNE INTERPRÉTATION JUDICIAIRES.

A. Le recours obligatoire au droit comparé lors de l'application des règles à caractère international.

par Christina Deliyanni-Dimitrakou

Mais, le recours du juge au droit comparé ne dépend pas seulement des caractéristiques générales du système juridique dans lequel il déploie ses fonctions. Il dépend en plus de la nature des règles qui régissent le litige en cause. L'usage jurisprudentiel du droit comparé est notamment obligatoire dans le cas des litiges régis des règles à caractère international. Avant d'examiner la façon avec laquelle le juge grec remplit l'obligation précitée, on essaiera de présenter la notion des règles à caractère international et les causes qui rendent obligatoire l'usage du droit comparé lors de leur application et de leur interprétation.

1. La notion de règle à caractère international.

Les règles à caractère international dont l'application judiciaire a besoin d'un recours obligatoire au droit comparé, peuvent être divisées en deux catégories principales: La première catégorie comprend des règles qui tirent leur caractère international de l'origine propre de leurs sources, sans égard du caractère interne ou international des rapports qui font l'objet de leur réglementation; il s'agit notamment ici des règles du droit international généralement admises ou bien les règles des traités internationaux. La seconde catégorie comprend des règles qui doivent leur caractère international plutôt à la nature de leur objet qu'à l'origine propre de leurs sources; il s'agit avant tout ici des règles du droit international privé.

Qu'elles résultent d'une coutume ou bien d'un traité international, les règles de la première catégorie ont besoin d'être appliquées de façon uniforme dans les ordres juridiques internes afin de produire leurs effets. C'est donc ce postulat de l'application uniforme qui oblige les autorités judiciaires nationales à examiner l'interprétation qu'ont donnée à ces règles la doctrine et la jurisprudence étrangères.

Le postulat de l'application uniforme n'est pas ignoré des règles du droit international privé[67], notamment dans le cas où celles-ci émanent d'un traité international visant à leur unification. Toutefois, c'est plutôt dans la nature par excellence internationale des rapports qui sont régis par ces règles qu'il faut chercher les causes qui rendent nécessaire l'utilisation de la méthode comparative lors de l'application de celles-ci. Le simple fait

[67] V. Batiffol, Lagarde, *Droit international privé*, (6ème ed.), T, I, (Paris 1974), nos, 23, 28,

que ces règles ont dans la plus part de cas pour but de déterminer lequel des ordres juridiques nationaux régira définitivement la relation privée en cause qui présente des éléments d'éxtranéité, met en contact le juge chargé de leur application avec au moins deux ordres juridiques et conduit inévitablement celui-ci à des réflexions d'ordre comparatif. La méthode comparative ne contribue pas, d'autre part, seulement à la solution de certains problèmes théoriques du droit international privé, telles que la qualification; elle aide en plus, à la mise en oeuvre des autres méthodes de réglementation des rapports internationaux développées par cette discipline. Il s'agit, en particulier, des méthodes qui ne se bornent pas à désigner de façon abstraite lequel des droits nationaux concurrents régira définitivement le rapport international en cause, mais elles examinent également du point de vue du droit matériel les solutions fournies par ces droits. Après l'examen du rôle de la méthode comparative lors de l'application des règles qui tirent leur caractère international de l'origine propre de leurs sources on examinera l'apport de cette méthode lors de l'application des règles du droit international privé.

2. Les règles d'origine international et le droit comparé.

a) L'utilisation de la méthode comparative lors de l'application des règles internationales jouissant d'une acceptation générale.

Les règles du droit international généralement acceptées jouissent d'une reconnaissance large dans l'ordre juridique hellénique. En vertu d'une jurisprudence qui remonte à la fin du siècle passé[68] les tribunaux consacrèrent l'application automatique de ces règles dans l'ordre juridique interne. Dans le but de confirmer et d'élargir la reconnaissance jurisprudentielle précitée, la Constitution hellénique de 1975 adopta une disposition spécifique qui a sa source d'inspiration dans l'article 25 par. 1 de la Loi Fondamentale allemande. Il s'agit, en particulier, de l'aricle 28 par. 1 de la Const. hellénique 1975 qui ne se borne pas à consacrer les règles du droit international généralement admises et les traitées internationaux ratifiés en tant que parties intégrantes du droit hellénique, mais elle prévoit, en plus, la supériorité hierarchique de ces deux catégories des règles internationales par rapport à toute disposition législative contraire.

D'après le système de contrôle de la constitutionnalité des lois en vigueur en Grèce, il appartient à toute juridiction étatique, sans égard de sa place dans la hierarchie judiciaire, d'examiner si une norme remplit les caractéristiques propres d'une règle internationale généralement admise. Or, parallèlement à ce contrôle juridictionnel diffus et casuistique, l'article 100 par. 1er *al fine* de la Constitution hellénique de 1975 reconnaît, en plus, le droit des juridictions nationales et des autorités administratives de recourir à propos de cette question auprès d'une haute juridiction spéciale.

---

[68] Aréopage, arrêt, 14/1896, cité par Ioannou, Economides, Rosakis, Fatouros, *Droit international public*, t. 2, (Athènes-Komotini 1990), p. 38, (en grec).

Il s'agit de la Cour suprême spéciale, qui a, parmi d'autres compétences, celle de trancher les contestations concernant la qualification d'une norme en tant règle internationale généralement acceptée.

Or, à propos de ce contrôle une double question se pose. Il s'agit tout d'abord de savoir quel est l'objet du contrôle que cette dernière Cour ainsi que les autres juridictions nationales effectuent en vue de qualifier une norme internationale de règle internationale généralement admise. Et puis, la question se pose quant au rôle que le droit comparé joue lors de la mise en place du contrôle en question. La réponse à ces questions dépend du contenu qu'on donne à la notion des "règles de droit international généralement admises", prévue par l'article 28 par. 1 Const. de 1975. D'après l'interprétation qui prévaut au sein de la doctrine[69] et de la jurisprudence helléniques[70], ces règles s'identifient avec l'ensemble des normes du droit international public général qui, vue leur qualité précitée, jouissent d'une acceptation générale incontestable. Le juge saisi de leur application n'a pas donc à contrôler l'acceptation de ces règles par la communauté internationale. Sa tâche exclusive consiste à voir s'il est admis par la majorité des sujets du droit international que la question litigieuse en cause est régie par une règle de droit international général. Or, pour répondre à cette question, le juge doit examiner le contenu que les ordres juridiques nationaux ainsi que les juridictions internationales conférant à cette règle. Il doit ainsi utiliser nécessairement la méthode comparative.

Toutefois, il est rare de trouver des analyses comparatives étendues dans la jurisprudence hellénique concernant la constatation et l'application des règles du droit international public général. Saisies de la qualification d'une réglementation de règle du droit international public, les juridictions helléniques se contentent dans la plus part de cas d attribuer ou de refuser cette qualification, sans examiner si la solution retenue par elles jouit d'une acceptation générale par la communauté internationale[71]. On entrevoit, certes, l'utilisation de la méthode comparative dans certaines décisions judiciaires[72] portant sur l'application des règles internationales relatives aux immunités de juridiction et d'exécution dont jouissent les Etats étrangers. Mais, cette utilisation reste sporadique et fragmentaire et ne caractérise pas l'ensemble de la jurisprudence concernant la constatation et

[69] Ioannou, Economides, Rosakis, Fatouros, *op. cit.,* p. 116 et s.

[70] AED, arrêt 68/1991, Journal Officiel, 13. 4. 1992. Fasc. spéciale de la jurisprudence du AED en vertu de l'article 100 Const hell., feuille no 8.

[71] V. les critiques de la doctrine sur l' attitude précitée des tribunaux et notamment sur l'arrêt no 359/1978 du Conseil d'Etat hellénique in Ioannou, Economides, Rosakis, Fatouros, *op. et loc. cit.,* p. 123 et s.

[72] V. par. exemple le jugement 2626/1965 du Tribunal de première Instance à juge unique d'Athènes, NoB, 1965, 886 et s. Ledit tribunal applique dans son jugement précité les règles iinternationales qui régissent la limite des immunités précitées ainsi que les conditions qui permettent de les écarter. Pour déterminer le contenu de ces règles, il utilise les enseignements des doctrines française, allemande et italienne et il fait en plus appel à la jurisprudence française.

l'application des règles du droit international public général.

La Cour Suprême spéciale de l'art. 100 par. 1 a. 6 de la Constitution, qui s'occupa une seule fois jusqu'à présent de cette question[73], hésita également à se livrer à des recherches comparatives étendues.

La Cour examina, en plus, la question de savoir, si l'exonération, de toute taxe et impôt, des produits américains, importés périodiquement en Grèce, pour les besoins des postes de radiodiffusion que les Etats-Unies avaient installés depuis la fin des années quarante dans le pays, constituait un comportement continuel et constant de l'Etat hellénique vis à vis à de l'Etat américain qui réunissait les caractéristiques propres d'une règle internationale généralement acceptée. Bien que la Cour reconnaisse au début de son jugement la nécessité d'un examen global des positions que la majorité des sujets du droit international adoptent en ce qui concerne la question précitée, elle abandonne ensuite la mise en place d'un tel examen. Elle se contente ainsi de déclarer l'inexistence d'une règle internationale imposant l'immunité fiscale des Etats pour les activités qu'ils développent en dehors de leur territoire, dans le territoire souverain des autres Etats, sans présenter les sources de droit nationales et internationales qui refusent expressément la reconnaissance d'une telle règle. La Cour déduit de façon indirecte l'inexistence de la règle précitée. Elle la déduit, notamment, d'une manière négative de l'ouvrage de Bishop *(Immunity from taxation of foreign state-owned property)* que la partie défenderesse (l'Etat américain) avait invoqué pour soutenir l'existence de la règle précitée. D'après le raisonnement de la Cour, le fait que l'auteur précité ne mentionne pas pour fonder son opinion une jurisprudence d'autorité émise par les juridictions internationales ou bien par la Cour suprême d`Etats-Unies, permet en effet de dégager la non reconnaissance de cette règle par la communauté internationale.

Mais, ce qui est le plus surprenant dans cet arrêt, est la façon sommaire dont se sert la Cour pour motiver l'écartement des allégations de la partie défenderesse concernant l'application au litige en question du principe de l'estoppel. Oeuvre de la jurisprudence anglaise du Chancelier, le principe de l'estoppel, interdisant le comportement contradictoire de la personne, exprime une règle générale qui jouit d'une reconnaissance large dans les ordres juridiques nationaux (*venire contra factum proprium*). C'est donc pour cette raison que la doctrine et les juridictions internationales mentionnent souvent ce principe parmi les principes généraux des Etats qui sont susceptibles de régler les relations internationales[74]. La Cour aurait dû, par conséquent, examiner avec attention, en utilisant la méthode comparative, la reconnaissance de ce principe par la communauté internationale, pour voir ensuite l'applicabilité de celui-ci au litige en cause.

---

[73] AED, arrêt 68/1991 v. supra, n., 70

[74] V. Gibbon, *Estoppel in international law*, ICLQ, 1958, p. 471

b) Le rôle limité du droit comparé lors de l' nterprétation par les tribunaux des conventions internationale ratifiées.

Bien que la Grèce ait ratifié un nombre important de conventions internationales qui introduisent des règles uniformes dans le domaine du droit commercial et maritime ainsi que dans le domaine du droit international privé, les juridictions helléniques n'utilisent pas, en principe, la méthode comparative lors de l'interprétation de ces instruments internationaux.

Les conceptions du droit hellénique à propos des conditions juridiques qui permettent l'entrée en vigueur des traités internationaux dans l'ordre juridique interne constituent la cause principale de cette attitude. Or, contrairement aux règles du droit international public général dont l'entrée en vigueur automatique dans l'ordre juridique interne fut reconnu en Grèce déjà pendant la fin du siècle passé[75], les traités internationaux, et notamment celles qui règlent des questions relevant de la compétence du législateur national, ont toujours besoin dans l'ordre juridique de ce pays d'une loi d'approbation pour produire leurs effets sur le plan interne[76]. Cette loi déploie une double fonction dans l'ordre juridique hellénique: elle autorise le chef de l'Etat de ratifier le traité international et elle introduit en même temps celui-ci dans l'ordre juridique interne.

Selon les concepts dualistes qui prévalurent dans la doctrine et la jurisprudence grecques avant l'entrée en vigueur de la Constitution de 1975 la loi d'approbation n'ordonnait pas seulement les organes étatiques nationaux d'éxécuter le traité international, mais elle transformait, en plus, les normes de celui-ci en règles du droit interne[77]. A la suite de ces concepts, les traités internationaux et, par conséquent même, les conventions internationales du droit uniforme, perdaient leur caractère international et s'assimilaient à la législation du droit interne. Cette situation fut, en plus, accentuée par le fait qu'un nombre important de conventions internationales du droit uniforme furent incorporées dans le Code de Commerce et le Code Maritime helléniques et perdirent ainsi leur caractère international[78].

---

75 V. supra n. 68

76 Art. 36 par 2 Const. hell. 1975

77 V. pour la doctrine et la jurisprudence de cette période, Yokaris, *La pratique des organes juridictionnels lors de l'application du droit conventionnel international*, (Athènes-Komotini 1986), p. 132 s., et notamment, p. 135, notes 134, 135.

78 Ce sont, notamment, les conventions internationales portant des règles uniformes dans le domaine du droit maritime privé qui se virent privées complètement de leur caractère international. Ces conventions qui étaient ratifiées et introduites dans l'ordre juridique hellénique avant l'entrée en vigueur du Code de droit maritime privé héllénique de 1958 (C. m. p. hell.), virent la plus part de leurs normes s'incorporer dans les articles de ce Code. Il s'agit, par exemple, des dispositions de la Convention internationale de Bruxelles de 1924 sur le connaisament qui furent incorporées dans les dispositions des articles 107 et s du C. m. p. hell., des dispositions de la Convention internationale de Bruxelles de 1910 en matière d'abordage qui furent incorporées dans les articles 235-245 du C. m. p. hell.; ou bien des dispositions de la Convention internationale de Bruxelles de 1910 sur l' assistance et les sauvetages maritimes qui furent incorporées dans les articles 246-256 du C. m. p. hell. La

C'est donc pour cette raison qu'il arrive de voir dans la jurisprudence hellénique de la période précédente la tendance des tribunaux d'appliquer la loi d'approbation des conventions internationales sans invoquer le texte officiel de celles-ci. [79]

La Constitution hellénique de 1975 atténua quelque peu la situation fâcheuse précitée. Ainsi qu'il a été déjà mentionné, cette Constitution se caractérise d'un ésprit favorable envers le droit international qui s'exprime avec la disposition de l'article 28 par. 1 qui consacre la supériorité hiérarchique des règles du droit international public général et des traités internationaux ratifiés par rapport aux lois ordinaires. Bien que la Constitution exige dans son article 36 par. 2 le vote d'une loi d'approbation pour l'introduction des traités internationaux dans l'ordre juridique interne, l'esprit favorable qu'elle adopte à l'égard du droit international a impliqué l'abandon progressif des concepts dualistes que la doctrine et la jurisprudence adoptaient auparavant quant à la nature de cette loi. D'après la conception qui prévaut à l'heure actuelle en Grèce, la loi en question ne transforme pas les normes du traité international en règles du droit interne, mais elle se contente à conférer à ses normes force de droit interne. Par suite de ce concept, le traité ratifié et entré en vigueur dans l'ordre juridique hellénique garde son caractère international. Ses normes ne sont pas assimilées aux dispositions du droit interne, mais elles sont considérées comme des sources de droit distinctes soumises à leurs propres règles d'interprétation[80].

Toutefois, si le tribunaux helléniques reconnaissent le caractère international des traités internationaux ratifiés et entrés en vigueur dans l'ordre juridique interne, ils hésitent pour l'instant d'appliquer le droit comparé lors de leur interprétation[81]. Et ceci, malgré le fait que la Grèce a ratifié certains instruments internationaux qui mentionnent expressément la méthode comparative parmi les méthodes d'interprétation des traités inter-

---

disparition du caractère international de ces conventions fut accentuée par la disposition de l'article 295 du C. m. p. hell. qui prévoit que les dispositions des Conventions internationales qui s'opposent aux dispositions de ce code ou bien qui portent sur des matières réglées par celui-ci sont considérées abrogées malgré le fait de leur ratification et de leur introduction dans l'ordre juridique hellénique. Bien que cet article se heurte à l'heure actuelle à la disposition de l'art. 28 Const. 1975 qui prévoit la supériorité hiérarchique des règles du droit inernational public général et conventionnel par rapport aux lois ordinaires, le tribunaux helléniques n'appliquent pas les dispositions des conventions qui n'ont pas été incorporées dans le C. m. p. hell dans le cas où celles-ci se heurtent aux dispositions de ce Code; V. Grammatikaki-Alexiou, Papassiopi-Passia, *The interpretation of international maritime conventions in Greek Law*, (National Raport au XIIIe Congrès international de droit comparé, Montréal, 1990), RHDI, 1991, p. 109, réponses nos 17-18.

[79] Yokaris, *op. cit*, p. 135, note 135, Gramatikaki-Alexiou, Papassiopi-Passia, *op et loc. cit*; Kiantou-Pampouki, *The interpretation of international maritime conventions in civil law and in common law*, in Rapport général au XIIe Congrès international de l'Académie internationale de droit comparé, Rapport général, Montréal 1990), RHDI, 1991, p. 7

[80] Ioannou, Economides, Rosakis, Fatouros, *op. cit.* t. 2, p. 129 et s., et 187 et s.

[81] Kiantou-Pampouki, *op cit*, p. 7 et s.

nationaux.

C'est, notamment, la Convention internationale de Vienne de 1969 sur le droit des traités internationaux et plus particulièrement, l'article 31 de celle-ci concernant les règles d'interprétation des dits traités qui effectue cette reconnaissance. Cette disposition prévoit l'obligation des Etats d'interpréter les traités internationaux en bonne foi et de donner à leurs termes le sens approprié qui résulte de l'objet et du contexte général du traité, auquel ils appartiennent. Se mettant à concrétiser les éléments qui composent ce contexte, ladite disposition mentionne, parmi d'autres, "toute pratique des Etats contractants concernant le traité international en cause qui, mise en place après la conclusion de ce traité, exprime la conception commune des Etats contractants quant à l'interprétation des règles de celui-ci". Il s'ensuit que les autorités judiciaires nationales, saisies de l'application d'un traité international, doivent utiliser la méthode comparative, afin de conférer aux termes de celui-ci une interprétation uniforme qui ne s'inspire pas des préoccupations nationales, mais qui jouit plutôt de l'acceptation unanime des Etats contractants.

C'est justement cette même idée de l'application uniforme que vise, d'autre part, à promouvoir également l'article 18 de la Convention de Rome de 1980 sur le droit applicable aux obligations contractuelles. Cette disposition prescrit, plus particulièrement, l'obligation du juge national de respecter le caractère international de ladite convention et d'éviter toute assimilation des règles de celle-ci aux dispositions du droit interne. Grâce à cette disposition, les parties contractantes ont la possibilité d'invoquer devant les juridictions du for l'interprétation que les tribunaux des autres Etats-membres ont donnée aux dispositions de la convention[82].

Toutefois, bien que les deux instruments internationaux susmentionnés jouissent, en vertu de l'aricle 28 par. 1 Const. hell, d'une valeur juridique supérieure par rapport aux lois ordinaires, la jurisprudence hellénique ne suit pas pour l'instant les règles d'interprétation prévues par eux. On aperçoit, certes, dans cette jurisprudence quelques décisions qui interprètent les termes des conventions internationales du droit uniforme, en faisant recours aux travaux préparatoires de ces conventions[83] ou bien à

[82] V. Giuliano/Lagarde, *Rapport concernant la Convention sur la loi applicable aux obligations contractuelles*, JOCE, 282 C 31. 10. 1980, Papassiopi-Passia, *La convention communautaire de Rome de 1980 sur le droit applicable aux obligations contractuelles*, (Thessaloniki 1991), p. 98 et s (en grec),

[83] V. par exemple Jugement du Tribunal de grande Instance d Athènes, 7029/ 1972, NoB, 1972 1081. Ce jugement interpréta l'article 20 de la Convention internationale de Varsovie de 1929 concernant la responsabilié du transporteur aérien, en faisant recours aux travaux préparatoires de cette Convention, V. également Grammatikaki-Alexiou, Papassiopi-Passia, *op. et loc. cit.*, qui mentionnent que les tribunaux hélléniques éxaminèrent les travaux préparatoires de La Convention internationale de Bruxelles de 1910 en matière d'abordage pour interpréter l'article 240 du C. m. hell. qui introduit l'obligation d'assistance réciproque des navires en collision en se fondant sur le fait que l'article précité eut sa source d'inspiration dans l'article 8 de ladite Convention.

l'interprétation qu'ont donnée à celles-ci la doctrine et la jurisprudence étrangères[84]. Mais, la pratique précitée reste pour l'instant exceptionnelle et n'altère pas l'image général de la jurisprudence hellénique qui se caractérise par la réticence des tribunaux à utiliser systématiquement la méthode comparative lors de l'interprétation des conventions en question.

c) L'application, par le juge, des instruments internationaux non ratifiés et le droit comparé.

La méthode comparative n'aide pas seulement le juge à interpréter correctement les conventions internationales ratifiées, mais elle permet également à celui-ci de se servir des conventions internationales non ratifiées comme éléments de comparaison, afin d'interpréter le droit interne ou bien pour combler les lacunes de celui-ci.

Les tribunaux helléniques ont ainsi appliqué des conventions internationales non ratifiées, en les considérant comme des éléments de fait soumis à la preuve, dans deux cas distincts, à savoir: lorsque un acte administratif ou législatif renvoie expressément à elles ainsi que dans les cas ou celles-ci sont expressément mentionnées comme droit applicable d'un contrat international précis.

C'est notamment l'art 2 de la Convention internationale de Bruxelles de 1926 "pour l'unification de certaines règles relatives aux privilèges et hypothèques maritimes" qui a été appliquée par les tribunaux comme un élément de fait, dans le cadre des procédures de saisie de navires, dans le but de la détermination par le juge des privilèges maritimes qui jouissaient d'une priorité par rapport aux hypothèques. Bien que ladite convention n'ait pas été ratifiée par la Grèce et ne fasse donc pas partie du droit hellénique, les tribunaux ont appliqué la disposition précitée en se fondant sur le fait, que celle-ci était mentionnée expressément par l'acte administratif qui approuvait l'enregistrement à port des navires en cause[85]. Il faut d'autre part mentionner que la Convention internationale de Genève de 1956, relative au contrat de transport international des marchandises par route (CMR) qui fut ratifiée par la Grèce en 1977, fut appliquée également par les tribunaux helléniques avant sa ratification dans les cas où elle était expressément choisie par le parties comme droit applicable d'un contrat international précis[86].

Toutefois, c'est surtout le droit communautaire et notamment les règles communautaires de la concurrence qui servirent de source d'inspiration pour l'interprétation, par le juge, du droit interne tout au long de la décen-

[84] V. par exemple arrêt du Tribunal de grande instance d'Athènes 4404/1966, NoB, 1966, qui détermina la notion du tranporteur aérien prévue par la Convention internationale de Varsovie en faisant recours à la doctrine et à la jurisprudence francaises et notamment à un arrêt de la Cour d'Appel de Lyon de 1951, publié à La Revue Francaise de Droit Aérien 1951 p. 440

[85] Aréopage 299/1983, END, 1984, p. 1978

[86] Cour d'Appel d'Athènes 7952/1980, NoB, 1980, 562

nie qui précéda l'adhésion de la Grèce à la Communauté. On aperçoit ainsi, pendant cette période, la tendance des tribunaux helléniques à prendre en considération le règles précitées bien que celles-ci n'eussent pas encore fait partie du droit interne. *L'ordonance no 1572/1967*[87] *du juge des référés de Thessaloniki* constitue un exemple éloquent de la tendance précitée ainsi qu'un des rares exemples d'utilisation correcte de la méthode comparative par le tribunaux.

Le juge en question s'était occupé plus particulièrement du problème de la qualification ou non de contraire aux bonnes mœurs – donc de déloyal au sens des dispositions de la loi hellénique sur la concurrence déloyale (Loi no 146/1916) – du fait d'un tiers d'avoir importé au marché hellénique dans le but de les revendre des marchandises d'une société étrangère, alors qu'il était en connaissance que cette société avait déjà conclu auparavant, pour ces mêmes produits, un contrat de vente exclusive avec un autre importateur. Les instances grecques, suivant jusqu alors le point de vue que la jurisprudence et la doctrine françaises avaient admis à propos de l'application de l'art. 1382 CC en la matière, qualifiaient le comportement précité de déloyal. Or, l'ordonnance concernée abandonna cette position, jusqu'alors constante de la jurisprudence hellénique, pour adhérer aux thèses de la jurisprudence et de la doctrine allemandes. Celles-ci, interprétant les dispositions respectives de la loi allemande sur la concurrence déloyale, ne qualifiaient, en effet, de déloyal au sens de cette loi, que l'acte du tiers, par lequel celui-ci faisait importer au marché intérieur les produits de la société étrangère après l'avoir incitée dolosivement à violer le contrat de vente exclusive qu'elle avait conclu antérieurement avec l'autre importateur; alors qu'il ne constituait point, selon ce même point de vue allemand, un acte déloyal le cas où le tiers avait importé au marché intérieur les produits de la société étrangère en profitant tout simplement du fait, que le contrat de vente exclusive, que ladite société avait conclu avec l'autre importateur, avait été déjà violé auparavant.

Ce qui est intéressant ici, c'est que l'ordonnance dont il est question ne se limite pas, dans son effort de motiver son adhésion au point de vue allemand, à se prévaloir du fait que la loi hellénique sur la concurrence déloyale avait eu comme modèle la loi respective allemande, mais il a en plus recours à la méthode comparative, voire même aux principes du droit communautaire, à une époque où la Grèce n'avait pas encore adhéré à la CEE. Il soutient, notamment, que la position modérée du droit allemand à l'égard de la qualification ou non du comportement en question comme un acte de concurrence déloyale – suivie, d'ailleurs, également, par la majorité des droits des autres pays-membres de la Communauté – est imposée même par le droit communautaire, notamment par la disposition de l'art. 85 du Traité de Rome, qui interdit, conformément à l'interprétation qui lui a été donnée par la Commission, les contrats de vente exclusive en tant

[87] ArchN, 1968, 735

qu'impliquant une déformation et une limitation de la libre concurrence. Or, cette disposition, bien que n'ayant pas encore en Grèce force de loi interne, pourrait être prise quand même, d'après l'ordonnance en question, en considération comme un élément de comparaison dans l'interprétation de loi hellénique, en vue de l'adhésion, ébauchée encore dans le temps et donc attendue, de la Grèce à la CEE.

3. Le rôle du droit comparé lors de l'application, par le juge, des règles du droit interne qui ont un caractère international.

Aux paragraphes qui suivent on essaiera d'examiner l'utilisation du droit comparé, par le juge grec, tant dans le cadre de la méthode classique des conflits de lois que dans le domaine des méthodes modernes qui visent à reconnaître aux juges la faculté de choisir le droit applicable en fonction de sa teneur substantielle.

a) Le droit comparé dans le cadre de la méthode classique des conflits des lois. [88]

Le droit international privé hellénique se compose de dispositions dans leur majorité écrites qui, insérées dans les articles 4-33 c. c. hell, présentent les caractéristiques propres des règles bilatérales de conflit.

Étant donné que le nombre des règles de conflit du système juridique hellénique fut toujours limité, la jurisprudence s'est vue obligée de compléter leurs lacunes. Elle a accompli cette tâche en recourant non seulement à l'esprit du droit international du forum mais également aux solutions admises tant par les systèmes de droit international privé étrangers que par les conventions internationales visant à unifier leurs règles. C'est ainsi que les tribunaux helléniques ont appliqué respectivement la *lex sedis* à une personne morale[89], et la *lex loci solutionis* à un contrat de prêt[90], alors que le droit international privé du forum ne contenait pas de dispositions écrites en la matière.

La méthode comparative présente, d'autre part, une utilité incontestable sur le domaine de la qualification. Bien que les tribunaux helléniques rejettent la doctrine des qualifications comparées[91], préconisée par la

---

[88] V. sur le rôle du droit comparé dans le domaine du droit international privé, entre autres, Evrigenis, *Droit comparé et droit internationl privé. Problèmes d'interdépendance méthodologique, Annales de la Faculté de Droit et des Sciences Économiques de l'Université de Thessaloniki, 1960-1962 offertes à la mémoire de P. Vizoukidis*, Vol. 7, p. 615et s (en grec); Batiffol, *Les apports du droit comparé au droit international privé, Livre du centenaire*, t. 1, Paris 1969, p. 131 et s; von Mehren, *L'apport du droit comparé à la théorie et à la pratique du droit international privé*, RIDC, 1977, p. 493 et. s; Beitzke, *Bemerkungen zur Kollisionsrechtsvergleichung in der Praxis*, RabelsZ, 1984, 623.; Drobnig, *op. et loc. cit.*, p. 613.

[89] Aréopage, arrêt 439/1954, Thémis, 1953, 788

[90] Cour d'Appel de Dodecanèse, arrêt 61/1954, EEN, 1954, 1235.

[91] Rabel, Das Problem der Qualifikation, RabelsZ, 1931, 241 et s.

théorie[92] en se prononçant pour la qualification *lege fori*[93], ils recourent malgré tout obligatoirement à la méthode comparative lorsqu'ils ont à qualifier des institutions ignorées de notre droit. Ce procédé a été suivi par les tribunaux helléniques avec plus ou moins de succès dans les cas où ceux-ci ont envisagé la détermination de la loi applicable à des institutions inconnues de l'ordre juridique hellénique telles que le testament conjoint[94] ou le trust[95].

L'application de la réserve d'ordre public implique également le recours intensif du juge à la méthode comparative. Celui-ci doit se servir de cette méthode tant au moment où il examine la compatibilité du droit applicable étranger avec les principes qui composent l'ordre public international qu'au moment où il se met à déterminer le contenu propre de cette dernière notion.

Pour s'aquitter de cette tâche, le juge ne doit pas se fonder exclusivement aux principes et aux valeurs de son propre système juridique, mais il doit, en plus, examiner si les principes et les valeurs en question jouissent d'une reconnaissance par les autres ordres juridiques, c'est à dire s'ils sont investis d'une valeur universelle.

Largement préconisée par la doctrine[96], cette détermination comparative de la notion d'ordre public international ne fut pas toujours suivie par le tribunaux helléniques qui ont donné dans certains cas un contenu nationaliste à cette notion. C'est notamment la jurisprudence rendue avant la réforme du droit de la famille qui exprime cette conception nationaliste des tribunaux helléniques quant au contenu de la notion d'ordre public international. On aperçoit ainsi, pendant cette période, des jugements qui ont écarté, pour des raisons d'incompatibilité avec la notion précitée, l'application des lois étrangères qui ne connaissaient pas l'institution de la dote[97] ou bien qui attribuaient le divorce pour des causes inconnues du droit hellénique[98].

---

92 Maridakis, *Droit international privé*, T I, (Athènes 1967), p. 237 et s. (en grec), Evrigenis, *Droit international privé*, (Thessaloniki 1968), p. 94 et. s (en grec).

93 Tribunal de première Instance à juge unique de Sparte, jugement 74/1981, NoB, 1982,. 376

94 Tribunal de grande Instance de Gythion, jugement 157/1959, NoB, 1960, 652, Cour d'Appel de Nauplie, arrêt 78/1960, NoB, 1960, 433. Tribunal de première Instance à juge unique de Samos, jugement 22/1971, Arch. Nom., 1971, 859.

95 Tribunal de grande Instance compétente en matière fiscale d'Athènes, arrêt 14150/1963, NoB,, 1964, 52, Tribunal de première Instance à juge unique d'Athènes, Hell. Dni, 1982, 42, Cour d'Appel compétente en matière fiscale d'Athènes, arrêt 4479/1972, NoB, 1973, 185 21, Cour d'Appel d'Athènes, 8301/1989, V. Vassilakakis, *La successsion testamentaire en droit international privé*, (Thessaloniki 1994), p. 310.

96 Evrigenis, *Droit comparé et droit internationla privé*, op. cit, p. 670 et s.

97 Tribunal de grande Instance d'Athènes, jugement 18682/1955, N D, 1956, 268 et s.

98 V. sur cette jurisprudence Vrellis, *Les réactions de la doctrine à la création du droit par le juge en droit international privé*, Rapport grec, Travaux de l'Association Henri Capitant, loc. cit, p. 405 et s. p. p. 409-410.

Mais cette conception nationaliste en matière de notion d'ordre public fut progressivement abandonnée[99], tant à cause de la modernisation législative du droit de la famille hellénique qu'en raison de l'augmentation du nombre des litiges internationaux, portés devant les juridictions helléniques. On aperçoit ainsi certains jugements qui essaient de donner une portée universelle à leurs conceptions concernant la notion d'ordre public international. *L'arrêt 653/1972 de l'Aréopage*[100] exprime la tendance précitée. Saisie d'une coutume étrangère qui reconnaissait comme héritier exclusif des biens immobiliers du père, son fils aîné, et de la mère, sa fille aîné, en excluant les autres descendants, la haute juridiction hellénique, a refusé l'application de cette coutume en invoquant l'incompatibilié de celle-ci avec le principe fondamental de l'égalité en matière successorale qui jouit d'une reconnaissance générale tant par le système juridique hellénique que par les ordres juridiques de tous les États.

b) Le droit comparé dans le cadre des méthodes qui déterminent le droit applicable en fonction de sa teneur substantielle.

L'utilisation jurisprudentielle du droit comparé est, en plus, favorisée par les méthodes nouvelles de réglementation que la discipline du droit international privé a développées pour atténuer la neutralité de la règle de conflit[101]. Ces méthodes ne se réalisent pas seulement par le moyen de la création, par le législateur ou par le juge, des règles matérielles de droit international privé régissant *ad'hoc* les rapports juridiques internationaux; elles sont également pratiquées par le biais de règles spécifiques qui ont comme but de permettre au juge d'appliquer, d'une part, les lois de police du for ainsi que les lois respectives étrangères et d'apprécier, d'autre part, les solutions matérielles offertes par les droits potentiellement applicables au litige en cause, en choisissant ensuite le droit qui lui paraît le plus approprié en l'espèce ou bien le plus apte à produire un résultat déterminé. Le juge doit examiner dans les méthodes précitées le contenu et les objec-

---

[99] Sous la pression des critiques de la doctrine l'arrêt 845/1969 de la Cour d'Appel de Thessaloniki, NoB, 1970, 710, affirma que le droit étranger compétent qui ignore l'institution de la dote n'est pas contraire à l'ordre public hellénique. Ainsi le Tribunal de grande Instance de Pirée, (jugement no 2162/ 1959, EEN, 1959, 970) et celui d'Athènes, (jugement 11552/1973, NoB, 1973, p. 1502) se sont contentés de ce que la cause du divorce du droit étranger se rengeait, comme notion générale dans les catégories de causes de divorce du droit hellénique, sans éxiger qu'elle soit complétement semblable à ces dernières. V. Vrellis, *Les réactions, op. et loc. cit.*, p. 411

[100] NoB, 1973, p. 39

[101] V. entre autres, Francescakis, *Lois d'application immédiate et règles de conflit*, Riv. dir. int. priv. proc., 1967, p. 691 et. s; Schwander, *Lois d'application immédiate, Sondernanknüpfungen, IPR Sachnormen und andere Ausnahmen von der gewöhnlichen Anknüpfung im IPR*, 1975; Goldman, *Règles de conflit, règles d'application immédiate et règles matérielles dans l'arbitrage commercial international*, Travaux du Comité Français du D. I. P., 1966-1969, p. 11et s; Papassiopi-Passia, *Règles d'application immédiate et règles matérielles de D. I.P*, (Thessaloniki 1989) (en grec).

tifs socio-politiques de l'ensemble des droits qui présentent un lien avec le litige en cause. Il doit ainsi utiliser largement la méthode comparative.

Malgré la reconnaissance que les codifications récentes du droit international privé ainsi que les Conventions internationales donnent aux méthodes précitées[102], celles-ci ont pour l'instant une place limitée dans le système du droit international privé hellénique. Les règles de ce système restent fidèles à la technique des conflits de lois classiques et ne reconnaissent que dans des cas tout à fait exceptionnels la liberté du juge d'examiner, avant le choix de la loi applicable au litige en cause, la teneur substantielle des droits qui présentent un lien avec ce dernier. Cette première constatation comporte tout de même d'exceptions.

L'article 11 Code civ. hell. fait partie de ces exceptions. Cet article utilise la technique des rattachements alternatifs en reconnaissant au juge la faculté d'appliquer pour l'appréciation de la validité quant à la forme de l'acte juridique, soit le droit de la nationalité de tous les parties, soit le droit du pays où l'acte est intervenu, soit le droit qui régit au fond cet acte. Visant à empêcher l'annulation des actes juridiques pour des raisons qui ont trait à leur validité quant à la forme, la disposition précitée a permis au juge grec d'examiner comparativement trois droits différents dans son oeuvre d'appréciation de la validité quant à la forme d'un acte juridique et d'admettre cette validité tous les fois qu'il constate que l'acte juridique en question a été conclu conformément au conditions de forme prévues par l'un au moins de ces droits[103].

Les tribunaux helléniques examinent, d'autre part, souvent la teneur substantielle des droits concurrents pour soutenir la validité quant au fond des contrats internationaux. Saisi de la validité d'une clause de vente exclusive insérée dans un contrat international entre une société à responsabilité limitée allemande et une société anonyme grecque, le juge des référés d'Athènes[104] à admis la validité de la clause précitée après avoir tenu compte, à coté du droit hellénique reconnu applicable en la matière en vertu de l'art. 25 al. 2 C. c. hell. comme le plus approprié à régir ledit contrat, du droit allemand qui bien que non applicable présentait, néanmoins, des liens de rattachement avec celui-ci.

Les règles des codifications récentes du droit international privé qui visent à permettre au juge d'élaborer des solutions conformes aux intérêts de certaines personnes ou bien de choisir parmi les droits susceptibles

[102] Vassilakakis, *op. et loc. cit.* p. 249 et s. (257).

[103] V. Aréopage, arrêt 126/1972, NoB, 1973, 737; Cour d'Appel d'Athènes, arrêt 3348/1971, NoB, 1973, 334, arrêt no 745/1971, NoB, 1972, 1156; Cour d'Appel du Pirée, arrêt 607/1984, PeirN, 1984, 261, concernant notamment la forme du mandat judiciaire des avocats.

[104] Tribunal de première Instance à juge unique d'Athènes jugement 2280/1970, NoB, 1970, 850 et s, V. également Bernitsas, *Vers une approche méthodologique nouvelle du droit applicable aux obligations contractuelles, (Analyse théorique et jurisprudentielle), Etudes offertes à la mémoire D. Evrigenis*, RHDEur., 1987, p. 314 et s., (343) (en grec).

d'être appliqués au litige, celui qui se présente le plus favorable à une catégorie de personnes déterminée[105], ont impliqué, d'autre part, un renforcement incontestable du rôle du droit comparé dans le processus de la détermination judiciaire du droit applicable[106].

Ces dispositions obligent le juge de faire des larges appréciations comparatives. Celui-ci ne doit pas seulement examiner, *in abstacto*, les droits potentiellement applicables au litige en cause comme il le fait quand il a à appliquer des règles qui utilisent la technique des rattachements alternatifs pour assurer la validité quant à la forme des actes juridiques[107], mais il doit en plus comparer *in concreto* les solutions offertes par ces droits pour trouver laquelle d'entre elles se présente plus favorable à la personne appartenant à la catégorie protégée[108].

Bien que jusqu'à une date très récente les règles de droit international privé précitées n'eussent pas trouver de place dans la législation hellénique, les tribunaux grecs ont confirmé dans la pratique les objectifs poursuivis par ces règles. Pour atteindre ce résultat ils utilisèrent les possibilités offertes par la méthode classique des règles bilatérales des conflits.

C'est, notamment, dans la jurisprudence concernant le droit applicable aux contrats de travail internationaux qu'on apercoit des tentatives des tribunaux d'examiner comparativement les droits concurrents et de trancher le litige conformément aux dispositions internes de la loi qui se présente comme la plus favorable aux intérêts concrets des travailleurs.

En se fondant ainsi sur l'aticle 25 C. Civ. hell., les tribunaux helléniques ont considéré le droit américain comme le droit le plus approprié pour régir un contrat de travail, passé entre une entreprise américaine et un travailleur américain, en vertu duquel ce dernier s'engageait de fournir ses services en Grèce malgré le fait que ce droit n'accordait pas au travailleur en question certaines gratifications prévues par la législation grecque[109]. D'après les motivations de l'arrêt sus-mentionné, le droit américain n'était pas contraire à - public hellénique étant donné que le niveau des salaires globaux prévu par celui-ci était plus élevé par rapport au niveau des salaires grecs y compris les gratifications précitées. Saisis, au contraire, des contrats de travail en vertu desquels des travailleurs grecs s'engageaient de fournir leurs services aux installations des entreprises grecques de construction au Proche Orient, les tribunaux helléniques soumirent lesdits contrats au droit hellénique en considérant ce droit comme le plus approprié pour régir ces

---

[105] V. pour ces règles Grammatikaki-Alexiou, *Règles matérielles du DIP et règles de conflit à caractère matériel, Etudes offertes à la mémoire de D. Evrigenis*, RHDEur, 1987, p. 299 et s. (en grec); Vassilakakis, *op. et loc. cit.*, p. 249 et s. (257).

[106] V. sur le rôle du droit comparé dans le cadre des méthodes précitées von Mehren, op. cit, p. 493 et. s.

[107] V. supra.

[108] V. Vassilakakis, *op. et loc. cit.* p. 265 et s.

[109] V. Cour d'Appel d'Athènes, arrêt 5709/1979, NoB, 1980, 1340; V. également, Aréopage, arrêt 204/1963, NoB, 1964, 1116.

contrats (art. 25 al. 2 C. civ. hell.). [110] Il résulte indirectement de ces arrêts que les tribunaux aboutirent à ce choix, afin de faire bénéficier les travailleurs concernés de certaines droits prévus par le droit du travail. Il s'agit, en pariculier, du droit de travailler huit heures par jour et quarante huit heures par semaine, du droit d'obtenir des majorations de salaire pour heures supplémentaires, etc. Pour atteindre ce but les tribunaux helléniques se virent dans certains cas obligés de déclarer nulles en tant que frauduleusement insérées dans les contrats précités, les clauses qui soumettaient ceux-ci au droit du travail des pays du Proche Orient [11].

C'est, également, par le biais de l'exception d'ordre public que les tribunaux helléniques réussirent d'assurer la protection des intérêts de certaines autres catégories de personnes. En se fondant sur cette clause, ils écartèrent ainsi l'application du droit hindou compétent du fait qu'il ignorait l'institution de la reconnaissance des enfants illégitimes[112] ou bien ils refusèrent l'application du droit roumain compétent, du fait qu'il n'attribuait pas aux membres de la famille d'une victime d'accident de circulation routière une indemnité pour dommages moraux[113].

La Convention de Rome sur le droit applicable aux obligations contractuelles de 1980 qui a été ratifiée par la Grèce en vertu de la loi de 1989, a favorisé, d'autre part, considérablement l'application du droit comparé lors de la détermination par le juge du droit applicable Cette convention[114] a introduit dans l'ordre juridique hellénique une série de dispositions intéressantes qui institutionnalisent le pouvoir du juge de choisir le droit applicable en fonction de la teneur substantielle de celui-ci ainsi qu'en fonction de la protection que ses règles offrent à certaines catégories de personnes. Il s'agit, notamment: d'une part de l'art. 3 par. 3 qui permet au juge d'écarter le droit le plus approprié au contrat désigné en fonction de la technique de la prestation caractéristique décrite dans le par. 2 de cette même article pour appliquer audit contrat un droit tiers présentant des liens plus étroits avec celui-ci; et d'autre part des articles 5 et 6 de la Convention qui reconnaissent la faculté du juge d'examiner comparativement la protection offerte par le droit potentiellement applicable au contrat des consomma-

---

[110] Cour d'Appel d'Athènes, arrêts 7894/1979, NoB, 1979, 1979, 10361/1979, NoB, 1980, 2035, 2000/1980, NoB, 1981,. 1210

[111] Cour d'Appel d'Athènes, arrêt 2000/1980, NoB, 1981, 1210.

[112] Tribunal de grande Instance d'Athènes, jugement 1140/1982, NoB, 1982, 1109.

[113] Cour d'Appel de Thessaloniki, arrêt 21/1988, Armenopoulos, 1988, p. 600.

[114] V. sur cette Convention, Giuliano, op et loc. cit; Gaudemet-Tallon, *Le nouveau droit international privé européen des contrats*, (Commentaire de la Convention CEE no 80/394 sur la loi applicable aux obligations contractuelles, ouverte à la signature à Rome le 19 juin 1980), Rev. trim. dr. eur., 1981, p. 215 et s.; Papassiopi-Passia, *La convention communautaire de Rome de 1980 sur le droit applicable aux obligations contractuelles*, (Thessaloniki 1991), (en grec). V. également en ce qui concerne les dispoditions de la Convention relatives au droit applicable au contrat de travail Grammatikaki-Alexiou, *Le droit applicable au contrat individuel de travail d'après la Convention communautaire de droit international privé de 1980*, (Thessaloniki 1984) (en grec).

teurs et au contrat du travail respectivement, pour choisir le droit qui se présente le plus favorable à chacune des deux catégories des personnes sus-indiquées.

Ces dispositions renforcent incontestablement l'utilisation du droit comparé lors de la détermination par le juge du droit applicable aux contrats internationaux. Cette utilisation est en plus favorisée par les dispositions de la convention qui règlent l'application aux contrats internationaux des lois de police étrangères. Il s'agit notamment de l'article 7 qui permet au juge d'appliquer, parallèlement aux lois de police du for, les lois respectives étrangères qui présentent des liens étroits avec le contrat litigieux, à condition que celles-ci ne soient pas contraires aux lois de police du for.

Pour décider s'il doit donner effet aux lois de police étrangères, le juge ne doit pas seulement examiner la nature et les buts des politiques législatives des États qui ont édicté ces lois, mais il doit en plus procéder à une comparaison et à une articulation des lois en question, avec le droit qui devrait normalemet régir le contrat en cause et éventuellement même avec les règles de police du for.

Il est intéressant de signaler ici que les tribunaux helléniques ont pris en considération les lois de police étrangères, même avant l'entrée en vigueur de la convention précitée dans l'ordre juridique interne. Saisie des contrats de travail conclus entre personnes d'origine grecque et exécutes en l'Iran, la Cour d'Appel d'Athènes[115] appliqua, parallèlement au droit hellénique compétent, les lois de police du lieu de l'éxécution desdits contrats, c'est à dire les lois de police iraniennes, qui préscrivaient, pour des raisons religieuses, comme jour de congé hebdomadaire le Vendredi au lieu du Dimanche.

B. Le recours facultatif au droit comparé lors de l'application des règles à caractère interne.

par Pénélope Agallopoulou

1. L'utilisation jurisprudentielle de la méthode comparative dans le domaine du droit civil.

a) Remarques préliminaires.

Les juristes grecs, notamment, ceux qui s'occupent du droit civil, se servent, pour rédiger des études ou des articles, de la méthode comparative, afin que le sujet de leur recherche soit examiné à fond. Cela est dû au fait que la rédaction, aussi bien du Code civil, que de la loi n° 1329/1983, apportant des modifications fondamentales au Code civil et particulière-

[115] Arrêt, 7894/1979, NoB, 1979, 1979; arrêt, 10361/1979, NoB, 1979, 2035; arrêt, 2012/1980, NoB, 1980, 2035.

ment au droit de la famille, fut précédée d'une large recherche comparative de divers droits; surtout des plus importants de l'Europe continentale, à savoir les droits allemand, suisse et français.

Si notre Code civil était, depuis très longtemps, orienté vers les droits des pays déjà cités, c'est parce qu'il existait entre lesdits pays et la Grèce une ressemblance significative portant sur les conceptions, les moeurs, ainsi que sur les différents problèmes socio-économiques. Or, il va de soi que la formation de notre Code civil fut fondée essentiellement sur les conditions sociales, les conceptions aussi, régnant en Grèce.

Ainsi notre Code civil, appartenant à la famille des codes des droits de l'Europe centrale de provenance germanique, conserve, pour n'avoir pas suivi aveuglément les modèles étrangers, son indépendance tant en ce qui concerne sa forme que le contenu[116].

Relativement aux modèles étrangers servant de sources à notre Code civil, on doit souligner les points suivants:

On a tenu compte surtout du Code civil allemand, car il était basé sur le droit des *Pandectes,* ayant constitué d'une certaine manière, la codification du droit romano-byzantin, comme celui-là était en vigueur même en Grèce. De surcroît, notre Code civil a respecté la division systématique du Code civil allemand en cinq parties, déjà mentionnées.

Puis on rappelle l'utilisation secondaire des Codes suisse (Code civil suisse, ainsi que le Code suisse des obligations), de même que, sporadiquement, d'autres droits[117].

Sur le cas spécial du droit de la famille, on doit indiquer qu'il n'a guère suivi de modèles étrangers pour le traitement de multiples sujets; car s'était déjà formé un droit national contenant néanmoins de fortes conceptions phallocrates, le rendant, même à cette époque, bien rétrograde.

Procédant à une comparaison de notre Code civil à d'autres droits-modèles, on considère qu'il demeure plus simple par rapport au Code civil allemand, tant sur la formulation que sur son élaboration. Notre Code civil s'inspire des dons gréco-latins de clarté, de simplicité et d'élégance d'expression, ce qui est plutôt attribué à l'influence du Code civil français.

Notre Code civil fait état d'une syntaxe telle que ses notions demeurent plus accessibles à un non-juriste, toujours en comparaison avec le Code civil allemand, sans toutefois que l'intense vulgarisation, caractéristique des Codes suisses, soit perceptible.

On reconnaît, en outre, que le Code civil hellénique tend à améliorer sur plusieurs points les modèles étrangers, évitant de se rendre épuisant, tel que le Code civil allemand qui inclut un très exhaustif examen circonstanciel ou lacunaire, tel que le Code civil suisse qui comporte un grand nom-

---

116 V. Gazis, *Notions générales de droit civil*, fasc. 1: *Introduction*, (Athènes 1970), p. 44 (en grec).

117 V. Gazis, *op. cit.*, p. 33.

bre de lacunes législatives[118].

Le Code civil hellénique manifeste, en conséquence, un esprit d'indépendance, par rapport aux codes précités étant donné qu'il a puisé ses sources dans l'expérience grecque.

Il est d'ailleurs à souligner qu'il contient un assez grand nombre de dispositions générales, comme celles se référant à un abus de droit, ou bien à une résolution ou réadaptation des contrats dues à un changement imprévu et sérieux des circonstances[119].

Certes, plusieurs années après la mise en vigueur de notre Code civil, datant du 23 février 1946, quelques modifications paraissaient plus que nécessaires. Elles ont été imposées, d'un côté par l'injonction constitutionnelle de l'article 4 de la Constitution en vigueur, celle de 1975, qui prévoit l'égalité entre hommes et femmes et d'autre coté par les conceptions et l'évolution sociales contemporaines prévalant déjà en Grèce. Ainsi, sans méconnaître la tradition en tant que facteur déterminant de la conscience sociale grecque, on a tenu compte, dans la modification du Code civil, de toutes les conceptions récentes régissant aussi bien la théorie internationale que les législations étrangères.

Par conséquent, avant que la loi n° 1329/1983 qui a modifié le Code civil et plus spécialement le droit de la famille, soit décrétée, on a effectué une étude comparative d'envergure se rapportant à tous ces droits qui, au long des dernières décennies, ont réformé leur propre droit de la famille. En parallèle, on a pris en considération les conceptions grecques, les conditions sociales ainsi que les moeurs dominantes[120]

b) La pratique judiciaire.

Relativement à la forme des décisions des tribunaux grecs, de même qu'à l'emploi par les tribunaux civils des droits étrangers, on se permet les remarques suivantes:

En ce qui concerne la formation de ces décisions, on respecte le modèle français selon lequel on met en avant la règle du droit (proposition majeure), suivie par le réel de l'affaire jugée (proposition mineure).

D'autre part, on doit faire quelques distinctions sur l'emploi des droits étrangers par les décisions des tribunaux civils, à savoir:

aa. Les arrêts de la Cour de Cassation ne se réfèrent pas, à quelques

---

[118] V. Triantafyllopoulos, *L'histoire des projets du Code civil hellénique*, AID, t. D, 1937, fasc. 3, p. 15; Litzéropoulos, *Les premiers dix ans du Code civil,* dans la revue NoB, t. 4, p. 240.

[119] V. Litzéropoulos, *op. cit.*, p. 237.

[120] V. Gazis, *Avant-projet*, et exposé des motifs de la loi concernant l'adaptation des dispositions du Code civil et spécialement du droit de la famille au principe constitutionnel de l'égalité entre hommes et femmes, dans l'édition du Ministère de la Justice grec sur le title "Introduction de l'égalité des droits et des devoirs entre hommes et femmes", Athènes 1979, p. 50 et s.

exceptions près portant sur des arrêts anciens, [121] aux droits étrangers et ne renvoient pas à la doctrine ou à la jurisprudence étrangères.

Il est à remarquer qu'ils ne se rapportent guère à la doctrine ou à la jurisprudence helléniques. A de rares exceptions les conclusions du Procureur Général ou bien du Procureur Général Assistant de la Cour de Cassation contiennent quelques références à la bibliographie étrangère[122].

bb. Au contraire, les décisions des tribunaux de fond (Tribunaux de Première Instance et Cours d'Appel) se réfèrent souvent à une bibliographie et à une jurisprudence étrangères, presque toujours allemandes.

On tire de l'étude d'un grand nombre de décisions des Tribunaux civils de la dernière décennie, publiées dans des revues juridiques, les conclusions suivantes:

On signale de moins en moins de décisions se référant à la doctrine ou à la jurisprudence étrangères. C'est parce qu'on dispose d'une bibliographie hellénique richissime en droit civil, ce qui rend le plus souvent toute autre référence inutile. En plus, la jurisprudence hellénique est extrêmement riche, étant donné que, comme il a été déjà mentionné, notre Code civil est en vigueur depuis environ un demi-siècle.

Quelques références à une bibliographie ou à la jurisprudence étrangères, plutôt allemandes, surviennent dans des cas particuliers, tels que:

aaa. Lorsqu'il s'agit de l'interprétation d'une disposition identique dans un droit étranger [123].

bbb. Lorsqu'il s'agit de l'interprétation d'une disposition semblable à celle comprise dans le droit étranger[124].

ccc. Dans les cas où le juge grec voudrait renforcer les positions soutenues par des juristes grecs[125]. Cela constitue une pratique habituelle,

---

[121] V. Aréopage, arrêts 708/1963 et 443/1964, publiés in Francescakis, Evrigenis, Syméonides, *Droit comparé, op. cit.*, annexe p. 485 et s. où on trouve une citation au droit suisse.

[122] V. Aréopage, arrêt 1381/1983, NoB, 1984, 1193.

[123] V. Cour d'Appel d'Athènes, arrêt 2824/1985, NoB, 1985, 833; Cour d'Appel d'Athènes, arrêt 538/1987, NoB, 1987, 1417.

[124] V. Cour d'Appel d'Athènes, arrêt 8935/1981, NoB, 1983, 221; Cour d'Appel d'Athènes, arrêt 6513/1985, NoB, 1986, 226; 14073/1988, NoB, 1989, 262; Cour d'Appel d'Athènes, arrêt 6077/1994, Hell. Dni, 1995, 391.

[125] Les décisions citées ci-dessous renvoient à la bibliographie et à la jurisprudence allemandes: Cour d'Appel de Crète, arrêt 138/1965, EEN, 1966, 366; Tribunal de première Instance de Thessaloniki, jugement 2530/1967, EEN, 1968, 56; Tribunal de première Instance d' Athènes, jugement 9363/1975, NoB, 1976, 92; Cour d'Appel d'Athènes, arrêt, 6581/1979, NoB, 1979, 1646; Tribunal de première Instance à juge unique d' Athènes, jugement 30/1980, Arménopoulos, 1981, 471; Tribunal de première Instance à juge unique d'Athènes, jugement 957/1984, NoB, 1984, 1055; Cour d'Appel de Patras, arrêt 639/1984, NoB, 1984, 1234; Cour d'Appel d'Athènes, arrêt 1541/1985, NoB, 1985, 1195;Cour d'Appel d'Athènes, arrêt 11518/1986, Hell. Dni, 1988, 916; Cour d' Appel de Larissa, arrêt 594/1987, NoB, 1987, 1646; Cour d'Appel d'Athènes, arrêt 5752/1988, NoB, 1990 p. 454; Cour d' Appel d' Athènes, arrêt 12364/1990, NoB, 1990, 766; Cour d'Appel d'Athènes,

puisque le juge s'efforce de démontrer une connaissance profonde du sujet à examiner.

On devrait, toutefois, préciser que les références à la bibliographie ou la jurisprudence étrangères sont souvent d'importance minime, soit parce qu'elles sont erronées, soit parce qu'elles n'apportent rien à la bibliographie hellénique.

Deux exemples concrets nous semblent assez révélateurs:

Premièrement, en ce qui concerne la détermination du montant de l'indemnité en cas de responsabilité civile, les références étrangères puisent leurs sources uniquement dans la bibliographie allemande, alors qu'on y trouve une homogénéité notable de solutions et de tendances dans tous les droits contemporains développés, voire ceux qui appartiennent aux familles latine et allemande. Il en résulte qu'on pourrait sans encombre mentionner des références tirées de l'ensemble de la bibliographie étrangère.

En deuxième lieu, concernant les conditions de la responsabilité délictueuse, les références sont à la bibliographie allemande; or, le Code civil grec règle la responsabilité par une clause générale, comme d'ailleurs les Codes civils français et suisse, sans adopter le système circonstanciel du Code civil allemand[126].

ddd. Lorsque le juge grec aborde d'autres paramètres du sujet. Un exemple caractéristique est dans le cas où il s'efforce de déterminer la notion de maladie mentale, ainsi que les conditions dans lesquelles cette maladie empêche l'usage de la raison. Le juge grec invoque, pour répondre à ces questions, d'ouvrages psychiatriques qui ne proviennent pas toujours de la bibliographie grecque. C'est alors qu'il faut noter qu'il fait des références concernant toujours la bibliographie allemande relative aux troubles psychiques, sans noter l'existence d'autres ouvrages américains, anglais ou français qui sont aussi et parfois plus approfondies[127].

eee. Lorsque le juge grec tâche de définir les notions inclues dans la loi

---

arrêt 12263/1990, NoB, 1991, 583; Cour d'Appel de Larissa, arrêt 1173/1990, NoB 1991, 937; Cour d'Appel d'Athènes, arrêt 4404/1991, NoB 1991, 1396; Cour d'Appel d'Athènes, arrêt 9560/1991, NoB, 1991, 1407; Cour d'Appel d'Athènes, arrêt 10753/1991, NoB, 1992, 574; Tribunal de première Instance à juge unique d'Athènes, jugement 1641/1993, Hell. Dni, 1995, 893, Citons à titre d'exception les décisions de la Cour d'Appel d'Athènes, arrêt 5746/1987, NoB, 1988, 1231 et de la Cour d'Appel du Pirée, arrêt 38/1995 Hell. Dni, 1995, 1313 qui renvoient à la bibliographie française.

[126] Les décisions citées ci-dessous renvoient à la doctrine et la jurisprudence allemandes: Cour d'Appel de Patras, arrêt 256/1984, NoB, 1984, p. 1567; Cour d'Appel d'Athènes, arrêt 9376/1984, NoB, 1985, 655; Cour d'Appel d'Athènes, arrêt 2073/1987, NoB, 1987, 1066; Cour d'Appel d'Athènes, arrêt 10396/1989, NoB, 1991, 403; Cour d'Appel d'Athènes, arrêt 12263/1990, NoB, 1991, 583. Citons en guise d'exception la décision de la Cour d'Appel d'Athènes, arrêt 1718/1987, NoB, 1988, 932 qui renvoie à la bibliographie française.

[127] V. Cour d'Appel de Patras, arrêt 466/1984, NoB, 1984, 1049; Cour d'Appel d'Athènes, arrêt 10867/1986, NoB, 1987, 560; Cour d'Appel d'Athènes, arrêt 4017/1988, NoB, 1988, 1659.

n° 1329/1983 ayant modifié le Code civil et, notamment, le droit de la famille. Afin que le nouvelles dispositions soient interprétées, le juge grec évoque souvent la doctrine et la jurisprudence allemandes. Sur ce dernier point, on voudrait observer que le droit allemand n a pas servi de modèle unique lors de la modification de notre droit civil et, notamment, des nouvelles dispositions du droit de la famille. En effet, plusieurs autres droits ont servi d'exemple au fur et à mesure qu'ils ont réformé récemment leur droit de la famille. Etant donné que cette dernière branche de droit se présente toujours liée avec le contexte socio-politique et culturel national, le juge grec devrait co-estimer les conditions sociales et les conceptions idéologiques grecques lors de l'interprétation des dispositions précitées[128].

fff. Lorsque le juge grec tâche de définir des notions générales[129]. Comme il a été, déjà, mentionné, le Code civil grec fait preuve d'esprit novateur vis-à-vis de son homologue allemand, car il règle, en vertu des dispositions spéciales, des questions telles que l'abus de droit et le changement imprévisible des circonstances. Etant donné que le Code civil allemand, ne règle point ces sujets, la doctrine et la jurisprudence allemandes s'efforcèrent de combler la lacune en interprétant la disposition générale de la bonne foi. Pour quelle raison, en conséquence, le juge grec devrait-il recourir à la doctrine et à la jurisprudence allemandes précitées, lorsqu'il interprète les dispositions du Code civil hellénique concernant les matières de l'abus du droit ou bien du changement imprévisible des circonstances ?

2. L'application judiciaire du droit comparé dans le domaine du droit administratif.

Jusqu'au moment où commence à fonctionner le Conseil d'Etat, en 1929 (institué par la loi n° 3713/1928), le droit administratif s'occupait uniquement des principes généraux, tout en négligeant l'étude des différends administratifs.

Nous tenons à rappeler que les tribunaux administratifs réguliers, soit les tribunaux de fond, commencent à fonctionner en Grèce en 1962 (fondés

[128] Les décisions mentionnées ci-dessous renvoient à la doctrine et à jurisprudence allemandes: Cour d'Appel de Patras, arrêt 368/1984, NoB, 1984, 1758; Cour d'Appel d'Athènes, arrêt 6974/1985, NoB, 1985, 1435; Cour d'Appel d'Athènes, arrêt 2087/1986, NoB, 1986,. 1242; Cour d'Appel d'Athènes, arrêt 10372/1986, NoB, 1987, 555; Cour d'Appel d'Athènes, arrêt 1311/1987, NoB, 1987, 930; Cour d'Appel de Larissa, arrêt 210/1987, NoB, 1987, 1415; Cour d'Appel d'Athènes, arrêt 5094/1988, Hell. Dni, 1992, 171; Cour d'Appel de Larissa, arrêt 897/1991, NoB, 1992, 92. Comme exceptions, on peut citer les décisions suivantes qui renvoient à la doctrine française: Cour d'Appel d'Athènes, arrêt 15715/1988, NoB, 1990, 80 et Cour d'Appel d'Athènes, arrêt 13484/1988, Hell. Dni, 1992, 189.

[129] V. Cour d'Appel de Thrace, arrêt 211/1984, NoB, 1985, 668 et Cour d'Appel d'Athènes, arrêt 8999/1984, NoB, 1985, 299 qui concernent l'abus de droit. V. aussi Cour d'Appel d'Athènes, arrêt 2718/1992, NoB, 1992, 882 qui concerne le changement imprévu des circonstances.

par le décret législatif n° 3845/1958), premièrement en tant que Cour des Comptes; dès 1976[130], ils se sont transformés en tribunaux administratifs, mais le jugement de la totalité des différends administratifs de fond leur échoit à partir du 11. 06. 1985[131].

Lorsqu'en 1929 le Conseil d'Etat ouvre ses portes, il n'existait aucune infrastructure scientifique pour soutenir ses décisions. Etant donné que le Conseil d'Etat hellénique avait été mis en place sur le modèle de son homologue français, ses premiers membres s'étaient fondés sur l'enseignement du droit français portant sur les différends administratifs[132]. Certes, un effort de longue haleine fut entrepris pour que le droit administratif français soit assimilé dans la réalité grecque.

Or, le Conseil d'Etat agit progressivement de manière constructive. Tout en formant une nouvelle notion de la légalité, il s'est efforcé de protéger le citoyen face à toute sorte d'injustice. Ladite notion a fourni la base du fonctionnement de l'Etat-justice[133].

Il est évident que, pour la formation de cette nouvelle notion de légalité, le Conseil d'Etat grec utilise, de manière créative, les données de la jurisprudence de son homologue français.

Par le mot de "créatif" on entend que les principes généraux, décrétés à travers ses décisions présentent un esprit novateur qui ne copie point la jurisprudence française.

Cela est dû au fait que le Conseil d'Etat a appliqué parallèlement aux institutions déjà existantes dans le droit administratif français, des institutions propres à la Grèce, comme par exemple la consolidation de la permanence des fonctionnaires publics; sans éviter, toutefois, de valoriser les données de la jurisprudence allemande[134].

Il est à noter, relativement aux institutions régissant le droit administratif français, qu'elles ont été interprétées, réformées et adaptées en vue de répondre aux particularités de la réalité juridique grecque.

On se permet, d'autre part, d'indiquer que la principale tâche du Conseil d'Etat, durant l'exercice de la juridiction annulative des actes administratifs, consiste en son pouvoir de contrôle de la compatibilité des préceptes d'une loi avec la Constitution. Il s'agit d'un élément caractéristique du Conseil d'Etat grec qui a, ainsi, des pouvoirs de contrôle de la légalité des

---

130 V. loi n° 505/1976.

131 V. loi n° 1406/1983.

132 V. Stassinopoulos, *op. et loc. cit.* n. 33, p. 3

133 La jurisprudence du Conseil d'Etat, à travers la récente interprétation de la notion de légalité, a imposé la causalité des actes administratifs, l'impossibilité de leur révocation lorsqu'ils ont été créées certaines conséquences en faveur des administrés ainsi que l'exercice de la notion distinctive de l'Administration. Cela signifie une liberté d'action administrative coïncidant avec la protection des droits du citoyen. C'est ainsi que le terme d'"administration honnête" est apparu. V. Stassinopoulos, *op. et loc. cit.*, p. 6 et s; Vegleris, *op. et loc. cit.* n. 33, p. 25 et s.

134 V. Stassinopoulos, *ibidem.*

actes administratifs plus larges par rapport à ceux du Conseil d'Etat français.

Ainsi, en France, un acte administratif ne peut pas être annulé sans avoir aucune inconvénient, en revanche en Grèce, le Conseil d'Etat se réserve de ses droits si lesdits actes ne sont pas conformes à la Constitution. Par conséquent, le Conseil d'Etat grec est investi d'un plus grand pouvoir juridique façe à son homologue français[135].

Disposant d'une si large autorité de contrôle, le Conseil d'Etat influe énormément sur l'évolution de la législation nécessitant de nouvelles dispositions législatives.

Par conséquent, on souligne que le Conseil d'Etat a fait ses premiers pas en se basant sur le modèle du droit administratif français; or, durant ses travaux, il a su développer un droit administratif grec pleinement adapté à la réalité sur place.[136] Ce dernier se dégage, même à travers la bibliographie grecque si large et la jurisprudence relative si riche.

Pour ce qui est des décisions juridiques de cette dernière décennie, il serait utile de retenir ce qui suit:

a. Les décisions du Conseil d'Etat ne font nullement appel à un droit étranger, ni à une quelconque bibliographie, ou jurisprudence étrangères. La doctrine étrangère, et notamment, la doctrine française, est parfois mentionnée dans les conclusions des Conseillers d'Etat.

Quelquefois, la bibliographie étrangère est utilisée pour renforcer l'avis soutenu[137]; quelquefois en revanche, on s'en sert, afin que la répulsion d'un avis soit justifiée [138].

Enfin, parfois au cours des conclusions des Conseillers d'Etat, on effectue un aperçu général en comparant divers droits de sorte que l'avis suivi soit pleinement justifié[139].

b. Les décisions des tribunaux administratifs de fond (Tribunaux de première instance et Cours d'Appel), ne se réfèrent pas aux droits étrangers, ni même à la bibliographie ou la jurisprudence étrangères.

3. Utilisation judiciaire du droit comparé dans les litiges du droit pénal.
Notre Code pénal est plutôt d'influence allemande et italienne[140]. En ce qui

[135] V. Vegleris, *ibid.*, p. 16 et s.

[136] Il a été, toutefois, soutenu que l'influence de la jurisprudence du Conseil d'Etat français sur la jurisprudence de notre Conseil d'Etat c'est ammoindrie, mais n'a jamais cessé d'exister, V. Arnaoutoglou, *op. et loc cit.* p. 577 et s. 584.

[137] V. Conclusions du Conseiller d'Etat B. Botopoulos sur l'arrêt du Conseil d'Etat 3944/1987, NoB, 1988, 610 et s.; Conclusions générales du Conseiller d' Etat S. Nicolaou sur les arrêts du Conseil dÉtat 2786, 2787 et 2788 / 1984, ToS, 1984, 592 et s.

[138] V. Conclusions du Conseiller d'Etat B. Botopoulos sur les arrêts du Conseil d'Etat 686 et 687 / 1987, ToS, 1987, 545 et s.

[139] V. Conclusions du Conseiller d'Etat B. Botopoulos sur l'arrêt du Conseil d'Etat 297/1985, NoB, 1985, 184.

[140] V. Chorafas, Notions générales du droit pénal, Athènes 1962, p. 39.

concerne l'utilisation du droit comparé par les tribunaux pénaux, il faut faire la distinction entre les arrêts rendus par la Cour de Cassation d'une part et le jugements rendus par les tribunaux de fond, d'autre part:

a. Il a été déjà mentionné que les arrêts de la Cour de Cassation ne renvoient pas à la doctrine et à la jurisprudence étrangères. Néanmoins, on trouve des références au droit étranger et notamment à la doctrine et à la jurisprudence allemandes, suisses, italiennes et françaises dans les conclusions des Procureurs Généraux Assistants.

On aperçoit, plus précisément, des références, à la doctrine ou à la jurisprudence étrangères dans les cas suivants:

aa. Lorsqu'il s'agit de l'interprétation d'une disposition qui a sa source d'inspiration dans une disposition identique étrangère[141].

bb. Lorsqu'il s'agit de tentatives du juge de combler les lacunes de la loi[142].

cc. Lorsque le juge essaie de renforcer une opinion ou une solution soutenues par la doctrine grecque[143].

b. Les tribunaux de fond, saisis des affaires du droit pénal, ne se référent qu'à titre exceptionnel au droit étranger. Ils le font, notamment, dans les cas où ils essaient de renforçer les opinions et les constructions théoriques, soutenues par la doctrine grecque[144]. Sur ce point il faut noter le fameux arrêt de la Cour d'Appel d'Athènes no 477/ 1975 qui condamna les responsables de la junte militaire, imposée en Grèce en 1967[145]. Cet arrêt contient un nombre important de références à la doctrine et à la jurisprudence allemandes.

---

141 V. Conclusions du Procureur Général Assistant G. Plagianakos, Aréopage, arrêt, 1438/1983, NoB, 1984, 123; Conclusions du Procureur Général Assistant C. Stamatis, Aréopage, arrêt 18/1986, NoB, 1986, 583.

142 V. Conclusions du Procureur Général Assistant C. Stamatis, Aréopage, arrêt 462/1983, NoB, 1983, 571.

143 V. Conclusions du Procureur Général Assistant C. Stamatis, Aréopage, arrêt 1360/1984, NoB, 1984, 1279; Conclusions du Procureur Général Assistant C. Stamatis, Aéopage, arrêt 7/1985, NoB, 1985, 328; Conclusions du Procureur Général Assistant C. Stamatis, Aréopage, arrêt, 376/1985, NoB, 1985, 696; Conclusions du Procureur Général Assistant C. Stamatis, Aréopage, arrêt, 1029/1985, NoB, 1985, 1460; Conclusions du Procureur Général Assistant S. Stamoulis, Aréopage, arrêt, 725/1986, NoB, 1986, 913.

144 V. Cour d'Appel de Larissa, arrêt, 320/1985, NoB, 1985, 1749; arrêt du Procureur de la Cour d'Appel d'Athènes 45/1990, NoB, 1990, 854; arrêt de la Cour d 'Appel d'Athènes 4054/1992, NoB., 1992, 923.

145 EEN 1975, 940.

HALLDÓR E. SIGURBJÖRNSSON[1]

Application of a Comparative Method by Icelandic Courts

1. INTRODUCTION: LEGAL HISTORY

Comparative law has special meaning in Icelandic law due to its legal history. Iceland is a former colony of Denmark which gained independence in 1944. In many areas, Icelandic and Danish law share similarities due to their historical ties but, to some extent, the law has gained different characteristics in each country even though they were *ab initio* the same. This difference in character is due to translations of varied quality, different interpretations by the courts and different scholarly views; further, the countries are different in nature. Iceland was and is dependent upon natural resources while Denmark is a more modern industrial country; thus, the societies and in turn the law and legal issues tend to be different.

The law has its origin in the legal co-operation between the Nordic countries[2] and this gives comparative methods in Iceland and the other Nordic countries features different from those in many other countries. This co-operation can be traced back as far as the 17th century and takes the form of triennial meetings of the Nordic Countries Lawyers' Conference where a legal topic ripe for unification is discussed and structured. Then, special Nordic committees and special committees in each country are formed to prepare a Nordic draft. This draft, along with a report, is then submitted to the Parliaments of each country. The draft is not final *per se* as each country's Parliament may make changes to the draft as it sees fit. Thus, the Nordic laws enacted as a result of this co-operation are not totally uniform even though they are generally the same. Of note is that some Nordic law may have its origin in other legal systems, such as German law,

[1] c.j., (U. Iceland). M.C.L (Calif. W. Sch. of Law), LL.M. (U. Hamburg), Research Fellow and guest of the Max Planck Institute, Hamburg. The writer is an Icelandic lawyer. This work is partly based on practical experience in Icelandic courts and to some extent on the methods applied by Icelandic judges and legal practitioners.

[2] The Nordic countries are Iceland, Norway, Sweden, Finland and Denmark. Further Aaland, Kalaallit Nunaat (Greenland) and the Faroe Insels form to some extent autonomous legal territories.

U. Drobnig and S. van Erp (eds.), The Use of Comparative Law by Courts, 189–195.

particularly Nordic contract law.[3]

The most extensive Nordic legal co-operation is found in early maritime law, the earlier laws of drafts and cheques, the law of contracts, the law on sale of goods, family law and the law of succession. The climax of this co-operation was reached in the thirties when five Nordic conventions on private international law and international civil procedure law were ratified.[4]

The recent influence of "European law" has led to, and may lead to further, adoption of many new Icelandic laws that have their origin in the *acquis communautaire*. This applies particularly to recent legislative bills on corporation law.

2. Uniform Application?

The issue of uniform application is raised particularly with regard to comparative law. In the Nordic countries, there is no supranational tribunal that is responsible for uniform application and interpretation of the Nordic law which results from Nordic legal cooperation. This causes particular problems regarding Danish law which are rectified to some extent by the methodology explained below:

a) The method used in Iceland to interpret *law of Danish origin* in particular is akin to comparative law. An Icelandic judge, when solving legal problems, is accustomed to reading Nordic, particularly Danish, legal materials in certain fields of law. This is especially evident with legal issues in the law of civil procedure where Danish case law is used as the basis of legal pleadings by skilled litigants in a court of law or when an Icelandic judge *ex officio* investigates the latest Danish case law or legal writings to ascertain his judicial competence and jurisdiction. Sometimes, Icelandic case law may be overlooked in favor of Danish case law which is more easily accessible in the form of printed case reports. This particularly applies to cases of the Icelandic district courts which are available at each local court but are not published or distributed widely. The application of this comparative method is largely based on the extent to which the Danish law in question is similar to or different from Icelandic law. Sometimes the

[3] *Sigurðsson* states that parts of Nordic contract law have their origin in the German BGB (1896): Art. 2 par. 1 of the Icelandic Contracts Act (no. 7/1936) corresponds to Art. 148 of the German BGB; Art. 3 corresponds to Art. 147 BGB; Art. 4 par. 1 corresponds to Art. 150 par. 1 BGB; Art. 4 par. 2 corresponds to Art. 149 BGB; Art. 5 corresponds to Art. 146 BGB and Art. 6 par. 1 corresponds to Art 150 par. 2 BGB. *Páll Sigurðsson*, Um þysku borgaralögbókina [BGB] og um þyskan samningarétt (Reykjavík, 1983) 32 ff.; *idem*, Kringsjá (Reykjavík, 1989) 72 ff.

[4] *Philip, Allan*, The Scandinavian Conventions on Private International Law: Recueil des Cours 96 (1959 I) 241 ff.

judge may base his comparative analysis on old Danish case law or legal writings if the Danish law has recently been changed but Icelandic law has not. The investigation and analysis of the judge is obviously dependent, to a large extent, on whether or not he has an *ex officio* duty to ascertain the law regarding procedural issues.[5]

b) Comparative analysis is obviously much more difficult for the judge when applying law that has its origin in the *legal co-operation of the Nordic countries* (Nordic law). One source of information for the judge is the Nordic Case Reports ("Nordisk domssamling") that have been published since 1958. The Reports only include case law from the Supreme Courts of each country, generally where the applicable law is based on Nordic legal co-operation, i.e. the law regarding obligations (law of contracts and sale of goods etc.) and family law. The Nordic Case Reports also contain case law from other fields, such as tort and intellectual property law. Occasionally, the Reports include cases from administrative law and the law of obligations which is not uniform but is of general interest.[6] Cases concerning maritime law are published in separate reports, i.e. Nordic Case Reports in Maritime Law ("Nordiske domme i Sjøfartsanliggender"). Here the judge is limited in his investigation as the Reports only have a limited number of Nordic cases, including those decided by the Supreme Court of each country but not by the district courts.

With the exception of the judges of the Supreme Court and the District Court in Reykjavik, Icelandic judges do not have access to large legal libraries for further information on Nordic law. Thus, the judges' investigations may sometimes be limited to the arguments and information provided by the litigants. A typical Icelandic judge is able to read Nordic legal scientific writings regarding particular issues in Nordic law. A limitation is that the Finnish language is not similar to the other Nordic languages. This limits the uniform application of Nordic law to the Nordic Case Reports in which Finnish cases have been translated into Swedish and to scholarly writings on Finnish law in languages other than Finnish.

How can the approach of the Icelandic courts be characterized? Snævarr,[7] a leading Icelandic scholar, characterizes the approach taken in Iceland as a "direct" application of Nordic laws and legal writings. That may be an overstatement and a better and more appropriate definition may be comparative methodology of a different kind, i.e. the Nordic Comparative Method. This terminology is different from the comparative method conventionally used by courts, since it is based on the unique nature and origin of Nordic law.

Nordic law is *ab initio* the same but due to changes in the Nordic Draft

---

[5] *Eiríkur Tómasson*, Úlfljótur (1987) 248.

[6] Nordisk domssamling 1 (1958) 1 f.

[7] *Ármann Snævarr,* Almenn lögfræði (Reykjavík,1989) 177.

made by the legislature of each country, through translations, and certain differences in social and legal systems, the law will gain a different character in each country. This different character acquired by Nordic law may require a critical and reasonable comparative analysis[8] before application in Icelandic courts; thus, the application cannot be defined as direct; rather, it is comparative and often indirect.

Regarding Icelandic law of "European-law" origin, the same applies as for Nordic law, i.e. no supranational tribunal exists. The impact of "European law" on the practice of the Icelandic courts remains to be seen but the interpretation and application of Icelandic law of that origin would usually call for more extensive comparative analysis than is generally employed by modern Icelandic courts.

3. The Practice of Icelandic Courts

It is not often that Icelandic courts do refer directly to the comparative method, for either Nordic law or law from other countries. Icelandic courts rarely refer directly to decisions by Icelandic or Nordic courts or to particular legal writings or legal theories of Icelandic or Nordic writers.[9] In most cases, the use of comparative methods by Icelandic courts has to be assumed, either from the pleadings of the litigants or from particular statements made by courts in their holdings and whether or not the legal issues involve Nordic law or perhaps "European law".

An important issue is that foreign law needs to be proven by the parties according to Art. 44 par. 2 of the Civil Procedure Act (no. 91/1991) and thus the judge will usually not *ex officio* investigate or apply foreign law.[10] On the other hand, an Icelandic judge's use of the comparative method does not seem to be limited by this provision and the judge appears to be free to use this legal technique in reaching his conclusion as he finds appropriate. Further, it may be argued that the judge is not normally limited by the pleadings of the parties or burden-of-proof principles regarding his investigation and application of the comparative method when analyzing the content and application of a rule of law. In practice, however, the judge may limit his investigations due to lack of time or resources, or based on common sense. As stated above (*supra* 2), the comparative method is bound to be different for Danish or Nordic law compared with foreign law in general. The following factors should be considered when comparative law is used by Icelandic courts:

(1) When issues of a procedural nature appear, comparative analysis with similar Danish law comes strongly into consideration – this is probably

---

[8] *Zweigert und Kötz*, Einführung in die Rechtsvergleichung I (1971) 47 f.

[9] *Ármann Snævarr* (n. 7) 275.

[10] *Eiríkur Tómasson* (n. 5) 248.

the field of law where the comparative method is most frequently applied;

(2) When Nordic law is considered, the Nordic Comparative Method should be applied by the judge;

(3) The judge, through his education, should be aware of similar laws in the other Nordic countries;

(4) The judge should be aware that Icelandic law is of foreign origin, particularly that law which has its origin in the *acquis communautaire*.[11]

In very few Icelandic cases do the courts directly employ some kind of comparative analysis. In one case, the Supreme Court[12] referred to an Icelandic indictment being served according to practice of Scottish law in Scotland but the manner of service was also deemed appropriate according to Icelandic laws.

In another Supreme Court[13] case regarding a foreign taxation decree that was sought to be enforced in Iceland, the District Court stated in its statement that accompanied the Supreme Court judgment that, according to views set forth by Nordic scholars and as evidenced by practice, such claims are not enforced. Of particular note is that the judge cited a Nordic Lawyers' Conference Report and the legal writing of a Norwegian scholar. In both instances, the courts compared the foreign laws and theories in question and considered the effect of application in Icelandic law. In neither case was the application "direct"; rather it was comparative, critical and indirect. Several more cases can be found, often involving private international law where the issue of application of comparative law arises frequently.[14]

A case decided by the Icelandic Supreme Court[15] in 1984 may serve as an illustration of the problems involved in using Nordic law, in this instance one of the Nordic Conventions on private international law. The case involved an adoption license issued by Icelandic authorities based on the applicant's domicile in Iceland according to Art. 1[illegible] of the Nordic Convention on Marriage, Adoption and Legal Guardianship of 6 February 1931. The applicant was in fact the step-father of the child in question who had been studying in Sweden and had filled out a Common Nordic Transportation Notification before moving from Iceland because he intended to move his legal domicile to Sweden. The Supreme Court interpreted the facts of the case to indicate a change of domicile in the meaning of private interna-

---

[11] A fifth instance is when Icelandic private international law determines that foreign law should be applied. This issue is not covered in this paper.

[12] Supreme Court 20 May 1964, no. 84/1964, H.1964.42[illegible] (pp. 429 and 460 (District Court) of the Judgment). "H" stands for "Hæstiréttur" (the Icelandic Supreme Court).

[13] Supreme Court 13 November 1967, no. 85/1967, H.1967.1011 pp. 1012 f. (District Court).

[14] *Davíð Þór Björgvinsson*, Tímarit lögfræðinga (1990) 206.

[15] Supreme Court 21 December 1984, no. 25/1983, H.1984.1444.

tional law, mainly based on arguments derived from legal principles regarding changes of legal domicile. Legal domicile is based on laws of public law origin and is not the same as a domicile in the meaning of private international law. The Court seems to have ignored the Nordic domicile concept which is largely based on the Norwegian and Danish concepts of domicile.[16] According to the Nordic domicile concept, people who study abroad for a number of years do not lose their original domicile provided there are no additional facts to affect that conclusion. The advocates did not plead, nor did the District Court or the Supreme Court refer to or compare, the legal theories or case law of the other Nordic countries regarding this issue.

This approach taken by the Icelandic courts violates the Nordic case law and the theoretical and scholarly views of the other Nordic countries.[17] This case is a good illustration of the problems that occur within the Nordic legal system due to the lack of uniform methods of application of Nordic law. This demonstrates a need either for stricter use of methods of comparative law, i.e. the Nordic Comparative Method, or for the establishment of a supranational tribunal *de lege ferenda* to avoid miscarriages of justice.

With "European law", the use of the comparative method may call for a new approach from Icelandic judges and, in turn, all legal practitioners, leading to the more extensive application of comparative law than is seen in modern Icelandic law at present. This particularly applies to law that has its origin in international conventions of which Iceland is a member state, such as the Lugano Convention on Jurisdiction and the Enforcement of Judgments in Civil and Commercial Matters of 16 September 1988 which may be ratified by Iceland in 1994[18] (the Convention was incorporated by Act

[16] *Philip, Allan*, Dansk international privat- og procesret (ed. 3, 1976) 162 f.

[17] *Þorgeir Örlygsson*, Tímarit lögfræðinga (1984) 221 ff.

[18] *Stefánsson* has advocated the uniform interpretation of the Lugano Convention and suggests several solutions, such as establishing a special institution that interprets the Convention in a manner binding for the Member States; a special party would be appointed to give advice regarding the interpretation of the Convention; the structure would be similar to that of the European Convention on Human Rights which allows for pleading of individuals; a special committee would be established to interpret the Convention; the Member States would impose upon their courts a duty of uniform interpretation; and then, finally, arbitration would be possible. The solution set forth in the Lugano Convention is found in a supplementary Protocol no. 2, art. 1 to the Convention. It states that the judges of each Member State "shall" take into consideration the main principles found in the case law of the other Member States. This is further outlined in art. 2 and 3 of Protocol no. 2 that set forth principles regarding establishment of an information and co-operation institute. In Protocol no. 2 of the Brussels Convention a similar statement appears which refers to the knowledge of the contracting parties of the case law of the EC Court and of the close connection between these two Conventions regarding the interpretation of the Brussels Convention. *Stefánsson* finds Protocol no. 2, art. 1 to the Lugano Convention to have value and finds generally that the intention of the Member States is that the Conventions should be interpreted in the same or a similar manner. *Stefán Már Stefánsson*, Tímarit lögfræðinga (1993) 33 ff.

no. 68/1995). For Nordic law also, either judges should be required to use an intensive comparative method or a supranational tribunal is required *de lege ferenda* to secure the uniform application of "European private law".

RENÉE SANILEVICI*

The Use of Comparative Law by Israeli Courts**

I. INTRODUCTION

One of the most important functions of comparative law is to aid legislation and law reform. This is especially true for western legal systems, for which comparative law constitutes an indispensable working tool of the legislature[1]. The Israeli legislature has made extensive use of comparative law in preparing new statutes and in reforming existing legislation[2].

The courts have been slower to liberate themselves from nationalism, and have generally remained reluctant to turn to foreign law. What is called *"horror alieni juris"* continues to exist even when foreign law is applicable according to conflict-of-law rules[3].

This report concerns the stage of the application of the law. But the use of comparative law by the courts is closely linked to the problem of its use in the preparatory work of legislation. When an institution, a provision, or their underlying concept are based upon or inspired by foreign legal sources, those sources may influence the application of the respective

* Senior Research Fellow, The Harry and Michael Sacher Institute for Legislative Research and Comparative Law, The Hebrew University of Jerusalem.

** *Abbreviations*:

L.S.I . – Laws of the State of Israel

P.D. – Piskei Din (Judgments)

Isr. L. Rev. – Israel Law Review

P.G. – Palestine Gazette.

[1] B. Aubin, "Die Rechtsvergleichende Interpretation Autonom Internen Rechts in der Deutschen Rechtsprechung," 34 *Rabels Zeitschrift fuer Auslaendischen und Internationlen Privatrecht* (1970) 458; H. Doelle, "Rechtsdogmatik und Rechtsvergleichung," 34 *Rabels Zeitschrift* (1970) 403; L. Constantinesco, *Traité de Droit Comparé, La Methode Comparative* (Paris, 1974, vol II) 289–370; K. Zweigert and H. Koetz, *An Introduction to Comparative Law,* (1989, vol I) 13.

[2] G. Tedeschi and I. England, "Les problèmes de la codification a la lumière des expériences et situations actuelles," *Israeli Reports to the VI International Congress of Comparative Law (Jerusalem 1962) 1*; U. Yadin. "The Use of Comparative Law by the Legislator," *Israeli Reports to the XI International Congress of Comparative Law* (Jerusalem, 1982) 10.

[3] E. Kramer, "Topik and Rechtsvergleichung," 33 *Rabels Zeitschrift fuer Ausländisches und Internationales Privatrecht* (1969) 1.

U. Drobnig and S. van Erp (eds.), The Use of Comparative Law by Courts, 197–221.

provisions by the courts.

The geographical area of the systems of law the courts refer to, the frequency of the references, and their significance in the creative development of Israeli law are in large measure dependent on the use of comparative law in all the stages of the adoption of statutes.

The extent of the use of comparative law by the courts in Israel, its purpose and its results are a consequence of the special historical conditions that accompanied the creation and development of Israeli law, as we intend to show in this report.

We think it necessary to present a brief account of these special historical conditions, as well as a short description of the character of the existing system of Israeli law.

During the British Mandate 1922–1948, in conformity with art. 46 of the Palestine Order in Council[4], the law in force in Palestine on the 1 of November, 1914 as well as later Ottoman laws remained in force. This provision preserved the Ottoman civil code – the Mejelle – composed of Moslem law, as well as other Turkish statutes, which were influenced by European codification, especially by the French Civil Code. Besides material law provisions, the Mejelle contained evidence and procedural rules[5].

The existing Ottoman law was gradually replaced by English common law. In some fields the administration of the British Mandate enacted local statutes called Ordinances which established rules similar to those of English law. The changes in the legal system occurred mainly by way of absorption of English common law through the courts, manned primarily by English judges, which interpreted the local law in the light of common law rules and principles. The infusion of English law was of such dimensions that, in Israeli legal literature, authors refer to it as "Anglicization" of the law of the Land (Eretz) Israel[6].

With the establishment of the state of Israel, art. 11 of the Law and Administration Ordinance, 1948[7], the existing law remained in force "insofar as there is nothing therein repugnant to this Ordinance or to other laws which may be enacted by or on behalf of the Provisional Council of State and subject to such modifications as may result from the establishment of the State and its authorities".

However, the existing law was insufficient to serve as the basis for the entire area of private law, and reliance upon foreign sources was inevitable. Besides, local law itself was based, to a great extent, on foreign sources.

---

[4] Laws of Palestine, vol III, p. 2569.

[5] For details see D. Friedman, *The Effect of Foreign Law on the Law of Israel,* (Jerusalem,1975).

[6] D. Friedman. *supra* n. 5, at p. 21; A.M. Rabello "The Harmonization of Common and Civil Law in the Private Law of the State of Israel" *Israeli Reports to the XIII Congress of Comparative Law* (Jerusalem, 1990) 2.

[7] 1 L.S.I. 7.

In the first years of independence, the law of the state of Israel continued to be connected to the common law by art. 46 of the Palestine Order in Council which provided application of the principles of common law and equity in cases of lacunae in the local law. This connection was gradually severed by provisions of some of the new statutes, which established that "in matters dealt with by the law, art. 46 no longer applies."

The formal statutory link was severed by the abrogation of art. 46 by the Foundations of Law 1980[8].

We should mention that, even before this link was formally severed, the judges displayed a tendency toward independence in the application of the existing law, restricting the application of English law and the remaining Ottoman law.

The date of abrogation of art. 46 (or other, prior dates of abrogation of its applicability by newly enacted statutes, each in its own field) is significant for this report, because, until that date, English common law remained partially the law in force, not foreign law. Thus, not all references in court decisions to English law can rightly be viewed as use of comparative law.

During the 1960s, the Ministry of Justice began a broad, long-term programme of piecemeal legislation regulating various fields of private law. The new legislation was adopted in stages. A great number of statutes in different branches of private law have since been enacted[9].

All these new statutes, which marked the development of the independent system of Israeli law, were planned and prepared by comparative research work.

In addition to general factors in the development of the use of comparative law in the preparation of new legislation or in law reform, there are also some special causes, determined by the historical conditions of the development of the Israeli legal system. These special conditions account, not only for the great extent of the use of comparative law in the preparation of new statutes, but also for its use in the application of new legal provisions by Israeli courts.

The newly enacted legislation has various sources of inspiration – conti-

---

[8] 34 L.S.I. 181.

[9] Those will be: Capacity and Guardianship Law, 1962, 16 L.S.I. 106; Succession Law, 1965, 19 L.S.I. 58; Agency Law, 1965, 19 L.5.1. 231; Bailees Law, 1967, 21 L.S.I. 49; Guarantee Law, 1967, 21 L.S.I. 41; Pledges Law, 1967, 21 L.5.1. 44; Gift Law, 1968, 22 L.S.I 113; Sale Law, 1968, 22 L.5.1. 107; Land Law, 1969, 23 L.S.I. 283; Transfer of Obligations Law, 1969, 23 L.S.I. 277; Contracts (Remedies for Breach of Contract) Law, 1970, 25 L.S.I. 11; Movable Property Law, 1971, 25 L.S.I. 175; Hire and Loan Law, 1971, 25 L.S.I. 152; Contracts (General Part) Law, 1973, 27 L.S.I. 117; Restoration of Lost Property Law, 1973, 27 L.S.I. 187; Spouses (Property Relations) Law, 1973, 27 L.S.I. 313; Sale (Housing) Law. 1973, 27 L.S.I. 213; Contract for Services Law 1974, 28 L.S.I. 115; Trust Law, 1979, 33 L.S.I. 154; Unjust Enrichment Law, 1979, 33 L.S.I. 44; Adoption of Children Law, 1981, 35 L.S.I. 3M; Insurance Contract Law, 1981, 35 L.S.I. 91; and Standard Contracts Law, 1982, 37 L.S.I. 6.

nental codes, ULIS, English law, Jewish law and Israeli case law[10].

In 1980, the Ministry of Justice initiated the preparation of a new code of Israeli private law by unification and harmonization of the existing laws, taking into account developments in the interpretation of their provisions by the courts, as well as changes possibly needed. The adoption of the principle of codification of private law is based on the continental civil codes. The influence of continental law is felt in the systematization of the various institutions of private law and partly in the content of the regulation.

In his report to the eleventh Congress of Comparative Law, U. Yadin, one of the initiators of the new Israeli legislation, mentions two reasons for the use of comparative law by the Israeli legislature: a) When Israel embarked on its law reform, there was no coherent system of law in force and no continuous tradition. Thus, the legislature was more open to consider other systems of law. b) Due to massive immigration, the majority of Israel's first lawyers, acting as advocates, judges, law teachers and members of parliament, had trained abroad and they brought with them their legal education and thinking (both continental and common law). During the Mandate, even those born in the country had to study law abroad and most of them studied in England or other common-law countries. All these people, coming from different legal backgrounds, could only work together by making comparisons[11].

In his essay on the system of Israeli law, "The Tradition and Culture of the Israeli Legal System", Justice A. Barak described the existing law in Israel as an independent system of law of "mixed jurisdiction", which has developed under the influence of common law and continental law and which is part of the western legal culture. Israeli law is also influenced by the Jewish cultural heritage, but Jewish religious law, which has remained in force in matters of marriage and divorce, draws its legally binding force from the statutes of the secular state of Israel.

Analysing these influences and the existing differences from the systems of law from the two aforementioned modern families of law, Barak reaches the conclusion that, due to its specific characteristics, the Israeli legal system is a separate, *sui generis* system of law, which belongs neither to the common-law or continental families of law, nor to the culture of Jewish law. Because every system of law of ''mixed jurisdiction", has its own historically-determined, specific traits, we cannot speak of a family of mixed systems of law[12].

---

[10] D. Friedman, *supra* n. 5, at p. 195.

[11] U. Yadin. *supra* n. 2 at pp.11–12.

[12] A. Barak, The Tradition and Culture of the Israeli Legal System, *European Legal Traditions and Israel,* (Jerusalem, 1994) 484; See also I. Englard, "The Law of Torts in Israel: The Problems of Common Law Codification in a Mixed Legal System" 22 *American Journal Of Comparative Law* (1974) 302; U. Yadin From Piecemeal Legislation to a

Usually, judges use comparative law considerations in order to support the interpretation given by them to the provisions applicable in the case before them, and particularly to support a new solution in the direction of the development of law.

Due to the historical conditions of the creation and development of the Israeli legal system, comparison with foreign law also represents a comparison between existing law and past law. What looks like a comparison, or what we might call a "comparison of different systems of law in space", is at times actually a comparison "in time" of successive laws in force in Palestine and the State of Israel. Such comparisons made by judges are aimed at an independent interpretation of Israeli law, by stressing the differences from the foreign law that was in force in Palestine, that remained in force in the first years of the State, or that was the source of the new legislation. In the following, by analysing court decisions in the different fields of private law motivated by comparative law, we will distinguish between categories of comparative law references in which foreign law is invoked in a positive way, in order to give additional support to the opinion of the judge concerning the interpretation of Israeli law, and references used in a negative way, in order to stress the differences between foreign law and Israeli law.

In preparing this report, we have scanned the published decisions of the Supreme Court for the last twenty years, and we have selected those to be presented only from decisions in civil appeals.

Because we have restricted our report to the field of private law, we only mention that, compared with legislative activity in the field of private law, legislative activity in public law has been rather scarce, and public law remains primarily the product of judicial law making by the Supreme Court. In carrying out the task of filling in gaps and developing law, the judiciary has made relatively frequent use of the tool of comparative law in the field of public law. The enacted Basic Laws which, at this stage, represent the fundamental principles of an Israeli constitution in the making, were also influenced by foreign legal sources.

II. Court decisions concerning the relationship between Israeli law and Jewish law

A special problem which the Supreme Court had to solve in using comparative law, concerned the relationship between Israeli law and Jewish law. On one hand, as already mentioned, Jewish law is one of the sources that has influenced the Israeli legislature. On the other hand, The Foundations of Law, 1980, mentions Jewish tradition, providing in Article 1 that:

Modern Code, The Israeli Experience," *In Memoriam* Uri Yadin (Jerusalem, 1990, vol II) 363.

"Where the court, faced with a legal question requiring decision, finds no answer to it in statute law or case-law or by analogy, it shall decide in the light of the principles of freedom, justice, equity and peace of Israel's heritage". In the interpretation of this provision and its application, the Supreme Court has expressed diverging opinions.

One opinion holds that Jewish law is the most important source to which the judge has recourse in interpreting Israeli law and in completing *lacunae.* The other opinion, held by the majority of judges of the Supreme Court, states that this provision establishes neither a general obligation of the judge to resort to Jewish law in the interpretation of Israeli law, nor any preference by the legislature for Jewish law when using comparative law in the process of establishing the proper law. According to this opinion, the Israeli legislature has not integrated Jewish legal rules but only ideas as a source of influence in the interpretation of Israeli law.

Justice Barak writes in his book *Interpretation in Law* that the principles mentioned in the Foundations of Law, 1980, are universal principles to which the judge has to give the meaning they have in Jewish tradition[13].

The controversy finds its expression in a number of decisions, primarily in the reasons for the decision. Since the discussion is ongoing in the decisions of the Supreme Court, and because it represents a characteristic problem of Israeli law, we chose to present the decisions, not according to their respective branches of law, but in a separate section.

In the Supreme Court's decision in *Bank Kupat Haam v. Handeles*[14], concerning the rules which apply to lost objects, the judges make ample references to comparative law in interpreting the provision of the Israeli Restoration of Lost Property Law, 1973, including the applicability of Jewish law. In the discussed case, a person found a bundle of debentures on the floor of the bank's vault. The finder inquired at the bank as to whom they belonged. As the owner was not found within the four-month period provided by Israeli law, the finder claimed a declaratory judgment recognizing his ownership of the debentures. The bank also claimed ownership because the debentures were found on its premises. The discussion focused on the question of whether the right belongs to the owner of the premises or to the finder.

Justice Elon, who also quoted American and English solutions, was of the opinion that the expression in art. 3 of the Restoration of Lost Property Law, 1973, that "a person who finds lost property in another person's domain" must be read according to Jewish law rules, which provide that lost objects belong to the first possessor.

Justice Barak was of the opinion that the lost debentures belonged to the bank as owner of the premises. He arrived at this conclusion by interpreting the law according to the purpose of its provisions, which is to enable

---

[13] A. Barak, *Interpretation in Law*, (Jerusalem, 1992, vol I in Hebrew) 527.

[14] (1980) 34(iii) P.D. 57.

the owner, as far as possible, to retrieve his lost property. This is more likely to happen when the lost object goes to the owner of the place where it was lost.

He criticizes the reference to Jewish law for the interpretation of the above mentioned expression as unnecessary, and he points out that:

a) Reference to Jewish law for interpreting Israeli law is not obligatory but only permitted;
b) Reference to Jewish tradition is meant to apply not to the norms of Jewish law, but to the treasure of its legal thinking to which we are to turn as a source of inspiration. The reference is to Jewish heritage in its cultural significance, not in its normative significance. We are permitted to look to Jewish law not in order to find rules but only as a source of inspiration for our rules;
c) In this case, the judge is allowed to refer to Jewish law in order to discern the meaning of the mentioned words, or as one of the possible solutions from which he may choose the appropriate law, and not as the end of the process. This creative choice has to be made in conformity with existing rules of interpretation, among which interpretation according to the purpose of the law is the most important.

The third judge sitting in the case, Justice Landau, then president of the Supreme Court, concurred with the opinion of Justice Barak that Israeli law has to be interpreted, first of all, in light of the aim of its own provisions. He also stressed that, in this instance, Jewish law could not serve as a guide and source of inspiration in the interpretation of Israeli law because its basic premises differ from the aims of the Israeli statute.

The *Dicker v. Moch* case[15], in which the Supreme Court used comparative law considerations, concerns public order. It refers to an agreement between business partners limiting a quitting partner from carrying on an activity similar to that of the partnership. One of the partners quit the partnership, but, as he continued the same activity on his own, the other partners sued him for damages for violation of the agreement. The defendant's plea, that the agreement was void according to art. 30 of the Contracts (General Part) Law, 1973, as it violated public order, was rejected by the Supreme Court.

Justice I. Kahan, reiterating the considerations of Justice Shamgar in a prior decision concerning public order[16], also emphasized that the determination of a concept like public order is the result of unique independent analysis, characteristic to every system of law, and that the concept of public order is permanently enriched by court decisions on various cases. At the same time, he was of the opinion that, in the case before the court, reference must first be made to decisions of common-law courts concerning the voidance of agreements limiting the freedom of occupation. He also

---

[15] (1978) 32(ii) P.D. 141.

[16] See n. 19 *infra*.

mentioned that the principles adopted in the problem of limitation of freedom of occupation are similar in common law and in continental law and that they are based on striking a balance between the binding force of the contract and the freedom of occupation.

Justice Elon expressed a different opinion on comparative law considerations concerning the concept of public order. He was of the opinion that, in this matter, we must turn to the Jewish legal tradition.

The third judge sitting in the case – Justice Asher – concurred with the opinion of Justice Elon that we cannot give a global theoretical answer to the question of what is contrary to public order, and that the answer depends on the circumstances of the case. But he dissented from the opinion of Justice Elon that there is only one source of inspiration for the judge, even if this source is very important from the moral point of view. The courts have to determine what is contrary to public order in accordance with the economic, cultural and ideological development of a civilized enlightened society. The judge must be aware that something which was just in the past may not necessarily be so in the present.

In a further hearing of *Koenig v. Cohen*[17], the legal problem under discussion was the interpretation of art. 25 of the Succession Law, 1965, which provides expressly that a will is valid even if there are defects in the signature, date and declarations of the witnesses. In this case, the question was whether a note, written by the deceased before committing suicide, that was not signed and bore no date, and by which she disinherited her husband, could be considered an enforceable will. Based on the interpretation of the provisions of art. 25, a majority of three judges stated that a note with no signature, no date, and unwitnessed cannot be considered an enforceable will.

In the minority opinion, the other two judges argued that the note had to be considered as the will of the deceased because of the circumstances in which the note had been written (the authenticity of the handwriting was not contested). Each of the two judges – Justice Elon and Justice Barak – who dissented from the solution of the majority, stated a different reason for his interpretation of the provisions of the Israeli law of succession. Both of them used comparative law in support of their reasons and the discussion between them focused on the more general question concerning the role of the Jewish heritage in completing *lacunae* and interpreting Israeli law.

Justice Elon based his interpretation on Jewish law, while Justice Barak referred to English and American scholars who express the liberal opinion that, in rare cases, it would be appropriate to admit the proof of an unsigned will. He considered the case under discussion to be one of these rare cases. He also quoted the opinion of an English scholar that an unsigned will might cause suspicions but not the nullity of the will. Justice Barak

---

[17] (1982) 36 (iii) P.D. 701, at p. 725.

argued that the Israeli legislature adopted a liberal view and rejected the more formal solutions adopted in other systems of law (the French, German, Swiss, and Italian codes) as the Succession Law generally admits the validity of a will despite its defects.

In contesting the opinion expressed by Justice Elon in this and other decisions, that, in interpreting the law, the judge must generally turn to Jewish tradition, he stressed two points: a) the text of the Foundations of Law, 1980, refers the judge to a number of general principles, not to all the theological and religious principles of Jewish law and b) the judge is bound to resort to these principles only in the second stage of filling in a *lacunae,* after having established that it is not possible to fill the *lacunae* by analogy to other provisions of Israeli law.

The comparative-law considerations of the presented decisions are of general importance for understanding the rules of interpretation of Israeli law and they may also give the reader some insight into the struggle between secular law and religious law, as reflected in the activity of the judiciary.

III. General Questions

In a number of decisions with comparative law references, the Supreme Court has discussed the meaning of the concept of public order. Besides the decision quoted above in the *Dicker v. Moch* case of the partnership agreement[18], we shall present two other decisions of the Supreme Court on the interpretation of "public order".

One decision is in connection with an agreement between divorced parents concerning the father's obligation for his child's maintenance.

In *X. v. Y.*[19], there was an agreement between the spouses concerning the support the father was to pay for his child (300 IsL.). Under the agreement, the mother of the child promised to return all the money paid as child support if she introduced any judicial claim to change the amount. When the mother introduced an action against the father of the child, claiming support according to the needs of the child, the father counter-claimed for restitution of the money already paid, according to the agreement. The mother pleaded nullity of the agreement by violation of public order. The Supreme Court admitted that the agreement was void but for another reason.

In discussing the concept of public order Justice Shamgar, President of the Supreme Court, compared "ordre publique" according to French law and English law and reached the conclusion that, although French law is more severe in this field (maintenance of children), it shares common

[18] *Supra* n. 15.
[19] (1977) 31(iii) P.D. 85.

ground with English law in that the courts of both countries will not recognize the validity of such an agreement when it violates social values and is "injurious to society". He also stressed that, even if Israeli law has historical connections with the mentioned systems (the agreement was made prior to the enactment of the Contracts (General Part) Law, 1973, and the consequences of a violation of "ordre publique" were therefore regulated by art. 64(1) of the Ottoman Civil Procedure, of French influence), public order is specific to every system of law depending on the actual circumstances. Quoting Lord Denning's statement that "public order is a wild horse", he preferred to nullify the agreement because it violated the principle of the best interest of the child.

A more recent decision in which comparative law was used in a discussion of the concept of public order[20] concerned the validity of the provision of a will by which the testator denied the right of one of her daughters to the inheritance, should she contest the will.

The Supreme Court rejected the plea of nullity of this provision and disinherited the daughter who had contested the will. Each of the three judges sitting in the case, based the decision on different reasons and employed comparative law in support of their conclusions.

Justice Maltz, who delivered the decision, was of the opinion that although the Succession Law, 1965, does not mention public order as a cause of nullity of a will, the principle may be applied to wills, but the criteria for evaluating a provision as contrary to public order are different from those used for contracts.

In giving a different reason for the decision, Justice Barak entered into details concerning the concept of public order and its effects. He stressed that public order is a general principle of Israeli law that applies by force of art. 61(b) of the Contracts (General Part) Law, 1973, to all legal acts, including wills. In agreeing with Justice Maltz that the criteria can be different in regard to different legal acts, he presented an extensive survey of French, English and American law. In analysing the reasons that can support the recognition of the validity of a provision of a will that imposes a condition against an attack on the will, he noted: the principle of honoring the intention of the testator and protecting the interest that the testator wanted to defend, the public interest is to encourage the conflicting parties to try to settle the conflict outside the court, and the defence of the family cell. He also mentioned a set of arguments that could motivate the nullity of such a condition. In concluding the discussion for and against the validity of such a condition, he presented three possible solutions to the conflict among various principles, values and interests adopted in different systems of law: unlimited recognition of a condition denying the right to inherit of the heir who contests the will, its voidance, and a restricted admission of its validity, depending on the circumstances. From these possible solutions,

---

[20] Angelman v. Klein (1986) 43(i) P.D. 772.

he chose the third. In explaining his choice he wrote:

> "Comparative law does not oblige us. This is the rule. This rule surely applies when the problem in discussion is 'public order' which reflects the national character of the system. But comparative law is a mirror through which the interpreter is able to look more deeply into his own system. As a result of this double look – at us from inside and to us from outside – I come to the conclusion that the proper solution is the middle one"[21]

Justice Bejski, agreeing with the solution, also added comparative law considerations, showing that the problem under discussion is controversial also in other systems of law, and he went into some detail, concerning the opinions expressed in English and American law. He described the evolution of the English solution from general recognition of the validity of provision denying the right of an heir who contests the will, toward a more restricted solution in which such a condition will not be enforced against the heir who contests the will in good faith and for reasonable cause. Adopting this distinction as a proper one, Justice Bejski explained the decision to reject the plea of nullity of the provision of the will by the fact that the heir who had contested the will did not act in good faith.

I have presented this decision in great detail because it employs comparative law considerations on a larger scale and it illustrates the way the Supreme Court of Israel uses comparative law in establishing the law, as well as the conceptions of the judges on the significance of reference to foreign law.

Another general question, in which the Supreme Court invoked comparative law in support of its interpretation, concerns the effects of *res judicata.*

In *Alrarbia v. The Custodian of Absentee Property*[22], the problem was whether *res judicata* functions in cases in which one party to the process is guilty of fraud. The Supreme Court stated that, in a case of a conflict between *res judicata* and equity and justice, *res judicata* must withdraw. In support of this conclusion, the Supreme Court referred not only to Israeli precedents but also to English and American court decisions, as well as to the opinions of English and American scholars.

In *The Development Authority v. Ezam*[23] the question to be answered was similar to the *res judicata* rule, namely whether the decision of an arbitrator can be invoked against a person who has not participated in the arbitration process. The Supreme Court admitted the possibility of pleading *res judicata* against a person who has interests close to those of the parties to the process (legal proximity). The decision was based on Israeli prece-

---

21 *Ibid.*, at p. 785.
22 (1991) 45(iv) P.D. 641.
23 (1977) 31(i) P.D. 253.

dents, inspired by common law.

Comparative law was referred to, regarding questions concerning the interpretation of provisions of the Arbitration Law, 1968[24], by the Supreme Court in *Shemen Industries v. Tavlin*[25]. In this case, there was a conflict between six producers of edible oil, all affiliated to the same company, about the apportionment of the damages from the state received by the company for injury caused to the producers. They designated an economist to decide about the apportionment of the damages among them. As some of them contested the decision about the distribution of damages, a preliminary question the court had to decide was whether the designated economist was an arbitrator or a valuer, as only in the first case are the rules on arbitration applicable. In looking for a solution to the question, Justice Shamgar referred to the concept of quasi-arbitrator, which performs quasi-judiciary functions, adopted in English decisions, (employing the words "I will add for comparison") which have also influenced prior Israeli court decisions. Although the conflicting parties designated him as a valuer, since their intention was that the decision would be final, the court deduced that he acted as an quasi-arbitrator and stated, without hearing the parties in conflict, that the decision given was voidable according to arbitration rules.

Comparative law considerations and references are to be found in questions concerning legal institutions and legal rules typical of the common-law system, which Israeli law inherited from English law, for example estoppel, and contempt of court.

In *Hadar Taxis v. Biton*[26], the Supreme Court faced for the first time the problem of whether the action of a third party, who participated in the infringement of an injunction not directed against him, but of which he knew, can be seen as contempt of court. In this case there was a temporary injunction in favour of an association of taxi drivers against another association, which forbade the defendant association to transport passengers from the airport. The question was whether a taxi driver, who was not party to the process, but who knew about the injunction against the drivers' association, could be held responsible for contempt of court for having infringed the injunction.

Art. 6 of the order concerning contempt of court, adopted in 1929 and amended in 1947, was inspired by English law. In analysing the provision of Section 6, Justice Barak stressed that the text speaks about "obedience to any order." In addition, he referred to the aim of the regulation – to defend a public interest. Based also on the interpretation given in a number of prior Israeli court decisions, he reached the conclusion that even a third person can be liable for contempt of court

24 22 L.S.I. 210.
25 (1985) 39(I) P.D. 561.
26 (1980) 34(iv) P.D. 232.

In regard to the matter of a third party, who was not a party to the process, Justice Barak analyses English and American solutions according to which a person who aids and abets the defendant in breaking the court's order and had knowledge of the injunction is committing contempt of court, although he is not party to the process. As far as Israeli law is concerned, Justice Barak preferred to leave the question open. He stated that the driver committed contempt of court, but the reason for the decision was the express language of the injunction, that it was given "against the defendant association and its drivers."

In *The Estate of Pnina Tenenbaum v. Bank Leumi*[27], a client claimed damages from his bank for negligence in honouring falsified cheques. The defendant pleaded estoppel and invoked English solutions. The bank argued that the client could have observed the mistake, because he did not have a large sum of money in his current account. The Supreme Court rejected the appeal, stating that the client could have noticed that false cheques had been drawn upon his account and should have warned the bank.

IV. Contract Law

One component of contract law during the British Mandate was the Ottoman law that remained in force, specifically, the provisions of the Mejelle, which regulated a number of particular contracts, and also some substantive provisions of the Ottoman Code of Civil Procedure, as for example freedom of contract. The second component of contract law was absorbed from English contract law via the directive of art. 46 of the Palestine Order in Council regarding the filling of *lacunae*, so that the contract law applied in the country in 1948 was almost identical to English contract law.

English law has remained an important source of new legislation, but is not as predominant as before and its influence has decreased gradually[28]. English influence is particularly noticeable in specific laws, such as assignment of obligations, agency, trust, and some provisions of the Contracts (General Part) Law, 1973, and the Contracts (Remedies for Breach of Contract) Law, 1970[29].

The influence of continental law is felt in the legislative technique – in the use of broad provisions like those of the French Civil Code – and in the adoption of some substantive provisions, such as the principle of good faith from the BGB and the theory of *culpa in contrahendo,* or the provisions

[27] (1977) 31(iii) P.D. 141.

[28] D. Friedman *supra* n. 5. at p. 102.

[29] We will hereinafter refer to the Contracts (General Part) Law, 1973, as the "General Contracts Law" and to the Contracts (Remedies for Breach of Contract) Law, 1970, as the Remedies Law.

concerning contracts for the benefit of a third party. Some provisions are of mixed influence – common law and continental law – as, for example, the rule that gives the creditor a right to claim specific performance of the contract, which is similar to the continental law principle, but the exceptions to the rule are also influenced by common law, especially the discretion of the court to reject the claim for specific performance due to considerations of equity.

There are also some influences of Jewish law but, as Professor Gabriela Shalev states, "it is less than its proponents hoped for"[30]. The influence of Jewish law is particularly felt in legislation and case law in the adoption of terminology, as it is the source of Hebrew legal terms.

Sometimes comparative law considerations have been used to support a dissenting opinion of one of the judges.

A fundamental problem concerning the rules governing the making of a valid contract was the object of controversy in *Sonenstein v. Gabaso*[31], which focused on the interpretation of art. 8 of the Land Law, 1969, which demands a written agreement for every real-estate transaction. The question before the court was whether or not the rule to negotiate in good faith, established by art. 12 of the General Contract Law, took precedence over the demand for a written agreement. The parties had orally agreed upon the sale of a flat. They had also agreed on its price, but some details remained to be discussed concerning the payments. The vendor refused to continue the negotiations and to conclude a written contract. The buyer claimed specific performance of the oral agreement. The decision, delivered by former Deputy President Ben-Porath, Justice Beisky concurring, upheld the decision of the District Court, which had ruled that the agreement was void because it violated the demand for a written agreement.

Justice Barak dissenting, argued that the court ought to have given preference to the obligation to negotiate in good faith over the demand for written contract. In support of his view he invoked common-law solutions based on promissory estoppel and the opinions of German legal scholars, and urged that one of the consequences of the infringement of the good faith rule can be recognition of the validity of the contract.

Comparative law was also referred to in regard to a problem concerning the validity of an agreement in the field of company law regarding the right to rescind an agreement between partners in a company because of gross disparity ("lesion"). In *Rabinovich v. Shlav*[32], the appellant was a partner to a company from which he withdrew and, according to the decision of the general assembly, the company bought his shares for an agreed price. Later, he sued for a declaratory judgment recognizing his right to the real value of his shares, on the grounds that he was misled and on the grounds

---

[30] G. Shalev, "Israel Law – 40 Years, Contract Law," *24 Israel L. Rev.* (1990) 665.

[31] (1988) 42(ii) P.D. 278.

[32] (1986) 40(iv) P.D. 533.

of gross disparity. In appealing the decision of the District Court, which rejected his request, he pleaded that because of his lack of experience he did not know that he had a right to a re-evaluation of his shares.

Justice Shamgar, who delivered the decision, analyzed the preconditions established by the General Contracts Law, 1973, for the existence of gross disparity as a cause of recision. He observed that lack of experience, in itself, does not constitute sufficient grounds for a claim of gross disparity. He referred to the conditions established by § 138 of the German BGB (which is the source of inspiration for the similar provision of Israeli law) and its interpretation, as well as opinions expressed in an English essay. Concluding that the lack of experience in the instant case was not of sufficient weight to constitute grounds for rescission, the Supreme Court rejected the appeal.

In the field of remedies for breach of contract, Israeli law has abandoned the prior rule adopted from English common law according to which specific performance of a contract was a discretional remedy. As in the continental systems, art. 3 of the Remedies Law has adopted specific performance as a remedy by right. Art. 3 also establishes common-law-inspired exceptions in which the court may refuse to grant enforcement of a contract.

In a case concerning the claim for specific performance of a service contract, comparative law considerations were used to distinguish between an obligation "to do" and the obligation "not to do". In the case of *The Public Committee for the Construction of Porath-Yosef Yeshiva v. Safdie*[33], disagreements arose between the beneficiary of the construction contract and the architect entrusted with the planning and supervision of the project. The conflicting parties submitted the disagreement to arbitration. Meanwhile, pending the settlement of the conflict, the architect obtained an injunction to stop the work on the building which, in his opinion, did not suit the project. In the appeal to the Supreme Court the beneficiary contested the legality of the injunction, arguing that it violated the provisions of art. 3(2), which creates an exception for obligations of personal services, which cannot be enforced. In interpreting this exception, the court also made recourse to English case law, which distinguishes between the enforcement of a personal obligation "to do" and an order "not to do". In adopting this distinction, the Supreme Court came to the conclusion that only in cases in which the injunction "not to do" would lead to a personal obligation "to do" could it fall under the exception established by art. 3(2).

References to comparative law can also be found in decisions concerning the good-faith principle. We will present one example: In *Roth v. Yeshupe*[34], a contract for the sale of an apartment contained a clause according to which taking possession of the apartment by the buyer would

---

[33] (1980) 34(iii) P.D. 505.

[34] (1979) 33(i) P.D. 617.

constitute conclusive and final proof of the performance of the contractual obligations by the vendor. According to this clause, the District Court rejected the buyer's claim for damages for breach of contract, namely for delay in performance and for defects in construction (non-conformity). In his claim, the buyer argued that the aforementioned clause was void according to the rules that govern standard contracts. The District Court rejected this argument, saying that such a clause does not figure among the void clauses listed in the Standard Contracts Law, 1964, then in force[35].

Justice Shamgar, delivering the decision of the Supreme Court, rejected the appeal on the basis of the good-faith rule introduced in Israeli law by the General Contracts Law. This rule allows the courts the possibility of examining the provisions of contracts in light of the requirements of good faith and public order. Justice Shamgar entered into some detail concerning the requirements of good faith, quoting prior Israeli decisions as well as the German law concerning § 242 of the BGB, which is the source of inspiration for the Israeli good-faith rule.

Justice Elon, concurring, added to the decision's rationale additional arguments based upon the provisions of Jewish law on good faith.

In *Leibowitz v. Eliahu*[36], the question was whether a distributor who had an exclusive agreement with a producer was entitled to an injunction against an Israeli firm which bought the same product directly from the producer and sold it at a lower price. The distributor argued that he had incurred advertising expenses and based his claim on his real right to the good name of the product. He also argued unjust enrichment in support of the claim. The District Court admitted his claim.

On appeal, Supreme Court President Shamgar, delivering the opinion of the Court, rejected the first argument, stating that the real right to the reputation of the product belonged only to the producer of the product and not to the distributor. In reasoning the opinion, Justice Shamgar analysed English case law and legal literature as well as the opinions of French and Italian scholars who reached a similar conclusion. In rejecting the other arguments, Justice Shamgar also discussed English and American solutions.

In *Israel Air Industry v. Zur Gat*[37], the question under consideration was whether compensation operates according to art. 53a of the General Contracts Law, 1973, which provides that two reciprocal obligations deriving from the same contract can be set-off, or according to art. 20 of the Remedies Law, which does not mention the condition of "the same contract".

Justice Bach, delivering the opinion of the court, stated that Section 20 of the Remedies Law cannot avoid the application of Section 53a of the

---

35 18 L.S.I. 51. The law was replaced by the new Standard Contracts Law, enacted in 1982.

36 (1990) 42(ii) P.D. 309.

37 (1988) 42(ii) P.D. 725.

General Contract Law because it represents *sedium materiae.*

Justice Barak, concurring, added comparative law considerations to the Court's rationale, pointing out the differences between current Israeli law, in which compensation is a result of a unilateral declaration, inspired by German law as opposed to French law, in which compensation can operate by law. He also stated that the provisions of prior laws concerning compensation established only the right to compensation, but the rules governing compensation are those established by the General Contracts Law.

There are also many cases concerning specific contracts in which the courts turn to comparative law.

Thus the courts make frequent references to foreign law in the field of insurance, because of the heavy influence of English law.

In *Zion Insurance v. Tshuva*[38], the question before the Supreme Court rested on the interpretation of the "peril-of-the-sea" risk provided for in an insurance policy. Although the insured boat was not found, the District Court admitted the claim to insurance indemnity made by the owner of a motor-boat which was lost at sea.

In its appeal, the insurer claimed that the boat sank because of motor failure, a risk not covered by the insurer. In rejecting this argument, Justice Or (joined by Justice Barak) analysed a number of decisions of English courts, as well as English legal literature, and deduced that the term "perils of the sea" covers all events for which the immediate cause is being at sea.

In order to illustrate the relative frequency of comparative-law references in the field of insurance law, we will present a non-exhaustive list of some of the other problems regarding which the Israeli Supreme Court resorted to comparisons with foreign law as a means of verifying its own solutions: the obligation of the insured to provide necessary information to the insurer, the interpretation of various risks provided for in the insurance policy, if the indemnity owed to the owner of a boat includes the salaries of the crew, if a communication made to the insurance agent can be seen as having been made to the insurer, the liability of the insurer for the acts of his agent, subrogation of the victim's rights by the insurer, and preconditions for the obligation of the insurer to pay indemnities for labour accidents.

Israeli law has no general regulation of obligations but according to art. 61b of the General Contracts Law, its provisions apply *mutatis mutandis* to other obligations that do not have their source in a contract. We will, therefore, include them under the heading of contract law.

In *The State of Israel v. Barad*[39], the claim concerned the right to be paid for salvage operations at sea according to the Israeli Law of Unjust Enrichment, 1979. Justice Bach, who delivered the decision, also referred

---

[38] (1992) 46(i) P.D. 63.

[39] (1992) 46(iii) P.D. 223.

to the Wrecks and Salvage Ordinance[40], adopted during the British Mandate, in 1926, and modelled on the English salvage law. After analysing the provisions of the English salvage law, Justice Bach noted that English law may serve as a "source of inspiration" in the interpretation of Israeli law, especially in view of the scarce local case law. He then showed that the position of English and American law is unequivocal in recognizing the right of the ship owner and his crew, who are acting professionally in the field of salvage at sea, to be paid for the salvage operations even if they act on their own initiative. Based on the provisions of the Israeli Unjust Enrichment Law, 1979, and on the arguments drawn from comparative law, he concluded that the Israeli Salvage Service of the Ashdod seaport and its crew had the right to be paid for the operation of salvage of the ship in danger, executed at the order of the commander of the Sea Service of the port.

V. Family law and succession

During the Ottoman period, Jewish religious law was the applicable personal-status law of Jewish residents. This situation was preserved during the British Mandate period.

The legal system of the state of Israel is secular, although Jewish religious law remains in force in some family matters, such as marriage and divorce, as the personal-status law of Jews.

At present, we are witnessing a process in which the secular legislature is removing many matters from the framework of personal-status law (Jewish law) by way of legislation, as did the courts by way of interpretation. New statutes enacted by the Israel legislature have established a secular territorial regime in the fields of maintenance obligations, financial relations between spouses, paternity, adoption, guardianship and succession[41].

The Supreme Court made use of comparative law in interpreting the Israeli Adoption of Children Law.

In *X v. Y*[42], the discussion focused on the conditions under which the courts may approve adoption of a child without the parents' consent (or the parent's consent, as was the case in this appeal). These conditions were regulated by section 11 of the Adoption of Children Law, 1960, then in force[43]. In this case, the Supreme Court admitted the plea that the father

---

40 Laws of Palestine, vol II, p. 1566 (English ed.).

41 For details see P. Shifman, "Israel Law – 40 Years, Family Law," 24 *Israel L. Rev.* (1990) 537.

42 (1978) 32(iii) P.D. 225.

43 14 L.S.I. 93. The law was replaced by the new Adoption of Children Law, enacted in 1981.

did not fulfil his obligation to care for his children. In support of the decision, Justice Etzioni mentioned the English Children Act, 1975, and the Adoption Act, 1976, the amendment of the BGB in 1977, and French law concerning cases in which the parents' consent is not necessary. In the case before the court, there existed a prior declaratory judgment of the court establishing that the children had been abandoned by their father for more than a year. In its decision, the court also quoted the definition of the term "abandoned child" provided in the American Uniform Adoption Act, which, like the other provisions of foreign law cited by the Court is based on the principle of the benefit of the child. In accordance with this principle, the Court allowed the adoption of the children without the consent of their father.

In another adoption case, *X v. Tel-Aviv City Council*[44], the court was asked to approve the adoption of a six-year-old child who had been abused by his natural parents. After spending two years in an institution for abandoned children, the child was entrusted by the social services to a family that wanted to adopt him. The social services initiated adoption procedures, but the District Court refused to approve the adoption without the parents' consent. The Supreme Court allowed the appeal, holding that art. 11 of the Adoption of Children Law, 1960, which established the cases in which the parents' consent was not needed, is applicable in this case. Justice Witkon, who delivered the decision, based it upon the principle of the benefit of the child, finding support for his reasoning in comparative case-law and literature.

In *X v. The Attorney General*[45], the question concerned the conditions under which adopting parents can claim the annulment of an adoption. The District Court rejected the adopting parents' claim of rescission, which was based upon their allegation that their consent to the adoption was given under the influence of error. After comparing the solutions offered by various legal systems, some of which make no allowance for the dissolution of an adoption, the appeal was denied on the basis of the interpretation of art. 19 of the Israeli Adoption of Children Law, 1981, which regulates the conditions under which such a dissolution is possible.

In a relatively large number of decisions, the Supreme Court has employed comparative law when looking for the right solution to complete a *lacuna* or for the proper interpretation of a provision of Israeli succession law.

In *Aharonian v. Haliska*[46], the testator left a will under which all his properties and money passed to his nephew. In a later will, he named his lawyer as his heir. The beneficiaries of both wills laid claim to the estate. The beneficiary of the first will alleged undue influence on the part of the

44 (1978) 32(iii) P.D. 393.
45 (1991) 45(iii) P.D. 302.
46 (1991) 45(v) P.D. 705.

lawyer, who was the beneficiary of the second will. The District Court accepted the allegation. Justice D. Levin, stressed the difference between English law and the present Israeli succession law, which did not adopt a presumption of undue influence for cases of a confidential relationship. Rather, the rule was that the burden of proof rested with the party claiming undue influence. However, citing Israeli Supreme precedents admitting an exception to that rule in cases in which the testator was dependent on the beneficiary, the Court rejected the appeal upon a finding that in the case before the court such a dependency existed.

VI. Tort Law

In 1944, during the mandatory period, the Civil Wrongs Ordinance[47] was enacted, and has remained in force ever since. The Civil Wrongs Ordinance represents a sort of restatement of the common law of torts as developed by English case law. Its provisions have been amended on several occasions and augmented by such new regulations as the Defamation Law, 1965[48], the Road Accident Victims (Compensation) Law, 1975[49], Defective Product (Liability) Law, 1980[50], and the Consumer Protection Law, 1981[51].

The historical roots of the Ordinance explain the tendency of the judges to turn to English law in interpreting its provisions, although this tendency has decreased over time, as judges have come to interpret the Ordinance in accordance with the needs of Israeli society. Indeed, some of the solutions of the Israeli Supreme Court have even preceded the adoption of similar decisions by English courts, as was the case with liability for negligence, which the Israeli Supreme Court recognized as a general principle, before it was acknowledged in English law.

Nowadays, recourse to English law is made "solely for the purpose of comparison" (as was stressed in one of the decisions we shall present) without giving it any particular preference. But comparative references to English law and to the law of other common law countries remain almost exclusive in this area of law.

A claim for damages for bodily injury in *Shaps v. "Prima" Prizner*[52] presented the Supreme Court with a case of product liability, before the adoption of the Defective Product (Liability) Law, 1980 (which established the strict liability of manufacturers). The question facing the court was

---

47 P.G. of 1944, supp. 1, p. 129.
48 19 L.S.I. 254.
49 29 L.S.I. 311.
50 34 L.S.I. 92.
51 35 L.S.I. 298.
52 (1978) 32(iii) P.D. 119.

whether or not the manufacturer could be held liable for negligence for having used the wrong model in the production of the product – a deck-chair. The District Court obliged the producer to pay damages to the victim for having violated his obligation not to market defective products. Each of the two parties quoted English and American case-law in support of their arguments. On appeal, the Supreme Court entered into a detailed discussion of the comparative case law and legal literature of common-law countries.

Justice Asher, who delivered the decision of the Supreme Court, based the rejection of the producer's appeal on the grounds that the manufacturer bore a duty of care toward all consumers. In support of this, he cited American case law in similar cases. In analysing the standards for defining a defective product, Justice Asher referred to a Canadian decision. He concluded his review of comparative law with the words: "as the circumstances are similar, we have to draw similar conclusions."

In *The Estate of Freilich v. The State of Israel*[53], the Supreme Court faced the question whether an estate can claim damages for pain and suffering and for the loss of expectation of life of the deceased, if the victim was unconscious until his death. The case concerned an accident that occurred before the enactment of the Road Accident Victims (Compensation) Law, 1975, and the estate argued that Israeli law recognized a right for loss of life expectancy. Justice Barak, who delivered the decision, made detailed reference to comparative legal literature and to the case law of common-law countries. He demonstrated that a separate claim for loss of expectation of life is recognized to a limited extent only in England, whereas in America it is linked to a claim for damages for pain and suffering. Justice Barak also took note of intermediary solutions provided by Canadian and Australian law, which recognize such separate right only if the victim is conscious, but this right does not devolve upon the heirs. After reviewing prior Israeli court decisions, which also left the question open, he concluded that the recognition of such a right must be left to the legislature inasmuch as the existing Israeli law does not justify such a claim.

In *Alshua v. Estate of Dahan*[54], the court was asked to recognize a claim for damages for mental anguish caused to relatives of a road accident victim, who did not, themselves, witness the accident.

The case concerned the parents of a 6-year-old boy who died 24 hours after an accident. The parents arrived at the hospital shortly after the accident and witnessed their son's dying agonies. Subsequently, their mental state deteriorated: they suffered from depression, fears, and nervousness, were often absent from work, and required physical and mental treatment. The Magistrates Court allowed the claim for compensation under the Road

[53] (1982) 36(iv) P.D. 816.

[54] (1990) 44(iii) P.D. 397.

Accident Victims (Compensation) Law, 1975, but the claim was subsequently rejected by the District Court, which held, however, that they had a good claim in negligence against the driver, under Section 35 of the Civil Wrongs Ordinance (New Version)[55]. Supreme Court President Shamgar, delivering the opinion of the Court, presented an extensive survey of English and American law in connection with the question: whether mental injury caused to a relative of the victim is subject to compensation, that is, whether a relative can be considered a victim of the road accident under the Road Accident Victims (Compensation) Law, 1975. English courts approached such claims with caution, apparently fearing a flood of compensation claims and lacking confidence in the ability of the medical profession to adequately treat cases of this kind. The conclusion drawn from English case law is that the claimant must have been at the scene of the accident or very near to it and must be closely related to the victim of physical injuries. Justice Shamgar also presented American law and literature on the subject.

Justice Shamgar then argued that the distinction between mental injury caused to a relative at the scene of the accident and mental injury arising at a later stage is largely artificial, stating that the determining factor should be causal proximity, clear proof of real and defined mental injury, and not necessarily proximity in place and time. He therefore concluded that mental injury of a relative is comprised by the concept of damage caused "in consequence" of a road accident and can entitle a relative to compensation under the Road Accident Victims (Compensation) Law, 1975. Nevertheless, he suggested that at the present stage it would be reasonable to limit the right only to first-degree relatives, explaining that the court must balance competing interests and take into account legal policy and the effects of the judgment on future patterns of behaviour, as well as its general economic impact.

The case was therefore remanded with instructions that the lower court reconsider the action in accordance with the principles outlined above relating to the application of the Road Accident Victims (Compensation) Law, 1975.

Dr. Zaitzov v. Katz[56] presented the question of a physician's liability for negligent advice given to a woman suffering from a hereditary disease. The woman had sought medical advice before marrying. She subsequently gave birth to a child who inherited her disease. A suit was therefore brought by the parents and on behalf of the child against the physician and the medical dispensary for the wrongful life of the child. The District Court rejected the child's claim but admitted the parents' claim.

The Supreme Court was confronted with this problem for the first time

---

[55] The new version of the original mandatory ordinance was published in 2 L.S.I. (New Version) 5.

[56] (1986) 40(ii) P.D. 85.

and the case was argued before a five-judge bench. Deputy President Ben-Porath, who delivered the decision, mentioned that the problem has arisen in other systems of law. She and the other judges who participated in the discussion, made ample reference to English, American, and Canadian case law and legal literature. The legal literature and case law of other countries treat the issue in terms of what is better: not to be born at all or a "wrongful" life? Opinions vary, not only in regard to the answer to this question, but also in regard to the possibility of making such a comparison. In its decision, the Supreme Court recognized the liability of the physician, in principle but, by a four-to-one majority, rejected the appeal made in the name of the child. Each of the judges added his reasons for admitting such liability in principle. Two expressed the opinion that the child's right to damages for wrongful life exists only in extreme cases, while the other two argued that such a distinction is relevant only for the extent of damages.

In the defamation case of *Avneri v. Shapira*[57], the claimant appealed against a temporary injunction issued against the publication of a biography of member of parliament, Shapira. The injunction was granted to Shapira, the defendant in the present appeal, on the grounds of alleged defamation.

In granting the appeal, Justice Barak described the evolution of the remedies granted for the tort of defamation in common law. In the past, courts recognized only a claim for damages, considering that injunctions could be contrary to freedom of expression. However, this is no longer the accepted view in Israel or in England. Toward the end of the last century, injunctions were permitted at the discretion of the court. Conceptions changed in the course of time and the courts tend to restrict the discretion of the court.

Following this historical-comparative law description, and after stressing the separation of Israeli law from English common law, Justice Barak turned to the provisions of art. 3 of the Israeli Defamation Law, which grants remedies to the victim of defamation, and deduced that the victim had a right to an injunction. Because an order to do or not to do could contravene a basic right, such as liberty, or freedom of the press, or a public interest, all legal systems place restrictions on the right to forced execution of such orders. Sections 73 and 74 of the Civil Wrongs Ordinance (New Version) list cases in which an injunction cannot be granted. The list is not exhaustive, and the restriction may apply in other cases. In the case under discussion, in exercising its discretion, the court has to strike a balance between freedom of expression and a person's good name, while taking the public interest into consideration. Justice Barak made ample references to American, Canadian, and English case law concerning the need for balancing conflicting basic rights and he concluded that in the instant case the public interest must prevail because the person involved is

[57] (1989) 43(iii) P.D. 840.

a public figure.

Justice Barak added that the arguments in favour of the rules adopted in common-law countries are equally valid in Israel. Making a general pronouncement on the use of comparative law, he wrote: "it is true that English rules are no longer binding, but to the extent that English law is based on the same basic principles that exist in our law, it is proper for us to draw inspiration from what goes on at the other end of the world"[58].

The other judges joined Justice Barak in holding that when liability for defamation has not yet been established by the court, the refusal to grant an injunction to the alleged victim of defamation properly expresses the necessary equilibrium between freedom of expression and the dignity of the person in Israeli law and thus granted the appeal.

Comparative law consideration plays a prominent role in the reasoning of numerous Supreme Court decisions concerning such issues of tort law, as negligence and its criteria, medical malpractice, contributory negligence, work-related accidents, vicarious liability of employers for damage caused by employees, and strict liability.

VII. CONCLUSIONS

In conclusion, it may be said that comparative law is used in Israel much as it is used elsewhere. Primarily, it serves as an auxiliary tool in applying the domestic law of the State as a means for lending support to the courts decision. The manner in which comparative law is used by Israeli courts and the purpose of that use are reflected in the characteristic formulae invoked by judges in introducing or concluding their comparative law references: "There are similar provisions in other countries, and although they do not bind us, the approach of other systems of law may be instructive for the case before us"; "Comparative law does not oblige us. This is the rule...but comparative law is also a mirror through which the interpreter may look more deeply into his own system"; "I will add for comparison that English law has adopted a similar solution"; "As the circumstances are similar we ought to reach similar conclusions," and others.

However, compared with that of other countries, Israeli case law seems to be characterized by more frequent reference to foreign law[59]. The relatively extensive use of comparative law by Israeli courts can be attributed to a number of circumstances:

---

[58] *Ibid.*, at p. 868.

[59] The German author B. Aubin analyses 31 decisions of the Supreme Court from 1909–1961 which contain comparative law references, *supra* n. 1; For the purpose of a numerical comparison, we will give an example picked at random from the volumes of decisions of the Israeli Supreme Court: in the three volumes of 1979 (33 i–iii P.D.) there are 45 decisions in civil appeals with foreign law references, some of them being short references and some of them detailed.

a) The historical roots of the Israeli legal system, mentioned in the introduction, may explain not only the openness of the legislature to modern solutions but also that of the courts;
b) The adoption of the doctrine of "stare decisis" in Israeli law. As a consequence of the binding force of precedent, some important common-law rules became an integral part of our legal culture. Thus, for example, it is but natural that, in referring to its own precedents in tort law, the Supreme Court also quotes similar decisions of English courts;
c) The discretionary power expressly granted the courts in numerous provisions of the new statutes, as, for example, the discretion given the court in deciding upon restitution in cases of frustration of contract, or in regarding the obligation to pay damages in cases of prohibited contracts;
d) The inclusion of such open-ended concepts as "good faith", "reasonableness", "justice", and "public order" in the new statutes;
e) The process of "codification in stages" creates legislative gaps. When judges are confronted with a question that is not covered by existing legislation, they have to fill the lacuna in order to provide an answer.

In the situations mentioned in paragraphs c, d, and e, Israeli judges sometimes turn to comparative law in order to check their exercise of discretion, or to check or support their own interpretation of the general concepts of Israeli law, or the solution they propose for filling a *lacuna.*

A great number, we would even venture to say the lion's share, of comparative law references made by Israeli courts are to English law or to the law of other common-law countries. This is partly a consequence of the strong historical links to English law. Initially, part of English law was introduced to Palestine in the way comparative law describes as "forced reception". In time, as in other countries, this evolved into voluntary reception, as common law was absorbed into the law of Palestine and of Israel by the courts and by the legislature in ways and for the reasons we mentioned in the introduction. Another reason for the preference of the courts for common law is the legal background of the judges and lawyers and the language barrier presented by continental law.

We have presented not only "leading cases" ("les grands arrêts de la jurisprudence") but also ordinary cases in which the courts have resorted to comparative law, in order to illustrate the use of comparative law by Israeli courts almost as a regular working tool. We can only regret that the geographical area of reference does not include more continental law. In this regard, Comparative Law Institutes around the world may be able to make an important contribution by initiating translations of the leading case law of their countries.

KIICHI NISHINO*

The Use of Foreign Law by Courts in Japan

SUMMARY

In Japan, various systems for assimilation of foreign law in court have been developed in recent decades but their practical and systematic use is still insufficient. Cases in which judges have to apply foreign law are still rare and many judges and court practitioners are not very interested in foreign law, other than in some particular fields.

I. INTRODUCTION

In the latter half of the 19th century, Japan started to modernize generally, modeling on Western countries; later, modern law from Western countries was also studied and absorbed. The objects of this kind of study and absorption have been German, French and Anglo-American law. So, "foreign law" in this paper means these laws, unless otherwise indicated.

II. JUDICIAL STUDY OF FOREIGN LAW

A. Judges and foreign law

(i) In general, judges in Japan do not need to know foreign law at all, either before or after becoming judges. They are only required to study Japanese law in the Japanese language. They have the opportunity to study foreign law at college as law students before taking the bar examination, and at the Legal Training and Research Institute as legal apprentices after passing the bar examination but these courses are just elective subjects. They neither have to study foreign law for the bar examination nor for judicial practice after becoming judges.

* Professor of Law, Niigata University; ex-judge of Niigata District Court.

U. Drobnig and S. van Erp (eds.), The Use of Comparative Law by Courts, 223–230.

Fundamental codes in Japan have been influenced to a variable extent by foreign law, e.g. the present Civil Code and Civil Procedure Code were enacted after the German Codes, and the present Constitutional Code and Criminal Procedure Code adopted much of American constitutional law and criminal procedure.

Judges in Japan do not have to study the original foreign law for themselves for the following reasons. Firstly, these fundamental codes were made many years ago (40 to 100 years) and each department of law in Japan has made its own changes over these periods. So, judges do not need to know current foreign law in order to interpret these Japanese codes, and almost every legal problem has already been resolved by the precedents of the Supreme Court. Secondly, as research by foreign law scholars has been quite prudent and their interpretations of Japanese law are necessarily based on the study of foreign law, it is enough for judges to study only the Japanese scholars' books themselves.

(ii) Some judges study foreign law, individually or in study groups. It is usual for them to choose either German law or Anglo-American law, and, since World War II, American law has become more popular than German law. Rarely, they may choose French law or general comparative law.

The reasons for studying foreign law are usually personal and academic interest, not to use a knowledge of foreign law in the courtrooms. The academic level of judges who study foreign law varies. Some of these judges, including several doctorate degree holders, are excellent, and usually they, as judges, are interested in positive law, rather than philosophical aspects of law, and in civil or criminal procedure, rather than substantive law. But, the number of judges who are interested in foreign law and who study it actively is less than a few per cent of the total number of judges in Japan.[1]

In the first half of this century, some judges studied foreign law eagerly, particularly German law. At that time, German law was much more important for judges than it is today because German codes were the direct models for all of the fundamental codes of Japan. Many judges understood the German language and they read German law books, especially German Commentaries of BGB and ZPO, for their judicial practice. At that time, studies of foreign laws by scholars were insufficient, so judges had to study foreign law for themselves. It has been reported that a judge once said that he would not reach a judgment until he received a book he had ordered from Germany. However, this kind of event was quite rare even then, and now certainly there are no such judges in Japan.

(iii) Nowadays, as international trade develops, the number of international

---

[1] The total number of judges in Japan is about 2800 (1400 fully-fledged judges, 600 assistant judges and 800 summary court judges).

disputes in Japan is increasing quite rapidly. Attorneys at law sometimes need a knowledge of foreign law, and the number of attorneys experienced in international disputes has increased in the big cities. In the courts, there are many civil cases in which parties are foreigners, and criminal cases in which the accused are foreigners.

The law that is applied in these cases is usually Japanese. It is still unlikely that foreign law would be applicable to these cases. And, for these cases, if any, the judges do not have to look for the applicable foreign law themselves because it is the burden of the parties or their counselors to find and demonstrate the applicable law for the case. However, if judges want to look for a rule applicable to the case for themselves, the General Secretariat of the Supreme Court can help.

B. Systematic assimilation of foreign law in the court system

1. The General Secretariat of the Supreme Court

In the system of courts of Japan, there are no standing offices to study foreign law generally and comprehensively. But, some departments of the General Secretariat of the Supreme Court, such as the Civil Affairs Bureau, Criminal Affairs Bureau and System Research Office, research foreign law when needed, for example, when making court rules, making a draft of a new code or answering inquiries from lower courts about a particular foreign law. This kind of research comes from books in the Library.

Most of the officers in these departments are lawyers and have experience as judges of lower courts; some younger officers have studied abroad.

2. Dispatch of judges abroad

a. Training

(i) Since the mid-1960s the Supreme Court has been systematically dispatching young lower court judges (assistant judges[2]) to the United States, England, Germany, France and Canada[3] for training in foreign law. The number of these young judges is about 15 every year, and this means that about one quarter of newly appointed young assistant judges have the chance to study abroad.

Selection is usually by designation of the Supreme Court, and only a few are chosen by open examination. The period of training is usually one year, although one or two may stay for two years.

This training system has been popular among young assistant judges because it is the only chance for them to study abroad while they are in office. Also, after completing their training, they are more likely to be promoted earlier in the bureaucracy of the judicial department.

They are sent to certain universities or lower courts in these countries. At

[2] Most of them are in their late 20s.

[3] Canada was added to this list in the late 1980s.

the universities, they study the law of that country as law students or visiting scholars. At court, although each court varies in how it treats the trainees, they are usually given an office or desk inside the court-house, and are given the opportunity to see the records, to observe trials or pretrial procedure, and to ask questions of judges and other court officers.

(ii) The assistant judges have to submit reports of their studies to the Supreme Court after completing their terms, but these are not published, except for a few which are worthy of publication. This kind of training abroad enables them to acquire knowledge of foreign law and widens their horizons, but there has been no systematic attempt to utilize the studies for judicial practice in Japan. The Supreme Court does not appear to expect them to become experts in foreign law, and is satisfied if they gain a fundamental knowledge of foreign law and ability in a foreign language.

b. Research

The Supreme Court has also dispatched judges of lower courts to foreign countries, such as the United States, Germany, England and France, so that they can make a specialized study of judicial situations and conditions in that country. The Supreme Court needs this information for making court rules, participating in the legislative process and resolving big important cases at the Supreme Court.

For example, a few years ago, the Supreme Court dispatched a judge for the criminal court of the Tokyo District Court, who is an expert in American criminal law, to the United States for more than one year to study actual situations of jury trial in the US. Japanese people now take a great interest in the jury system, and jury trial, which has been suspended since 1943, may be resumed.

Currently, an overall amendment of the Civil Procedure Code is under way, so the Supreme Court is dispatching several judges of lower courts to foreign countries every year to study civil practice in those countries.

3. Judicial Research Report

Every year since World War II, the Supreme Court has designated several lower court judges as judicial researchers so they can study certain judicial themes.[4] All the reports have been published. At first, it was quite common for them to choose aspects of foreign law as their topics, because, at that time, the whole judicial department was eager to absorb foreign law and foreign legal systems. For example, for the first 10 years (from 1947 to 1956) about one third of these reports (27 out of 78) handled foreign top-

---

[4] Until the 1970s they were exempted from their case load and devoted all their time to research for one year. Since then, they have done their research as well as working as judges.

ics,[5] and some of them were equivalent to doctoral dissertations.

However, recently, ordinary judges have had less interest in foreign law and it is quite common for these researchers to choose domestic, practical and technical themes[6] rather than academic ones. In the last 10 years (from 1981 to 1990), only two reports[7] (out of 13) have handled foreign law topics.

4. The Supreme Court Library

The Supreme Court Library is one of the best law libraries in Japan. It has 215,000 law books and 40% of them (84,000 books) are foreign books. It subscribes to 730 legal periodicals and 30% of them (about 220 magazines) are foreign ones. These are important materials for the practice and research of the Supreme Court and its General Secretariat.

All High Courts, District Courts and Family Courts[8] have their own law libraries, but they concentrate on Japanese law books only, so collections of foreign law books at these libraries, if any, are fragmentary.

III. JUDICIAL PRACTICE AND FOREIGN LAW

A. Lower courts

(i) As stated already, it is rare for judges in Japan to have to apply foreign law to their cases, though the number of foreign parties is increasing rapidly. In cases to which foreign law will be applied, the parties have the burden to find and demonstrate the applicable law, and it is not so difficult for the counselors to find some relevant rule from books or from the foreign parties. But, in these cases, it is also quite common for judges to have wide and free discretion of interpretation in every field of law, including the field of international private law, because they do not normally have knowledge of or access to the original rule. And, when they cannot find an applicable foreign rule, judges may apply "reason" as law, since a judge cannot refuse to handle a case because of the lack of an applicable law.

---

[5] E.g. Criminal Evidence in the U.S. (1947) by J. Kawahara, History of the Rule Making Power of the Court of England (1947) by J. Hosono, Cross Examination in Anglo-American Civil Procedure (1948) by J. Kawano, Divorce in the U.S. (1948) by J. Ooe, Professional Ethics in the U.S. (1949) by J. Fujii, Constitutionality of the Juvenile Court in the U.S. (1949) by J. Nakagawa, etc.

[6] E.g. Credibility of Confessions (1984) by JJ. Tazaki et al., Admissibility of Illegally Obtained Evidence (1985) by JJ. Takagi and Oobuchi, Civil Trial Practice (1986) by JJ. Iwasa et al., Summary Handling of Small Claims (1988) by JJ. Hirate et al., etc.

[7] Court System for Constitutional Issues of Western Countries (1989) by JJ. Chiba et al. and Civil Court Practice in France (1990) by JJ. Yamasita et al.

[8] There are 8 High Courts, 50 District Courts and 50 Family Courts. Also, there are about 400 Summary Courts.

Divorce cases are the exception. Judges have handled many and various international divorce cases so far, so many judges, in particular judges of the family law division of the Tokyo District Court, are familiar with the divorce laws of many countries, such as China, Korea, the Philippines and many states in the US.

Cases in which foreign law has been applied are usually reported by law magazines and they are useful precedents when judges have to handle similar cases.

Study of foreign fundamental law is so popular among scholars now that Japanese commentaries of them, such as the UCC of the United States and BGB or ZPO of Germany, have been published here although they are seldom necessary for the cases in court.

(ii) It has been rare for judges to make direct use of knowledge of foreign law when interpreting Japanese law. Knowledge of foreign law is quite helpful to interpret the law of Japan because, as said before, the fundamental codes of Japan were greatly influenced by foreign laws. But it is rare for counselors to argue about foreign law in courtrooms except in some cases to which foreign law is applied directly. Many judges and practicing lawyers think law in Japan can be interpreted in a Japanese way without any direct help from knowledge of foreign law because of the courts' own development of the law and the large number of precedents. Judges and court practitioners are not very interested in foreign law.

Some attorneys at law in big cities need a knowledge of foreign law because the number of foreign clients is increasing, but their major fields are in making agreements and preventing conflicts outside the court so they seldom appear at the courthouse.

B. Supreme Court

Although, at the Supreme Court, the fundamental practice situation is similar to that of the lower courts, there are some differences.

First, in the Supreme Court, there are about 30 judicial research officers. All of them are recruited from judges of the lower court and they make preparations for the judgments, and perform relevant research when necessary to assist the Supreme Court Justices.[9] Some of them may research foreign law when they think it is necessary for a particular case. However, it depends upon their personal knowledge, and not all judicial research officers will necessarily research into foreign law. Knowledge of foreign law or of a foreign language are not requirements for appointment as a

[9] Their role resembles that of law clerks in the United States, but all research officers have judgeship of lower courts and have had more than 10 years' experience as a lower-court judge. Their term is usually three to five years, and after that they are appointed as lower court judges again. Only the Supreme Court has this kind of research officer.

judicial research officer.

Second, in some particular cases, parties argue directly, citing foreign law, precedents and academic theories. Typical of these cases are those in which fundamental human rights, under the Constitution of Japan, are disputed. The American Constitution was a model for the present Constitution of Japan and we have had similar issues, so counselors sometimes cite American constitutional cases or theories as persuasive authority.[10] Usually, parties who submit this kind of argument are the accused and their defenders in criminal cases, and public prosecutors have seldom made these kinds of arguments or citations.[11]

By contrast, the Supreme Court usually handles only original issues which are problems of Japanese law, and mention is seldom made of foreign laws or cases. In one case,[12] the Supreme Court stated that, although foreign law can be an important reference material, it is not correct to interpret the Constitution of Japan by adopting a foreign authority directly without considering the differences between social conditions of Japan and that other country. This is almost the only occasion on which the Supreme Court has made an official comment on this kind of argument.

There was another exceptional case[13] in which both majority opinion and minority opinion cited foreign laws. The issue was whether a ban on political activities of public servants was constitutional. In this case, both sides found a convenient foreign rule or authority for their conclusions and used it to reinforce their arguments. Each side hoped to make their interpretation more significant by the use of foreign jurisprudence.

---

[10] E.g. Sogo Taxi Co. v. Director of Tax Administration Office, Judgment of the Supreme Court on June 24, 1966, 20 Supreme Court Civil Reporter 1145; Japan v. Koh, Judgment of the Supreme Court on Apr. 30, 1970, 24 Supreme Court Criminal Reporter 196; Japan v. Boku (so-called Takada case), Judgment of the Supreme Court on Dec. 20, 1972, 26 Supreme Court Criminal Reporter 631; Hanober Ins. Co. v. Oosaka Shosen, Judgment of the Supreme Court on Mar. 15, 1974, 28 Supreme Court Civil Reporter 222; Japan v. Ooba, Judgment of Supreme Court on May 6, 1977, 31 Supreme Court Criminal Reporter 544; Japan v. Hashimoto, Judgment of the Supreme Court on Sep. 7, 1978, 32 Supreme Court Criminal Reporter 1762; Matsumoto v. Soka-Gakkai (so-called Itamandara case), Judgment of Supreme Court on Apr. 7, 1981, 35 Supreme Court Civil Reporter 443; Natsume v. Land Register, Judgment of Supreme Court on Dec. 16, 1986, 40 Supreme Court Civil Reporter 1236; Japan v. Makieda, Judgment of the Supreme Court on Dec. 18, 1989, 43 Supreme Court Criminal Reporter 882, etc.

[11] Japan v. Ogawa (Judgment of the Supreme Court on May 21, 1976, 30 Supreme Court Criminal Reporter 1178) is just such a rare case.

[12] Japan v. Oosawa (so-called Sarufutsu case), Judgment of the Supreme Court on Nov. 6, 1974, 28 Supreme Court Criminal Reporter 393.

[13] Japan v. Tsuruzono, Judgment of the Supreme Court on Apr. 25, 1973, 27 Supreme Court Criminal Reporter 547.

IV. Some Comments

Although various systems for the assimilation of foreign law in court have been developed and improved in recent decades, their practical and systematic use is still insufficient

The reason is, as stated previously, that cases to which foreign law is applicable are few, and judges do not need to know foreign law in order to interpret Japanese law.

One more reason should be added to this. One of the characteristics of Japanese jurisprudence is that the distance between practice and academic theory is large. There have been few interchanges between scholars and court practitioners, including judges. Most professors of law have no experience as practitioners and, equally, it is rare for professors of law to become practitioners. So, most judges are not interested in studying foreign law, and only scholars have studied and tried to utilize foreign laws systematically. I believe that, in order to make good use of foreign jurisprudence, active interchange between practice and academy should be one of the objects of the legal world in Japan in the future.

MARC ELVINGER*

Le recours, par les juridictions luxembourgeoises, aux techniques de droit comparé dans l'interprétation et l'application du droit luxembourgeois

Il s'agit, ci-après, de cerner dans quelle mesure les juridictions luxembourgeoises recourent à la doctrine et la jurisprudence étrangères, voire aux techniques du droit comparé, pour l'interprétation et l'application du droit luxembourgeois. On ne traitera donc pas, ci-après, le problème de *l'application,* par les juridictions luxembourgeoises, du droit étranger en vertu des règles luxembourgeoises de droit international privé.

Les quelques développements qui suivent ne sont pas le fruit d'une analyse systématique de la jurisprudence luxembourgeoise. Ce sont plutôt des constats fondés sur l'expérience professionnelle de l'auteur en tant qu'avocat.

1. Il est utile de rappeler, pour commencer, les particularités de l'environnement juridique luxembourgeois, particularités qui font que le recours à la jurisprudence et à la doctrine étrangères relèvent de la pratique quotidienne du juriste de droit luxembourgeois:

1.1. – A l'instar de la Belgique, le Luxembourg a, au début du 19e siècle, été doté de pratiquement tous ses grands "monuments" législatifs (Code civil, Code de procédure civile, Code de commerce, Code pénal, Code d'instruction criminelle) français, puisqu'il faisait partie intégrante du Ier Empire à l'époque de la promulgation des codes napoléoniens.

1.2. – A l'exception du Code pénal – remplacé en 1879 par un Code inspiré de celui alors en vigueur en Belgique – aucun de ces codes n'a fait l'objet d'une réforme d'ensemble. Les nombreuses réformes ponctuelles intervenues ont été très largement calquées sur celles opérées en France et parfois sur celles opérées en Belgique.

1.3. – Les lois particulières (non codifiées) dont le pays a été doté s'inspirent tantôt du droit français (p. ex. loi sur le droit d'auteur) tantôt

---

* avocat au barreau de Luxembourg

U. Drobnig and S. van Erp (eds.), The Use of Comparative Law by Courts, 231–234.

du droit belge (p. ex. loi sur les associations; sur les sociétés commerciales, sur la protection de la jeunesse) et parfois même du droit allemand (p. ex. loi sur les brevets). L'ensemble du droit fiscal est d'origine allemande.

1.4. – Il n'y a pas, au Luxembourg, d'Université (sauf de 1ère année) avec cette double conséquence que les juristes sont formés dans des universités étrangères (c. 70% en France et c. 30% en Belgique) et que la recherche et la production doctrinales restent tout compte fait limitées bien qu'elles aient connu un essor appréciable au cours des dernières années.

1.5. – Compte tenu de la relative exiguïté du pays et, en conséquence, du nombre relativement limité des décisions de justice rendues, une "jurisprudence" proprement luxembourgeoise – au sens d'un ensemble jurisprudentiel à la fois relativement complet et cohérent, unifié par les décisions de la Cour de cassation – ne pourrait guère se constituer. Cette affirmation ne doit cependant pas être comprise comme niant toute autonomie à la jurisprudence luxembourgeoise et encore moins comme impliquant un rattachement systématique de celle-ci à *un* système juridique étranger. Elle signifie seulement que la jurisprudence luxembourgeoise n'est pas "autosuffisante" et qu'elle se nourrit systématiquement de celle des pays dont sont inspirés les textes à appliquer.

1.6. – Jusqu'il y a récemment, l'accès aux décisions rendues par les juridictions luxembourgeoises était difficile, à l'exception des décisions relativement peu nombreuses publiées dans la Pasicrisie luxembourgeoise. Un progrès substantiel a cependant été réalisé dans ce domaine par la mise en place d'une banque de données et la publication périodique de sommaires de jurisprudence.

1.7. – Il existe un nombre non négligeable de dispositions en vigueur au Luxembourg dont le texte est encore actuellement identique en France et en Belgique mais sur l'interprétation desquelles les jurisprudences française et belge ne coïncident pas. Le prototype en est l'article 1384 du Code civil sur la responsabilité du fait des choses mais il ne s'agit que d'un exemple parmi d'autres.

2. Pour les besoins de l'examen à effectuer, il convient de distinguer entre 1) le recours des tribunaux luxembourgeois à la doctrine et la jurisprudence d'*un* ordre juridique étranger en vue de l'interprétation et de l'application du droit luxembourgeois et 2) l'adoption, par les juridictions luxembourgeoises, d'une approche comparatiste proprement dite, c'est-à-dire consistant dans la comparaison des normes, doctrine et jurisprudence d'au moins *deux* ordres juridiques différents en vue de l'interprétation et de l'application du droit luxembourgeois.

2.1. La première des démarches envisagées est – par la force des choses – systématiquement pratiquée par les juridictions luxembourgeoises. Sauf en certaines matières peut-être (surtout le droit du travail et le bail à loyer), peu de décisions de justice qui ont à se prononcer sur une question de droit tant soit peu sujette à controverse ne contiennent pas de référence à de la doctrine et/ou de la jurisprudence étrangères.

Quant à la question de savoir à la doctrine et/ou à la jurisprudence de *quel* pays référence sera faite, le premier critère est bien évidemment celui de la source d'inspiration – c'est-à-dire de l'origine – des dispositions qu'il s'agit d'appliquer. De ce point de vue la référence au droit français est la plus fréquente, la référence au droit belge figurant en – bonne – seconde place.

Il ne fait pas de doute cependant que des critères moins scientifiques interviennent à leur tour, le poids de ces critères "seconds" étant bien sûr fonction de la possibilité même de s'inspirer d'ordres juridiques différents, c'est-à-dire de l'existence, dans plusieurs ordres juridiques étrangers, de normes similaires à celles en vigueur au Luxembourg. Parmi ces critères on signalera par exemple:

– la question de savoir si le juge a été formé en Belgique ou en France;

– celle de savoir si, dans le domaine dont s'agit, la Bibliothèque de la Magistrature est mieux équipée en ouvrages français ou belges, étant précisé qu'il y a un à priori pour les livres français parce qu'ils sont beaucoup moins chers (!);

– celle de savoir si les avocats ont fourni au juge des références à l'un ou l'autre système juridique étranger auquel il eut été possible de se référer.

Enfin, un autre critère non scientifique qui joue certainement un rôle appréciable est celui de l'*opportunité*. Il est permis de partir de l'hypothèse que fréquemment un juge connaît déjà la solution qu'il entend donner à un litige à un moment où il ne sait pas encore exactement comment motiver, en droit, cette solution. Si, dans un tel cas de figure, il peut justifier la solution préconisée par lui par référence à un droit étranger donné (p. ex. le droit français), tandis que la référence à un autre droit (p. ex. le droit belge) conduirait à une solution différente, son choix sera vite fait!

A vrai dire, ce cas de figure aura souvent impliqué une approche de droit comparé proprement dite, sans pour autant que celle-ci ne transparaisse à la lecture de la décision rendue, pour la simple raison que le juge omettra de signaler qu'une autre solution eut été envisageable par référence à un autre système juridique dont il n'a cependant pas retenu la solution.

2.2. S'agissant des approches de droit comparé proprement dites, il faut à mon sens faire une sousdistinction entre

1) l'interprétation d'une disposition de droit luxembourgeois par voie de confrontation de cette disposition avec une disposition similaire de droit étranger;

2) la recherche d'une solution à une question de droit luxembourgeois à la lumière des solutions consacrées par différents droits étranges.

2.2.1. Le premier cas de figure se présente assez fréquemment lorsque des dispositions luxembourgeoises, bien qu'inspirées de dispositions d'un droit étranger, *n'ont pas été reprises telles quelles de celui-ci.* L'interprétation de la norme de droit luxembourgeois sera alors souvent faite à la lumière de ce qui, précisément, la distingue de la norme étrangère dont elle est par ailleurs inspirée.

2.2.2. Il est assez fréquent que pour justifier une solution qu'il adopte, une tribunal se réfère aux solutions et opinions jurisprudentielles et doctrinales *conformes et concordantes* de plus d'un système juridique étranger et plus particulièrement des ordres juridiques français *et* belge.

Il est par contre relativement rare – sans pour autant être réellement exceptionnel – qu'en vue de la recherche d'une solution de droit luxembourgeois, un tribunal compare – dans la motivation même de son jugement – les solutions en vigueur dans deux ou plusieurs systèmes juridiques étrangers pour ensuite opter soit en faveur de la solution consacrée par l'un de ces systèmes juridiques soit consacrer une solution propre au droit luxembourgeois.

Le constat qui précède ne préjuge cependant en aucune manière de la *démarche de recherche* adoptée par le juge et qui ne trouve pas nécessairement à s'exprimer dans le texte de sa décision (cf. aussi ci-avant sub. 2.1. in fine). On peut prendre pour acquis qu'à l'image des avocats, les juges luxembourgeois font *souvent* des recherches parallèles en droit français *et* belge[1].

Les constats qui précèdent ne devraient d'ailleurs présenter qu'une originalité toute relative par rapport à l'approche qu'un juge adoptera généralement lorsqu'en jurisprudence et doctrine – même nationale – il existe des positions discordantes relativement à la solution d'une même question de droit: une fois que le juge aura opté pour l'une ou l'autre de ces solutions, il ne fera généralement pas même état de la position doctrinale et/ou jurisprudentielle qui va à l'encontre de la solution retenue par lui.

---

[1] Des recherches en droit allemand sont par contre bien plus rares, à la fois parce que les systèmes juridiques sont beaucoup plus différents et parce que pour un juriste luxembourgeois, l'allemand juridique est, sinon impénétrable, du moins très difficile à digérer.

SJEF VAN ERP*

The Use of the Comparative Law Method by the Judiciary – Dutch National Report**

I. INTRODUCTION

If comparative law and its impact on cross-border legal thinking were depicted in the form of a triptych, its three panels would have to portray doctrine, case law and legislation. When asked which of the three parts then should be the middle panel, the reply can, I believe, only be: case law. History shows, reaffirmed by modern practice, that the use of the comparative law method as a way of deciding a case can influence legal practice equally or even more deeply than a legislator might do by introducing abstract legal solutions based on foreign legal examples. Looking at the comparative law method from this perspective, it is not surprising that after discussing "the use of comparative law by the legislature" (Caracas, 1982) and "doctrine as the source of the international codification of law" (Sydney/Melbourne, 1986) the 1994 International Congress of Comparative Law (Athens/Delphi) will re-examine "the use of comparative law by courts" after its first examination in 1966 (Uppsala).[1]

Before going into further detail about the comparative law method as used by the Dutch judiciary, I should first of all explain what is meant by "comparative method". The comparative method is a voluntarily or non-voluntarily chosen approach to the solution of a given case by which non-

* Professor of civil law and European private law University of Maastricht, the Netherlands; Deputy Judge, District Court of Amsterdam.

** I would like to acknowledge my debt to N.A. Florijn, legal researcher at the Netherlands Council of State, for his willingness to discuss his thoughts on the use of comparative law by the Dutch legislature (the subject of his doctoral thesis "Rechtsvergelijking in het wetgevingsproces", published by Tjeenk Willink, Zwolle, 1993). Also, I would like to thank my student-assistant Jack Withaar for his help and ardent interest.

[1] See L. Baudoin, L'usage qui est fait en jurisprudence du droit comparé, in: Rapports Généraux au VIIe Congrès international du droit comparé, Acta Instituti Upsalliensis Jurisprudentiae Comparativae (ed. Å. Malmström) (Stockholm, 1968). Regrettably there were only five national reports: Canada (Québec), Greece, Japan, Poland and the United States (Louisiana).

U. Drobnig and S. van Erp (eds.), The Use of Comparative Law by Courts, 235–25[illegible].

binding foreign law constitutes a substantial factor – with a potentially positive or negative impact – in the decision-making process leading towards the resolution of a question governed either by Dutch law or by the Netherlands binding internationally harmonized or uniform law.[2] This attempt to describe what the comparative law method stands for touches upon several aspects of this approach to the solution of legal problems, some of which will be dealt with in further detail.

First of all the aspect of (non-)voluntariness.[3] One can speak of voluntary use in a case where foreign law is followed only because of its, what common lawyers would call, persuasive authority. The background here can be manifold: e.g. because other legal systems have encountered the same type of problems which they may already have solved in a specific way, or because

---

[2] Cf. J.M. Polak, Theorie en praktijk der Rechtsvinding (doctoral thesis) (Zwolle, 1953), p. 40/41 with references to older Dutch literature, of which I particularly would like to mention E.M. Meijers, Uitlegging en toepassing in Nederland van aan den Code Civil ontleende voorschriften, in: Mededeelingen der Koninklijke Academie van Wetenschappen, Afdeeling Letterkunde, Deel 74, serie B, no. 5 (Amsterdam, 1932), also published in: Verzamelde Privaatrechtelijke Opstellen I, p. 45 ff. (Leyden, 1954). See also I. Kisch, Statutory construction in a new key, "harmonizing interpretation", in: K. Nadelmann *et al.* (eds.), XXth century comparative and conflicts law, Legal essays in honor of Hessel E. Yntema (Leyden, 1961), p. 262 ff.; P.L. Wery, De autonomie van het eenvormig privaatrecht (public lecture) (Deventer, 1971), p. 15 ff.; H.J.M. Jeukens, Rechtsvergelijking in de jurisprudentie van het Hof van Justitie van de Europese Gemeenschappen, in: Publicaties van de Nederlandse Vereniging voor Rechtsvergelijking no. 11 (Deventer, 1973), p. 1 ff.; H.U. Jessurun d'Oliveira, Rechterlijke rechtsvorming en rechtsvergelijking, in: Publicaties van de Nederlandse Vereniging voor Rechtsvergelijking no. 24 (Deventer, 1977), p. 1 ff.; J.H. Snijders, Rechtsvinding door de burgerlijke rechter (doctoral thesis) (Deventer, 1978), p. 15 ff., p. 34 ff.; E.H. Hondius, Het burgerlijk wetboek in rechtsvergelijkend perspectief, in: Bijleveld et al. (eds.), Recht vooruit, Opstellen verzameld ter gelegenheid van 150 jaar BW (Deventer, 1988), p. 59 ff.; B.W.M. Trompenaars, Pluriforme unificatie en uniforme interpretatie (doctoral thesis) (Deventer, 1989), p. 128 ff. and p. 149 ff. (with further references to comparative literature); J.H. Dalhuisen, Wat is vreemd recht? (inaugural lecture) (Deventer, 1991); A.S. Hartkamp, Wetsuitleg en rechtstoepassing na de invoering van het nieuwe Burgerlijk Wetboek (inaugural lecture) (Deventer, 1992), p. 18 ff.

[3] Cf. H. Patrick Glenn, Persuasive authority 32 McGill Law Journal/Revue de droit de McGill, 261 (1987), p. 265, arguing that, on final analysis, all reception of law is neccesarily voluntary. In his own words, when discussing the introduction of the law of a colonizing country in the respective colonies, he formulates it as follows: "A reception in a colonial structure also represents (...) local adherence to an external model of law, since in the absence of adherence or acquiescence there can be no reception, only ongoing struggle." A thesis which could apply in any case of reception. For a further elaboration upon his ideas see also H. Patrick Glenn, Harmonization of private law rules between civil and common law jurisdictions, in: International congress of comparative law (13th: 1990; Montréal, Québec), General reports to the XIIIth Congress of comparative law, (Cowansville, 1992), p. 79 ff. and (same author) Reception and reconciliation of laws, in: P. Sack (ed.), Monismus oder Pluralismus der Rechtskulturen, Anthropologische und ethnologische Grundlagen traditioneller und moderner Rechtssysteme (Berlin, 1991), p. 209 ff. An interesting view is also offered by C. Mouly, Le droit peut-il favoriser l'intégration européenne, 37 Revue internationale de droit comparé 895 (1985), esp. p. 935 ff. and p. 945, stressing the importance of reasoning, as being the essential element in any process of legal thinking.

case law or a given statute (perhaps even a whole code) is based on a foreign example.[4] However, its use can also be non-voluntary. In the latter situation, a further distinction can be made between direct and indirect non-voluntary use. Direct non-voluntary use of the comparative legal method can be found in cases concerning the interpretation of an EC directive – which has to be construed in a "European-autonomous" way[5] – and in cases where an international treaty obliges the parties to the instrument to interpret it in such a way that its unifying nature is being promoted. Indirect non-voluntary use occurs when a judge is compelled to apply foreign law because of his own rules of private (or public) international law. A good example of what is meant here is offered by the obligatory acceptance of a foreign legal decision by reason of conflict-of-laws rules concerning recognition and enforcement of foreign legal judgments or arbitral awards. The procedural and substantive foreign law applied in that foreign decision is – as a consequence of that recognition – also made a part of Dutch law, other than in the well-known exception of cases where the law applied is contrary to public order ("ordre public"). Another example, this time from a public law perspective, can be found in extradition cases. The extradition of the alleged criminal has to be based on facts which are punishable under the criminal laws of both the requesting and the requested state, thus compelling the court, that has to give a ruling on the admissibility of the extradition, to compare its own and foreign criminal law.[6] Because of its narrow relationship with both conflict of laws and public international law and its lack of impact on substantive Dutch law, indirect non-voluntary use of comparative law will generally be left aside in this report.

Secondly, the above attempt to describe the comparative method tries to make clear that this approach is nearly always only one factor in the decisi-

---

[4] Cf. Patrick Glenn, Persuasive authority, p. 265 where he distinguishes reception of a legal system as alliance (e.g. Roman law in Europe before the codification movement, French law in colonial Québec) and reception as construction (e.g. the nineteenth century codifications which encapsulated Roman law in a petrifying national code). Based on this classification scheme he goes on to distinguish two types of "continuation of law": law as enquiry, in the case of reception as alliance, and law as a national response, in cases where persuasive authority has turned into (nationally) binding authority. By clarifying in this way the reasons behind the use of foreign legal sources – which, if falling under the category "persuasive authority" are not really "foreign" – Patrick Glenn certainly offers a helpful insight into the historical background of the comparative method. But he also makes clear how this method can help to create a truly open legal mind which will stimulate a more deeply rooted evolution of the law.

[5] Cf. in this respect the following recent studies regarding the developments towards a European private law: J.H.M. van Erp, Europees privaatrecht in ontwikkeling, in: Themis en Europa/Een opening van nieuwe grenzen?, p. 61 ff. (Zwolle, 1989); F. De Ly, Europese gemeenschap en privaatrecht (inaugural lecture) (Zwolle, 1993); E.H. Hondius, Naar een Europees burgerlijk recht and L.A.D. Keus, Europees privaatrecht-Een bonte lappendeken, Preadviezen uitgebracht voor de Vereniging voor Burgerlijk Recht en de Nederlandse Vereniging voor Europees Recht (Lelystad, 1993).

[6] See for the Netherlands A.H.J. Swart, Uitleveringsrecht (Zwolle, 1986), p. 95 ff.

on-making process, along with other methods, such as reasoning by analogy, as well as historical and teleological interpretation. This aspect of the comparative law method will also not be discussed here, as it belongs more to the general theory of law and legal methodology than to the practical use of comparative law in specific cases. However, I would like to make one remark to avoid any possible misunderstanding. The use of the comparative law method does not mean *per se* that the foreign solution is always used as an example of how a given problem can be solved under Dutch law. It could also be used to demonstrate how *not* to solve that problem. Consequently, the comparative method may have either a positive or a negative impact on the decision-making process.

The focus of this report will, as indicated earlier, be on voluntary and direct non-voluntary use of comparative law. It is here that substantive Dutch law might, to a lesser or greater degree, be determined by foreign law. The degree will depend on the purpose for which the comparative law method is used. It could be that the objective is mere orientation to gain more elaborate insights into the relevant field, but it could also be that foreign law is used as support or justification (or both) for the final decision of the case at hand. The degree will also depend on the relative weight of the comparative law method amongst other methods of interpretation, as was mentioned earlier. This makes it clear from the outset, beyond any reasonable doubt, that no general conclusions can be drawn from the following analysis of Dutch case law. In each case, only differing shades of authority bestowed on foreign law can be sketched and only a limited number of cases can be discussed, given the limits of this report. Furthermore, this report will, also by necessity, mainly focus on private law, although public law examples will be given where available. The reason is that the comparative law method seems to have developed more in private law areas than in the field of public law. A possible explanation could be that, as a result of the pervasiveness of Roman legal thinking with regard to private law, even after the codification movement on the continent of Europe, a feeling of comity remained alive. This feeling was no doubt strengthened in those areas where international trade demanded cooperation. A common "*ratio scripta*", on the other hand, never existed to the same degree in public law. For this reason, public law could develop more locally, and this development was intensified both by the rise of the nation state and by the need to disentangle public law from the "general" theory of private law, thus securing its expansion into a field of its own. As far as criminal law is concerned, it should be added that here the fundamental maxim of "*nulla poena, sine lege*" has a far-reaching influence. The consequence of this maxim is that judge-made substantial criminal law will not be found in Dutch law. Comparative criminal law is, as far as I have been able to establish, never used by the Supreme Court, although it occasionally happens that the Public Ministry[7] at the Supreme Court will put forward

[7] In Dutch: "Openbaar Ministerie", French: "Ministère Public". The English translation

comparative legal arguments in its advisory opinion.[8] A few examples will be given in Section V.

Before elaborating further upon the comparative law method along the lines just indicated, I will make some introductory remarks concerning the role of the Netherlands Supreme Court. These will concern: (1) the special relationship between on the one side Dutch law and on the other side the law of the Netherlands Antilles and Aruba, as well as (2) the supervisory role of the Supreme Court when it comes to decisions by lower courts in which comparative legal arguments have been used. Then the "hidden" use of comparative law will be dealt with, followed by a topical review of cases where the comparative law method has been used openly. This review will be followed by some tentative conclusions.

II. The Supreme Court as highest court for the Netherlands, the Netherlands Antilles and Aruba: inter-regional comparisons

The Netherlands Supreme Court (Hoge Raad der Nederlanden) is not only the highest court for that part of the Kingdom of the Netherlands which is in Europe (usually referred to as "the Netherlands"), but also for the parts of the kingdom in South America: the Netherlands Antilles and Aruba. The importance of this lies in the fact that the three parts of the Kingdom are separate jurisdictions when it comes to matters of substantive law. Consequently, one common Supreme Court may prevent unnecessary divergence. The role of the Supreme Court as the highest court for the Netherlands Antilles and Aruba is limited, however. The Supreme Court only has jurisdiction in, generally speaking, civil and criminal cases. Excluded are, among other matters, tax and bankruptcy cases.[9] The possibility of legal divergence in the

of "Openbaar Ministerie" as "Public Prosecutions Department", which sometimes can be found in an English language version of Dutch legal texts, can only be used if the "Openbaar Ministerie" at the level of District Courts or Courts of Appeal is meant. The legal status of the "Openbaar Ministerie" at the Supreme Court is very different compared to the status of their counterparts at a lower court level. The Procurator General and the Advocates General at the Supreme Court submit advisory opinions to the Court in both criminal and civil cases and are independent from the Ministry of Justice.

[8] Cf. D. Hazewinkel-Suringa/J. Remmelink, Inleiding tot de studie van het Nederlandse strafrecht (Alpen a/d Rijn, 1991, p. 71 (comparative law method is used by the Public Ministry as an argument in traffic law cases, because of international uniform regulation).

[9] Cf. Regulation concerning Cassation for the Netherlands Antilles and Aruba (Cassatieregeling voor de Nederlandse Antillen en Aruba), Kingdom Act 20 July 1961, Bulletin of Acts and Decrees 1961, 212 (with amendments). See W.E. Haak De blik vooruit na 25 jaar Cassatieregeling Nederlandse Antillen, Tijdschrift voor Antilliaans Recht-Justicia 1990, issue 3, p. 1 ff.; reply by F.B.M. Kunneman (Concordantie en cassatie) and J.A.B. Janus (een "gegarandeerde" cassatieregeling (?)) with a rejoinder by Haak, Tijdschrift voor Antilliaans Recht-Justicia 1990, issue 4, p. 17 ff. See also Veegens/Korthals Altes/Groen, Cassatie in burgerlijke zaken (Zwolle, 1989), nrs. 31 and 86.

fields of civil and commercial law has become more likely since the promulgation of a new Civil Code for the Netherlands, which does not apply in the Netherlands Antilles and Aruba. There, the old Civil Code is still in force. This means that decisions by the Supreme Court given in cases under Dutch private law are no longer necessarily decisive for the same question under the law of the Netherlands Antilles or Aruba and *vice versa*. The Charter for the Kingdom (Statuut voor het Koninkrijk), which governs the relationships between the constituent parts of the Kingdom, nevertheless obliges the courts to make great efforts to keep the various legal systems in the fields of civil and commercial law, criminal law, civil and criminal procedural law and some parts of intellectual property law as close together as possible.[10]

An example of this effort can be found in H.R. 13 March 1981, N.J. 1982, 57 (*Steward v. Williams*)[11], a case concerning immovable property on the island of St. Maarten (Little Bay District), where English is the prevailing language. The question to be answered was whether the, according to the N.A. Civil Code, invalid transfer of immovable property by merely handing over a "receipt" could still be considered as a transfer based on a "legal title".[12] If so, the invalidity could no longer be invoked; possession in good faith based on a "legal title" led to the acquisition of the property right after 20 years. If not, the usual prescription period of 30 years would apply. The Supreme Court denied the applicability of the 20-year prescription period, arguing solely on the basis of Dutch law, asserting that the relevant law of the Netherlands Antilles was equal to Dutch law. The requirement of public registration of a notarial deed of transfer is such an essential condition for the transfer of immovable property that it cannot be evaded by possession in good faith during a period of twenty years in a case where only a receipt had been handed over. The Advocate General Haak, in his advisory opinion, argued the same on the basis of article 2265 French Civil Code which was the basis of both article 1982 N.A. C.C. and article 2000 N. C.C. [13]

---

[10] Art. 39 Charter for the Kingdom; cf. also art. 38 of the Charter. Article 38 does not apply to private international law nor to inter-regional law (i.e. the rules to decide the law of which consituent part of the Kingdom has to be applied in a – to use an American term – "diversity" case).

[11] H.R.: Hoge Raad (Supreme Court); N.J.: Nederlandse Jurisprudentie (Netherlands Law Reports).

[12] The receipt read as follows (English is the original language): "Received from Miss Catherine Stewart the sum of Twenty dollars on a Piece of Land situated (...). Sale to be given when called for, and also the am't of Ten dollars to be paid."

[13] As is probably well known, the former Dutch Civil Code was to a large degree based on the French Civil Code. For an early comparison of the two codes see C. Asser, Het Nederlandsch Burgerlijk Wetboek vergeleken met het Wetboek Napoleon (2nd ed., The Hague/Amsterdam, 1838). Where foreign law is taken as a more-or-less direct model, it is sometimes difficult to clearly distinguish the historical from the comparative method of interpretation. Of course the two are closely related, but they are not the same. If, in the case of the Dutch Civil Code, the comparisons with French law include developments in France after the promulgation of the Civil Code, the method of interpretation becomes less historical and more comparative. Other examples of important civil cases where French law has

An example of a recent case where Dutch law differs from the law of the Netherlands Antilles and Aruba is H.R. 26 November 1988, N.J. 1989, 421 (*X v. Y*), a case about inter-regional conflicts of law. Here the Supreme Court held that the Dutch inter-regional rule to decide which law would apply to the grounds for a divorce, requested in the Netherlands, between a husband living in the Netherlands and a wife living in the Netherlands Antilles, should be based on the Dutch private international law rule. That rule, in turn, was based on international conventions. It is not certain if this inter-regional conflicts-of-law rule will be followed in a case governed by Antillean or Aruban law.

Growing divergence between Dutch and e.g. Antillean civil and commercial law is now (as mentioned earlier), in spite of the efforts to harmonize the laws of the different constituent parts of the Kingdom more than ever possible.[14] This results in questions not just about which authority has to be given to Dutch law when determining questions of Antillean or Aruban law, but also the other way round: how to deal with differing Antillean and Aruban law in a comparable case under Dutch law. It can be said with near absolute certainty that those areas which have been developed for the most part in case law, both under the old and the new Civil Code, will hardly be affected. A prominent example is pre-contractual liability and, closely related, the liability for unilateral undertakings, in particular by public authorities. Pre-contractual liability was developed under Dutch law whereas several very recent Supreme Court decisions on liability for undertakings have been given in cases governed by Aruban and Antillean law.[15] Legal practitioners consi-

---

influenced the interpretation of the comparable articles in the Dutch Civil Code are H.R. 3 March 1905, Weekblad van het Recht 8191 (*Blaauboer v. Berlaos*, deciding that a contract can only confer rights upon third parties, but cannot impose duties upon them) and H.R. 31 January 1919, N.J. 1919, 161 (*Lindenbaum v. Cohen*, deciding that the tort of negligence included cases where the action or inaction was against principles of proper behaviour in society, now codified in article 6:162 C.C.).

[14] But cf. A.S. Hartkamp, De betekenis van de invoering van een nieuw vermogensrecht (Boeken 3-8 NBW) in Nederland voor de rechtspraktijk in het Koninkrijk, Tijdschrift voor Antilliaans Recht-Justicia 1991, issue 2, p. 65 ff, who believes that, even with a new Civil code in the Netherlands, the differences will remain minimal. A good illustration of the way this might work out in practice can be seen in H.R. 22 January 1993, N.J. 1993, 597 (*Windward Islands Bank v. Jongsma*). Here the Court upheld a clause in general bankconditions creating liability of the client, who had lost a case against the bank, for court expenses above the amount of legal costs due to be paid by any losing party as determined by the N.A. Code of Civil Procedure. The argument which the Court gave was that developments under Dutch law even from before the new Civil Code had created a regime which would protect that client against abuse of this general clause, to which was added that Antillean law in this respect was compatible with Dutch law. To put it briefly: "old" and "new" Dutch law were not basically different and "old" (or "new"?) Dutch law was equal to Antillean law, so Antillean law is actually "new" Dutch law. A truly remarkable outcome.

[15] See e.g. H.R. 27 November 1992, N.J. 1993, 287 (*Felix v. Aruba*) and H.R. 10 September 1993, N.J. 1996, 3 (*Den Dulk v. Curaçao*). The abbreviation "R.v.d.W." means "Rechtspraak van de Week" (Weekly Law Reports).

der all these cases applicable under Dutch, Antillean and Aruban law. In other areas, where the new Civil Code brought fundamental changes, the situation is unclear.

III. PROCEDURAL REMARKS: THE SUPREME COURT AND FOREIGN LAW

According to Art. 99 Law concerning the Organization of the Judiciary (Wet op de Rechterlijke Organisatie)[16], the Supreme Court has to reverse a lower court judgment if its decision is given in disregard of formal requirements, the violation of which is sanctioned with nullity, or if its decision is given in violation of the law, with the exception of the law of foreign states.[17] Dutch procedural law in this respect follows the French system of "cassation": the Supreme Court only rules on questions of law, not on questions of fact. The application of foreign law by a lower court is considered to be a question of fact, which means that the Supreme Court will not vacate a judgment which is based on an incorrect application of foreign law, unless the lower court argued that foreign law and Dutch law did not differ and, in the opinion of the Supreme Court, Dutch law had been misapplied.[18] Nevertheless, the Supreme Court will reverse a decision if the use of foreign law has not been based on a proper reasoning. In the latter case, the judgment is given in violation of a basic rule of civil procedure, i.e. the rule that every judgment must be based on solid and reasonably understandable arguments.

It may be useful to look at an example of a case where the Supreme Court refused to give a ruling on the application of foreign law by the lower court as well as a case where the Supreme Court did give such a ruling, reasoning that the decision was based on insufficiently clear arguments. The first case is H.R. 27 June 1969, N.J. 1969, 365 (*Carl Zeiss Jena/GDR v. Jenaer Glaswerk Schott & Gen/FRG*). In this case, the Court of Appeals in The Hague had decided that, according to the law of the Federal Republic of Germany, the Carl Zeiss Stiftung Heidenheim a/d Brenz was a legal person

[16] Bulletin of Acts and Decrees 1827, 20 (with further amendments).

[17] In cases where the Supreme Court sits in its capacity of ulterior court in an Antillean or Aruban case, not only the violation of Antillean or Aruban law, but also the violation of Dutch law is a ground for annulment of the decision of the lower court. In an Antillean or Aruban case, the lower court is the Joint Court of Appeal of the Netherlands Antilles and Aruba. (The Joint Court decides cases coming from a Court of First Instance.) Cf. art. 1 Regulation concerning Cassation for the Netherlands Antilles and Aruba.

[18] See Veegens/Korthals Altes/Groen, Cassatie in burgerlijke zaken nr. 87 ff. and H.R. 4 April 1986, N.J. 1987, 678 (*Ragetlie v. SLM*; presumption by the lower court that under the circumstances of that particular case the relevant rule of Surinam and Dutch labour law was not essentially different). This refinement, however, does not imply that it can be argued that, given that the Dutch and the foreign rule are the same, misapplication of Dutch law would allow the Supreme Court to vacate the judgment on the basis of misapplication of foreign law. See H.R. 20 April 1990, N.J. 1991, 439 (*Eurasian express line et al. v. Oulu Osekeyhtio*).

under West German law and, as such, was a legal person according to Dutch law. The Supreme Court refused to rule on the argument that the lower court had misapplied foreign (in this case, West German) law. The second case is H.R. 2 April 1976, N.J. 1977, 124 (*Stadtjugendamt Iserlohn v. the estate of X*). In this case, the Stadtjugendamt had, on behalf of a child living in Iserlohn, applied to the court to give a maintenance order against the father, living in the Netherlands, who had declared that he was the biological father. The Court refused this, on the advice of the Child Care and Protection Board, on the grounds that the father had to pay maintenance to other children in the Netherlands and had a relatively low income. The Supreme Court vacated the decision, arguing that the Court of Appeals had not given any reasons why the relevant provision of the German Civil Code, which would have led to a different conclusion, should not be applied.[19]

IV. "HIDDEN" USE OF THE COMPARATIVE LAW METHOD

So far, the cases used merely to illustrate the first part of this report seem to suggest that Dutch judges use the comparative law method more and more often. Before proceeding with a further survey of relevant cases to find out whether this first impression is indeed an adequate description of the situation in the Netherlands, a complicating factor must be discussed: the sometimes "hidden" use of comparative law.

First of all, the least hidden use of the comparative law method by the Supreme Court can be found where, although the court itself does not give foreign law as an argument, it is obvious that the justices could have gained inspiration from the advisory opinion of the Public Ministry, which did present comparative insights. A good illustration is offered by the decision in *Steward v. Williams*, a case which was discussed earlier (Section II). Another example, although less hidden than in the previous case, can be found in H.R. 9 October 1992, N.J. 1994, 535 (*B. v. Bayer Nederland et al.*, the "DES daughters" case). In that decision, the Supreme Court, while accepting joint and several liability of the pharmaceutical industry for the damage caused by the use of DES during pregnancy, rejected the possibility of a so-called "market-share liability" as developed in American law, saying: "(...) such a system of market-share liability – which was elaborated in the advisory opinion of the Public Ministry, nrs. 17–21 – cannot be accepted".

A truly hidden use of comparative law can be found in cases where an advocate, presenting his case before the Supreme Court, refers to comparative research, which, if one looks at the arguments upon which the decision is based, could have influenced the court. An example is (perhaps?) H.R. 9 March 1990, N.J. 1990, 561 (*Kacar-Kisacik v. Stegeman*). The question

---

[19] § 1603 German Civil Code states that in a case like this the father was obliged, be it within certain limits, to maintain all his children.

which had to be answered was when, as a question of law, a woman was deemed to be pregnant, in a case where she had been dismissed at a time when her pregnancy was still unknown to her. The relevance of the question lies in the fact that, during pregnancy, dismissal is not allowed. The ruling which the Supreme Court gave was that, under the present circumstances, it could be unfair that the burden of proof would fall solely on the employee. For this reason, the general principle of the Dutch law of evidence that the burden of proof rests upon the person who states a claim might be departed from. That decision comes, at least in its reasoning, very close to a judgment by the German Bundesarbeitsgericht, although finally there a more specific rule was given. The German court decided that a pregnancy should be deemed to have begun 280 days before the expected birth of the child as predicted by a medical doctor.[20] It might seem that the similarity of reasoning in these two cases is somewhat accidental, given the difference in final ruling. However, if one reads the arguments presented by one of the advocates – specifically discussing German law – the submission that comparative arguments might have influenced the court becomes more tenable.

The use of comparative research by counsel is sometimes less concealed in cases where references to this research can be found in the advisory opinion of the Public Ministry. See e.g. H.R. 19 April 1991, N.J. 1991, 690 (*Dienstenbond FNV v. Kip and Sloetjes*, which will be discussed below in Section V.B.6), p. 2974 (advisory opinion by the Advocate General Koopmans) and the already mentioned Des daughters case, p. 2488 and p. 2491 (advisory opinion by the Advocate General Hartkamp).

V. THE USE OF THE COMPARATIVE LAW METHOD: A TOPICAL REVIEW

Research using modern technology (CD-ROM) has made it instantly clear that discussing all cases in which foreign law has played a role in the decision-making process, even limited to those decided by the Supreme Court in the five year period 1989–1993[21], would prove to be a task far beyond my reach, given the time available and the limits of this report. For this reason, I have decided to offer a few examples in areas which seem most influenced by the use of the comparative law method. To avoid the impression, however, that this method has only been used frequently in recent years, and, until then, was for the most part limited to comparisons with French law, I

---

[20] Bundesarbeitsgericht 27 October 1983, Neue Zeitschrift für Arbeits- und Sozialrecht 1985, p. 222 ff.

[21] Two areas where lower court decisions are of great practical importance should at least be mentioned here: admiralty law (particularly cases decided by the District Court of Rotterdam) and private international law. I can only refer to the journals in which admiralty law and private international law cases are published: Schip en Schade (abreviated: S & S) and Nederlands Internationaal Privaatrecht (abreviated: NIPR).

would like to start this topical review with a discussion of a few relatively older cases.

A. Growing use of comparative law beginning in the first half of this century

The first cases in which the comparative law method, in the broad sense as defined earlier, became more settled all date – remarkably enough – from 1941 and later. I will briefly discuss five cases: H.R. 28 November 1941, N.J. 1942, 205 (*Buma v. Jogchem's Theaters*), H.R. 2 April 1942, N.J. 1942, 468 (*Jurgens v. Van Heesch*), H.R. 21 May 1943, N.J. 1943, 455 (*Van Kreuningen v. Bessem*), H.R. 25 June 1943, N.J. 1943, 498 (*Henkel v. Sikkens*) and H.R. 17 October 1946, N.J. 1947, 33 (*Vlamoven v. Van de Pol*). These decisions concern industrial property law (Buma, Henkel and Vlamoven), private international law (Jurgens) and the law of damages (Van Kreuningen).

In each of the three industrial-law cases, a point arose as to the existence or non-existence of protection under the relevant statutes and all three demanded a policy decision with potentially far-reaching financial consequences, not just for the case at hand but also in future cases. The Buma case was about the question of whether a transferee of a copyright could be bound by a previous contract made by the transferor, limiting that copyright. According to a previous ruling (see *Blaauboer v. Berlips*, mentioned previously), a contract could not bind third parties, but, should this rule also apply here? The answer was negative: commerce, especially in an area which was regulated internationally, demanded that "rights in rem" – like a copyright according to Dutch law – could be limited by previous contracts as long as no public register existed in which these agreements could be published, and that this was in accordance with the system of the Dutch Copyright Act. Consequently a policy choice which was at the basis of Dutch private law was abandoned here for reasons of incompatibility with other legal systems. In the Henkel case, the question which arose was under which conditions a trade mark could be registered under the Dutch Trade Mark Act. Henkel had registered a trademark "Imi" with the description: "chemical products for industrial purposes". According to the Supreme Court this was specific enough. The Trade Mark Act required that the kind of goods for which the trademark was registered would be mentioned and international use, important for this internationally regulated area, made it clear that this description was not unacceptably vague. The third industrial property case was about the annulment of a patent. If a request for a patent was modified in some essential respect, should the patent given on the basis of the changed request be annulled or should the patentability be judged at the moment of the requested change? The answer was, with a reference to the English Patent and Design Act as well as the German legal practice, that the patent should not be annulled, but its validity be decided as of the moment of modification.

Jurgens v. Van Heesch was a case about the private international law rule "*locus regit actum*". If a gift had not been offered and accepted in a notarial deed and for that reason was void according to Dutch law, being the "locus", did this imply that the gift might also be held formally invalid under the law applicable to the gift itself, in this case English law? The Supreme Court did not agree with this latter conclusion, as, in most European countries, statute and case law were in favour of a multiple rule of formal validity as was here submitted and also because the interests of international dealings required acceptance of such a rule.

Finally a case in the field of tort law, which, to stress its importance, was recently reaffirmed. Van Kreuningen had suffered personal damage because of a car accident caused by Van Bessem. The question to be decided was whether art. 1407 (old) C.C. allowed the judge to award damages for pain and suffering. The Court ruled that, in case of any doubt as to the meaning of art. 1407 C.C., the decision should be in favour of allowing such an award. The arguments given were that both the law as it was before the introduction of the Civil Code and the law in our neighbouring countries were in favour of such a decision.[22] This decision was followed in the recent case of H.R. 8 July 1992, N.J. 1992, 714 (*Academisch Medisch Centrum Amsterdam v. O.*). The facts of the case are extremely sad. A young medical doctor at the Amsterdam Medical Centre (a university hospital), which specializes in helping AIDS patients, by accident used an unclean intravenous needle for a blood transfusion to a 57-year-old married patient with an average life expectancy. The patient became infected with the HIV virus and sued, among others, the Amsterdam Academic Medical Centre for damages because of pain and suffering. The Supreme Court, while stressing that a decision to award immaterial damages has to be based on Dutch standards, did not find any violation of a rule of law in this case when the Amsterdam Court of Appeals had taken into account developments in other countries, without the parties even having made this a point of their argument.

Even after this short case review, it already seems clear that the comparative law method is used mostly in those areas where Dutch law interacts with the laws of neighbouring countries as well as legal rules laid down in treaties. This is particularly true in areas of international commerce, but – as can be seen in the torts cases – not only there. The following topical review will elaborate upon this further.

---

[22] Again, I have already made an earlier reference to this; it can be seen how the historical and the comparative method of interpretation sometimes come very close or even overlap. See the interesting remarks made by N.A. Florijn in his thesis, when discussing this case. *Van Kreuningen v. Van Bessem* has been codified in art. 6:106 C.C.

B. Traditional and more recent areas where the comparative law method is used

For the reasons given earlier, only a few examples can be discussed here. Given my impression that the comparative law method is more widely used than these cases show, particularly by the Supreme Court, I have included decisions where comparative legal research was undertaken by the Public Ministry, as can be found in advisory opinions. In spite of this, I have to admit that, strictly speaking, in these cases, use of the comparative law method by the judiciary cannot often be ascertained.[23]

1. Private (and public) international law[24]

In H.R. 23 September 1988, N.J. 1989, 743 (*Mines de Potace d'Alsace v. Onroerend Goed Maatschappij Bier et al.*), the Supreme Court decided that the French Mines de Potace were liable in tort under Dutch law against the growers of vegetables in the western part of the Netherlands because of pollution of the Rhine with salt. The decisions of the District Court of Rotterdam are especially intriguing, since this liability was also based on public international law arguments. This aspect was no longer a part of the argument when the case came before the Supreme Court.

H.R. 6 December 1991, N.J. 1992, 669 (*H. v. M.*) was a case about international matrimonial property law. At the time of marriage, both husband and wife had been of Spanish nationality, with the consequence that, according to Dutch private international law, Spanish law would be applicable to their matrimonial property regime. In a case of differing nationalities, however, the law of the first matrimonial domicile governs, which would have been Dutch law in this case. The wife stated that there was no true common nationality and for that reason Dutch law should govern the matrimonial property regime. The argument she put forward was that she had acquired her Spanish nationality involuntarily at the moment of her marriage and hence her other (Dutch) nationality should be considered as "effective". This argument was rejected by the Supreme Court. Legal certainty was needed in this area and weighing the "effectiveness" of a nationality would jeopardize that. The Advocate General Strikwerda discussed, among other aspects, the views of A. E. von Overbeck in his "*rapport explicatif*" con-

---

[23] Excluded were cases which, despite the fact that they drew comments from a comparative perspective, did not offer any indication at all that comparative legal insights might have influenced the final outcome. Cf. e.g. H.R. 2 February 1990, N.J. 1991, 1 (*Staat der Nederlanden v. Stichting Natuur en Milieu*) in which it was decided that judges can ask for expert testimony also on questions of law. In a case note, published in the Nederlandse Jurisprudentie 1991, p. 6, J.B.M. Vranken discusses the uniqueness of this ruling from a comparative perspective, an aspect not taken into consideration by the Supreme Court nor the Public Ministry.

[24] See also H.R. 2 April 1942, N.J. 1942, 468 (*Jurgens v. Van Heesch*), mentioned earlier.

cerning the Hague Convention on Matrimonial Property.

H.R. 30 October 1992, N.J. 1993, 117 (*Vandervoodt v. Indosuez Bank België*). With an explicit reference to the comparative research done by the Advocate General Strikwerda, the Supreme Court gave a ruling on the interpretation of the Geneva Convention for the settlement of certain conflicts of laws in connection with bills of exchange and promissory notes 1930. The holder of a bill of exchange was allowed, in a case governed by Belgian law because the bill of exchange had been issued in Belgium, to demand payment from the drawee/debtor in a situation where the drawer was involved in bankruptcy proceedings. The Advocate General, in his advisory opinion, presented an elaborate discussion of comparative legal literature concerning the aforementioned Geneva Convention.

2. International commercial law[25]

Cases falling within this category very often also belong to the group of decisions discussed under the heading private (and public) international law (see e.g. *Vandervoodt v. Indosuez Bank België*). Similarly, the example I would like to discuss here is, partially, a case about private international law. At the same time, however, the decision offers a very clear illustration of the way in which the Supreme Court decides questions concerning uniform commercial law. The case is H.R. 29 June 1990, N.J. 1992, 106, also published in Revue de droit uniforme/Uniform Law Review 1990, I, p. 457 ff (*Nilsson & Noll v. Delta Lloyd*). Nilsson & Noll (a transport company in Sweden) had concluded a contract of transport with Volvo-Car Produktie Born (Netherlands). The goods were to be transported in trailers partly by road and partly by sea (roll-on/roll-off ship). For the transport by sea, Nilsson & Noll had concluded a contract with Tor Lloyd AB which had issued a non-negotiable waybill. During the voyage, the goods in four trailers, which had been stored on deck, were severely damaged because of a heavy storm. The insurers paid the damages and then sued Nilsson & Noll as road carriers arguing that, although this was so-called "piggy back" transport, the liability regime of the Convention on the contract for the international carriage of goods by road (CMR) should govern. Nilsson & Noll replied that, in this case, the exception laid down in art. 2 (1) CMR was applicable. According to that article the liability regime under the present circumstances was not governed by the CMR but by "the conditions prescribed by law" for the carriage of goods by sea, here the so-called Hague-Visby Rules. One of the difficulties which arose was that the equally authentic French text of art. 2 (1) CMR used an at-first-sight different terminology. It said that the "*dispositions impératives de la loi*" concerning the transport of goods by sea should govern. Could that lead to a different regime from that under the English

[25] Cf. also H.R. 28 November 1941, N.J. 1942, 205 (*Buma v. Jogchem's Theaters*), H.R. 25 June 1943, N.J. 1943, 498 (*Henkel v. Sikkens*) and H.R. 17 October 1946, N.J. 1947, 33 (*Vlamoven v. Van de Pol*).

text? The Supreme Court first of all referred to the advisory opinion given by the Advocate General Haak, who had made it clear beyond doubt that there was no internationally accepted uniform interpretation of art. 2 (1) CMR to solve this conundrum. As there were also no "*travaux préparatoires*" available, the Court based its decision on the object and purpose of the CMR and ruled that, if no bill of lading had been issued and consequently the Hague-Visby rules would not apply by themselves[26], these rules would still govern the liability regime in the present case. A uniform interpretation of art. 2 (1) CMR demanded, in the view of the Court, a highly objectivist approach, leading to the applicability of the regime on which the parties could have been expected to agree in an average case of transport of goods by sea. The fact that the actual contract between the parties would lead to a different result was thus no longer relevant.

3. *Interpretation of "open" norms*

In the new Dutch Civil Code, which in this respect only continues an already existing trend, several matters, especially those which require an *ad-hoc* balancing of interests, have been left to the judges' discretion. This is very often done by avoiding detailed rules and instead formulating an open-ended norm, like for example the duty of creditor and debtor to comply with what good faith requires. Some decisions show that the Supreme Court in cases involving these open-ended rules takes a close look at the position of the respective parties in society, taking into regard the specific group to which they belong. This sometimes means that a factor influencing the decision can be that a party has a foreign legal background. Thus notions originating in foreign law can enter the decision-making process almost unnoticed.[27] Let me give an example: H.R. 18 November 1983, N.J. 1984, 345 (*Shu v. Lam*). The case was about the famous (or notorious?) problem of how to solve the dilemma which arises when someone declares something which he later denies to have been in conformity with what he truly wanted, whereas the party to whom the declaration was made had relied on that same statement supposing that this was what the other party truly intended. Shu, who worked as a cook in a Chinese restaurant, thought he had a contract of employment with Lam, the *de-facto* business manager. Lam, however, stated that not he but his sister was the employer, as she was the owner of the restaurant. According to the Supreme Court, questions of justified reliance had to be solved taking into consideration all the relevant circumstances of the case. These included the fact that both parties were Chinese and, as such, had

---

[26] And even if a bill of lading had been issued, the Hague-Visby rules would not apply (at least not by way of mandatory rule) because the trailers with the goods were stored on deck.

[27] This is not the "hidden" use of the comparative law method mentioned earlier. Once the foreign background of the parties has become a relevant factor, the comparative law method is used openly. Cf. in this respect also S. Rutten, Moslims in de Nederlandse rechtspraak (Kampen, 1988), p. 264 ff.

certain expectations about who could be considered to be the "employer".

4. Tort law

See the cases earlier examined: H.R. 21 May 1943, N.J. 1943, 455 (*Van Kreuningen v. Bessem*); H.R. 8 July 1992, N.J. 1992, 714 (*Academisch Medisch Centrum Amsterdam v. O.*); H.R. 9 October 1992, N.J. 1994, 535 (*B. v. Bayer Nederland et al.*, the "DES daughters" case): H.R. 23 September 1988, N.J. 1989, 743 (*Mines de Potace d'Alsace v. Onroerend Goed Maatschappij Bier et al.*) and the case which will be discussed under the heading Labour law: H.R. 19 April 1991, N.J. 1991, 690 (*Dienstenbond FNV v. Kip and Sloetjes*).

5. Environmental law

See: H.R. 23 September 1988, N.J. 1989, 743 (*Mines de Potace d'Alsace v. Onroerend Goed Maatschappij Bier et al.*).

6. Labour law

H.R. 19 April 1991, N.J. 1991, 690 (*Dienstenbond FNV v. Kip and Sloetjes*). Under pressure from a strike organized by a labour union, Kip and Sloetjes had sold their shares in a limited company of which they were the single owners; moreover they had resigned as its directors. The labour union hoped, by forcibly changing the legal control and management of the company, to secure its further existence. Kip and Sloetjes later sued the labour union for damages, arguing that the union had committed a tort by using undue pressure, causing them to sell below the actual value of the shares. The labour union rejected this contention, saying that article 6 (4) of the European Social Charter (ESC) gave them judicial protection against claims such as these which were based on strikes they had organized. The Supreme Court rejected this interpretation of article 6 (4) ESC, saying that case law and legal literature in the countries which were a party to the Charter showed that this type of strike, directly aimed at a change of management without demanding e.g. a pay rise, was a-typical and, as such, not protected by the ESC.

7. Criminal law

Two cases can be mentioned in which the representative of the Public Ministry at the Supreme Court used comparative law as an argument in his advisory opinion. In both cases, the Supreme Court did not give any indication whatsoever of the extent to which the submitted comparative law arguments might have influenced its decision.

H.R. 15 January 1991, N.J. 1991, 668 (computer crime). From a comparative law point of view, two interesting questions arose in this case. First of all, the case presented a formal question. Can a Procurator General at a Court of Appeals ask the Supreme Court to reverse a decision in which a positive ruling has been given on a request by that same Procurator General? The argument put forward by the Procurator General was that the legal questions which had to be answered in this case were of the utmost practical importance and a ruling by the Supreme Court was badly needed. The Advocate General at the Supreme Court Meijers denied that the Procurator General had standing, citing French case law. The Supreme Court disagreed with its Advocate General. The second question was whether art. 225 Criminal Code, declaring it unlawful to counterfeit documents, could apply in a case where computer data stored on a disk had been used improperly. Could such a disk, on which data were stored for a limited period of time only, be considered as a document intended as evidence? Based in part on comparative research, the Advocate General concluded that this was possible. The Supreme Court agreed, without any reference to foreign legal materials or the advisory opinion.

H.R. 1 October 1991, N.J. 1992, 197 (the case of "Psychiatrist F."). The question was whether art. 249 Criminal Code, forbidding impudity (especially sexual intercourse) between a doctor and a patient under his care, could be applied in a case where a psychiatrist had behaved in a highly indecent and professionally improper way towards a patient in a psychiatric hospital who had been admitted by her own volition. The Procurator General Remmelink gave as his advisory opinion, referring to German law, that this was indeed the case. He was followed by the Supreme Court, again without any reference to foreign law or even to the advisory opinion.

VI. FINAL REMARKS

The traditional areas where the comparative law method is used by the Dutch judiciary are private and public international law (e.g. the interpretation of treaties) and international commercial law (which is strongly connected with the aforementioned areas). Alongside these traditional areas, the comparative law method has, more recently, also been used in other areas. An aspect which seems to be common to all of these is that they are connected with problems shared by nearly all industrialized societies (e.g. mass marketing of products, pollution of the environment, computer crime).

It would be mere speculation if I attempted to predict the specific areas which, in the near future, might show a rise in the use of the comparative law method. Only a few, rather general, remarks can be made. The comparative law method will no doubt be used more and more in those areas where a common legal culture exists or is coming into existence. This common legal culture can be very old (e.g. based on a shared heritage, such as Roman law or Common law) but it can also be fairly recent. An example of the latter type of situation can be found in countries whose markets are integrating and, for that reason, are compelled to harmonize or even unify parts of their legal systems. Partial legal integration may create an atmosphere of mutual understanding and hence a more far-reaching movement towards convergence of legal solutions.

Traditionally, private-law areas, such as contract, tort and property law, have been more open to influences from abroad than family law, matrimonial property law and succession, as well as public-law areas, like procedural law, criminal law and administrative law. But even here changes are in the air. Nowadays, cohabitation without marriage very often results in purely contractual arrangements between the partners, thus removing these relationships from the reach of family law and matrimonial property law. The problems caused by this phenomenon, which can be seen throughout the western world, are much the same in every legal system. Also, in traditionally public-law areas, a change can be felt. It could well be that, in (civil and criminal) procedural law, the idea of a fair trial and the principles resulting therefrom, as laid down in the Rome Convention on Basic Human Rights and Fundamental Freedoms, will influence Dutch case law even beyond the reach of that treaty. Foreign notions of a fair trial might be taken into consideration, perhaps at the level of advisory opinions by the Public Ministry or during judicial deliberations in chambers. Criminal law, by contrast, will probably remain far less open to foreign non-binding influence because of the absolutely fundamental principle of "*nulla poena, sine lege*". As far as administrative law is concerned, the situation might be different again. It would not be surprising if the coming years were to show a growing tendency to look for inspiration from abroad, especially in those areas where common social and economic problems occur, for example illegal immigration. It could also happen that European administrative law will have an increasing influence on Dutch administrative law. A good example here may be the way in which the principle of proportionality is applied under European law; this might show the direction for its application by Dutch courts in strictly national cases. On the other hand, it should be remembered that administrative law is typically an area where statutory solutions are preferred to solutions developed by case law.

Perhaps it is not too much of an oversimplification to conclude this report by saying that, as far as the Netherlands is concerned, the opening of national markets and the creation of an open economy is reflected in the opening of our national legal system, resulting in an increasingly more open legal mind and hence an ever-growing use of the comparative law method by the judiciary. It could well be that this change in attitude leads to what Tancelin[28] regards as vital to a more deep-seated understanding of comparative law: "La vision du droit des comparatistes est révolue: les systèmes auxquels on n'appartient pas tournent autor du système du rattachement, à la façon dont le soleil tournait autor de la terre pour les anciens. Le droit comparé a besoin de sa révolution copernicienne."

---

[28] M. Tancelin, Contribution du Québec à la recherche des causes du déclin ou de l'éclipse du "jus commune", Il Foro Italiano 1983 (September volume), V, 207.

ESIN ÖRÜCÜ*

Comparative Law in British Courts**

I. INTRODUCTION

1. In this study[1] the phrase comparative law is used in its broadest sense, that is, not just as a theoretical distillate and an abstraction, *the tertium comparationis*, but as covering even a passing reference to foreign law by a court, or the use of merely a single solution offered by foreign law, *secundum comparatum*. Comparative law does not here imply a comparison of differences and similarities carried out by the courts but solely the use of a foreign solution either in its entirety or as a guide to interpretation. Even a cursory reference to foreign law, subsequently rejected, is considered. More accurately therefore, the topic dealt with here is 'the use of foreign law by the courts'. It is possible to find cases where the court, comparing different rules of foreign and domestic systems thoroughly, opts for one of these as the 'better' answer to the problem under consideration. It is realistic to say however, that by the nature of the process applied by courts, comparative law can only be utilised as a method of interpretation or as an approach to case law and legislation, that is, as a method, a legal technique, rather than as a distinct branch of legal science. By extending the survey here to 'characterisation and alternative connecting factors' in private international law, the use of comparative law by courts embraces even situations where the competent jurisdiction or the proper law is selected, and the judge is not called upon to examine the foreign law and to compare it with his own, but only to exercise the selection process. Comparative law

* Professor of Comparative Law, University of Glasgow and Erasmus University, Rotterdam

** *List of abbreviations used in this study:*

ALL ER, All England Law reports

SLT, Scots Law Times

SC, Session Cases

I.C.L.Q., International and Comparative Law Quarterly

MLR, Modern Law Review

Ox.J.L.S., Oxford Journal of Legal Studies

[1] This is an updated and extended version of the paper given at the International Congress of Comparative Law in Athens, 1994, published in Bridge, Banakas, Gardner & Carey-Miller (eds) *United Kingdom Law in the Mid-1990's* (London, 1994)

U. Drobnig and S. van Erp (eds.), The Use of Comparative Law by Courts, 253–2■5.

proper, however, as Gutteridge puts it, "is not concerned with the selection of appropriate jurisdictions or with the choice of law"[2], it covers a far wider area. Here though, all such cases are placed within the scope of 'the use of comparative law by courts'.

As examples of the application of comparative method to domestic problems, all situations where the courts seek foreign law solutions for UK problems, examine the content of foreign law for UK law reform purposes, suggest developments along foreign law lines or choose to follow such authority rather than English ones, are considered. As to applying the comparative method to international transactions, all situations are considered where the courts are involved in conflict of laws cases, establishing the relevance of foreign law to domestic litigation, transnational litigation, unification or harmonisation particularly under the EC, or seeking the common core of legal systems, that is, 'general principles of law recognised by civilised nations'.

Apart from trying to ascertain how far foreign law is referred to, for what purposes, when and in what way, it is interesting to try to detect existing patterns. One way of doing this, could be to determine whether membership of the European Community has affected the number of cases where reference is made to a continental legal system or a rule of such when new areas of law are being built up or in cases where common law is not clear. To this end all the published[3] decisions rendered in 1972, 1982 and 1992 are looked at in this study. Another time span for consideration is 1990-1995, the six year period following the 1990 International Congress of Comparative Law. Looking over a period of years would be one way of approaching the topic. Another approach could be to investigate various areas of law. Are there more references to foreign law in tort, negligence, contract and competition law for example, then in tax, divorce or adoption? Yet another approach would be to determine which laws are referred to most; more to commonwealth and common law perhaps or is there a changing trend as suggested by Bingham?[4] Apart from in cases when there has to be a reference for reasons of conflict of laws or because a foreign law is applicable to the case, why are references made? Is the aim of the courts to fill the gaps of domestic law, to clarify the law or to seek support and guidance?

In this study, the method chosen to deal with the topic is to consider all decisions rendered in 1972, 1982 and 1992 and between 1990 and the end of 1995[5], published in the All ER[6], rather than to look at isolated decisions here and there in which it is known that reference to foreign law was made

[2] Gutteridge, *Comparative Law* (Cambridge: Cambridge University Press, 1949) p. 40

[3] 'Published' for the purpose of this research means in the All England Law Reports.

[4] Bingham, ' "There is a World Elsewhere": The Changing Perspectives of English Law' : [1992] 41 *I.C.L.Q.*, p.515

[5] Some 1996 cases have also been looked at, though not in the same systematic manner.

[6] For the Scottish cases included, the S.L.T. and the Session Cases.

by borrowing[7] and adopting a foreign solution or concept, or seeking guidance, and then to attempt to derive meaningful conclusions from these lone cases. The years 1972, 1982 and 1992 are chosen, as stated above, to test whether entry to the European Community in 1972 made any difference to the pattern of references. Obviously looking at the scene at ten yearly intervals is a crude method, and a large chance element is involved. This may be corrected however, by looking intensively at the period between 1990-1995 which is chosen for three reasons The first is to test the findings of the ten yearly search. The second, as indicated above, is that this period roughly corresponds to the time span between International Congresses of Comparative Law. The third is to look at the most recent six year period, a period long enough to attempt meaningful analysis and to formulate reliable hypotheses. In this way one can look at tendencies appearing consistently, if any, and make predictions, using both statistical and substantive information. One might also find the answer to the question: Have things changed in the 1990s?

By combining the time element and the substantive element, certain patterns are apparent and certain general conclusions may be drawn. The choice of this methodological approach is in addition to the one suggested by Professor Drobnig, the General Reporter for this Topic in the 1994 International Congress of Comparative law. A combination of both approaches is used.

II. Preliminary Considerations

It is important to stress at the outset four distinct elements pertaining to the UK position in the matter of courts using comparative law.

a. One is the matter of language skills. English is a world language. There is little incentive to learn foreign languages in the UK. Until recently the importance of this skill was not stressed in either legal education or the legal profession. The result is that it is easier for a person unfamiliar with foreign languages to have access to common law materials. As Gutteridge said it is "regrettable that civil law and sources should not be utilised to the same extent, but this can, no doubt, be explained, by linguistic difficulties, and by the fact that the technique of continental legal authority is apt to be baffling to one who has been trained in methods of approach of the common law"[8].

b. The second element is the difficulties created by the rules on proof of

---

[7] For example it is well known that Viscount Haldane LC derived the concept of the 'directing mind and will' from German Law in *Lennards Carrying Co Ltd and Asian Petroleum Co Ltd* (1915) AC 705

[8] Gutteridge, *op. cit.*, pp. 44-45

foreign law.

> "Foreign law is a question of fact. It must be pleaded and proved by expert evidence. The court cannot take judicial notice of foreign law, though it be notorious. In the absence of evidence, foreign law is presumed to be the same as English law."[9]

This means that an awareness and the use of foreign cases and foreign material by counsel is more important than the judges' knowledge of them for the purpose of reference to foreign law in a particular case. Although a foreign legal rule is not one of the facts of the case and therefore must be decided by the judge and not the jury, when there is one, the judge cannot deal with such a question *ex officio*. The courts are restricted by what is presented to them by the parties. As Lord Mustill states:

> "It is perhaps just permissible to take notice that the contemporary Belgian Law of arbitration differs from the law of other European countries, but beyond this I would certainly not be willing to go since, most remarkably, no evidence of Belgian law is before the court."[10]

So, even though the judge may be perfectly aware of the existence of the foreign rule, in default of the parties, he must assume that the foreign law is the same as English law. The rules of foreign law are to be proved by the testimony of experts giving evidence in the same way as other expert witnesses. When there is a conflict in the evidence of the experts, the court decides what the foreign law actually is on the basis of that evidence and material cited by the experts. Thus, when experts disagree the judge has to decide between them, so he may pursue his own inquiries into the sources of foreign law if he is equipped to do so, and draw his own conclusions. The court applies foreign statutes literally, on its own reading, despite conflicting testimony of experts.

c. The third element can be summarised in the following statement quoted by Markesinis: "Why bother with foreign cases when we have so much material of our own".[11] This may not be solely an English attitude but as Lord Justice Bingham says of the period when he started practice, "it was an almost universal article of faith that English law and legal institutions were without peer in the world with very little to be usefully learned from others (save, on occasion, the High Court of Australia)"[12]. This he characterises as the proud, confident and self-reliant spirit.

---

[9] *El Ajou v Dollar Land Holdings plc & another* [1993] 3 All ER, 717, Millett J at 739 (Chancery Division)

[10] *Channel Tunnel Ltd. and another v Balfour Beatty Construction Ltd. and other* [1993] 1 All ER, 683 at 691 (House of Lords)

[11] Markesinis, 'Comparative Law - A Subject in Search of an Audience': (1990) 53 *MLR*, p.4

[12] Bingham, *op. cit.*, p.514

d. The fourth is an element more particular to the common law family than to any other, save maybe to the Islamic and is of the utmost importance. It is the consciousness that common law is a whole. The unity of common law is a very real tie between the jurisdictions within the common law family and the citing of decisions from another common law jurisdiction as authority is very frequent, though usually for the purpose of 'help' or 'comfort'. David says that using comparative law as a means of improving national law, English courts cite Canadian, Australian and New Zealand judgments "with an authority almost equal to that they would enjoy had they been rendered in English Courts"[13]. The feeling of oneness is so strong that in one case the judge found it difficult to refer to New Zealand law as foreign and apologised to his New Zealand friends for using the word 'foreign'[14]. Figures and examples will be looked at below. In 1995 there were 118 cases in which there was reference to other jurisdictions, international conventions or EC law. In these cases 174 references were made to other common law jurisdictions of which, 64 were instances where the judge was looking for help, support or authority. This sense of affiliation is a special characteristic of this family of laws as is reflected in the results of this study. In *Cheah v Equiticorp Finance Group Ltd and another* [15], Lord Browne-Wilkinson stated that: "It is manifestly desirable that the law on this subject should be the same in all common law jurisdictions". In *Vasquez v R* the Privy Council expressed the view: "This conclusion will bring Belize into line with other commonwealth countries of the Caribbean..."[16]. The Privy Council however, expressed regret "that there should be any divergence between English and New Zealand law on a point of fundamental principle."[17] British courts also regard it as desirable that the law north and the south of the border should be the same or similar as far as possible[18].

This element is also tied to the shared language, culture and appreciation of mental constructs of these jurisdictions. Lord Bridge stated in *Bennett v*

---

[13] David, & Brierley, *Major Legal Systems in the World Today*,(3rd ed., London: Stevens, 1985), p.8

[14] *Attorney General of New Zealand v Ortiz and others* [1982] 3 All ER 432

[15] [1991] 4 All ER, 989 (Privy Council)

[16] [1994] 3 All ER, 674 (Privy Council). Again in the House of Lords, in *R v Clegg* [1995] 1 All ER, 334, Lord Lloyd at 343 expressed his satisfaction with the decision by saying: "Thus the consequence of the use of excessive force in self-defence will be the same in the laws of England, Scotland, Australia, Canada and West Indies."

[17] Lord Lloyd at 773 in *Invercargill City Council v Hamlin* 1996] 1 All ER, 773 (Privy Council). He goes on 'whether Pirelli should still be regarded as good law in England is not for their Lordships to say. What is clear is that it is not good law in New Zealand.'

[18] See for example *Larner v British Steel plc* [1993] 4 All ER, 102 (Court of Appeal, Civil) where Peter Gibson J says at 113: "I recognise the importance of construing statutory provisions applicable both sides of the border in a consistent fashion, but...". Also see cases cited and the point made by Bingham, op.cit., p. 517

Horseferry Road Magistrates' Court and another[19], "Whatever differences there may be between the legal systems of South Africa, the United States, New Zealand and this country, many of the basic principles to which they seek to give effect stem from common roots". Again, as will be seen later, when there is no domestic authority to help them, courts do not hesitate to rely on other commonwealth and common law authorities[20] for example by saying:

> "Curiously enough, there appear to be no reported English decisions ... A number of decisions in other commonwealth countries have, however, considered such a state of affairs ... In the absence of any countervailing authority in English courts, I am of the opinion that the principles to be derived from the foregoing sources should be accepted as valid in English law."[21]

Even when there are domestic solutions but these are old and unsatisfactory in dealing with contemporary problems, courts will refer to these same foreign commonwealth and common law jurisdictions[22].

Looked at from this perspective, English courts[23] appear to refer, discuss and use foreign law and cases in solving domestic problems more frequently than courts of any other jurisdiction.

III. THE VIEWS OF LEGAL WRITERS

Before looking at views expressed by legal writers in this country on issues related to the use of comparative law by courts, I turn to two eminent comparatists. Zweigert and Kötz,[24] when discussing the practical use of comparative law in the interpretation of national rules of law and the position of an interpreter of national rules, first raise the question of whether the interpreter is able to, or entitled to, invoke a superior foreign solution. In the face of an unequivocal national enactment, they contend that foreign material cannot be used to by-pass these rules. However, when the construction is doubtful or there is a lacuna, the judge is acting as the

---

[19] [1993] 3 All ER, 138 (House of Lords)

[20] See for example, *Banque Bruxelles Lambert SA v Eagle Star Insurance Co Ltd.* [1995] 2 All ER, 769; *R v Linekar* [1995] 3 All ER, 69; *British Diabetics Association v Diabetics Society Ltd* [1995] 4 All ER, 812; *R v Dryden* [1995] 4 All ER, 987; *R v Humphreys* [1995] 4 All ER, 1008

[21] Lord Keith at 562 and 566 in *Martin v Watson* [1995] 3 All ER, 559 (House of Lords)

[22] See for example, *Mercedes-Benz AG v Leiduck [1996]* 3 All ER, 929 (Privy Council); *Attorney General for Hong Kong v Reid and others* [1994] 1 All ER, 1; *Connaught Restaurants Ltd v Indoor Leisure Ltd* [1993] 4 All ER, 834

[23] Scottish courts to a much lesser extent, to be discussed later.

[24] Zweigert & Kötz, *An Introduction to Comparative Law* (2nd ed. Oxford; Clarendon Press, 1987), p. 18.

legislator and the modern legislator sometimes takes his solutions from comparative law. So it is suggested that the comparative method must be included among the criteria traditionally applied to the finding and interpretation of national rules[25]. Then the important question to be posed is: 'How far can or should this go?' After questioning whether only related systems should be consulted or only whichever foreign solution seems best to the judge or the solution common to a number of other systems, Zweigert and Kötz advocate a bold answer[26]. They suggest that comparative law helps the courts to clarify and amplify the law and used in conjunction with normal methods, it serves to confirm and support a result reached by a traditional route. In their view however, merely to juxtapose the laws of various jurisdictions without comment is not comparative law, and to compare only parts of a solution could be unprofitable as well as misleading.[27] Zweigert and Kötz's general research has led them to the conclusion that courts are on the whole timid; however, the situation is better when uniform laws are being interpreted.[28] Here, the judges modify national rules to arrive at an internationally acceptable result which promotes legal uniformity. Although according to Zweigert and Kötz this activity calls for a comparative law interpretation, they ask whether it is beyond the powers of the national judge.[29] In relation to the common law they state that the unity of common law, the basic unity of legal science in the Anglo-American world still exists.[30]

After these general remarks, I would like next to refer to an early English comparative lawyer of great importance, Gutteridge who points out that since by virtue of a 'pious fiction' there are supposed to be no gaps in common law, in laying down the rule which he applies to the facts, the judge must avoid any suspicion that he has borrowed his law from a foreign system.[31] This observation is supported by Forsyth's analysis of 'legitimate expectations' when he shows that Lord Denning used the concept of 'legitimate expectations' a borrowing by English law from German law, without mentioning any authority, and said in a letter written to Forsyth, "it came out of my own head and not from any continental or other source"[32] It is also interesting however, to note that Lord Diplock, whose many judgments contain references to continental, especially French and German law, and American positions, did not seem to adhere to this 'pious fiction' when he openly used Evans' translation of Pothier in devel-

[25] *id.*
[26] *id.*
[27] *id.*, p.41
[28] *id.*, p.19
[29] *id.*
[30] *id.*
[31] Gutteridge, *op. cit.* p.37
[32] Forsyth, 'The Provenance and Protection of Legitimate Expectations': (1988) 47(2) *The Cambridge Law Journal*, p.241

oping 'primary and secondary obligations' and 'synallagmatic and unilateral' contracts, saying, "I have borrowed it from French law and the Civil Code arts. 1102-1103."[33]

Gutteridge also says that a historical analysis would show that Roman law has been resorted to frequently by judges of the Chancery Courts and that English commercial law is largely derived from foreign sources, partly by its descent from the Lex Mercatoria of the Middle Ages[34]. However, he goes on to say that it is only natural that the Anglo-American system should take the place of Roman law as a general guide to the English courts whenever they desire such guidance. Gutteridge again points out that the citation of foreign authority is not usually encouraged by English judges. When dealing with references made by the counsel to the laws of other jurisdictions a judge would say, "it must not be forgotten however, that these other systems of jurisprudence are relevant only so far as they throw light on our law"[35]. This position is much the same today as we see for example, in a 1993 case where the Privy Council decision reads:

> "... such discussions can give valuable guidance as to the proper approach to the interpretation of ... particularly where the decisions in the other jurisdictions are in relation to an article in the same or substantially the same terms. However, it must not be forgotten that decisions in other jurisdictions are persuasive and not binding authority and that the situation in those jurisdictions may not necessarily be identical to that in ... ."[36]

Gutteridge, talking of the position in 1949 also says that English judges do not resort to Roman law and the writings of Pothier as they did in the 19th century, but that they have a distinct tendency "to lend a willing ear to the citations of American authorities"[37], more by way of testing the soundness of their conclusions than in reliance on the American decisions. He also points out that Irish and Scottish cases are cited frequently in argument as they have great persuasive effect. Again in 1949 it seems that Canadian law reports were not resorted to as frequently as they might have been and the South African, Australian, New Zealand and British Indian law reports, containing valuable material, were overlooked. Gutteridge hopes that "at some future date more extensive use will, no doubt, be made of foreign law for the purpose of assisting our judges to fill the gaps that are still to be

---

[33] *United Dominion Trust (Commercial) Ltd v Eagle Aircraft Services Ltd* [1968] 1 WLR 74 in Rudden: (1990) 10 *Ox.J.L.S.*, p.449 and Dickson, 'The Contribution of Lord Diplock to the General Law of Contract': (1989) 9 *Ox.J.L.S.* pp.441-462

[34] Gutteridge, *op. cit.* p.38

[35] *id.*, p.39

[36] *Attorney General of Hong Kong v Lee Kwong-Kut, Attorney General of Hong Kong v Lo Chak-man and another* [1993] 3 All ER, 939 (Privy Council)

[37] *id.*, pp. 39-40

found in our law"[38]. He also stresses the question of international co-operation in that there should be no contradictory decisions emanating from courts of various countries and that the intent on underlying treaties would be defeated if different interpretations were given by courts of contracting countries. Gutteridge is realistic in saying that judges cannot all be expected to be comparatists, so those who practice in the courts "if they themselves have not the qualifications to enable them to place before the court an accurate synopsis of solutions which have been arrived at or proposed in other jurisdictions, it is their duty to consult others who are in a position to supply the information which is needed"[39]. Today this plea is still being made:

> "if it be objected that our judges do not have clerks, are not presented with Brandeis briefs, nor benefit from the kind of work that avocats généraux perform in some systems, then a partial solution lies in the greater use of the academic's ability to collect and synthesise information ... a partnership with the academic profession could thus provide more benefits to judges than many have hitherto been willing to recognise."[40]

Markesinis and Deakin say that not only legal scholars but courts also often use comparative law to see how legal systems of the past and the present deal with similar problems, "especially when they are called upon to interpret international conventions where uniformity of interpretation may be an added incentive for them to undertake such comparative studies".[41] However, "this task, worthy, if not at times essential, is fraught with obstacles"[42]. Among these obstacles they cite a judge's mentality and his unwillingness to be guided by foreign experience probably related to a kind of intellectual arrogance or a genuine belief that the foreign system, being very different, will not be of practical use; the enormous pressures under which judges and counsel work because of lack of time, volume of work; and an increasing awareness of expenditure on the part of clients.[43]

Lord Goff of Chieveley says:

> "Strongly though I support the study of comparative law, I hesitate to embark in an opinion such as this upon a comparison, however brief, with a civil law system, because experience has taught me how very difficult, and indeed potentially misleading, such an exercise can be. Ex-

---

[38] *id* p.40

[39] *id.* p.45

[40] Markesinis and Deakin, 'The Random Element of their Lordships' Infallible Judgment: An Economic and Comparative Analysis of the Tort of Negligence from Anns to Murphy': (1992) 55 *MLR*, p. 633

[41] Markesinis and Deakin, *op. cit.* p.632

[42] *id.*

[43] *id.*

ceptionally however, in the present case, thanks to material published in our language by distinguished comparatists, German as well as English, we have direct access to publications which should sufficiently dispel our ignorance of German law and so by comparison illuminate our understanding of our own."[44]

Markesinis points out in an earlier article[45] that comparative law has failed to excite the imagination of students and practising lawyers including judges. According to him the reason for this is that teachers of comparative law have undervalued and understressed the importance of case law and ignored the practice of the courts in everyday cases. The role he attributes to foreign case law is as a means of correcting and improving national law and as help in shaping the development of national law.

Lord Justice Bingham[46] would like to see the 1990's as a period when English lawyers cease to regard Europe as 'somewhere else'. Looking at developments in the fields of staying English actions, the law of sovereign immunity, British accession to the European Community, the distinction of private law and public law, the 'Mareva injunction' and procedural changes, he claims that things are changing and that there is greater awareness and use of continental materials today. In answering the question, 'Why is there now an increased internationalism?', Lord Justice Bingham points to several factors: the membership of the Community which has brought England into closer contact with the continent and with Scottish lawyers, the growing importance of international conventions, the growth of international commercial practice, the settlement in England before and after the Second World War of very distinguished legal scholars bringing with them a rich legal culture fertilising the English one, and finally to the work of comparatists. This development is characterised by Bingham not as establishing a new tradition but reverting to an old one, and according to him a preferable one.[47] Here it is interesting to note that Markesinis and Deakin are making a (paradoxical) suggestion that "this insular mentality may have been greater in the 20th century then it was in the 19th" indicating however, by reference to Lord Chief Justice's article discussed above, "it may now, again, be about to give way to a greater degree of internationalism".[48]

Recently, Koopmans, looking at Comparative law and the courts, com-

44 *White and Another v Jones and others* [1995] 1 All ER, 691 at 705 (House of Lords).

45 Markesinis, *op. cit.* p.5

46 Bingham, *op. cit.*

47 Bingham, *op. cit* p.527

48 Markesinis and Deakin, *op. cit.*, p.632. See more recently the claim that, at least in conflict cases, the "practice of English courts accords ill with their 'Chinese wall' reputation" and that English courts have shown far more internationalism in this field than they have been given credit for, especially compared to French courts. Enonchong, 'Public Policy in the Conflict of Laws: A Chinese Wall Around Little England?': (1996) 45 *IC.L.Q.*, p633.

mented that national courts in many jurisdictions have been more interested in using the comparative method over the last fifteen years or so, that the climate is changing and that this is apparent also in the English courts. This he purports, by looking at *White v Jones*, referred to above, which he sees as characterised by a lack of suitable precedent where the House of Lords looked at German law while assessing solutions adopted by other jurisdictions.[49]

The findings of the present study which will now be presented, discussed and analysed will throw some empirical light on the above views related to this topic. Some views will be strengthened and others weakened.

IV. JUDICIAL PRACTICE

A. The Results of Statistical Analysis

a. At ten yearly intervals since the UK joined the EU.

Year	*Number of cases with reference to foreign law and the breakdown of references*		
1972	26 cases -		3 conflict
	(Total 602)		0 ECJ or EC
			3 international convention
			12 continental law/civilian
		*	30 common law/commonwealth
			1 other

*(Of the 30 references 23 were for support and authority; USA 8 of 10; Australia 7 of 7; Canada 2 of 2, NZ 3 of 3, Scotland 3 of 3)

1982	29 cases -		2 conflict
	(Total 438)		3 ECJ or EC
			4 international conventions
			4 continental/civilian
		*	42 common law/commonwealth
			0 other

*(Of the 42 references 22 were for support and authority; USA 7 of 9; Australia 6 of 6; Canada 4 of 7; NZ 3 of 5; Scotland 0 of 0)

1992	25 cases -		6 conflict
	(Total 362)		7 ECJ or EC
			4 international conventions
			7 continental/civilian
		*	33 common law/commonwealth

[49] Koopmans, 'Comparative Law and the Courts': (1996) 45 *I.C.L.Q.* p. 544

0 other

*(Of the 33 references 19 were for support and authority; USA 6 of 9; Australia 4 of 7; Canada 4 of 7; NZ 1 of 2; Scotland 1 of 2)

b. The Last Six Years.

1990	29 cases -		3 conflict
	(Total 346)		4 ECJ or EC
			5 International Conventions
			5 continental/civilian
		*	29 common law/commonwealth
			9 other

*(Of the 29 references 23 were for support and authority; USA 3 of 8; Australia 9 of 10; Canada 2 of 2; NZ 3 of 3; Scotland 4 of 4)

1991	18 cases -		3 conflict
	(Total 293)		2 ECJ or EC
			0 international conventions
			2 continental/civilian
		*	30 common law/commonwealth
			0 other

*(Of the 30 references 28 were for support and authority; USA 6 of 8; Australia 6 of 6; Canada 6 of 6; NZ 3 of 4; Scotland 4 of 4)

1992	25 cases -		6 conflict
	(Total 362)		7 ECJ or EC
			4 international conventions
			7 continental/civilian
		*	33 common law/commonwealth
			0 other

*(Of the 33 references 19 were for support and authority; USA 6 of 9; Australia 4 of 7; Canada 4 of 7; NZ 1 of 2; Scotland 1 of 2)

1993	30 cases -		1 conflict
	(Total 314)		8 ECJ or EC
			14 international convention
			7 continental/civilian
		*	125 common law/commonwealth
			0 other

*(Of the 125 references 45 were for support and authority; USA 8 of 18; Australia 12 of 28; Canada 9 of 180; NZ 10 of 21; Scotland 6 of 13)

1994	99 cases		1 conflict
	(Total 269)		7 ECJ or EC
			16 international conventions
			15 continental/civilian
		*	145 common law/commonwealth
			4 other

*(Of the 145 references 38 were for support and authority; USA 4 out of 10; Australia 11 out of 49; Canada 7 out of 17; NZ 8 out of 23; Scotland 8 out of 15)

1995	119 cases		3 conflicts
	(Total 285)		2 ECJ or EC
			17 international conventions
			3 continental/civilian
		*	174 common law/commonwealth
			2 other

*(Of the 174 references 64 were for support and authority; USA 12 out of 28; Australia 25 out of 53; Canada 6 out of 16; NZ 12 out of 25; Scotland 6 out of 19)

B. Fields of Law where foreign law is used

The areas of law where 'the use of comparative law by courts' is observed are extremely varied because of the factors discussed below, which affect the reference to especially commonwealth and common law decisions as authority. Generally the fields into which the statistically analysed cases fall are: substitution, company mergers; company, winding up; proper law of contract; wills; occupier, negligence, duty owed by occupier to trespasser; negligence, causation, duty to take care, breach of duty; negligence, duty to share holders; vicarious liability; gaming, lottery; libel; slander; contract, waiver; divorce, living apart; maintenance order; divorce, recognition; marriage, validity; division of matrimonial property; income tax, double taxation; stay of proceedings; currency control, debt in foreign money; foreign defendant, foreign plaintiff, vessel visiting English port; contempt of court; local authority, rate payer; criminal evidence, hearsay; boundary, doctrine of accretion; troves, right of possession, finder; crown, divisibility; carriers, loss or damage to goods; option to purchase; criminal law, trial, evidence in the absence of the jury, interpretation of EC Treaty; extradition, committal; EC law, competition; employment, equal pay, equal work, EC Treaty; goods removed unlawfully, enforcing foreign law; constitutional law, long delay in executing of sentence; statute, validity, Treaty rights; sale of land, fraud; limitation of action, public authorities; shipping, carriage by sea, jurisdiction of English courts; gift, *donatio mortis causa*; title to foreign copyright; compulsory purchase; right not to be hindered in the enjoyment of freedom of expression; Bill of exchange, proper law; minor, abduction; minor, custody; bye-law, validity, severability; pre-trial, post judgment relief; Mareva injunction; contract, illegality, performance; copyright, infringement; company, director, breach of duty, forum non convenience; company, compulsory winding up; mental health, patient, recall to hospital; refusal of medical treatment; medical treatment, withdrawal of consent; criminal law, assault, occasioning bodily harm, consent; malicious falsehood, negligence; false imprisonment, residual liberty; criminal law, blasphemy; criminal law, conspiracy; abortion, medical negligence; rape, marital exemption; easement, right of way; EC law, Sunday trading, proportionality; restitution, money paid to the crown; judicial review; drug trafficking; insurance; trustee, constructive trust; abuse of process; solicitor, negligence; tort, harassment; arbitration.

C. When and how is foreign law used?

1. In cases where foreign law is indicated

a. Conflict of Laws

In all the years covered there were twenty two such cases. When conflict of laws points to foreign law or when the case has a foreign element such as recognition of a foreign divorce any relevant foreign law will be referred to. In conflict of laws cases English law will preferably be used and foreign law will be assumed to be the same as English law unless evidence is brought to show otherwise. This was stated clearly in *Bumper Development Corp Ltd v Commissioner of Police of the Metropolis and others* (Union of India and others, claimants)[50] from which I quote:

> "Ian Kennedy J reviewed at length not only the evidence of Hindu law as set out by textbook writers and in judgments delivered in the Indian courts, but also the oral evidence given before him by the expert witnesses before reaching his conclusions as to which claimants would be acceptable as juristic entities in the courts of Tamil Nadu, and whether, and if so in what circumstances, such a party could claim a title to Nataraja. However, before coming to consider the evidence on this aspect of the case, it is convenient to consider the position in the English courts. It is trite law that foreign law in our courts is treated as a question of fact which must be proved in evidence. In the absence of any evidence to the contrary, it is to be assumed to be the same as English law. It is however the duty of the judge when faced with conflicting evidence from witnesses about a foreign law to resolve those differences in the same way as he must in the case of other conflicting evidence as to facts. What is not so plain, however, is how he should deal with documentary evidence in the form of textbooks and reports of judgments and decisions in foreign courts.... We have come to the conclusion that the learned judge was not entitled to reject the evidence of experts...and was not entitled to rely upon his own researches... without having the assistance of the expert witnesses and the submissions of council."

There is a presumption that law of another jurisdiction is the same as the forum's where no proof to the contrary is presented. Also, insufficient proof of foreign law may result in the application of forum law. Often

---

[50] [1991] 4 All ER, 638 (Court of Appeal, Civil). For a more recent but similar statement see *El Ajou v Dolar Land Holdings plc and another* [1993] 3 All ER, 717 (Chancery Devision)

natural justice and public policy grounds may show that foreign judgments cannot be enforced. This was the case in *Adam and others v Cape Industries plc and another.*[51] It is also a fact that, for example in international child abduction cases, the existence of prior orders from foreign courts is not significant; the principles should be acceptable to English courts as seen in *Re F (minor)*[52]. The courts also ask whether there are considerations of European law or comity. In many such cases ECJ rulings serve as a guide. Good examples are *Webb v Webb*[53], *Union Transport*[54], *Dresser UK Ltd and others v Falcongate Freight Management Ltd and others The Duke of Yare*[55] and *Johnson*[56]. Usually the determination of applicable law depends on the public interest of the forum in dispute the parties' access to foreign law materials, clarity of choice of law rules and the nature of the foreign legal system involved[57]. It is interesting to note that in *Collister v Collister*[58] it was held that since Scotland was not outside the United Kingdom, the 1920 Maintenance Orders Act did not apply.

As seen in *Montreosso Shipping Co Ltd v International Transport Workers' Federation*[59], the important question in conflict of laws cases is 'With which system of law has the person involved the closest and most real connection'? In a 1972 case[60], Lord Denning said:

> "To determine the proper law of the contract, the courts at one time used to have a number of presumptions to help them. Now we have to ask ourselves; what is the system of law with which the transaction has the closest and most real connection? This is not dependent on the intention of the parties. We study every circumstance connected with the contract and come to a conclusion. When the circumstances point to more than one country, then..."

In yet another case[61] Lord Denning said:

> "If the plaintiff considers that the procedure of our courts or the substantive law of England may hold advantage for him superior to that of any other country, he is entitled to bring his action here, provided he can serve the defendant or arrest his ships within the jurisdiction of these

---

51 [1991] 1 All ER, 929 (High Court, Chancery)

52 [1990] 3 All ER,97 (Court of Appeal, Civil)

53 [1992] 1 All ER, 17 (High Court, Chancery)

54 [1992] 1 All ER, 161 (House of Lords)

55 [1992] 2 All ER , 450 (House of Lords)

56 [1992] 3 All ER, 14 (High Court, Queen's Bench)

57 The so-called Schlesinger's 'multi-factor-approach' in the United States of America.

58 [1972] 1 All ER, 334 (High Court, Family)

59 [1982] 3 All Er, 841 (Court of Appeal, Civil)

60 *Coast Lines Ltd v Hudig and Veder Chartering NV*[1972] 1 All ER, 451 (Court of Appeal, Civil)

61 *The Atlantic Star - The Owners of the Bona Spes v the Owners of the Atlantic Star* [1972] 3 All ER, 705 (Court of Appeal, Civil)

> courts and his action is not vexatious or oppressive. You may call this 'forum shopping' if you please, but if the forum is England, it is a good place to shop in, both for the quality of the goods and the speed of service....This does not breach international comity, for they have received international recognition."

According to Enonchong, however, contrary to the popular opinion, English courts have an internationalist attitude, nurtured by the doctrine of international comity[62], because of which they are reluctant to invoke public policy against the normally applicable foreign law. In *Re Maxwell Communications Corporation plc (N.Z.)* Vinelott J says:

> "I have not been referred to the law of any continental jurisdiction except Switzerland. It seems to me unlikely that in any system derived from the civil code, the law will differ in this respect from the position under Swiss law. It seems from the speech of Lord Kilbrandon that under Scottish law a creditor can contract out of or waive his right to set-off and if so, he can presumably validly agree that his debt be subordinated. I have set out the leading authorities in South Africa, The United States and Australia. It would, I think, be a matter of grave concern if, at a time when insolvency increasingly has international ramifications, it were to be found that English law alone refused to give effect to contractual subordination. I have reached the clear conclusion that such a clause is valid and effective and is not avoided by any consideration of public policy and I shall so declare."[63]

b. International Conventions

"Although international conventions do not have the force of law unless embodied in municipal legislation, they may in the field of international law be valuable as a guide to the rules of international law which this country as a signatory respects"[64]. In this case, writers such as Grotius and Wolff, and French, German, Italian and Australian law and cases were looked at for "any indication as they may give to the view taken in foreign and commonwealth civilised states." English courts look at foreign law and the convention concerned to understand its application or for the sake of comity[65]. In *Michael Galley Footwear Ltd (in liq) v Iaboni*[66], Belgian, Dutch and German cases were looked at to understand the application of the Contract for the International Carriage of Goods by Road, in view of the comity. In *T v Secretary of State for the Home Department*, Lord Lloyd said: "In a case concerning an international convention it is obviously

---

[62] Enonchong, *op.cit.*, p.640

[63] [1994] 1 All ER, 737 (Chancery) at 754, 755.

[64] *Radwan v Radwan* [1972] 3 All ER, 967 (High Court, Family)

[65] English courts refer frequently to the idea of comity. See for example, *Hewitson v Hewitson* [1995]1 All ER, 472 (Court of Appeal, Civil)

[66] [1982] 2 All ER, 200 (High Court, Queen's Bench)

desirable that decisions in different jurisdictions should, so far as possible, be kept in line with each other[67]". When a convention has to be used, then other interpretations may be looked at. In *Re A and another (minors)* [68] for example, Balcombe J said:

> "Since French and English are both official languages of the Hague Convention, we were referred also to the French version of art 13(a).....We were also referred to a judgment... in the High Court of Australia... where Deane J gave a comprehensive dissertation on the various meanings which 'acquiescence' can have at common law. Since we are here concerned with the meaning of 'acquiesced' in an international convention to which many countries, not only those with a common law background, have adhered, it cannot be right to attempt to construe 'acquiesced' by reference only to its possible meaning at common law or equity."

Again, this time in *Antwerp United Diamonds BVBA v Air Europe*, Phillips J said:

> "While the balance of academic opinion and foreign decisions tilts in favour of the plaintiffs, it does not do so in a manner which is decisive. In this circumstance, I propose to follow the approach advocated by Bingham J in ..., namely to approach the convention in an objective spirit in order to try to discover what its true intent is".[69]

This is especially important when there is no clearly established rule of English law on the matter.

The Brussels Convention is now part of English Law (the 1982 Act) and is regarded as essential for the furtherance of comity as seen in *Macaulay v Macaulay* [70].

In general it can be said that a restrictive interpretation and a limited application of conventions is preferred by English courts which try to keep purely domestic cases out of the scope of the conventions as seen in *Re G (minor)* [71].

c . The European Convention of Human Rights

The European Convention of Human Rights does not form part of UK

---

[67] [1996] 2 All ER, 865, at 889 (House of Lords). This was the Convention relating to the Status of Refugees, 1951. Phillip J said in *Kinnear v Falconfilms NV*: "In a convention case it would not be proper for the court to apply domestic rules to decline jurisdiction under 6(2) simply because the third party was domiciled abroad". [1994] 3 All ER, 42 at 50 (Queen's Bench)

[68] [1992] 1 All ER, 929 (Court of Appeal, Civil)

[69] [1993] 4 All ER, 469 at 474

[70] [1991] 1 All ER, 865 (High Court, Family)

[71] [1993] 3 All ER, 657 (Court of Appeal, Civil)

law[72]. When a reference has been made to it and there is no unambiguous or no established or certain English law on the matter, then the Convention is used, as can be seen in *Derbyshire County Council v Times Newspapers Ltd and others*[73]. The "Convention may be deployed for the purpose of the resolution of an ambiguity in English primary or subordinate legislation."[74] Otherwise it cannot be directly applied or administered by the courts of this country as stated in *Weldon v Home Office*[75]. It is accepted however, that English law should develop alongside ECHR, as stated by Lord Scarman in *Home Office v Harman*[76]:

> "We believe the true path forward is to ensure that our law develops in a way which is consistent with the obligations accepted by the UK in the European Convention and with the developments of the common law achieved in America ... Of course, neither American law nor the convention can be decisive of this appeal. But both are powerfully persuasive, the convention because its observance is an obligation of the United Kingdom, and American law because of its common law character. Each reinforces conclusions which we draw independently from our own legal principles."

In *R v Secretary of State for the Home Department, ex parte K*[77] ECHR was relied upon by counsel, but failed to convince. It furnishes 'valuable guidance' as accepted in *Attorney General of Hong Kong v Lee Kwong-Kut*[78] and sometimes can be 'relied upon' as in *L'Office Cherifien des Phosphates and another v Yamashita–Shinnihon Steamship Co Ltd,*

[72] However, "The fact that the convention does not form part of English law does not mean that its provisions cannot be referred to and relied upon as persuasive authority as to what the common law is, or should be ... For my part, I am prepared unreservedly to adopt this approach but I hope that it is not unduly insular, or even parochial, to remind oneself at the outset that the object of the inquiry is to establish the relevant rules of the common law." *R v Mid Glamorgan Family Health Services* [1995] 1 All ER, at 365 (Evans LJ).

[73] [1992] 3 All ER, 65 (Court of Appeal, Civil) and [1993] 1 All ER, 1011 (House of Lords).

[74] *Rantzen v Mirror Group Newspapers* (1986) [1993] 4 All ER, 975 Neill LJ at 993 (Court of Appeal, Civil)

[75] [1990] 3 All ER, 672 (Court of Appeal, Civil). Also see *Brind v Secretary of State for the Home Department* [1991] 1 All ER, 720 at 735. Also reiterated recently in *R v Cowan* [1995] 4 All ER, 936 where Lord Taylor LJ said: "We stress that decisions of the Commission and indeed of the European Court of Human Rights itself are not binding upon this court. They are of assistance to resolve ambiguity in our domestic law ... Nevertheless, the Commission's observations are of interest." at 945.

[76] [1982] 1 All ER, 532 (House of Lords). Another such case *Re D and another (minors)* [1995] 4 All ER, 385 at 397 (House of Lords). Also see *R v Secretary of State for the Home Department, ex parte Wynne* [1992] 2 All ER, 315 (Court of Appeal, Civil)

[77] [1990] 3 All ER, 562 (Court of Appeal, Civil)

[78] [1993] 3 All ER, 939 (Privy Council) and *R v Brown* [1993] 2 All ER,75 (House of Lords)

The Boveraa[79]. Lord Goff for example, feels 'fortified' in his view "by the fact that in ... the European Court of Human Rights expressed the opinion..."[80]. It is also stated in *R v Adverting Standards Authority Ltd, ex parte Vernons Organisation Ltd*[81] that human rights are 'as much a sinew of common law as of ECHR'. In *Derbyshire County Council v Times Newspapers Ltd and others,*[82] Balcombe J said:

> "Article 10 (of ECHR) has not been incorporated into English domestic law. Nevertheless it may be resorted to in order to resolve some uncertainty or ambiguity in municipal law ... also, it does not establish any novel proposition under English law ... It has been stated on high authority that art 10 is in effect the same as the English common law ... In my view, therefore, where the law is uncertain, it must be right for the court to approach the issue before it with a predeliction to ensure that our law should not involve a breach of art 10. .. Even if the common law is certain, the courts still, when appropriate, consider the United Kingdom is in breach of art 10."

There is yet another context in which the impact of this Convention can be discussed. In *R v Secretary of State, ex parte McQuillan*[83], Sedley J (at 422) looks at the Convention through the jurisprudence of the Court of Justice of the European Community and says:

> "... if on the wider scale it is for the courts of the United Kingdom to apply principles of European law whenever appropriate, the principles and standards set out in the convention can certainly be said to be a matter of which the law of this country now takes notice in setting its own standards. ... Once it is accepted that the standards articulated in the convention are standards which both march with those of the common law and inform the jurisprudence of the European Union, it becomes unreal and potentially unjust to continue to develop English public law without reference to them ... . Such an approach is indeed already en-

---

[79] [1993] 3 All ER, 686 (Court of Appeal, Civil)

[80] *Wynne v Secretary of State for the Home Department* [1993] 1 All ER, 574 at 581 (House of Lords). Also in *R v Secretary of State for the Home Department, ex parte Leech* [1993] 4 All ER, 539, Steyn LJ, expressed the opinion that, ". . the decision, although not directly binding in England, reinforces a conclusion that we have arrived at in the light of the principles of our domestic jurisprudence" at 555, having said earlier, "The principle was laid down by the ECtHR in ... and it was clearly enunciated as a part of our domestic jurisprudence by the Divisional Court in ..." at 548

[81] [1993] 2 All ER, 202 (High Court, Queen's Bench)

[82] [1992] 3 All ER, 65 (Court of Appeal, Civil). In the same case in the House of Lords [1993] 1 All ER, 1011, where it is conceded that the law of England was uncertain, Lord Keith at 1021 states: "I have reached my conclusion upon the common law of England without finding any need to rely upon European Convention. .. Common law of England is consistent with obligations under the Treaty." See along similar lines, *R v Advertising Standards Authority, ex parte Vernms* [1993] 2 Al ER, 202 (Queen's Bench)

[83] [1995] 4 All ER, 400 (Queen's Bench)

joined by Ex p Bugdaycay in relation to a predominant value of the common law – the right to life – which, as it happens, the convention reflects."

d . EC and ECJ

When there is an involvement of EC law, English courts look at ECJ cases and via these to cases involving foreign systems of law, this, being done within the scope of ECJ decisions. The courts are keen to keep to meanings explained by the ECJ, especially if the matter is not covered by English authority. ECJ decisions give guidance, and a judgment obtained in a member state on a matter of EC law has a special weight, particularly again if not covered by English authority. In *R v Ministry of Agriculture and Fisheries and Food, ex parte Hamble (Offshore Fisheries)* [84], Sedley J sees the fact that Britain is a relative latecomer to the Community doctrine of 'legitimate expectations' as "an advantage, at least to the extent that our case law on the topic has not had a chance to ossify and because it enables us to learn from our neighbours."

In *Petereit v Babcock Int. Holding Ltd,* [85] and *Emi Records Ltd v Modern Music Karl-Ulrich Walterbach GmbH* [86], where there was little guidance as to the circumstances in which the court should exercise its discretion to stay the enforcement obtained in a member state, the English court looked to ECJ for guidance. Again in *Arkwright Mutual Insurance Co v Bryanston Insurance Co Ltd and others* [87], the English court compared English law and EC law in determining *lis alibi pendens*, as one aspect of *forum non conveniens*. Lord Goff remarked in *Woolwich Building Society v Inland Revenue Commissioners (No 2)* [88], "I only comment that, at a time when Community law is becoming increasingly important, it would be strange if the right of the citizen to recover overpaid charges were to be more restricted under domestic law than it is under Community law". Certainly, EC law is regarded as part of domestic law through the European Communities Act 1972, thus a chief constable's decision was quashed for contravening art. 34 of the EC Treaty[89]. Sedley J states: "If each member state were governed in carrying out its part of this joint exercise by no jurisprudence but its own domestic law, a major objective of the policy (in this case common agriculture) would be frustrated."[90] Thus:

"Distinct issues may well be raised by the rights possessed by the appli-

[84] [1995] 2 All ER, 714 (High Court, Queen's Bench)

[85] [1990] 2 All ER, 135 (High Court, Queen's Bench)

[86] [1992] 1 All ER, 616 (High Court, Queen's Court)

[87] [1990] 2 All ER, 335 (High Court, Queen's Bench)

[88] [1992] 3 All ER, 737 (House of Lords)

[89] *R v Chief Constable of Sussex, ex parte International Trader's Ferry Ltd* [1995] 4 All ER, 364 (High Court, Queen's Bench) at 378

[90] *R v Ministry of Agriculture, Fisheries and Food, ex parte Hamble Fisheries* [1995] 2 All ER, 714, at 725

> cant as a citizen of the European Union. Not only the rights themselves but the powers of derogation from them are matters primarily of European law, to which the jurisprudence of the United Kingdom's courts must conform."[91]

However, in *Johnson v Coventry Churchill International Ltd*[92], a conflict of laws case, after analysing the purpose of the foreign law, in this case German, and the ECJ decision, it was decided that this would be an exception to the rule and English law should apply.

e. Through the Privy Council

Sixteen jurisdictions within the commonwealth still use the Privy Council for ultimate appeal. On the whole the Privy Council prefers the English law's understanding of rules and to understand foreign (commonwealth) law as English law. However, the Privy Council also gives special weight to the views of judges in the lower courts in so far as they reflect the advantage which those judges enjoy of familiarity with prevailing local conditions, this with the proviso that the courts have used that advantage, as seen in *Hector v. Attorney General of Antigua and Barbuda and others*[93] in 1990. So the Privy Council applies and interprets foreign law and seeks guidance from the local courts, though their decisions are not binding, as stated in *Ali v R* and *Rassool v R*[94], where the Privy Council was dealing with Mauritius law. The Privy Council plays a crucial role in maintaining the harmony of the common law within the commonwealth world, laying down paths for cross fertilisation. This was so in *Mercedes-Benz A.G.*, where the Privy Council preferred the approach of the Australian courts when deciding Hong Kong law[95]; or in *Vasquez v R* and *O'Neil v R*[96] where they brought the laws of the individual jurisdictions of the commonwealth into line with others, especially within their specific regions.

In *R v Clegg*[97] it was recognised by the House of Lords that the law of England was settled in accordance with a decision of the Privy Council and that the laws of England, Scotland, Australia, Canada and the West Indies were now the same as to the consequence of using excessive force in self-defence. However, Lord Lloyd queried "whether, despite this uniformity, some changes in the laws may, nevertheless be desirable?"[98]

---

91 *R v Secretary of State, ex p McQuillan* [1995] 4 All ER, 400 at 425
92 [1992] 3 All ER, 14 (High Court, Queen's Bench)
93 [1990] 2 All ER, 103 (Privy Council)
94 [1992] 2 All ER, 1 (Privy Council)
95 [1995] 3 All ER, 929 (Privy Council)
96 [1994] 3 All ER, 674 (Privy Council)
97 [1995] 1 All ER, 334 (House of Lords)
98 *id.* at 346

2. In developing English law when there is no statutory law

When there is not and has never been any statutory provision expressly conferring a right, then other common law jurisdictions are consulted by way of judge-made law by interpretation, as for example, in the case of *Hughes v. Doncaster Metropolitan Borough Council*[99] when the Scottish Court of Sessions provided guidance. In *United City Merchants (Investments) Ltd and others v Royal Bank of Canada and others*[100] it was pointed out that, "although there does not appear among English authorities any case in which this exception has been applied, it is well established in the American cases". When the area under scrutiny is one of common law, counsel introduces decisions from other common law or commonwealth jurisdictions. In *Sen v Headley,*[101] Mummery J remarked:

> "In the course of his lucid submissions counsel for Mrs Sen took me on an instructive world tour, visiting various common law and civil law jurisdictions which have developed the doctrine of donatio mortis causa. I was referred to decisions of the courts in Australia and Canada, and also to statements of the law in textbooks on the law of South Africa and Scotland."

Judges use these decisions for 'support', 'aid' and 'guidance' or because they give 'comfort'. The decisions are referred to 'with great respect' as 'powerful', 'persuasive', 'helpful', 'illuminating' or 'applicable'. This respect arises sometimes because the principle was first developed in the jurisdiction referred to. These decisions are sometimes preferred over English law. For example, in interpreting the Copyright Act 1982, the view expressed by the High Court of Australia was preferred[102] and again an Australian case was followed, departing from English law in sale of land and date of performance, when Nourse LJ said: "In my opinion there is ample justification for a departure from the conventional view ... . I would prefer to say that the conventional view, at all events in modern conditions, is inconvenient and therefore unjust; and, there being no binding authority in point, to hold that it ought no longer to be adopted".[103] These decisions are sometimes 'accepted unreservedly' as in an Australian case related to abduction and an illegitimate child[104], sometimes used to 'clarify defini-

[99] [1990] 2 All ER, 53 (Court of Appeal, Civil)

[100] [1982] 2 All ER, 720 (House of Lords)

[101] [1990] 1 All ER, 898 (High Court, Chancery)

[102] *Express Newspapers plc v News (UK) Ltd and others* [1990] 3 All ER, 376 (High Court, Chancery). For a recent case see *Galoo Ltd (in liq.) v Bright Grahame Murray (a firm)* [1995] 1 All ER, 16 where Glidewell LJ says at 26 "The answer in my judgment is supplied by the Australian decisions to which I was referred, which I hold to represent the law of England as well as of Australia, in relation to a breach of duty imposed on the defendent whether by contract or in tort..."

[103] *Behzadi v Shaftesbury Hotels Ltd* [1991] 2 All ER, 477 (Court of Appeal, Civil)

[104] *C v S (minor)* [1990] 2 All ER, 449 (Court of Appeal, Civil)

tions' and almost always for the furtherance of common law. When there is no statutory law and a common law principle is being developed, the courts tend to look at developed commonwealth jurisdictions such as Australia, Canada and New Zealand, and to the common law jurisdiction of the United States of America. For example in *Director of Public Prosecutor v Hutchinson and others*[105], it is stated that the fullest exploration and exposition of the general principle was given by the US Supreme Court and the High Court of Australia. In *Murphy v Brentwood District Council*[106] when negligence and duty to take care was considered, American, Australian, Canadian, and New Zealand positions were compared and, looking at the *Anns* doctrine in the commonwealth, it was stated that the choice was either to follow Australia, reject *Anns,* or follow Canada and New Zealand. Sometimes a Scottish case is regarded as applicable in England as in *R v R*[107] when rape in marriage was discussed.

This being the area in which the comparative method is of most importance, for the sake of clarity, it will be considered under nine categories. British courts extensively discuss commonwealth and common law cases as 'authority' and use them for 'assistance'.

i. Common law jurisdictions provide unity and uniformity of common law[108]. In one case the court followed American solutions to provide uniformity in the whole common law world as seen in *Cheah v Equiticorp Finance Group Ltd and another*[109]: "Their Lordships' conclusions accord both with what they understand to be the generally accepted view of the law affecting subordination of debts and the law of the United States... It is manifestly desirable that the law on this subject should be the same in all common law jurisdictions." In another case[110], in the name of comity in common law, the Australian position was followed. Another aspect of this approach is that the English courts use decisions from other common law jurisdictions as English law as in *R v Lord Chancellor's Department, ex parte Nangle*[111]. In view of a Scottish procedure different from the English, the court trying to secure uniformity of the common law, stated that in the UK one law of procedure should apply.[112] The court also found no

[105] [1990] 2 All ER, 836 (House of Lords)

[106] [1990] 2 All ER, 908 (House of Lords)

[107] [1991] 2 AllER, 257 (Court of Appeal, Criminal)

[108] For a general review see: *R v Birmingham City Council, ex parte Ferrero Ltd* [1993] 1 All ER, 530; *McAllister v General Medical Council* [1993] 1 All ER, 982; Daley v R [1993] 1 All ER, 86; *R v Morhall* [1993] 4 All ER, 888; *Yip Chiu-cheung v R* [1994] 2 All ER, 924; *Galoo v Bright Grahame Murray* [1995]1 All ER, 1[illegible]; *Dhak v Insurance Co of North America (UK) Ltd* [1996] 2 All ER, 609

[109] [1991] 4 All ER, 989 (Privy Council)

[110] *Attorney General v Sport Newspapers Ltd and others*, [1992] 1 All ER, 503 (High Court, Queen's Bench)

[111] [1992] 1 All ER, 897 (High Court, Queen's Bench)

[112] *McAllister v General Medical Council*, [1993] 1 All ER, 9[illegible]2 (Privy Council)

difference in the application of the doctrine of *volenti* in *Pitts v Hunt and another*[113] and support for this from Scottish law.

ii. When there is no modern decided English case[114] as in *Woolwich Building Society*[115] and *Airedale NHS Trust v Bland*[116], or when English law has not moved on since 1861 as in *White and another v Jones and others*[117], the courts search for a general principle by looking at other developed common law jurisdictions[118]. For example, in *Woolwich*[119] Lord Browne-Wilkinson in the House of Lords remarked:

> "Although as yet there is in English law no general rule giving the plaintiff a right of recovery from a defendant who has been unjustly enriched at the plaintiff's expense, the concept of unjust enrichment lies at the heart of all the individual instances in which the law does give a right of recovery."

He then looked at other common law jurisdictions. Earlier, in the Court of Appeal in the same case, it was pointed out that this issue, which was of considerable importance, was much discussed by distinguished academic commentators, but had not been directly the subject of any modern decided case.

iii. When there is no direct English authority other common law authorities are helpful and persuasive such as *Sen v Headley*[120] where Australian, Canadian, South African and Scottish cases were used. In *Martin v Watson* McCowan LJ says:

> "I have found no English authority which is directly in point in the present case. ... In the Commonwealth however, there have been a number of cases which posed similar problems. ... I find myself in complete agree-

---

[113] [1990] 3 All ER, 344 (Court of Appeal, Civil)

[114] For such cases refer to: *Ancell and another v McDermott and others* [1993] 4 All ER, 355 (Court of Appeal, Civil); *R v Secretary of State for the Home Department, ex parte Bentley* [1993] 4 All ER, 442 (Queen's Bench); *Coppee-Lavalin SA/NV v Ken-Ren Chemicals and Fertilizers Ltd (in liq) Voest-Alpine AG v Ken-Ren Chemicals and Fertilisers Ltd* [1994] 2 All ER, 449 (House of Lords); *Connaught Restaurants Ltd v Indoor Leisure Ltd* [1994] 4 All ER, 834 (Court of Appeal); *T v Secretary of State for the Home Department* [1996] 2 All ER, 865 (House of Lords)

[115] [1991] 4 All ER, 577 (Court of Appeal, Civil) and [1992] 3 All ER, 737

[116] [1993] 1 All ER, 821 (High Court, Family Division; Court of Appeal; House of Lords). This case illustrates well all the types of references and relationships that exist between the legal systems in the common law world and therefore, is an all-rounded excellent example to study.

[117] [1993] 3 All ER, 481 (Court of Appeal, Civil)

[118] And civilian jurisdictions when it reached the House of Lords, as will be seen later in this study. See [1995] 1 All ER, 691

[119] [1992] 3 All ER 737 (House of Lords)

[120] [1990] 1 All ER, 898 (High Court, Chancery)

ment with these views (Australian, Canadian, New Zealand and American cases were looked at)."[121]

Again Lord Mustill in *R v Kingston* says:

> "In the absence of guidance from English authorities it is useful to inquire how other common law jurisdictions have addressed the same problem. I begin with two decisions of the High Court of Justiciary, neither of which was cited in the Court of Appeal. The reasoning of the HCJ cannot be applied directly to the present case, since the law of Scotland concerning the mental element of crime and the effect on it of a disturbance of the defendant's mental condition is not precisely the same as that which prevails in England. Nevertheless the closely reasoned judgment contains much the most extensive treatment of the problem in any of the materials before the House, and if read with appropriate caution gives valuable guidance both on general principle and on the solution to the particular problem on hand."[122]

In a negligence, damages and collapse of the property market case the courts faced a similar situation and in the absence of an English case, this time adopted the Canadian position[123].

In *Mulcahy v Ministry of Defence*, while looking into negligence and duty to take care, Neill LJ says:

> "It was accepted on behalf of the defendants that there was no direct English authority to support the proposition that no duty of care in tort is owed by one soldier to another when engaging the enemy in battle conditions. Reliance was placed however, on ... decisions of the High Court of Australia... I consider that an English court should approach this claim in the same way as the High Court of Australia in the Shaw Savill case."[124]

iv. When English common law is inadequate such as in *Simmonds v Dobson and another* [125], *Derbyshire County Council v Times Newspapers Ltd and others* [126] and *Khorasandjian v Bush* [127], again reference was made to other common law jurisdictions[128].

---

121 [1994] 2 All ER, 606 at 627 (Court of Appeal, Civil)

122 [1994] 3 All ER, 353 at 365 (House of Lords)

123 *Banque Bruxelles Lambert SA v Eagle Star Insurance Co Ltd* [1995] 2 All ER, 769 (Queen's Bench; Court of Appeal, Civil). Similarly in *Martin v Watson* [1995] 3 All ER, 559 (House of Lords), Lord Keith at 562 says: "Curiously enough, there appears to be no reported English decision... A number of decisions in other Commonwealth countries have however, considered such a state of affairs".

124 [1996] 2 All ER, 758 at 766, 770 (Court of Appeal, Civil)

125 [1991] 4 All ER, 25 (Court of Appeal, Civil)

126 [1992] 3 All ER, 65 (Court of Appeal, Civil)

127 [1993]3 All ER, 669 (Court of Appeal, Civil)

128 Other cases of interest are: *Giles v Thompson* [1993] 3 All ER, 321 (House of Lords);

v. To extend the law as in *Bennet v Horseferry Road Magistrates' Court and another*[129], or to move the law on as in *White and another v Jones and others*[130], or in furtherance of common law in novel cases of negligence and damages, great weight is given to Australian, Irish, Canadian and United States cases such as in *Burton v Islington Health Authority*[131] and *Jones and Others v Wright*[132]. In *Jones*, Hidden J, remarked:

> "The first thing to say is that, though we sit here in Liverpool in the summer of 1990, the journey will take us around the world and back over the years. It will involve Australian buggies, Irish trains, and even Canadian snowmobiles. It may be asked:'What have these to do with Hillsborough?' The answer is: 'Surprisingly, everything'."

He then found it necessary to see how the courts of some other countries have dealt with the problems thrown up by such cases in their own jurisdictions in this century. Attaching great weight to an Australian case, he went on to say:

> "This case is of significance, not only in demonstrating that a court in a common law jurisdiction has widened the categories of relationship where damages can be recovered ... This may be a timely reminder of the way in which courts can deal with such problems when they are presented to them, and the way in which, even when the line as to particular relationships is extended by a court, the court can nevertheless differentiate between genuine and unestablished claims."

In *Giles v Thompson*[133], looking at 'champerty' rooted in mediaeval history, the House of Lords looked at Australia when seeking improvements and a new approach in the field of non-fault accidents in the light of contemporary public policy.

vi. When there is much to learn from imaginative legal developments, from for example Australia, New Zealand, Canada and the United States as in the case of *White and another v Jones and others,*[134] English courts refer to such other common law jurisdictions. In this case, as will be seen below, German, French and Dutch positions were also considered at a later stage in the House of Lords. In another recent case[135] Dillon LJ said:

Tinsley v Milligan [1993] 3 All ER,65 (House of Lords)

[129] [1993] 3 All ER, 138 (House of Lords)

[130] [1993] 3 All ER, 481 (Court of Appeal, Civil); [1995] 1 All ER, 691 (House of Lords)

[131] [1992] 3 All ER, 833 (Court of Appeal, Civil)

[132] [1991] 1 All ER, 353 (High Court, Queen's Bench)

[133] [1993] 3 All ER, 321

[134] [1993] 3 All ER, 481 (Court of Appeal, Civil); [1995] 1 All ER, 691 (House of Lords)

[135] *R v Devon County Council, ex parte Baker; R v Durham County Council, ex parte*

"The law in this field is still developing, and it may be that the process of development has at present time gone somewhat further in Australia than the decided cases have so far taken in this country. For my part, however, I have found generally helpful the observations of Deane J in the High Court of Australia in ... ."

Lord Keith, looking at negligence and the duty to take care looked extensively to cases from New Zealand and said:

"The views expressed in these three cases decided in a jurisdiction which is well known to be tender in its approach to claims in negligence involving pure economic loss are of great importance. The process of reasoning which they contain is in my opinion entirely sound and apt to be followed and applied in the present case."[136]

However, Thorpe J in *Secretary of State for the Home Department v Robb* [137], looking at hunger strike and medical treatment said:

"There has been a fuller development in other common law jurisdictions, particularly in the United States, and all counsel have drawn my attention to and relied upon a number of decisions all of which consider the right of the individual to refuse nutrition in different circumstances. The most recent, and for me the most helpful is the decision ... these decisions are obviously relevant and helpful in reaching a decision as to how the law stands in these jurisdictions ... It seems to me that within this jurisdiction there is perhaps a stronger emphasis on the right of the individual's self-determination when balance comes to be struck between that right and any countervailing interests of the state ... In this case there is no countervailing state interest to be set in the balance."

vii. When seeking to soften the impact of an English rule in *British Railways Board v Herrinton* [138] it was pointed out that, "there is a growing tendency of courts both in England and Scotland to try to soften the impact of the rule in *Addie's* case. Australian authorities are even more persuasive and far reaching than those in this country. ...The House of Lords should re-examine the whole problem and reconsider its decision in *Addie*".

viii. When seeking support for the position of the English court[139] devel-

---

Curtis [1995] 1 All ER 73, at 88 (Court of Appeal, Civil)

[136] *Spring v Guardian Assurance plc and others* [1994] 3 All ER, 129 at 141 (House of Lords) However his Lordships did not agree with him though they all fully discussed the NZ cases.

[137] [1995] 1 All ER, 677 at 682, 683 (High Court, Family Division)

[138] [1972] 1 All ER, 749 (House of Lords)

[139] For some examples also see: *Lockheed-Arabia Corp v Owen* [1993] 3 All ER, 641 (Court of Appeal, Civil); *Re Dorman (deceased)* [1994] 1 All ER 804 (Chancery Devision); *Re Barn Crown Ltd* [1994] 4 All ER, 42 (Chancery Division); *White and another v Jones* [1995] 1 All ER,691 (House of Lords); *T v Secretary of State for the Home Department*

oping the law, such as in the area of negligence and duty of care, Australia provided 'inspiration' as in *Caparo Industries plc v Dickman and others* [140]. In this case Lord Bridge said:

> "Whilst recognising, of course, the importance of the underlying general principles common to the whole field of negligence, I think the law has now moved in the direction of attaching greater significance to the more traditional categorisation of distinct and recognisable situations as guides to the existence, the scope and the limits of the varied duties of care which the law imposes. We must now, I think, recognise the wisdom of the words of Brennan J in the High Court of Australia in *Sutherland Shire Council v Heyman.*"

When seeking support to push the law further, in areas such as marital rape in *R v R* [141,142], Scottish law was used. In *Wai Yu-tsang v R* [143] (1991) Canadian law gave comfort. In confirming the views of the judge in a case dealing with proportionality, in addition to the jurisprudence of the ECJ, Canadian judgments were referred to in *Stoke-on-Trent City Council v B & Q plc, Norwich City Council v B & Q plc* [144]. Such cases also help the judge to make up his mind as in *R v Croydon Justices, ex parte Dean* [145].

Lord Jauncey, in a case involving personal injury and nervous shock, looked at Scotland, Australia and the United States and said: "My Lords, as is so often the case, in the field of negligence valuable contributions to the discussion are to be found in judgments of the High Court of Australia and in the context of this appeal I propose and refer to two"[146].

ix. There are also situations where the court compares but rejects[147] foreign decisions, such as when in *R v Governor of Pentonville Prison, ex parte Naghdi* [148] American law was found not to satisfy the conditions of English law on extradition and fugitive offenders. Again, in *Halifax Building Society v Thomas,* Glidewell LJ dismissing the appeal, said:

> "Despite his able argument, I cannot discern that there is any such general established principle. Indeed, Mr Waters has to concede that there is

[1996] 2 All ER, 865 (House of Lords)

140 [1990] 1 All ER, 568 (House of Lords)

141 [1991] 4 All ER, 481 (House of Lords)

142 [1991] 2 All ER, 257 (Court of Appeal, Criminal)

143 [1991] 4 All ER, 664 (Privy Council)

144 [1991] 4 All ER, 221 (High Court, Chancery)

145 [1993] 3 All ER, 129 (High Court, Queen's Bench)

146 *Page v Smith* [1995] 2 All ER, 736 at 745 (House of Lords)

147 For some further examples see: *Pepper (Inspector of taxes) v Hart* [1993] 1 All ER, 42 (House of Lords); *Antwerp United Diamond BCBA v Air Europe* [1993] 4 All ER, 469 (Queen's Bench, Commercial Court); *Bank of America National Trust and Savings Association v Chrimas The Kyriaki* [1994] 1 All ER, 401 (Queen's Bench, Commercial Court)

148 [1990] 1 All ER, 256 (High Court, Queen's Bench)

no English authority upon which he can rely to establish his right to succeed either in the law of restitution, under the head of unjustified enrichment, or in the law of constructive trusts. The sole American decision which appears to be directly in point, that of the New York District Court in *Federal Sugar Refining Co v US Sugar Equalisation Board Inc* (1920) 268 F 575 is not sufficiently persuasive to secure a visa for admission into English jurisprudence ... I cannot conclude that the principle for which Mr Waters contends is at present established as part of our law."[149]

In *Pitts v Hunt* [150], comparing English and Australian positions, it was held that in car drivers' negligence and duty of care, the two jurisdictions reached their different solutions from common law principles. Also in *Caparo* [151], for example, it was stated that, "Now, of course, any decision of the Court of Appeal of New Zealand is entitled to the very greatest respect, but it has to be observed that the majority view was based on an interpretation of Lord Wilberforce's observations in the *Anns* case which has since been severely qualified by subsequent decisions of this House". In *Attorney General v London Weekend Television Ltd* [152] it was stated:

> "Whether the words complained of create a serious risk ... in each case the test must be applied in the light of the surrounding circumstances and arguments presented by counsel ... those cases in the Supreme Court of the United States where alternative formulae appear to have been preferred ... Such judgments are always respected by this court and in cases where the law in the UK has moved more rapidly than here, often followed. In this case however, we cannot and see no need to do so even assuming that the disciplines of contempt of law in England are similar to those in the US as affected by the 1st and the 14th Amendments of the American Constitution to which reference has been made. For the law of contempt in England had been defined for us 30 years before the founding fathers in Philadelphia signed the Declaration of Independence which predated the making of the American Constitution and its amendments."

The following is also a useful observation:

> "In my judgment the case (English) is clear authority in favour of the lex loci actus and against the application of the law of incorporation for the purpose of deciding questions of priority while the transfer remains unregistered. There is also strong persuasive authority to the same effect in the United States. All the witnesses who gave expert evidence before me

---

[149] [1995] 4 All ER, 673 at 682 (Court of Appeal, Civil)
[150] [1990] 3 All ER, 344 (Court of Appeal, Civil)
[151] [1990] 1 All ER, 568 (House of Lords)
[152] [1972] 3 All ER, 1146 (High Court, Queen's Bench)

> on New York conflict of laws were agreed that in the last 25 years there has been a revolution in the approach of the New York courts to choice of law questions in favour of what has been described as a 'functional and teleological methodology'. Old decisions may, therefore, no longer be a safe guide to the present law. But in my judgment they may still provide persuasive authority for an English court where they reflect the traditional approach which still prevails in Commonwealth and European jurisdictions."[153]

Two further quotations should suffice under this head:

> "Thus whatever the United States courts now regard to be the scope of waiver of privilege, the reasoning in *Hearn v Rhay* (US District Court) certainly does not represent English law."[154]

> "In my respectful opinion the principle enunciated by Sheppard J (NSW SC) in the last passage I have cited from his judgment is not established by any English authority. I appreciate that the English law of restitution should be flexible and capable of continuous development. However, I see no good reason to extend it to apply to ..."[155]

3. Reference to Continental law and civil law

i. It is easily demonstrated that continental law is usually mentioned only in passing by English courts when brought to their attention and is not normally used in the sense of (b) above, that is, for support or guidance. Looking at 1972, 1982 and 1990-1995 cases shows no real change in the pattern. Yet, for example, in *Antwerp United Diamonds BVBA v Air Europe,* a Dutch and a Belgian case was presented together with a case from the US and another one from British Columbia as foreign authority to the Court of Appeal and there was no English decision on the question prior to the decision of the lower court in the present case. Hirst LJ said:

> "Of these by far the most significant decision, both by virtue of its high authority and by virtue of its close reasoning and analysis, is in my judgment *Insurance Co of North America v Royal Dutch Airlines* in the Supreme Court of the Netherlands ... I find (this decision) very strongly persuasive ... even though it is not of course binding upon us or conclusive."[156]

Again in *Barclays Bank plc v Glasgow City Council* and *Kleinwort Benson*

---

[153] *MacMillan v Bishopsgate* (No.3) [1995] 3 All ER, 747 at 766 (Millett J) (Chancery Devision)

[154] *Nederlandse Reassurantie Groep Holding NV v Bacon and Woodrow (a firm)* [1995] 1 All ER, 976 at 987 (Colman J) (Queen's Bench, Commercial Court)

[155] *Regalian Properties plc v London Dockland Development Corp* [1995] 1 All ER, 1005 at 1024 (Rattee J) (Chancery Division)

[156] [1995] 3 All ER, 424 at 428

plc v Glasgow City Council, where a question arose as to the meaning of a term taken from the Common Customs Tariff and used as part of German tax law, Lloyd LJ said: "But there is precedent for the course we propose to take, provided by the German courts (case cited in c - 231/89).[157]

However, *Woolwich Building Society v Inland Revenue Commissioners (No 2)* [158], is more typical where Lord Goff pointed out in his judgment:

> "An instructive example of this approach is to be found in German law, in which we find a general rights of recovery which is subject to the principle that an administrative act is, even if in fact unlawful, treated as legally effective unless and until it is cancelled, either by the authority itself or by an administrative court. Furthermore a citizen can only enforce the cancellation by making a formal objection within one month of notification; and if that objection is rejected by the authority, the citizen must take legal action within another month. In addition, one citizen cannot benefit from the successful formal objection of another citizen,; he must object in due time himself. Such draconian time limits as these may be too strong a medicine for our taste; but the example of a general rights of recovery subject to strict time limits imposed as a matter of policy is instructive for us as we seek to solve the problem in the present case. At this stage of the argument I find it helpful to turn to recent developments in Canada."

A more recent example is the case of *White and another v Jones* and others, where the House of Lords dealt with negligence and duty of care in relation to solicitors. Lord Goff looked at the experiences in other countries in this developing area where law has moved on and stated that the question was "much discussed, not only in this country and other common law countries, but also in some civil law countries, notably Germany."[159] Pointing out also to similar conclusions reached by French and Dutch courts, he extensively discussed all cases, civilian and common law, reserving extensive treatment to German law. However his solution is based on tort and English authority. In the same case, Lord Browne-Wilkinson stresses that the law in this area is not ossified[160]. Lord Mustill, dissenting, is rather concerned about the building of new law on the basis of *Hedley Byrne* which he sees as a 'bold development of a new doctrine' and wants to survey the foundations and create a solid intellectual basis[161].

However, when a civil law maxim has become part of a common law jurisdiction, such as when the Supreme Court of Canada decided on the basis of a civil law maxim because the case was a Quebec case and the

---

[157] [1994] 4 All ER, 865 at 889 (Court of Appeal, Civil)
[158] [1992] 3 All ER, 737 (House of Lords)
[159] {1995] 1 All ER, 691 at 697
[160] *id.* at 719
[161] *id.* at 724, 725

Civil Code of Quebec was applicable, in the case of *Burton v Islington Health Authority, de Martell v Merton and Sutton Health Authority*[162], Dillon LJ said:

> "For my part, I think it would be open to the English courts to apply the civil law maxim directly to the situation we have in these two appeals, and treat the two plaintiffs as lives in being at the time of the events which injured them as they were later born alive, but it is not necessary to do so directly in view of the effect which the Montreal Tramways case has already had in the development of the common law in this field in other common law jurisdictions."

Nearly all the references to Continental systems occur however, in cases where that foreign law is indicated in the dispute. Child abduction cases, extradition cases, cases revolving around recognition and enforcement of judicial decisions and double taxation cases, are the types where we see such references. For example, in *G and H Montage GmbH v Irvani*[163], English, German and Iranian laws were compared in relation to a signature placed on a bill.

In one case[164] where the concept of proportionality was being discussed within the context of EC law, although EC law was extensively used, reference was made to Canadian, American and Australian understandings of the concept to guide the court and confirm the judges' views, rather than the German, though the concept itself entered the English scene from German law via the ECJ[165].

In terms of years, there are 8 out of 12 cases in 1972, 4 out of 8 in 1982, 5 out of 5 in 1990, 2 out of 2 in 1991, 4 out of 7 in 1992, 6 out of 7 in 1993, 10 out of 15 in 1994 and 3 out of 3 in 1995 where a continental system of law is referred to because the specific law or legal system is relevant or pivotal for the case. Even then there are problems. For example in *Webb v Webb*[166], Judge Paul Baker QC, after stating, "It is said that under the law of the European Community the French courts have exclusive jurisdiction in the case", said that the conferment of exclusive jurisdiction could lead to great inconvenience for the parties and therefore there was sound reason for limiting it as far as possible. He then complained, "Article 16 is couched in the concepts of the civil law systems of the original member states. It does not readily fit in with the system of legal and equitable interests in property obtaining in England and Wales and in

---

[162] [1992] 3 All ER, 833 (Court of Appeal, Civil)

[163] [1990] 2 All ER, 225 (Court of Appeal, Civil)

[164] *Stoke-on-Trent City Council*, [1991] 4 All ER, 221 (High Court, Chancery)

[165] For a case where practices and other instruments of France, Spain, Portugal, the Netherlands and Denmark were looked at for the purposes of implementing the Treaty of EU see: *R v Secretary of State for Foreign and Commonwealth* Affairs, ex parte Rees-Mogg [1994] 1 All ER, 457 (Queen's Bench).

[166] [1992] 1 All ER, 17 (High Court, Chancery)

both parts of Ireland." Further, in *R v Governor of Pentonville Prison, ex parte Chinoy* [167], it was held:

> "However, if the methods of obtaining evidence were legitimate by reference to English law and appropriate to the situation under investigation, the fact that the evidence had been obtained abroad unlawfully according to foreign and international law did not require the court to exclude the evidence so obtained. Since English law acknowledged the fact that the detection and proof of drug trafficking offences might necessitate the employment of covert and unlawful means, the means employed by the United States agents to obtain evidence against the applicant were appropriate to the drug trafficking offences which they were investigating and, as such, were legitimate by reference to English law irrespective of whether they gave rise to breaches of French law and European human rights legislation."

Nolan J also said:

> "In saying this, I do not forget that crucial evidence against the applicant has been obtained by means which are criminal in France, at any rate according to French law, are in breach of the ECHR. I bear in mind the principle that, in civil cases, our courts do not enforce a contract if its performance would involve doing an act in a foreign and friendly state which violates the law of that state. But the collection of evidence for the purposes of a prosecution in a criminal case seems to me to raise very different considerations."

In this context, as well as in the context of giving effect to conventions, the following quotation from the judgment of Bingham LJ in *Dresser UK Ltd and others v Falcongate Freight Management Ltd and others The Duke of Yare,*[168] is interesting:

> "Although (as recognised in *Zelger v Salinitri*) practice on the continent of Europe varies from country to country, Mr Leggatt accepted that courts in those countries would not ordinarily regard themselves as seized of proceedings until (at earliest) the proceedings had been actually served on and thus brought to the attention of the defendant. But he pointed out that service and notice were not in all cases coincident. Thus under Dutch procedure, for example, a defendant resident abroad is treated as served when a copy of the proceedings is served on the officer van justitie for the issuing court, and French procedure provides in similar circumstances that service is complete when the huissier delivers the proceedings to the ministère public. While grateful to be told of these departures from the ordinary rule, it does not affect my conclusion.

[167] [1992] 1 All ER, 317 (High Court, Queen's Bench)
[168] [1992] 2 All ER, 450 (Court of Appeal, Civil)

> We are concerned to analyse and apply English procedure, and we will review that of other countries only when an issue under the convention falls to be decided. We must then accept their interpretation of their procedural law. It may, however, be that in other countries as well as this, procedural rules will call for reconsideration in the light of the convention. Mr Leggatt urged that it would be contrary to the ratio of *Zelger v Salinitri* to force English procedure into a strait-jacket of European design. I agree. But procedural idiosyncrasy is not (like national costume or regional cuisine) to be nurtured for its own sake and in answering the question before us we must have regard to the realities of litigation in this country and the purpose of the convention, not to tradition, nomenclature or rules developed for other purposes."

In *Continental Bank NA v Aeokos Cia Naviera SA* Steyn LJ said:

> "In construing the 1968 Convention, it is important to put aside preconception based on traditional English rules. The convention is a radical new regime governing the international legal relationships of the contracting states ... The genesis of the convention is the jurisprudence of civil law rather than the common law. Since the original states were all civil law countries ... The idea that a national court has discretion in the exercise of its jurisdiction does not generally exist in the civilian systems: Schlosser Report (1977). Article 17 follows the civilian approach. Article 17 has mandatory effect."[169]

ii. In a very few cases (4 in 1972, 4 in 1982, 0 in 1990, 0 in 1991, 3 in 1992, 0 in 1993, 6 in 1994 and 2 in 1995) brief comments are made in general reference to continental or civilian tradition, to indicate background and the origin of legal rules[170].

Even Roman law and Justinian are mentioned when showing sources of laws, but never for help. For example, in *Sen v Headley*,[171] discussing gifts and donatio mortis causa, Roman law was cited as the origin of the concept:

> "Although donationes mortis causa were taken from Roman law, it is only the first two requirements which now bear evidence of that ancestry. They are embodied in the definition given in Justinian's Institutes (2 Just Inst, tit vii) which was adopted by Lord Loughborough LC in *Tate v Hilbert* (1793) 2 Ves III at 119 ... We can therefore turn away from Ro-

169 [1994] 2 All ER, 540 at 549

170 See *Henderson v Merrett Syndicates Ltd* [1994] 3 All ER, 506 where the development of the common law and civil law are considered, specifically in relation to concurrent claims and German law is praised after French law as to the doctrine of non cumul is criticised (Lord Goff at 524, 525). In *El Ajou v Dollar Holdings* [1994] 2 All ER, 705 English law and German law are compared in the use of the term 'directing mind' derived originally from German law.

171 [1991] 2 All ER, 636 (Court of Appeal, Civil)

man law and give our whole attention to the English authorities."

Again, in *Southern Centre of Theosophy Inc v State of South Australia* [172], the doctrine of accretion was shown to be derived from Justinian, and yet guidance is sought from Australia and the United States.

In The *Funabaski Sycamore Steamship Co Ltd v Owners of the Steamship White Mountain and others* [173] Dunn J said that the Admiralty Court always awarded interest on a limitation fund and then quoted from Lord Denning; "Court of Admiralty did not apply common law. It followed the civil law and gave interest on damages whenever the non-payment was due to the wrongful delay of the defendant. Ex mora the obligor; ex mora means 'on account of the delay'. It is so stated in the Digest 21.1.32(2)."

V. Scottish Courts

While English courts are often reproached for being unduly insular in their attitude to foreign law, which has been seen not to be the case at all, especially if the vast number of references to the other common law jurisdictions is looked at, "Scots lawyers are usually excluded from the charge, since they are generally regarded as being 'more internationally-minded'"[174]. This is not true either as far as the Scottish courts are concerned. More Scottish cases are dealt with solely on Scottish authority than English cases on English authority.

Where cases make reference to foreign law, this is mostly understood to be English, commonwealth and other common law, in that order. All non-Scottish law is regarded as an extraneous source of law. Though in the long established and non-statutory branches of law Roman law[175] was traditionally the appropriate foreign law to look at today the significance of Roman law has diminished. Occasionally South African and continental systems may be considered because of the historical ties. However, as Lord Coulsfield said in *Sharp v Thomson* [176]:

> "Although weight should be given to the arguments that the purity of Scots law, as a system based on the civil law, should be maintained and the unitary conception of ownership preserved, the arguments should not be overemphasised or treated as in themselves decisive."

On some occasions American authorities may be discussed[177]. However,

---

172 [1992] 1 All ER, 283 (Privy Council)

173 [1972] 2 All ER, 181 (Admiralty, Queen's Bench)

174 Enonchong, *op. cit.*, p.633 referring to Markesinis, *The Gradual Convergence* (1994) p.2

175 See *Fortune v Fraser* 1995 SC 186 where Roman law is looked at for a distinction

176 1995 SC 455 at 505

177 See *Abnett v British Airways plc* 1995 SC 439 where Lord Allanbridge said: "We

the first foreign system to be consulted is the English one. In *Mains v Uniroyal Englebert Tyres Ltd*[178] the Court of Justiciary said: "While English authorities are not binding on us, I consider where the Scottish authorities conflict we are entitled to pick which of the cases with which we find favour."

It is interesting to note that references to Scottish law are not extensive in England, as we have seen above. Lord Justice Bingham said:

> "Eventually, as we know – in no small part due to the work of Lord Goff, both as advocate and judge, and the wisdom of Lord Diplock – the Scottish rule was adopted in England. But it took three appeals to the House of Lords to put the law where, one feels, it should always have been and might have been had English lawyers of the time been willing to look north of the border and acknowledge that acceptance of jurisdiction by the English court is not necessarily an unmixed blessing for all concerned."[179]

Again, in choosing the appropriate forum, the *forum non conveniens* principle, so well established in Scotland, has recently become available in England.

It can be said that in Scotland it is customary to look south of the border first. Especially in cases involving commercial and industrial law, Scottish courts tend to look to England. In as diverse areas as judicial review, company, takeover, damages, constructive lease, recognition of foreign divorces, bankruptcy, compulsory purchase, compensation, reparation and negligence, just to name but a few, we see how Scottish courts find 'powerful support' from English cases. For example, in *Centri-Force Engineering Ltd. v Bank of Scotland*[180], the Outer House held:

> "The considerations which give rise to the basic rule in England apply equally in Scotland in my opinion. The only exception to the basic rule recognised in English law, drawing on authority from USA, is where the beneficiary himself presents the documents required by the letter of credit and they are forged or fraudulent ... I have no reason to doubt that for the same reason that exception would apply in Scots law."

Again in *Morrison v Panic Link Ltd*[181] it was held:

> "If it was suggested that there was any difference between English law

---

were referred to a number of authorities, mostly American which ... gave different answers to this problem." Again in *Morgan Guarantee Trust Co of NY v Lothian Regional Council*, where there were no Scottish cases, and though Scots law was regarded lacking in clear and coherent structure in the field of unjustified enrichment, American, Canadian and South African cases did not provide aid since they were not unanimous. 1995 SC 165.

[178] 1995 SC 518 at 535

[179] Bingham, *op. cit.*, p. 517

[180] 1993 SLT 190 (Outer House, Court of Session)

[181] 1993 SLT 602 (Outer House, Court of Session)

> and Scots law in relation to the construction of this contract, it would be necessary for the defenders to aver what that difference was in the present action. They have made no such averments and accordingly it must be assumed that the English law is the same as Scots law as far as the construction of the contract is concerned."

In a Scottish appeal to the House of Lords, Lord Roskill said:

> "The Lord Ordinary started his opinion by stating that there was no Scottish authority directly in point and, while in argument before you much Scottish, English and indeed Commonwealth authority was cited, it remains the fact that no decision in any court that was cited conclusively shows the correct route to be taken, though many may be said greatly to illuminate the route."

The three main Commonwealth decisions in this case were of the Supreme Court of Canada, the High Court of Australia and the Court of Appeal of New Zealand, all before *Anns*. The New Zealand case reflecting the present law in New Zealand, and consonant with the views Lord Roskill expressed in his speech, was followed.[182]

As to figures, looking through 1995 Session Cases, for example, there are four House of Lords cases reported and in two of them, one English case each is cited and no other authorities by Scottish courts. Again in 1995 Session Cases, in the 41 Court of Justiciary cases reported and the 61 Court of Sessions cases reported, 20 cases referred to English cases, one to American law and one to Roman Law. In *Morgan Guarantee Trust Co of NY v Lothian Regional Council*[183] where there was no Scottish authority, English, American, Canadian and South African cases were looked at. Again in the case of *Anderson v HM Advocate*, the Court of Justiciary referred to the position in other countries and discussed decisions from England (including two by the Privy Council), New Zealand, South Africa, the US, Canada and Australia, and looked at the ECHR where they said that although its provisions were not part of domestic law, "the principles which they describe have, for a long time, been established as part of the law of this country[184]". Some of these cases were found 'useful', 'helpful' and 'of interest' in the search for 'support' to overrule a previous Scottish case.

---

182 *Junior Books Limited v Veitchi Co Limited* [1982] 3 All ER, 201(House of Lords)

183 1995 Session Cases 151

184 *Anderson v HM Advocate* 1996 Session Cases, 29 at 34 (The Court of Justiciary)

VI. Frontiers of Judicial Comparison or How Far Can Courts Go?

A. Departing from English Law and Following Another

We have seen instances of this above. In *Behzadi v Shaftesbury Hotels Ltd*[185] for example, the court departed from English law and followed Australian law. In *Khorasandjian v Bush*[186] the English judge, arguing that "relief must be had and common law does not have the resources", opted for a decision of the Alberta Supreme Court. The aim of this type of approach is to achieve improvement in the law and to create unity in all common law jurisdictions as seen in *Cheah v Equiticorp Finance Group Ltd*[187]. In keeping with this, commonwealth cases are sometimes treated as if they are English cases and cited as authority as seen in *R v Lord Chancellor's Department*[188] and in *Airedale NHS Trust v Bland*[189]. However, this could be a passing reference, dispersed among English authority.

B. When English law is well established and satisfactory

In *White and another v Jones*[190] it was stated that

> "In England we have much to learn from the imaginative legal developments in Australia in contract and tort, however, this categorisation does not advance substantive arguments."

In *Downsview Nominees Ltd and another v First City Corp Ltd and another*[191], the New Zealand case was compared to the law of the UK and it was held that the consequences in the UK would be harsher and therefore, there was danger in extending the bounds of negligence along New Zealand lines. Again in *Re T (adult: refusal of medical treatment)*[192], although the court agreed with the reasoning of the Canadian case, it was stated that in the UK the damages would not be so high.

In *Baytur SA v Finagro Holding SA*[193] it was said:

> "The effect of a scission in French law (traité de scission) is that the assets and liabilities of one company are transferred to two or more companies. In the present case the effect of the scission was to transfer all rights and obligations possessed by the buyer under the contract of sale

[185] [1991] 2 All ER, 477 (Court of Appeal, Civil)
[186] [1993] 3 All ER, 669 (Court of Appeal, Civil)
[187] [1991] 4 All ER, 989 (Privy Council)
[188] [1992] 1 All ER, 897 (High Court, Queen's Bench)
[189] [1993] 1 All ER, 821 (High Court, Family; Court of Appeal, Civil; House of Lords)
[190] [1993] 3 All ER, 481 (Court of Appeal, Civil)
[191] [1993] 3 All ER, 626 (Privy Council)
[192] [1992] 4 All ER, 649 (Court of Appeal, Civil)
[193] [1991] 4 All ER, 129 (Court of Appeal, Civil)

to ... But obviously that cannot affect our decision."

C. In developing English law when there is an Act of Parliament

When an area of English law is covered by statute not by common law, an English judge cannot benefit directly from foreign law, common law or otherwise. When there is a statute, foreign law is not significant. *Rance and another v Mid-Downs Health Authority and another*[194], *Sinclair v Director of Public Prosecutions and another*[195] and *Inland Revenue Commissioners v Herd*[196] are examples of the rule that when an Act of Parliament determines the question, the English judge cannot directly benefit from foreign case law. In *Rance and another v Mid-Downs Health Authority and another*[197], Brook J, after considering various American cases, said:

> "Apart from deriving satisfaction in the interests of comity from the fact that I am able to detect in the English statute very nearly the same concept of 'viability' as is used in the courts of the United States, I do not consider that American case law is of direct assistance to my task of interpreting English Acts of Parliament."

Again, in *Sinclair v Director of Public Prosecutions*[198], because there was the 1870 Extradition Act, there was no need to consider foreign, in this case American, law. However, when it is a matter of interpretation of a statutory obligation, judge-made law is important. Support and guidance is then sought from other common law jurisdictions. While relaxing the rules on interpretation and looking for support to commonwealth jurisdictions such as Australia and New Zealand, Lord Browne-Wilkinson said, in *Pepper (Inspector of Taxes) v Hart and related appeals*[199],

> "We have heard no suggestion that recourse to parliamentary history has significantly increased the cost of litigation in Australia and New Zealand and I do not believe that it will do so in this country .... Other common law jurisdictions have abandoned the rule without adverse consequences."

Here we can also cite *Hughes v Doncaster Metropolitan Borough Council*[200].

In *R v Morhall* Lord Taylor CJ said:

---

194 [1991] 1 All ER, 801 (High Court, Queen's Bench)
195 [1991] 2 All ER, 366 (House of Lords)
196 [1993] 3 All ER, 56 (House of Lords)
197 [1991] 1 All ER, 801 (High Court, Queen's Bench)
198 [1991] 2 All ER, 366 (House of Lords)
199 [1993] 1 All ER, 42 (House of Lords)
200 [1990] 2 All ER, 53 (Court of Appeal, Civil)

"Some guidance is to be found in ... (a NZ case) in which ... (the judge) sought to explain the word 'characteristics' used in a similar context in the NZ Crimes Act 1981 ... This case was cited with approval as stating the position in English law by Lord Simon."

However, in *Bank of America National Trust & Savings Association v Chismas The Kyriaki*, an Australian case was rejected as "there is no counterpart in New South Wales to s.35 and therefore this case does not assist the counsel in the main point."[201]

Finally, in *Luc Thiet Thuan v R* Lord Goff said:

"But in the respectful opinion of their Lordships, it must be unwise to impose uncritically upon an English statute an interpretation placed upon a statute from another jurisdiction, which is not expressed in the same words. Of course, there is a strong affinity between England and New Zealand law on this subject, reflecting their common origin; and anything which has fallen from North J is regarded with great respect in this country, as it is in New Zealand. But their Lordships feel compelled to say that the wholesale adoption, without analysis of a substantial part of this obiter dictum, which covers a whole range of points on a notoriously difficult subject with particular reference to the New Zealand statute, is not a satisfactory approach to the interpretation of the objective test in provocation as recognised in the English statute. Each point must, in Hong Kong as in England, fall to be considered by reference to the words of the statute, their historical derivation from the common law, and the legislative setting (where relevant) at the time of enactment."[202]

D. When Law should be developed by Parliament

In *Caparo*[203] for example, the foreign, in this case the American, position on duty of care and duty to shareholders was found preferable; however, the House of Lords suggested that it is the legislature which should develop this area. Again in *R v Kearley*[204], although there were illuminating New Zealand and Australian cases, it was pointed out that the law should be improved by Parliament. In *Tinsley v Milligan*[205], Lord Goff stated:

"These provisions of the Act (New Zealand) demonstrate how sweeping a reform was considered necessary by the New Zealand legislature in order to substitute a system of discretionary relief for the present system of rules founded upon the in pari delicto principle ... The real criticism

---

[201] [1994] 1 All ER, 401 at 417 (Queen's Bench, Commercial)

[202] [1996] 2 All ER, 1033 at 1042-43 (Privy Council)

[203] [1990] 1 All ER, 568 (House of Lords)

[204] [1992] 2 All ER, 345 (House of Lords)

[205] [1993] 3 All ER, 65 (House of Lords)

> of the present rules is not that they are unprincipled, but rather that they are indiscriminate in their effect, and are capable therefore of producing injustice. It is this effect which no doubt prompted the reform of the law in New Zealand, embodied in the 1970 Act; and it prompts me to say that, speaking for myself, I would welcome an investigation by the Law Commission, if this is desirable and practicable by the authorities concerned, and that I would be more than happy if a new system could be evolved ... ."

The courts are generally of the opinion that:

> "The enactment of this legislation does not, of course, lead inevitably to the conclusion that neither common law nor equity provides a means by which Mr Thomas could be prevented from enjoying the profit of his crime. Nevertheless, the readiness of Parliament to address the problem by legislation weakens the case for providing a solution by judicial creativity."[206]

E. Penal, Revenue and Public laws of Foreign States

English courts will not entertain directly or indirectly, a suit brought by a foreign sovereign state to enforce its own penal or revenue laws. English courts do not see themselves as 'sitting to collect taxes for another country or to inflict punishment for it'. This principle is extended to any act done in the exercise of sovereign authority. This position was fully discussed in 1982 in *Attorney General of New Zealand v. Ortiz and others*[207]. In this case there was argument *obiter* that English courts should enforce the New Zealand Historic Articles Act because comity required that English courts should respect the national heritage of other countries by according both recognition and enforcement to their laws affecting the title to property while it is within their territory.

VII. Justification of Judicial Comparison and Conclusion

The main judicial comparisons are between the members of the common law family. English courts make frequent reference to other commonwealth jurisdictions and the United States. Among these references, in the years under survey, most were made to Australia with 166, then to the United States with 102, New Zealand with 86 and Canada with 75. Scotland

---

[206] *Halifax Building Society v Thomas* [1995] 4 All ER, 673 at 683 (Court of Appeal, Civil)

[207] [1982] 3 All ER, 432 (High Court, Queen's Bench, Commercial; Court of Appeal, Civil)

comes behind with 60 references[208]. The reasons have been fully explored above. Since 1993, as new areas are being developed and as English law needs modernisation, references have increased four-fold to common law jurisdictions, especially to Australia, the United States and New Zealand, as the figures demonstrate. The major justification is the perceived unity of common law which allows the using of decisions from other common law jurisdictions as if they are English authority. This usage and reference does not extend however, to statutory laws.

In theory, there is ample justification for referring to laws of the other member states of the EU, especially in comparing their attitudes to the interpretation of EC law; however, it cannot be said that this is happening to any significant extent. There does not seem to be the kind of cross fertilisation between the member states of the EU as there is between the jurisdictions of the common law.

English and Scottish cases do not reflect an 'integrationist' approach with other member states of the European Union, except when the specificalities of a case so demand. However, references to commonwealth/common law jurisdictions abound in resolving domestic disputes, especially when there is no domestic authority or the topic is a new and expanding one. There are extensive quotations from the reasoning of these cases and they are regarded as of special value to fill in the gaps of English and, to a lesser extent, Scottish common law.

However, the years 1994 and 1995 have seen a change in this respect and yet, the overall picture is very similar to that of previous years. There is a general increase in reference to foreign law. The references to common law cases have more than quadrupled in the last three years, whereas references to civilian systems have doubled.

When comparisons are made between British law and other common law jurisdictions, this is essentially a 'functional use' of comparative law, whereas when civilian systems are considered, one may be forgiven for thinking that it reflects an 'ornamental use' of comparative law. In the first group, the British cases deal mostly with domestic law and domestic problems. In the second group the cases fall mostly within a wider ambit, usually of European law or an international convention. Again, in the first group, foreign cases are either directly used or used to give guidance and support reflecting the 'integrationist' approach in the common law world. In the second group, the moral and political considerations necessitate looking into the laws of the civilian states, especially if the case is related to EC law or a convention, at which point we even see:

"There seems no doubt that, while national laws of contract differ, there

---

[208] There are, of course, occasional references to Ireland, South Africa and India and also many other commonwealth jurisdictions such as Hong Kong, Malaysia, Nigeria, the Bahamas, Jamaica and Belize in Privy Council cases related to appeals arising from the courts of these.

is a general sense in which the word contract is understood by the signatories to the convention. English notions of consideration and privity must be discarded. But at its irreducible minimum a contract is a consensual arrangement intended to create legal relations and to be legally enforceable."[209]

Here certainly the 'internationalism' is manifest. As for seeking guidance or support from, or direct use of, civilian cases in preference to British law or other common laws, the same cannot be said. As foreign law is a question of fact in common law, it is worth repeating once more that it is the counsel who must be convinced of the value and relevance of comparisons, and, since the judges rely on counsel, the concept of 'the courts' used in the title of this study must be taken in the widest sense.

It only remains to be said that, while it is true that each year there are one or two cases where an exposé of a civilian doctrine is made and solutions thoroughly discussed, though not necessarily adopted, this should not be taken to mean that the trend has changed. Such a small number of swallows cannot make a summer. They may indicate a spring.

[209] *Kleinwort Benson Ltd v Glasgow City Council* [1996] 2 All ER, 257 at 273 (Court of Appeal, Civil)

DAVID S. CLARK*

The Use of Comparative Law by American Courts

I. INTRODUCTION

There is an increasing use of foreign law in American courts today associated primarily with the internationalization of civil procedure and criminal procedure. This internationalization – tied to the growth in trade and investment across national borders and the ease of long distance travel and communication – manifests itself when a domestic court must deal with a foreign law issue, collect evidence abroad, extradite a fugitive, or obtain jurisdiction over a foreign country defendant. A court's involvement with a foreign element will at least implicitly force the judge to face the matter comparatively: how does the foreign law or legal system differ from the American approach?

Outside the recently emerging fields of international civil procedure and international criminal law,[1] there is scant legal literature on the use of foreign and comparative law in United States courts because courts rarely cite foreign law. Historically, the situation was different. Before the Civil War courts regularly referred to Roman law, civil law, and English common law.[2] Much of this influence was carried through the great treatises of Blackstone (1723-1780),[3] (continued with American editions), James Kent

* Professor of Law and Director, Comparative and International Law Center, University of Tulsa and Vice President, American Society of Comparative Law. An earlier version of this chapter appeared in 42 *Am. J. Comp. L.* 23-40 (Supp. 1994)

[1] See, e.g., Gary B. Born, *International Civil Litigation in United States Courts: Commentary and Materials* (3d ed. 1996); Andreas F. Lowenfeld, *International Litigation and Arbitration* (1993); Ved P. Nanda & M. Cherif Bassiouni (eds.), *International Criminal Law: A Guide to U.S. Practice and Procedure* (1987); Bruno A. Ristau 1-6 *International Judicial Assistance* (with Michael Abbell, vols. 3-6, 1990).

[2] See Pound, "The Influence of the Civil Law in America," 1 *La. L. Rev.* 1 (1938).

[3] William Blackstone, 1-4 *Commentaries on the Laws of England* 1765-1769, repr. 1966).

U. Drobnig and S. van Erp (eds.), The Use of Comparative Law by Courts, 297–314.

(1763-1847),[4] and Joseph Story (1779-1845).[5] The comparative law leavening of indigenous American law largely came to an end by the 20th century due to the influence of the historical school of jurisprudence, the adequacy of the West Publishing Company's national reporter and digest system in accumulating a corpus of American law, and the general social force of nationalism.

An important exception to the eclipse of comparative law in American courts continues in Louisiana and Puerto Rico, the two mixed common law and civil law jurisdictions in the United States.[6] In addition, the civil law occasionally provides the rule for property law issues involving title, mining or water rights, or matrimonial property in the states of Arizona, California, Florida, New Mexico, and Texas, which were formerly controlled by Spain.[7] The special situation in these jurisdictions, however, is beyond the scope of this paper.

In the sections that follow, I review briefly those areas of the law in which American courts have come again to use foreign law and thus to at least implicitly compare foreign and domestic legal rules. These areas include international law, civil procedure, and criminal procedure. To keep the paper a manageable length I focus in particular on the internationalization of civil procedure. I also consider certain methods and sources of judicial comparison and end with three examples of episodic judicial comparison that more or less reflect the current parochial nature of American law and the American judiciary.

II. International Law

Of the three primary formal sources of international law mentioned in the Statute of the International Court of Justice,[8] treaties and international custom provide examples for the use of foreign and comparative law in

---

[4] James Kent, 1-4 *Commentaries on American Law* (1826-1830); see Watson, "Chancellor Kent's Use of Foreign Law," in, Mathias Reimann (ed.), *The Reception of Continental Ideas in the Common Law World, 1820-1920* at 45 (1993).

[5] Story published nine "Commentaries" on various subjects of American law between 1832 and 1845. See, e.g., Joseph Story, *Commentaries on the Conflict of Laws* (1834). See Hoeflich, "John Austin and Joseph Story: Two Nineteenth Century Perspectives on the Utility of the Civil Law for the Common Lawyer," 29 *Am. J Leg. Hist.* 36 (1985).

[6] See Fiol Matta, "Civil Law and Common Law in the Legal Method of Puerto Rico," 40 *Am. J Comp. L.* 783 (1992); Yiannopoulos, "Louisiana Civil Law: A Lost Cause?," 54 *Tul. L. Rev.* 830 (1980).

[7] See, e.g., Baade, "The Historical Background of Texas Water Law: A Tribute to Jack Pope," 18 *St. Mary's L.J.* 1 (1986).

[8] 59 Stat. 1055, signed 26 June 1945. Art 38(1) provides: "The Court … shall apply:
international conventions …;
international custom, as evidence of a general practice accepted as law;
the general principles of law recognized by civilized nations …"

American courts. The United States does not accept "general principles of law recognized by civilized nations" as a formal source of law to be applied by domestic courts, however, since there would always exist a state of federal rule on the particular point that would be applicable.

Treaties in the United States are the "supreme Law of the Land,"[9] prevailing over earlier inconsistent federal statutes and over all state law. The Warsaw Convention for the Unification of Certain Rules Relating to International Transportation by Air,[10] a multilateral treaty ratified by the United States, derives much of its meaning from French internal law. It provides an interesting illustration of the use of foreign and comparative law in American courts. The U.S. Supreme Court, in *Eastern Airlines, Inc. v. Floyd*,[11] recently interpreted article 17 of the Warsaw Convention and demonstrated the importance of foreign and comparative law.

Article 17 in English reads: "The carrier shall be liable for damage sustained in the event of the death or wounding of a passenger or any other bodily injury suffered by a passenger ...." The issue in *Floyd* was whether this article permits recovery for mental or psychic injuries unaccompanied by physical injury or the physical manifestations of injury. The plaintiffs were passengers on an Eastern Airlines flight while each of the three jet engines failed due to loss of oil pressure. The plane lost altitude rapidly, but after a period of descending flight without power, the crew managed to restart an engine and land the plane safely.

The Supreme Court began its analysis with the observation that the only authentic text of the 1929 Warsaw Convention is in French and therefore the French text must guide its analysis. In interpreting the article 17 phrase "toute autre lésion corporelle subie par un voyageur," the Court considered the following: (1) bilingual French-English dictionaries; (2) U.S. Senate and United Kingdom Parliament translations of "lésion corporelle" as "bodily injury"; (3) French statutes and Civil Code article 1382 in force in 1929; (4) pre- and post-1929 French judicial decisions using the term "lésions corporelle" (5) pre- and post-1929 French doctrine (treatises and scholarly writing); (6) the German translation of "toute autre lésion corporelle" as "sonst gesundheitlich geschädigt wird" (other injury to health); (7) the 1929 Convention's drafting history of article 17 beginning with the Paris Conference in 1925; (8) comparative law research showing the unavailability of compensation for purely psychic injury in many common law and civil law countries in 1929; (9) post-1929 conduct of the International Civil Aviation Organization; (10) the article 17 interpretation made by the Supreme Court of Israel; and (11) general purposes of the Convention. As a result of its treaty interpretation and comparative law research,

[9] U.S. Const. Art. VI, cl. 2.
[10] 49 U.S.C. App. § 1502.
[11] 111 S.Ct. 1489 (1991).

the Court concluded that the Warsaw Convention does not allow recovery for purely mental injuries.

Although the United States has signed only a few international agreements that have solely one authentic language that is not English, the Supreme Court has often stated that in interpreting English language or multi-language agreements one of its goals is to contribute to a uniform international interpretation of the document. This view is in conformity with the Vienna Convention on the Law of Treaties,[12] article 33(3) of which states: "The terms of the treaty are presumed to have the same meaning in each authentic text." The important United Nations Convention on Contracts for the International Sale of Goods,[13] which the U.S. has ratified, also promotes this idea in article 7(1): "In the interpretation of this Convention, regard is to be had to its international character and to the need to promote uniformity in its application ...." The goal of uniformity in interpretation thus frequently presents the opportunity for an American court to invite attorneys to present it with comparative law research on how other legal systems interpret the phrase or term in issue.

International custom provides American courts with another opportunity to use comparative law to clarify the content and meaning of an international legal norm. Custom has been part of United States law since at least *The Paquete Habana* (1900),[14] and consists of the general practice of nations accepted as law.[15]

An important example of the use of comparative law in this context occurred in the U.S. Court of Appeals case, *Filartiga v. Pena-Irala* (1980).[16] The plaintiffs, citizens of Paraguay, sued another Paraguayan – the Inspector General of Police in Asunción – for the death of their relative by torture. The court was asked to determine whether an act of torture committed by a state official against one of its own citizens violates the customary international law of human rights. In addition to examining numerous relevant treaties and United Nations resolutions, the court also found that the constitutions of 55 nations expressly or implicitly prohibit torture. The court then stated: "Having examined the sources from which customary international law is derived – the usage of nations, judicial opinions and the works of jurists – we conclude that official torture is now prohibited by the law of nations."[17]

---

[12] 1155 U.N.T.S. 331, concluded 23 May 1969, entered into force 27 Jan. 1980. Although the United States has not ratified the Convention, 82 nations are parties to it. Many of the Convention's provisions have been absorbed into U.S. law as part of international custom. See Frankowska, "The Vienna Convention on the Law of Treaties before United States Courts," 28 *Va. J. Int'l L.* 281 (1988).

[13] 3 *Martindale-Hubbell International Law Digest* IC-34 (1998).

[14] 175 U.S. 677 (1900).

[15] Supra. N. 8.

[16] 630 F.2d 876 (2d Cir. 1980).

[17] 630 F.2d at 884.

III. DEVELOPMENTS IN INTERNATIONAL CIVIL PROCEDURE

The increase in American law suits with a foreign element stimulated substantial changes in federal and state law affecting transnational civil litigation. On the federal level the Judicial Conference in 1963 approved amendments to the Federal Rules of Civil Procedure: Rule 4(i) – since 1993 Rule 4(f) – provided for alternative methods to serve American judicial documents abroad and Rule 28(b) governed taking depositions abroad and legitimized use of letters rogatory in federal cases. In 1964 Congress added 28 U.S.C. § 1696 and §§ 1781-1782 to improve judicial procedure for serving foreign documents in the U.S. and for obtaining evidence on behalf of foreign and international tribunals. The legislative sponsors hoped that such liberal provisions of non-reciprocal national rules might induce other countries to cooperate and follow the U.S. example. Lastly, in 1966 the addition of Rule 44.1 to the Federal Rules of Civil Procedure and Rule 26.1 to the Federal Rules of Criminal Procedure facilitated the proof of foreign law in federal courts.

Meanwhile, in 1963, the United States had joined the Hague Conference on Private International Law and the Rome International Institute for the Unification of Private Law (UNIDROIT), which marked its willingness to enter into treaties related to international civil procedure. Three such international agreements are now in effect for the United States: the Hague Convention on Service Abroad of Judicial and Extrajudicial Documents in Civil and Commercial Matters (1969); the U.N. Convention on the Recognition and Enforcement of Foreign Arbitral Awards (1970); and the Hague Convention on the Taking of Evidence Abroad in Civil and Commercial Matters (1972).

All of these developments have dramatically increased the number of foreign law issues that American courts must face. The next four sections illustrate the use of foreign law in discrete areas of international civil procedure.

IV. SERVICE OF PROCESS ON FOREIGN DEFENDANTS IN CIVIL CASES

In December 1993 the Federal Rules of Civil Procedure were amended to add Rule 4(f), which now suggests a preference for the use of the Hague Service Convention[18] and other service treaties that the United States has ratified or may later ratify. In addition, Rule 4(f)(2) requires compliance with the Hague Convention in cases in which it applies.[19] Article 1 of the

---

[18] 20 U.S.T. 361, T.I.A.S. No. 6638, concluded 15 Nov. 1965 entered into force for the United States 10 Feb. 1969.

[19] The Inter-American Convention on Letters Rogatory (concluded 30 Jan. 1975, entered into force for the United States 28 July 1988), by contrast, is not intended as mandatory, so

Convention, in turn, states that it "shall apply in all cases, in civil or commercial matters, where there is occasion to transmit a judicial or extrajudicial document for services abroad." Thirty-six countries are parties to the Hague Service Convention, including most European nations and Japan.

Several issues involving the law of the foreign country in which service is attempted under the Hague Convention have arisen in American courts. First, the Convention only applies in "civil or commercial matters."[20] Does that include administrative or tax cases? The United States will permit service of process in administrative cases, but France, Germany, and Japan will not. These countries, for instance, have refused to serve documents from the Environmental Protection Agency, the International Trade Commission, and the Federal Trade Commission. Egypt excludes family law cases from the concept of "civil." And what about service of a U.S. contract claim requesting punative damages? Is that essentially a civil or a criminal matter? The German state courts of appeals are split on this issue.[21]

An American court may also be asked to look at the internal law of a signatory to the Hague Convention to determine if a particular method requested by the applicant "is incompatible with the law of the State addressed,"[22] or to determine whether a default judgment is appropriate where the defendant has not appeared and service was "by a method prescribed by the internal law of the State addressed for the service of documents in domestic actions upon persons who are within its territory."[23] American courts have split on the issue of whether service by registered mail is permitted in Japan under article 10(a) of the Hague Convention. A federal court of appeals determined that the answer is no, partly on the basis of its finding that registered mail service is not allowed under Japanese law.[24]

In the U.S. Supreme Court's only case interpreting the Hague Service Convention, *Volkswagenwerk Aktiengesellschaft v. Schlunk* (1988),[25] it compared the American practice of substituted service on the defendant's corporate subsidiary (Volkswagen of America), reasoning that it was not the defendant's implicit agent, to the French practice of *notification au parquet*. After finding that the Hague Conference intended to *eliminate*

---

that an American plaintiff has the option of using Rule 4(f)(2)'s alternative methods of service.

20 Art. 1.

21 See, e.g., X. Co. v. Bavaria, Decision of 9 May 1989, 35 *RiW* 483 (1989), trans. by Ristau, 28 *Int'l Legal Materials* 1570 (1989).

22 Art. 5(b).

23 Art. 15(a).

24 Bankston v. Toyota Motor Corp., 889 F.2d 172 (8th Cir. 1989). Cf. Lemme v. Wine of Japan, Inc., 631 F.Supp. 456 (E.D.N.Y. 1986) (mail service permitted). See Kim & Sisneros, "Comparative Overview of Service of Process: United States, Japan, and Attempts at International Unity," 23 *Vand J. Transnat'l L.* 299 (1990).

25 486 U.S. 694 (1988).

notification au parquet – used in Belgium, France, Greece, Italy, and The Netherlands – as an approved method for the Convention, the Court concluded that substituted service is sufficiently different so that the Hague Convention did not apply under the *Schlunk* facts.

For service of process in countries that have not signed the Hague or Inter-American Conventions, or in other circumstances in which the Conventions do not apply, federal courts will follow the new Rule 4(f) and state courts will follow similar rules, often based on the previous Federal Rule 4(i). Federal Rule 4(f)(2) permits four alternative methods of service,[26] each of which requires the court (or initially the plaintiff) to investigate the foreign service of process law.[27]

V. Civil Discovery of Evidence in Foreign Countries

In December 1993 Federal Rule 28(b) was revised to draw the attention of lawyers to the Hague Evidence Convention[28] or to other treaties permitting civil discovery that the United States might sign. The Committee Notes to the Rule state: "The party taking the deposition is ordinarily obliged to conform to an applicable treaty or convention if an effective deposition can be taken by such internationally approved means, even though a verbatim transcript is not available or testimony cannot be taken under oath." Thirty countries have ratified the Hague Convention, including most European countries, Argentina and Mexico, but not Japan.

The Committee Notes show a more internationalist approach to the Hague Convention than the U.S. Supreme Court was willing to grant in its only case interpreting the relationship between the Federal Rules on discovery and the Hague Convention. In the *Aérospatiale* (1987) litigation,[29] the Court's majority rejected the French corporate defendant's argument

---

[26] The earlier Federal Rule 4(i) also permitted the same four alternative methods of service, except that the current Rule 4(f)(2)(C) options (i) and (ii) did not require an explicit comparative law inquiry. See infra n. 27.

[27] Fed. R. Civ. P. 4(f)(2): "[Service may be effected] if there is no internationally agreed means of service …:

(A) in the manner prescribed by the law of the foreign country for service in that country in an action in any of its courts of general jurisdiction; or

(B) as directed by the foreign authority in response to a letter rogatory or letter of request; or

(C) unless prohibited by the law of the foreign country, by

(i) delivery to the individual personally of a copy of the summons and the complaint; or

(ii) any form of mail requiring a signed receipt, to be addressed and dispatched by the clerk of the court to the party to be served …."

[28] 23 U.S.T. 2555, T.I.A.S. No. 7444, concluded 18 Mar. 1970, entered into force for the United States 7 Oct. 1972.

[29] Société Nationale Industrielle Aérospatiale v. U.S. District Court, 482 U.S. 522 (1987).

that the Convention mandates its exclusive use when evidence is located abroad, or even that the Convention or international comity requires the Convention's first use, with the Federal Rules providing a supplement to the Convention when it is ineffective or inapplicable. Instead, the Court found that comity only requires a trial judge to order the Convention's use when she deems it appropriate, after considering the situations of the parties and the interests of the foreign state and the United States. The exact line of reasonableness of a discovery request, the Court continued, is a matter for the trial judge's discretion: "American courts should therefore take care to demonstrate due respect for any special problem confronted by the foreign litigant on account of its nationality or the location of its operations, and for any sovereign interest expressed by a foreign state."[30] The Supreme Court seemed to invite trial courts, at least under some circumstances, to consider foreign law in the balancing process to determine whether a party should be required to use the Hague Convention.

Other issues arise that might involve foreign country law under the Hague Evidence Convention. As with the Service Convention, the Evidence Convention only applies to "civil or commercial matters."[31] Does this include requests for evidence in bankruptcy, antitrust, or probate cases? Is this question resolved under American law or the foreign country law where the evidence is located, or does a resisting witness have a right to rely on the law more favorable to his interest.[32]

Certain articles in the Hague Evidence Convention directly involve an American court in the comparison of local and foreign procedural rules. Article 9 states:

> The judicial authority which executes a Letter of Request shall apply its own law as to the methods and procedures to be followed.
>
> However, it will follow a request of the requesting authority that a special method or procedure be followed, unless this is incompatible with the internal law of the State of execution ....

Article 10 is even stricter on "measures of compulsion," which must comply with the requested state's internal law. Article 11 gives a foreign witness a "privilege or duty to refuse to give the evidence – (a) under the law of the State of execution; or (b) under the law of the State of origin ...." Under certain circumstances, article 11 may even recognize a third country's evidence law. Finally, article 12 provides the grounds for refusal of a letter of request, which involve a determination of whether execution

---

[30] 482 U.S. at 546.

[31] Art. 1.

[32] Cf. art. 11: "the person concerned may refuse to give evidence in so far as he has a privilege or duty to refuse to give the evidence –
(a) under the law of the State of execution; or
(b) under the law of the State of origin ...."

of the request would fall outside the functions of the requested state's judiciary or would prejudice its "sovereignty or security."

Article 23 of the Convention has caused American courts particular concern[33] and provides an interesting example of how far comparative law needs to progress to satisfactorily educate lawyers about foreign legal systems. Article 23 permits signatories to declare that they "will not execute Letters of Request issued for the purpose of obtaining pre-trial discovery of documents as known in Common Law countries." Inserted into the Convention by the British, it was aimed at the perceived excesses of American-style party-directed "fishing expeditions" and intrusive requests to discover evidence from non-parties. Several civil law delegations falsely believed that U.S. pretrial discovery could be used before commencing legal proceedings to build a case that might later be filed. As a result, virtually every contracting state except for the United States has entered an article 23 declaration. With regard to civil law nations, part of the problem concerns conceptual differences about when the "trial" begins. In the United States, all requests for foreign assistance would be seen as part of the pretrial discovery process, since a trial could not be interrupted for a lengthy period to gather admissible evidence. On the civilian side, civil proceedings are seen as a series of meetings at which evidence may be introduced. There is no sharp break between pretrial and trial in the American sense. United States courts, in determining whether the Convention is useful in obtaining documents located abroad, have to interpret article 23 declarations in the light of foreign countries' procedural systems. Some foreign courts have drawn a distinction between impermissible "pretrial discovery," which is a search for inadmissible information that may itself lead to admissible trial evidence, and allowable requests for documents actually to be used at trial that are described with specificity. From another vantage point, even a nation such as Germany, which reads article 23 literally to preclude the discovery of documents, will allow the compulsion of testimony concerning the contents of documents.[34]

American courts have traditionally favored the use of applicable federal or state rules of civil procedure to directly obtain evidence located abroad. This extraterritorial discovery under American procedural law can only be effectively ordered when the foreign litigant is subject to a U.S. court's territorial jurisdiction and the information is within his possession or control. Otherwise, a party must use Federal Rule 28(b) or its state equivalent, which if the Hague Convention is inapplicable authorizes a letter of request (rogatory), deposition by U.S. consular officer, or deposition by commission. Even a party who could rely on direct American

[33] See, e.g., Société Nationale Industrielle Aérospatiale v. U.S. District Court, 482 U.S. 522, 536-37 (1987)

[34] See, e.g., Siemens Aktiengesellschaft v. Bavaria, Decision of 27 Nov. 1980, 27 *RiW* 554 (1981), trans. by Ristau, 20 *Int'l Legal Materials* 1025 (1981).

discovery orders for foreign evidence may prefer using Rule 28(b) if the losing party will not have sufficient assets located in the United States. In this situation, the winner must take his U.S. judgment abroad for enforcement, which may be denied if the party used direct American discovery that violated the public policy of the enforcing nation.[35]

Whether to request a letter rogatory under Rule 28(b) usually implicates comparative law issues in the area of foreign procedural law and especially foreign discovery practice. For instance, are U.S. officials permitted to administer a deposition in the foreign country? If so, a party may prefer to use a U.S. consular official to administer a deposition under Rule 28(b)(3).[36] Since most countries do not permit this notice procedure for their own citizens, or will not permit it for compulsory evidence taking, an alternative method would be a deposition by commission under Rule 28(b)(4). This method is accepted in some nations because the American court appoints the person before whom testimony will be taken and only grants a commission "on terms that are just and appropriate." Some common law countries make compulsory process available to the commission upon petition to the foreign court. Most civil law nations, however, consider evidence gathering a governmental function and reject commissions as an affront to their sovereignty.

One is then left with the option of a letter rogatory.[37] Because letters rogatory employ the courts of a requested country, their use does not offend that country's judicial sovereignty. These courts often can compel a witness to appear. On the other side, foreign courts normally follow their own procedure. Thus, relevant foreign law questions include: How does a requested court respond to a letter rogatory and how fast can it be expected? Is a blocking statute or testimonial or document privilege applicable? Is oral examination permitted or is examination limited to written questions? Does a counsel have the right to confront or cross-examine the witness?

A recent case involving Switzerland illustrates how a discovery question may involve a foreign law issue. In *Roberts v. Heim*[38] a co-defendant requested a letter rogatory under Rule 28(b)(2) for what seemed to be a deposition upon written questions against the defendant Werner Heim in Switzerland. The letter was issued by the federal district court and executed nine weeks later by a Swiss judge. It is likely that the judge used local procedure and asked the questions rather than permitting the more invasive style of American direct and cross-examination. In the issue

---

[35] Gerber, "Extraterritorial Discovery and the Conflict of Procedural Systems: Germany and the United States," 34 *Am. J. Comp. L.* 745, 774-75 (1986) (ZPO § 328(4)); Ohara, "Judical Assistance to be Afforded by Japan for Proceedings in the United States," 23 *Int'l Law.* 10, 25-27 (1989) (CPC art. 200(3)).

[36] See U.S.C. §§ 4215, 4221.

[37] Fed. R. Civ. P. 28(b)(2).

[38] 130 F.R.D. 430 (N.D. Cal. 1990).

before the American court, the defendant Heim argued against an order compelling him to respond to additional discovery in the United States on the ground that he would be forced to violate Swiss criminal law. The special master charged with resolving this issue had the obligation of interpreting the meaning of "business secret" in article 273 of the Swiss Penal Code. He put the burden of proof on Heim to avoid the discovery order, so that Heim's attorney had the task discussed in the next section of proving a foreign law issue in an American court. The attorney failed to show that Heim's testimony would include protected business secrets and so the master ordered Heim to appear in the United States for his deposition.

VI. CHOICE OF FOREIGN LAW IN CIVIL CASES

The growing importance of international commerce and travel in the past three decades has had a dramatic impact on civil litigation in United States courts. Today individuals routinely name foreign firms as defendants in lawsuits seeking to enforce U.S. product liability, labor, environmental protection, or consumer protection laws. Equally prevalent are contract and corporate law actions arising out of transnational business activities as well as antitrust or other regulatory actions against foreign business. Foreign law may govern when an American state's choice of law rule points to the internal law of a foreign country. Examples include disputes involving contracts made or to be performed abroad, foreign property holdings, torts committed overseas, estates of foreign domiciliaries leaving assets in the U.S. or estates of Americans with real property abroad, and foreign marriages, separations, and child custody or support obligations.

The common law approach in the United States is that foreign law should be handled by the court as if it were a fact. The rationale for this classification is that judges could not reasonably be presumed to know the applicable foreign rule. Some of the logical consequences of treating foreign law as a fact are that it must be pleaded, the ordinary rules of evidence apply (which often excludes helpful material), parties present the relevant information and the judge cannot conduct her own investigation, review on appeal is highly deferential to the trial judge's "factual" determination, and the court's decision has no precedential value.

The inadequacies of the common law approach to foreign law issues, given the increasing level of transnational activities, led the federal courts and most states to adopt some form of judicial notice or quasi judicial notice provision to facilitate the determination of foreign law. Rule 44.1 was added to the Federal Rules of Civil Procedure in 1966, while a similar Rule 26.1 was inserted into the Federal Rules of Criminal Procedure at the same time. Today 22 states and the District of Columbia have a provision modeled on Rule 44.1.

Consider how Rule 44.1 modifies the common law approach. It reads:

> A party who intends to raise an issue concerning the law of a foreign country shall give notice by pleadings or other reasonable written notice. The court, in determining foreign law, may consider any relevant material or source, including testimony, whether or not submitted by a party or admissible under the Federal Rules of Evidence. The court's determination shall be treated as a ruling on a question of law.

Foreign law not need not be pleaded to withstand a motion to dismiss the lawsuit, but some "reasonable written notice" must be provided to the court and the other party to avoid unfair surprise. A foreign law issue is for the judge to determine as a question of law. The court, once an issue is properly raised, may consider any relevant source of information, even on its own initiative, and the Federal Rules of Evidence on admissibility do not apply. An appellate court may freely review a foreign law issue, without restriction by the clearly erroneous standard, and may substitute its own opinion for that of the trial court. Finally, a ruling on the foreign law issue constitutes a precedent under the doctrine of stare decisis.

California and New York enacted more elaborate statutes,[39] which provide that a party can compel a judge to notice foreign law if the party gives adverse parties sufficient notice of his request and furnishes the court with sufficient information to take judicial notice. The issue of sufficiency remains in the discretion of the judge, but these "mandatory" statutes have more bite than the "permissive" Rule 44.1. Nine states – including Florida, Michigan, and New Jersey – have one of these bifurcated permissive-mandatory judicial notice statutes.

Six states have enacted simpler judicial notice statutes that leave open important questions concerning the treatment of foreign law. For instance, it may not be clear whether a party who wants to rely on foreign law must raise it in a pleading or may simply request a judge to take judicial notice.[40]

Finally, 12 states – including Illinois – remain in the common law fact camp. Most of these states have provided, however, that a foreign law issue is for the court and not for the jury to determine, and some allow proof of the foreign law issue without use of expert witnesses. Nevertheless, the basic fact approach in these states remains intact. Consider a recent Illinois case:[41]

> While we respect the parties' request to consider Canadian law, we are compelled to remind the parties that it has long been the rule that courts will not take judicial notice of the laws of another country, but they must be alleged and proved as facts .... When a party interested in claiming

[39] Cal. Evid. Code §§ 310-311, 452-455, 459-460; N.Y. Civil Proc. L. & Rules, rules 3016, 4511.

[40] See, e.g., 12 Okla. Stat. §§ 2201, 2203.

[41] In re Marriage of Osborn, 564 N.E.2d 1325, 1327 (Ill. App. 1990).

> the benefit of a foreign law or statute fails to show by appropriate pleading and proof the status of the law of the place where the contract was made or was to be performed, the courts of the state where the suit is brought will apply the law of the latter state to the contract. [Citation omitted.] Under the circumstances, we apply the law of Illinois, without consideration of Canadian law, to determine the issues in this case.

Iowa, another fact pleading state, illustrates how extreme the presumption of equivalence between foreign law and local law can become. The Iowa Supreme Court, in a child custody case, declared: "Neither party pleaded any statute from another jurisdiction as required .... Neither party attempted to prove Vietnamese law was applicable to any issue raised in this case. Therefore it must be presumed foreign law both statutory and common law is the same as ours."[42]

The overall trend, nevertheless, has been one of increasing receptivity in American courts toward accepting foreign law arguments. In federal courts and elsewhere, judges have determined that a pretrial summary judgment hearing is often the most appropriate stage in a civil proceeding at which to resolve a foreign law issue. It is more efficient than waiting for a trial and summary judgment hearings are ideally structured to resolve legal issues.[43]

VII. Enforcement of Foreign Country Civil Judgments

We have already seen in section IV that an attorney who wishes to serve process on a foreign defendant must at the earliest stage of a lawsuit consider the law of that defendant's country if the plaintiff later must enforce his U.S. judgment there. A similar comparative law inquiry into the judgment enforcement law of another country is necessary if a plaintiff intends to use U.S. discovery rules to obtain extraterritorial testimony or documents.

In this section I discuss the reciprocal problem: recognition and enforcement of a foreign country judgment in a United States federal or state court. Foreign law issues may again appear: for instance, concerning the finality of the judgment, the impartiality of the tribunal, or the adequacy of the rendering court's subject matter or personal (territorial) jurisdiction.

Recognition and enforcement often go together, but they are distinct procedural concepts. If a U.S. court precludes litigation of a particular foreign claim because it was previously litigated abroad, and instead relies on the foreign judicial decision, the court recognizes the decree or judg-

---

[42] Doan Thi Hoang Anh v. Nelson, 245 N.W.2d 511, 516 (1976).

[43] See, e.g., Walpex Trading Co. v. Yacimientos Petroliferos Fiscales Bolivianos, 756 F. Supp. 136 (S.D.N.Y. 1991), 789 F. Supp. 1268 (S.D.N.Y. 1992).

ment.[44] If the plaintiff further requests that a court use its coercive power to compel the defendant to satisfy the recognized judgment, usually in money damages, the court may enforce the foreign judgment.[45] There is no uniform national standard governing these questions, unlike the full faith and credit due sister state or federal judgments. Instead, the recognition and enforcement of foreign country judgments is usually governed by a standard of comity as defined by individual states.

The usual starting point in most states under the common law approach is the classic dictum from the 1895 United States Supreme Court decision in *Hilton v. Guyot*.[46]

> [W]here there has been opportunity for a full and fair trial abroad before a court of competent jurisdiction, conducting the trial upon regular proceedings, after due citation or voluntary appearance of the defendant, and under a system of jurisprudence likely to secure an impartial administration of justice between the citizens of its own country and those of other countries, and there is nothing to show either prejudice in the court, or in the system of laws under which it was sitting, or fraud in procuring the judgment, or any other special reason why the comity of this nation should not allow it full effect, the merits of the case should not, in an action brought in this country upon the judgment, be tried afresh.

The Court also required reciprocity (the foreign court must enforce a U.S. judgment in similar circumstances), but only in the particular situation in which a citizen of the foreign country won a lawsuit against a non-citizen (for example, an American) defendant and brought the judgment to the United States for enforcement.[47] In order to bring more clarity to this area of the law, the Commissioners on Uniform State Laws proposed in 1962 the Uniform Foreign Money-Judgments Act.[48] Article 2 states: "This Act applies to any foreign judgment that is final and conclusive and enforceable where rendered ...." A judgment creditor must, if contested, prove a foreign law issue, that is, that the judgment under the law of the rendering country is "final," "conclusive," and "enforceable." Article 4 provides several mandatory grounds for non-recognition that involve foreign law determinations. Article 4(a) reads:

> A foreign judgment is not conclusive if

---

[44] See, e.g., Panama Processes, S.A. v. Cities Service Co., 796 P.2d 276 (Okla. Sup. Ct. 1990).

[45] See, e.g., Ackermann v. Levine, 788 F.2d 830 (2d Cir. 1986).

[46] 159 U.S. 113, 202-03 (1895).

[47] For this common law approach see, e.g., De la Mata v. American Life Ins. Co., 771 F. Supp. 1375, 1380-90 (D. Del. 1991).

[48] 13 U.L.A. 261 (1986).

(1) the judgment was rendered under a system which does not provide impartial tribunals or procedures compatible with the requirements of due process of law;

(2) the foreign court did not have personal jurisdiction over the defendant;[49] or

(3) the foreign court did not have jurisdiction over the subject matter.

An interesting feature of the Uniform Act is that it dropped *Hilton's* reciprocity requirement to recognize a foreign judgment. The Act has been substantially adopted in 29 states, but six of these states (including Florida, Idaho, Massachusetts, North Carolina, Ohio, and Texas) added lack of reciprocity as a discretionary (and Georgia added it as a mandatory) ground for nonrecognition. Federal courts have tended to view the recognition issue as a matter of substance for the purpose of the *Erie* doctrine, and thus have applied the law of the state in which the federal court is located rather than develop a uniform federal rule of comity for the recognition of foreign country judgments.[50]

VIII. References to Foreign Law in Criminal Proceedings

Many of the same circumstances that require a consideration of foreign law in civil cases also arise in criminal cases, most commonly in extradition proceedings or when necessary evidence is located in a foreign country. In addition, some other issues in criminal law and procedure have an element that may implicate a foreign law matter. For instance, a witness in an American criminal proceeding may be able to invoke the privilege against self-incrimination if he can show that his testimony would expose him to a substantial risk of prosecution in a foreign country.[51] Second, some recidivist statutes provide that all previous convictions – including those in a foreign country – count toward the increased penalty for a multiple offender. A search into foreign law might include an inquiry about whether there was a judgment of conviction, whether the judgment was in fact a criminal and not an administrative matter, and whether the proceedings met the minimum standard of fairness necessary for the U.S. Constitution's due process clause.

The most common instance of judicial inquiry into foreign law in the criminal context concerns extradition. In 1987, for instance, there were 572

---

[49] An American court's willingness to avoid a foreign law determination is illustrated (on the personal jurisdiction issue) by Nippon Emo-Trans Co., Ltd. v. Emo-Trans, Inc., 744 F. Supp. 1215 (E.D.N.Y. 1990).

[50] See, e.g., Somportex, Ltd. V. Philadelphia Chewing Gum Corp., 453 F.2d 435 (1971), cert. denied, 405 U.S. 1017 (1972).

[51] See In re Cardassi, 351 F. Supp. 1080 (D. Conn. 1972).

international extradition requests made and received in the United States. These are coordinated by the Office of International Affairs (OIA) in the Department of Justice Criminal Division, which oversees the 61 treaties that govern U.S. extradition relations. When a foreign country seeks extradition of one of its fugitives from the United States, it requests assistance from the OIA, which assigns an assistant U.S. attorney to represent it in court proceedings. A variety of foreign law issues may arise. First, most treaties require the United States to refuse extradition if prosecution is barred by the requesting country's statute of limitations. Second, these treaties also require a court to refuse extradition if the fugitive was convicted, acquitted, or being tried in the U.S. and the requesting country's law forbids double jeopardy under these circumstances. Third, the offense for which extradition is sought must be a crime in both the requesting country as well as in the United States. This dual criminality requirement today tends to focus on whether the act is a crime in both countries rather than on similar denomination of the offense under both laws. This element often becomes determinative in certain offenses of a regulatory nature.[52]

IX. METHODS AND SOURCES OF JUDICIAL COMPARISON

When choice of law rules determine that a claim or a defense is governed by foreign law, the problem of pleading and proving the relevant foreign law occurs. We have also seen that for a few treaties interpreted as foreign law, for international custom, and for certain procedural issues with an international contact – civil as well as criminal – the knowledge and perhaps proof of foreign law may be necessary or at least helpful. Where statutes do not prescribe the rules governing the process of pleading and proof of foreign law, the common law approach prevails. The basic principle of the common law has been that foreign law is a fact and must be pleaded and proved as a fact. However, in contrast to the firm adherence of the English to this "fact" treatment of foreign law, most American states and the federal courts have now adopted some form of judicial notice provision to facilitate the pleading and determination of foreign law.

Pleading or otherwise providing sufficient notice of a foreign law issue is, of course, only part of the difficulty. Legal proof must be thought of in terms of statutes, decisions, customs, scholarly commentaries, translations, and expert witnesses to support the necessary contentions. The competent lawyer must interview foreign law experts, study their qualifications, and integrate their knowledge into forms and elements familiar to courts in the United States.

---

[52] Morris Abbell & Bruno A. Ristau, 4 *International Judicial Assistance: Criminal* 12, 16, 51, 96-98, 183-84, 187 (1990).

The foreign law expert plays the key role in educating American judges about foreign law. An expert can attest to the authenticity of a source of foreign law, the applicable foreign rule in the particular case, its current interpretation, and which other laws might apply to the situation. Of course, the expert must perform a comparative function by explaining the foreign rules in terms that an American judge can comprehend. Normally this task is carried out with an affidavit. But the effectiveness of an affidavit is limited, since it cannot respond to the specific concerns of the judge and it is sometimes suspect because the witness has not been subject to cross-examination.[53]

Therefore, an expert may have to give a deposition, subject to cross-examination, or actually testify at a summary judgment hearing or a trial. This discussion implies what is obvious about the American judicial process: it is adversarial and each side in a dispute may well hire its own expert. There is then a tendency for experts to become partisans for the attorney who has hired them and for the resolution of foreign law questions to degenerate into a battle of the experts.[54]

A solution to this problem lies in judges willing to make use of impartial court-retained experts or special masters. Federal Rule of Evidence 706 permits a court on its own motion or on the motion of any party to appoint an expert witness. A witness so appointed shall advise the parties of his findings. His deposition may be taken by any party and he may be called to testify by the court or a party, subject to cross-examination in both instances. Judges also have the authority – under Federal Rule of Civil Procedure 53 in the federal system – to appoint a special master, who acts like a quasi-judge in investigating a foreign law issue. The masters may require the production of documents, put witnesses on oath and examine them, and hold hearings useful for the task at hand He then prepares a report for the judge and makes findings of fact and conclusions of law if required. A small number of reported cases have relied on a court appointed expert or a special master to resolve foreign law issues.[55]

X. EPISODIC COMPARISON IN JUDICIAL PRACTICE

In addition to the increasing number of references to foreign law in American courts required by the growth in international law and the recognition that civil and criminal procedure must confront cases that transcend the

[53] Sprankling & Lanyi, "Pleading and Proof of Foreign Law in American Courts," 19 *Stan. J. Int'l L.* 3, 43-45, 48-50, 58-60 (1983).

[54] Merryman, "Foreign Law as a Problem," 19 *Stan. J. Int'l L.* 151, 154-55, 172-73 (1983).

[55] Roberts v. Heim, 130 F.R.D. 430 (N.D. Cal. 1990); Corporacion Salvadorena de Calzado (Corsal), S.A. v. Injection Footwear Corp., 533 F. Supp. 290 (S.D. Fla. 1982).

boundaries of the United States, there are also significant examples of episodic judicial comparison of foreign laws and legal institutions for other reasons.

First, American states, outside of Louisiana, have received English common law as a residual source of law.[56] One still occasionally reads cases in which a judge will examine an English precedent or institution, such as the jury, as a comparative aid to resolve a case.

Second, there have been silent transplants of foreign law into the American legal system, which then provide a basis for comparison between the indigenous and foreign legal forms. Two examples must suffice. One was the result of David Dudley Field's borrowing of civilian ideas on procedure for his New York Code of Civil Procedure. This 1848 Code was revolutionary since it abolished the English feudal writ and bill system of pleading and replaced it with a single civil action guided by "code" pleading. It also implemented the merger of law and equity, a distinction that was a source of great confusion and delay. By 1873 more than half the American states had embraced civil procedure codes based on Field's model.[57] The other example concerns the German law sources for Karl Llewellyn's work on the Uniform Commercial Code. This Code has been adopted in all American jurisdictions, incorporating concepts of good faith, usages of trade, custom, and reasonableness into the field of sale of goods and other commercial law areas. Courts have grappled with these concepts, compared them with the rules of common law contracts, and evolved a peculiar blend of common law and civil law jurisprudence.[58]

Lastly, comparison may serve the goal of critique. Some judges discuss foreign models when confronted with controversial issues in, for example, criminal law and procedure. These issues include the use of the exclusionary rule of evidence to enforce rights found in the Fourth and Fifth Amendments to the U.S. Constitution, the prevalence of the guilty plea, and the desirability of the death penalty.

---

[56] See, e.g., 12 Okla. Stat. § 2: "The common law, as modified by constitutional and statutory law, judicial decisions and the conditions and wants of the people, shall remain in force in aid of the general statutes of Oklahoma ...."

[57] See Clark, "The Civil Law Influence on David Dudley Field's Code of Civil Procedure," in, Mathias Reimann (ed.), *The Reception of Continental Ideas in the Common Law World, 1820-1920* at 63 (1993).

[58] See Whitman, "Commercial Law and the American *Volk*: A Note on Llewellyn's German Sources for the Uniform Commercial Code," 97 *Yale L. J.* 156 (1987).

ALAIN A. LEVASSEUR*
with the assistance of Madeline Heber**

The Use of Comparative Law by Courts

INTRODUCTION

"The field of comparative law is dominated by academics rather than practitioners and is thought of as largely an academic discipline. Therefore its approach tends to be more theoretical than that of other fields that are more clearly connected with practice."[1] "In reviewing the reception of U.S. law in Germany, Stürner observed that there has been no comparable reception of European law in the United States. The prerequisite study of foreign law has not occurred. It is the rare American who has studied law in continental Europe. U.S. law schools pay foreign law little note."[2] "Today there is no excuse not to learn from others. It would be arrogant in the extreme to hold out U.S. law as a model for legal reform in Central and Eastern Europe and to refuse to recognise that other legal systems have much to offer the United States. Indeed, the possible contributions of the study of foreign law to legal reform in the United States are numerous".[3]

The above two recently expressed comments on the role of comparative law in the U.S. legal system and the identity of those who, in the United States, are promoting the benefits of the study and use of comparative law, should stand as a clear indication and warning that, outside the realm of some U.S. law schools, the relevance of comparative law is almost non-existent,

* Hermann Moyse, Sr. Professor of Law Louisiana State University.
** Reference Librarian (J.D., A.M.) Louisiana State University

1 Farnsworth, "Looking in from Outside your Garden: Another View of Comparative Law," in, Perméabilité des ordres juridiques: rapports présentés à l'occasion du colloque-anniversaire de l'Institut suisse de droit comparé – Osmose zwischen Rechtsordnungen: Berichte des Kolloquiums anlässlich des zehnjährigen Bestehens des schweizerischen Instituts für Rechtsvergleichung – The Responsiveness of legal systems to foreign influences: reports presented to a colloquium on the occasion of the tenth anniversary of the Swiss Institute of Comparative Law. (1992); p. 415.

2 Maxeiner, "'Address-1992: High Time for American Lawyers to Learn from Europe' or Roscoe Pound's '1906 Address Revisited'," 15 *Fordham Int'L. J.* 1 at 2 (1991-1992).

3 Id. at 5.

U. Drobnig and S. van Erp (eds.), The Use of Comparative Law by Courts, 315–333.

which is really a euphemism for "nil". Indeed, as far as the federal and most state courts in this country are concerned, foreign law is not considered as a relevant topic for consideration and even less for study. Today, and even since the last decades of the last century, these courts have shown no cultural inclination, intellectual bent or mere professional curiosity, to look into comparative law (in the sense of foreign legal systems) as a possible source of legal or natural law support of their own decisions or as a means of providing a more cogent rationalisation of their own rulings. And, yet, the history of the American legal system was, at one time, full of a legitimate optimism and authentic promises deeply rooted in the 19th century coexistence of the civil law and the common law. It could have become a contemporary modern legal system inherently built on the comparative, theoretical and practical, advantages of the still dominant two major legal systems, the civil law and the common law. "[I]n Wilson's Law Lectures (1791) Pufendorf is cited twenty-nine times and there are ten references to Grotius, ten to Vattel, four to Burlamaqui, and five to Rutherforth's Institutes of Natural Law, an exposition of Grotius. Again, in the first volume of Story on the Constitution, there are nineteen citations of Vattel, six of Heineccius, three of Burlamaqui, two of Grotius, and two of Rutherforth. We must remember that these books and others of the sort were the staple of the beginnings of American legal education ... When John Adams was studying law, Gridley told him that a lawyer in this part of the world had more to learn than an English lawyer. 'A lawyer in this country', he said, 'must study common law and civil law and natural law and admiralty law' ... one of the then leaders of the New York bar laid out a course of study in which, of nine general works, the first three were Wood's Institutes of the Civil Law, Domat's Civil Law and Pufendorf ... With the advent of historical and analytical jurisprudence in American legal thought after the Civil War, there was little patience with the ideas of the seventeenth and eighteenth centuries. It became the fashion to sneer at the great law writers of the formative era of our law. Even Gray attributes the decision in *Swift v. Tyson* not to Story's conception of natural law but to fondness for generalities and restless vanity."[4]

Thus, whereas the nineteenth century displayed all the wares and tools available to a comparative legal system (as exemplified by the fact that many courts searched for a comforting and rational support for their own views or for original sources of law in the French legal system in particular) the twentieth century abruptly changed course to turn the American legal system into an inward looking system where legal and rational comparisons are made within the internal legal order controlling in the United States. As a result, the study of foreign comparative law (as opposed to the comparative method used exclusively within the internal legal order) was moved to the attic where law professors delight in studies confined to the academic spheres. The identification of comparative law with the study of foreign law

---

[4] Roscoe Pound, *The Formative Era of American* Law 24-26 (1938).

may have become so "*foreign*" to the American courts that a scholar ventured to say, albeit tongue-in-cheek, that a true, authentic American would not have what it really takes to become a true comparatist: "Most of those in your garden are *not* Americans, and even those who are have wonderfully exotic names. This does not seem to be a field for the Smiths or the Joneses."[5]

I. Comparative Law and the Courts in the 18th and 19th Centuries

Samuel Champlain and Robert Cavelier Sieur de La Salle established the control of France on vast stretches of territories that extended from the Great Lakes down the Mississippi river to the Gulf of Mexico. The law then in force was the Custom of Paris and the Royal Ordinances of the Kingdom of France. Spain had possession of the territory of Florida spreading its influence along the Gulf of Mexico and in Louisiana in particular. In those territories under Spanish control, the law then governing was that of the Siete Partidas, la Recopilacion de las Indias and the Fuero Juzgo.

While France and Spain were enforcing the civil law system in the territories under their control, thirteen English colonies were settling themselves along the Atlantic coast. Twelve were English in their social and ethnic compositions whereas the thirteenth one was mostly Dutch. These thirteen colonies distinguished themselves from the territories under French and Spanish control in that they had a constitutional and administrative structure defined and regulated by a charter granted by the English crown. There existed therefore a certain coherence and homogeneity in the governmental and legal structures of these colonies. The English common law was the law of the land except where local circumstances and exigencies required that a more malleable legal system be applied such as the teachings of the Bible.

Whereas the immigration of populations from European civil law jurisdictions was reduced to a trickle, waves of migrants from England were settling in the colonies. These migrants started soon to move west onto the vast territories under French control where the population was extremely scarce and where the political and legal administrations were mostly symbolic. In 1787 Congress "organized the area from the Great Lakes down to the Ohio River east of the Mississippi into the Northwest Territory and passed for its government the measures known as the *Ordinances for the Northwest Territory*." These ordinances did not disturb the French private Civil Law so far as it was practiced among the French settlers ... They were soon greatly outnumbered by English speaking settlers from the east and among the separate units of government set up where French law had previously prevailed were those of Michigan, Wisconsin, and Illinois. The Territorial Legislature of Michigan in 1810 declared its English speaking people were unfamiliar with the untranslated "Custom" of Paris and there was no easy way of knowing it

[5] Farnsworth, supra n. 1, at 414.

and provided by law that neither it nor the French Ordonnances were binding, ... As late as 1860 the Supreme Court of Michigan recognized the influence of French Civil Law and attempted to show that the law of Michigan at that time on title to river bed ... corresponded to Justinian Roman Law as interpreted by Vinius ... The Supreme Court of Wisconsin in 1864 recognized the extension of French law into the state but held that the English speaking settlers had brought into the state the English Common Law in their affairs. In 1878 the Illinois Supreme Court held made-land in the middle of a stream derived its ownership characteristics from the shore land in accordance with the "Custom" of Paris. The far-reaching overhanging effect of the "Custom" is illustrated in a 1910 decision of the Supreme Court of Illinois ... These are given as examples of French law still being a factor in present day law of States carved out of the Northwest Territory ... [6]

A survey of the decisions handed down by the states' courts during the eighteenth and nineteenth centuries shows that, in a few instances and outside of the state of Louisiana, some courts did make use of comparative law in their search for a well grounded legal analysis of the issues raised before the court.[7]

In the reports of cases of the state of New York at the beginning of the nineteenth century, one can find a certain number of references to sources of French law and to French authors, particularly in the field of commercial law which was highly developed at the time in France and merely emerging as a special field of law in the USA. In addition French commercial law presented itself as a coherent and self contained branch of the law outlined in comprehensive and somewhat practical treatises.

In the first volume of the reports of cases of the State of New York by William Johnson, (1806-1809) one can find in the decisions of the Supreme

---

[6] Howard Milton Colvin, *Roman and Civil Law Elements in Sources of the Law of the United States* 123-125 (1935).

[7] For purposes of illustration as well as on account of the historical events described briefly above and because of this writer's particular and biased interest, the focus was placed, in this research, on the role played by French scholars and French cases in the investigation conducted by American judges in their research of the sources of the law applicable to a case. In addition, because in the eighteenth and nineteenth centuries those French sources of law were most likely to be available in the French language only, it was essential for any American judge to know that language. One can consider this requirement of knowledge of the language of the source of the law as essential in ascertaining the true influence of foreign law in an American judge's analysis of local legal issues. The reliance on translations of foreign legal materials into English may alter a judge's conscious determination to find out how a legal problem is handled abroad. A translator's slant and bent of mind, as well as his selection of the materials to be translated may alter the true legal regime and meaning of the foreign legal provisions which are translated. One could cite some translations by a particular Louisiana Supreme Court Justice to illustrate this problematic aspect of translations. This is not to say, however, that translations are useless and should not be taken into account. Quite to the contrary as we truly believe that translations should be encouraged and supported. However, before relying on a translation, one should ascertain that the translator was not only an expert linguist but also a person fully immersed in the legal cultures of the legal systems in whose languages he is working.

Court of Judicature of New York for the year 1806 some references to "foreign" sources of law, *i.e.* the French author Robert Joseph Pothier, mostly known for his treatise on the law of Obligations as applied to commercial contracts, Balthazard Marie Emérigon, known for his treatise on insurance published in Marseille in 1783, and René Valin who wrote a commentary on Louis the XIV's ordinance on commercial shipping:

D. and G. Ludlow v. Bowne and Eddy, Johns. Rep. p. 1:[8]

"Kent, Ch. J ... . The recent decisions in the English courts I consider as correct expositions on the common law, for they only illustrate more fully the same principles which we find recognized in the time of Lord Holt. We have not, nor ever had, any such rule in our law as that to be found in the civil and French law (Inst. 2, 1, 41, and Pothier, Traité du Contrat de Vente, n. 322) by which even a delivery does not transfer the property without payment, unless a credit be given.'

The United Insurance Company v. Scott and Seaman, Johns. Rep. 1 p. 106.[9]

"Kent, Ch, J ... . Abandonnement has this retrospective effect: and it amounts to a complete transfer of the property. (.. 2 Emerigon, 194-196; Pothier, Contrat d'Assurance, n. 138.)

N. L. & G. Griswold, v. The New York Insurance Company, Johns. Rep. 1 p. 205.[10]

"Livingston, J ... If the injury arise from the misconduct of the owner, ... , there is no hardship in depriving the owner of freight to the extent of the damage done, and render liable for further compensation ... Of the same opinion is Pothier (Charte-Partie, part 1, sec. 3, art 2. sec 1), in his Treatise on Charter-Parties.

Nancy Jackson v. Archibald Jackson, Johns. Rep. 1 p. 430[11]

"Mr. Woodworth, in reply ... Suppose the case of parties married in France, and that by the laws of that country the contract could not be dissolved for any cause whatever (this was the law in France, before the Revolution. See Pothier, Traité du Contrat de Marriage, part 6, ch. 1 art. 1) ... Different countries admit different causes of divorce. (Montesquieu, liv. 15, ch. 14, 15.)

Patrick v. Hallett and Bowne, Johns. Rep. 1 p. 239.[12]

---

[8] Case dealing with the insurance on goods shipped from New York to France.

[9] Case involving insurers on the cargo and freight on a ship on a voyage from New York to Savannah and to Jamaica. The ship was captured and the owners abandoned the ship to the underwriters.

[10] Case involving issues of marine insurance, damage to cargo, abandonment, sale of cargo.

[11] Case dealing with a divorce, issues of domiciles of the parties, evasion of the law of one state.

"Mr. Pendleton, for the defendant ... . The same doctrine is maintained by all the foreign writers on this subject. (... Emerig, Vol. I. p. 575, 557, 580). In France, where by a particular ordinance, a previous survey is necessary before a vessel proceeds on her voyage, ...

Kent, Ch. J ... . The same presumption is adopted by Valin (Vol. II3, p. 103); but the French law, had, in part, at least, drawn a different conclusion from one of the articles of the ordinance of 1682, . ."

Schmidt v. The United Insurance Company, Johns. Rep. 1. p. 247.[13]

"Kent, Ch. J ... . The interdiction of commerce with the port of destination, is stated by Emerigon (Vol. I. 542) to be a peril of the sea, ..."

In Book IV of Johnson's Reports (1810-1813), one can find some additional cases in which some references are made to "comparative law", i.e. French law as suggested above. Pothier is cited in three cases, at least, dealing with issues related to marine insurance and vessels or ships, the same general topics for which Pothier was a reference in the earlier New York cases:

Watson v. The Marine Insurance Company, Johns. Rep. 7 p. 57:

"Kent, Ch. J ... . and Pothier, in his Traité du Contrat d'Assurance, No 52, and 164, recognizes it as an established doctrine."

M'Bride v. The Marine Insurance Company, Johns. Rep. 7 p. 431:

"Per Curiam ... The foreign authorities on commercial law speak the same language. (Ord. de la Marine, lib. 3. . ; Pothier, Traité des Charte-partie, No. 85;. .)"

D. Merritt v. Johnson, Johns. Rep. 7 p. 473:

"Per Curiam ... . It is so laid down by Bracton (... .) and Pothier illustrates it by a variety of clear and apposite examples. (Traité du droit de Propriete, No. 169, 180)."

Besides those cases citing Pothier, five (5) other cases, at least, do cite Emérigon (and Valin). Again it is worth pointing out that all these cases deal with issues of marine insurance and that Kent Ch. J. either wrote the decision for the court (in four (4) cases) or was on the court in the per curiam ruling.[14] In the case of Jumel and Desobry, the lawyer for the plaintiffs, Mr. Hoffman,

[12] Case dealing with the seaworthiness of ship.

[13] Case involving marine insurance and the blockade of the port of destination.

[14] The Same v. The New York Insurance Company, Johns. Rep. 6 p. 107; Jumel and Desobry v. The Marine Insurance Company, Johns. Rep. 7 p. 370; Hallet v. The Columbian Insurance Company, Johns. Rep. 538; Bradhurst and Field v. The Columbian Insurance Company, Johns. Rep. 9 p. 646; Deidericks v. The Commercial Insurance Company of New York, Johns. Rep. 10 p. 1012.

even cited the Répertoire Dalloz[15] as a reference among many others.[16]

In the case of *Dash v. Van Kleeck*[17] the judges of the Supreme Court of New York all showed much scholarship and erudition in citing many different sources of a comparative law nature, but whereas all the other judges made references to English law (Blackstone in particular) and to the law of other states of the Union, Kent Ch. J. was the only one to make reference to an article in the constitution established for the French Republic, in the year 1795, that no law, criminal of civil, could have a retroactive effect: *"Aucune loi, ni criminelle ni civile, ne peut avoir d'effet rétroactif."* Even French despotism, ... for the same limitation is laid down as a fundamental truth in the code now in force under the sanction of the French Empire. (Code civil des Français, No. 2) ..."

If we switch, for a moment, to another New York court, the Court of Chancery in the years 1815-1819, one cannot but be struck by the observation that the references made to French law were made by the Chancellor who was no other than James Kent. In the particular matter of divorce, the Chancellor made numerous cross-references to Fournel, Traité de l'Adultère, as well as to Pothier in his Traité du Contrat de Mariage.[18] One most interesting case in which Chancellor James Kent made an extensive use of comparative law, French law in particular, is the case of *Campbell v. Mesier.*[19] The issue was one of contribution regarding a party wall in which two owners had an equal interest. After citing Papinian, the Chancellor stated that: "The rules and doctrines of the French law may be referred to by way of illustrations, and to show the prevailing equity and justice of the rule of contribution, in respect to party walls ... . this is not only a rule of positive ordinance, but is a principle of ancient law." Code civil, No 653. Fournel, Traité de Voisinage, edit. 1812, tom. 2, 217; Pothier, Contrat de Société Première Appendice, Nos 199, 203 ... . "If I necessarily," says Pothier, "deprive my neighbor of the profits of his business arising from the use of his side of the wall, ...".

Rather than proceed with more research on the use of comparative law by American courts in the second half of the nineteenth century and end up with the same observations others have made, two tentative conclusions can be stated here. Both have been expressed in scholarly articles on the influence of the civil law in America and can be reported here, in part, as they concur and are fully supported by our own investigation of this same topic. The first element of a conclusion is borrowed from Roscoe Pound's research on the Influence of the Civil Law in America: "One who reads the older American

---

15 4 Dall. Rep. , 446, cited at p. 371, Johns. Rep. . 7

16 Did Mr. Hoffman know that Kent Ch. J. was going to be asigned the case and, thus, attempted to seduce or please the Chief Justice?

17 Johns. Rep. 7 p. 391.

18 Isabella Mix v. M. P. Mix, 1 Johns. Ch. p. 79; Peter Williamson v. Jane Williamson, 1 Johns. Ch. p. 220; Barrere v. Barrere, 4 Johns. Ch. p. 811, 812.

19 4 Johns. Ch. 858

reports, particularly those of the State of New York, cannot fail to notice the unusual number of references to the writers and authorities of the civil law which they contain and the great deference which appears to be paid to such authorities. No less remarkable is the rapid falling off in this practice and practically complete cessation of it by the middle of the nineteenth century. At present, citation of the authorities of the civil law, except in cases involving some point of international law or of admiralty jurisdiction, is usually the merest pedantry, and is seldom indulged in. When in recent years an American judge does see fit to cite them he does so in the manner of one who is displaying his learning, and not, as many American judges once did, in the same manner in which he cites common-law authorities."[20] Roscoe Pound further elaborated on the vanishing influence of the civil law in these terms: "As one studies the text books and the reports of the formative era of American law, he may well wonder how it came about that notwithstanding its marked advantage of form and system, as compared with the common law, notwithstanding the appeal which the idea of codification made to the laity, ... the civil law was not received and the direct taking over of rules and doctrines from the French code and French treaties was so small.

There were many reasons and they are not without instruction for us when we come to consider what is to be the future of the two systems in this country.

Probably the reason which was primarily responsible is to be found in the nature of law as distinguished from laws. Law is characteristically a taught tradition and, as Maitland puts it, taught law is tough law. The law teaching of our formative era was of the apprentice type, ... Generations of apprentice trained lawyers handed down a tradition of the common law which resisted systematic text books, reform legislation, and popular demand for a code ... Until the end of the nineteenth century there were relatively few academic law schools in the United States. By far the greater number of lawyers came from apprentice training in offices or from apprentice type law schools ... The idea of the common law so transmitted was thoroughly congenial to the pioneer conditions and modes of thought ... When university teaching of law became the rule in the United States, the time had gone by when the civil law might have been received.

Again, American lawyers are not polyglot and translations were not at hand at the crucial time. If English books were not to be had easily, French books were doubly inaccessible ... Pothier on Obligations was translated by François Xavier Martin in 1802, but the translation was not widely known. Pothier's treatise on Sales was not translated till 1839, nor his treatise on Partnership till 1854. There was an American edition of Domat in 1850. Except in Louisiana, few read French, and the translations came too late. When they began to be available, equity had crystallized, the law merchant

[20] Pound, "The Influence of French Law in America," 3 *Ill L. Rev.* 354, (1908-1909).

had been absorbed, comparative law had become decadent, ..."[21]

A contemporary legal historian, Peter Stein, conveyed his observation as a conclusion of his own research as follows: "The branch of substantive law in which the common law offered least to the new nation was commercial law. At the time of the Revolution, the radical decisions of Lord Mansfield in this field had hardly made themselves felt in America. It was therefor particularly in this branch of the law that American jurists turned for guidance to the leading French writers on the civil law. Among them the outstanding figure was that of Robert Joseph Pothier (1699-1772) ... Two other French jurists, who were frequently cited with him by American writers, were Balthazard Marie Emérigon (1716-1785) and René Josué Valin (1695-1765) ... The 1820's and 1830's were the hey-day of the civil law in the United States. The publication of Edward Livingston's Civil Code for Louisiana in 1825 seemed to assert its ascendancy and to presage an extension of its influence among the common-law states. Yet by 1850, it had probably ceased to be a real force in the development on American law. Why? Various reasons may be suggested. First, the most zealous champions of the civil law were members of the legal establishment, and the older of them tended to be Federalists and Whigs in their politics. Story and Kent had held high judicial office, ... Their enthusiasm for the civil law never permeated down to the humdrum practitioner of the law ... Secondly, the intellectual leaders of the legal profession themselves turned away from the civil law as a means for developing American law ... Those whose tastes were more classical and "liberal", in the contemporary sense, were now less interested in the civil law as expounded by Domat and Pothier than in the law of the classical Roman jurists, seen as a manifestation of the culture of antiquity ... By the 1840's, however, the historical school was winning.[22]

---

[21] Pound, "The Influence of the Civil Law in America", 1 La. L. Rev. 1, 13-1-16 (1938), A survey of the use of comparative law, under the form of French law, by American state courts in the second half of the nineteenth century reveals that some courts did cite, here and there, the same commentator Pothier but mostly on the basis of the English translations of his works. Other authors are also cited. As illustrations, here are some statistics: 1) Supreme Court of Texas, 1886-1899, 5 cases cite Pothier on Obligations; 2) Supreme Court of Pennsylvania, 1886-1895, 7 cases cite Pothier on Obligations but also on Successions; are also cited in an 1895 case: Duranton, Marcadé, Domat, Toullier and the Code Napoléon; 3) Supreme Court of Illinois, 1894-1897, 2 cases mentioned Pothier; 4) Supreme Court of California, 1885-1896, 6 cases cited Pothier in his work on Obligations; 5) Court of Appeals of New York, 1884-1899, 13 cases referred to Pothier on Obligations, on Successions, on Louage; a case in 1889 added references to Toullier, Duranton, Marcadé and the Code Napoléon; 6) most interestingly enough, we found the greatest number of cases (outside of Louisiana) citing Pothier as a foreign source of law in the jurisprudence of the Supreme Court of Ohio, 1831-1898: 19 cases referring to Pothier on Obligations, on Contracts, on Insurance, on Propriété and one of these cases citing also Pardessus, Droit Commercial.

[22] Stein, "The Attraction of the Civil Law in Post-Revolutionary America," by Peter Stein, 52 *V. L. Rev.* 403-434, (1966) (see also Zaphiriou, "Use of Comparative Law by the Legislator," 30 *Am. J. Comp.* 71, (1982). The author states in particular that "The post-revolutionary period was the formative era and the golden age of American law. It was marked by an inten-

II. THE TWENTIETH CENTURY

In the conclusion of his article on the "*Use of Comparative Law by the Legislator*", Professor G. Zaphiriou invited legislatures and courts to resort more often to international law comparison rather than confine themselves, as has been the trend since the second half of the nineteenth century, to interstate law comparison:

> "The legislatures, the courts and the existing institutions of law reform and unification, have mainly used interstate comparison for the development of the law in the United States. However, interstate law comparison and international law comparison are methodologically very similar.
>
> Expanding international trade and business, the need to comply with international standards and the necessity to protect United States interests by appropriate legislative measures have made indispensable the increasing use of international law comparison. International comparison is also used to provide ideas for the introduction of new legislation."[23]

Another respected scholar in the field of comparative law, Mary Ann Glendon, expressed the same views on the benefits of a comparative analysis of the existing legal systems:

> "We can only benefit from a heightened awareness of the ways in which other nations have approached problems with which our own legal system is currently struggling. Even though legal devices developed in other countries are rarely suitable for direct transplant, they often serve the cause of law revision and reform by showing that our range of choice may be wider than we had imagined, and by alerting us to the potential drawbacks as well as the possible advantages of alternative methods of proceeding. The study of foreign experiences can also be a fertile source of inspiration and ideas. And even when it does not immediately move us into a new stage of thinking, it nearly always affords us a deeper understanding of, and a more balanced perspective on, our own law."[24]

Have the federal courts and the state courts in the United States, ever since the beginning of the twentieth century, listened, *ex tunc* to Chancellor Kent, Roscoe Pound and Joseph Story or *ex nunc* to the advice of these two contemporary scholars? Considering that case law has always been the primary source of law in the common law system, that in addition to the United States Congress and the state legislatures, the courts "legislate" at least "interstitially",[25] have these courts, which make law, taken advantage of their role as

---

sive use of international comparative law." at p. 80.

[23] 30 *Am J. Comp. L.* 71, 95, (1982).

[24] Mary Ann Glendon, *The Transformation of Family Law*, (1989).

[25] Zaphiriou supra n. 22, at 71-72.

promoters of legal reforms and initiators of legal changes to present "foreign" legal viewpoints and incorporate them, wherever feasible, into the indigenous legal, social, economic, constitutional, criminal, ... structures and patterns of this country?

Our quantitative investigation and qualitative research of the cases of American courts which, in this twentieth century, did make use of substantive international comparative law or even only dared to get involved in the methodological process of foreign comparative legal analysis, turned out to be somewhat disappointing to say the least.

A. U.S. Supreme Court and Federal Courts

One most interesting case, and certainly well known, is the case of *Muller v. Oregon*.[26] In this case the US Supreme Court held that the Oregon "maximum hours for women" law was reasonable. In what became known as a "Brandeis brief", the not-yet Supreme Court Justice Louis D. Brandeis, acting as counsel for the state of Oregon, called the attention of the Justices to a series of foreign statutes which imposed restrictions on the hours of labor that may be required of women. Mr Brandeis cited statutes from Great Britain, France, Switzerland, Austria, Holland, Italy and Germany. "Then follow extracts from over ninety reports of committees, bureaus of statistics, commissioners of hygiene, inspectors of factories, both in this country and in Europe, to the effect that long hours of labor are dangerous for women primarily because of their special physical organization. The matter is discussed in these reports in different aspects, but all agree as to the danger." In the presence of such an extensive, well documented and relevant research presented by an attorney's brief, Mr Justice Brewer could only be impressed, if not seduced, by the scholarship displayed by Mr. Brandeis. Making an analogy with patent cases, perhaps in the hope of providing a stronger legal "homelike" background to his opinion, Justice Brewer wrote that "In patent cases counsel are apt to open the argument with a discussion of the state of the art. It may not be amiss, in the present case, before examining the constitutional question, to notice the course of legislation as well as expressions of opinion from other judicial sources. In the brief filed by Mr. Louis D. Brandeis, for the defendant in error, is a very copious collection of all these matters, an epitome of which is found in the margin ... The legislation and opinions referred to in the margin may not be, technically speaking, authorities, and in them is little or no discussion of the constitutional question presented to us for determination, yet they are significant of a widespread belief that woman's physical structure, and the functions she performs in consequence thereof, justify special legislation restricting or qualifying the conditions under which she should be permitted to toil ..."[27] In the 1936 case of Van Beeck, *Administrator, v. Sa-*

[26] 208 U.S. 412 (1907).
[27] 208 U.S. 412 at 419-420, 1907.

bine Towing Co., Inc, et al.,[28] Mr. Justice Cardozo was called upon to decide whether an employer's liability abates "where the beneficiary of the cause of action, in this case, the mother of the seaman, dies during the pendency of a suit in her behalf." In his opinion, Justice Cardozo stated that, according to a case of the King's Bench in 1606, the rule was "that in action of tort damages are not recoverable by any one for the death of a human being". The rule is often viewed as a derivative of the formula "actio personalis moritur cum persona", a maxim which "is one of some antiquity," ... even in classical times, however, the Roman law enforced the principle that "no action of an essentially penal character could be commenced after the death of the person responsible for the injury." The post-classical maxim, taken up by Coke and his successors, gave a new currency to these teachings of the Digest, ... [29]

Some ten years later, in *New York v. United States*,[30] Mr. Justice Frankfurter writing for the court upheld the right of Congress to tax the state of New York on its sale of mineral waters. In discussing the constitutional power of the United States over State activities, Justice Frankfurter stated that "the essential nature of the problem cannot be hidden by an attempt to separate manifestations of indivisible governmental powers ... The present case illustrates the sterility of such an attempt." In two footnotes in support of his legal analysis, Justice Frankfurter referred to the law of Argentina, as well as to "attempts along similar lines to solve kindred problems arising under the Canadian and Australian Constitutions" which "proved a barren process ... Even where the Constitution of a federal system explicitly deals with the problem of intergovernmental taxation, as in Brazil, litigation is not escaped and nice distinctions have to be made."[31]

In two 1961 decisions of the U.S. Supreme Court, the Justices did find some guidance and inspiration in foreign substantive comparative law. Writing for the majority of the Court in *McGowan v. State of Maryland*,[32] Mr. Chief Justice Warren analysed the long history of Sunday legislation against the background of a British Bill of 1936 and the Parliamentary Debates in the House of Commons as well as in relation to the Reports of the International Labour Conferences.[33] In a concurring opinion, Justice Frankfurter commented that "even on the Continent the forces which in the latter half of the nineteenth century pressed for the amelioration of the working conditions of the laborer expressed themselves in part in Sunday legislation", citing the German, Austrian, Swiss, Danish, Norwegian and Russian experiences as well as the reports of the Congrès International du Repos Hebdo-

[28] 300 U.S. 342 (1936).

[29] Id at 344-345, (1936). In footnote 4 Justice Cardozo referred to Buckland, "A Text-Book of Roman Law," in, William W. Buckland & Arnold D. McNair (eds.), *Roman Law and Common Law* 345 (1936).

[30] 326 U.S. 572 (1946).

[31] Id. at 580, 583.

[32] 366 U.S. 1101 (1961).

[33] Id. at 1118 n. 21.

madaire.[34] In the same year 1961, in the case of *Poe v. Ullman*,[35] which dealt with the issue of the validity or invalidity of Connecticut statutes prohibiting the use of contraceptives, Justice Harlan found support for his dissenting opinion in an incursion in the field of foreign comparative law: "Although the Federal Government and many States have at one time or other had on their books statutes forbidding or regulating the distribution of contraceptives, none so far as I can find, has made the use of contraceptives a crime. Indeed, a diligent search has revealed that no nation, including several which quite evidently share Connecticut's moral policy, has seen fit to effectuate that policy by the means presented here". In the footnote supporting that statement, one can read that an "unqualified disapproval of contraception is implicit in the laws of Belgium ..., France ..., Ireland ..., Italy ..., Spain ..., Canada ..., Germany ..., Switzerland ..."[36]

Much scholarship and erudition was displayed by Justice Blackmun in the famous case of *Roe v. Wade*.[37] To resolve the issue of abortion "by constitutional measurement, free of emotion and of predilection",[38] Justice Blackmun "inquired into, and in this opinion place some emphasis upon, medical and medical-legal history and what that history reveals about man's attitudes toward the abortion procedure over the centuries".[39] We are told that at the time of the Persian Empire abortifacients were known and that criminal abortions were severely punished. We are also told, however, that abortion was practiced in Greek times as well as in the Roman Era ... Greek and Roman law afforded little protection to the unborn ...[40] It is undisputed that at common law, abortion performed before "quickening" ... was not an indictable offense.[41] A loose consensus evolved in early English law that these events occurred at some point between conception and live birth".[42] In many of the substantial footnotes which provide an abundance of references to a variety of sources on the many facets of abortion (philosophy, morality, religion, medicine, law ...), one will find citations to J. Noonan, Contraception: A History of Its Treatment by the Catholic Theologians and Canonists, *(note 22); to Augustine, De Origine Animae, to the Decretum Magistri Gratiani *(note 22), or to Tietze & Lehfeldt, Legal Abortion in Eastern Europe, ... *(note 44).

It is unquestionable that the comparative legal analysis of this highly emotional and sensitive issue of abortion enabled Justice Blackmun, not only to present the cold evidence and factual picture of how other civilizations

---

34 Id. at 1166 n. 40.
35 81 S. Ct. 1752, (1961).
36 Id. at 1783 n. 16.
37 410 U.S. 113 (1972).
38 Id. at 116.
39 Id. at 117.
40 Id. at 130.
41 Id. at 132.
42 Id. at 133.

faced this issue but also how the legal aspects of abortion were shaped and framed in the context of different societies, at different times and according to different levels of knowledge and culture. This extensive foray into foreign substantive comparative law played the role of a huge canvas on which Justice Blackmun felt more comfortable to add his personal contribution than if he had had to act as a pioneer exploring hostile and unknown territories.

The 1986 case of *Bowers v. Hardwick*[43] shows a timid attempt by some Justices to look beyond the borders of the United States to determine how other nations, societies and legal systems handle the issue of consensual sodomy in the privacy of a home. Justice Byron White, writing for the majority, confined himself to a survey and an inter-state comparative analysis of the statutes of different states to conclude that the Court was "unpersuaded that the sodomy laws of some 25 States should be invalidated on this [morality] basis."[44] Chief Justice Burger, in a concurring opinion, went a little further than Justice White in going "abroad" to trace the history of sodomy and the responses some societies have adopted. "Homosexual sodomy was a capital crime under Roman law. See Code Theod. 9. 7. 6. ; Code Just 9. 9. 31 ... . During the English Reformation when powers of the ecclesiastical courts were transferred to the King's Courts, the first English statute criminalizing sodomy was passed."[45] In his dissenting opinion, Justice Blackmun pointed out that "petitioner's invocation of Leviticus, Romans, St Thomas Aquinas, and sodomy's heretical status during the Middle Ages undermines his suggestion ..." for example: Pollock & Maitland, note 6, p. 211; Blackstone, note 3, p. 214). This opinion is far from being as well researched and scholarly documented as was Justice's Blackmun's decision in *Roe v. Wade*. No reference was made to foreign sources of law expressed in an other language than English and even to translations in English of foreign materials as if sodomy was a human behavior limited to the English speaking world of England and the USA. And, yet, it is unquestionable that such an issue as sodomy has raised as many important and emotional questions as abortion in many other countries and human societies than the United States. If the issue was essentially the constitutionality of a state statute and, as such, a matter of American constitutional law, it was also an issue of Human Rights and Privacy which is a matter of concern to the whole world. One may wonder why the Justices were so "provincial" and "home-tied" in this case?

Beyond these few cases from the US Supreme Court, we found two recent lower court cases of some interest, the second more than the first one.

In *United States v. Hall*,[46] the U.S. Army Court of Military Review was called upon to pass judgment on the issues of sodomy and right to privacy. While referring extensively to the case of *Bowers v. Hardwick*, the Court of

---

43 478 U.S. 186 (1986).
44 Id. at 196.
45 Id. at 197.
46 34 M. J. 695 (ACMR 1991).

Military Review added a personal touch of foreign comparative law where it stated that "the debate and uncertainty over the right to privacy are not purely American. There has been a sort of juridical trans-Atlantic volley in privacy law ever since the serve by the Vice Chancellor in Prince *Albert v. Strange* ... Until the European Commission and Court of Human Rights joined in on this side most of the smashes were coming from the United States, in the form of common law and statutory torts of invasions of privacy."[47]

In the case of *Aluminum Company of America v. Essex Group, Inc.*,[48] U.S. District Judge Teitelbaum was faced with the issue of the reformation of a long-term contract on the basis of several theories. Stating the obvious, but thereby showing great wisdom, humility and intellectual curiosity, Judge Teitelbaum acknowledged that "Happily some American cases and the law of many foreign countries take a different view of the problem. The problem of serious, sustained inflation is not unique to modern America ... And several other nations have recently experienced more severe inflation than America has. When the problem has arisen, here and abroad, courts and legislatures have repeatedly acted to relieve parties from great and unexpected losses."[49] In an Appendix to the case, the judge stated that "the Court has studied various remedies utilized by courts in foreign countries, when beset with contracts that are no longer deemed fair in light of changed circumstances:" Thereafter the judge surveyed the laws of Germany, Switzerland, Argentina, Brazil, Japan, Italy, Israel, Chile, Sweden.[50]

In light of the poor results we were apparently obtaining in this empirical research on the use of comparative law by federal courts, we undertook a more pointed research on the use by US federal courts of appeal of a few selected French sources of law. Here are some statistics collected on different sources:

a) under the title "droit civil français", there were 15 decisions between 1964 and 1992. Out of these 15 cases, 12 arose in Louisiana, 2 in Puerto Rico, and 1 from Georgia but it dealt with an issue of conflict of laws.
b) under the title "French Civil Code", there were 48 cases between 1952 and 1991. Out of these 48 cases, 19 came from Louisiana, 2 from Puerto Rico and 27 from other jurisdictions. However, most of these 27 decisions dealt with conflict of laws issues; some made a few references to French law merely to point out that the methods of interpretation at civil law are different from those known at common law.
c) under the names "Aubry et Rau", 16 cases were identified between 1955 and 1992. However, 14 of these cases concerned Louisiana law and the remaining 2 came from Puerto Rico.

---

[47] Citing Michael, "Homosexuals and Privacy", 138 *New L. J.* 831, 11 November 1988 in fn. 2 on p. 697.

[48] 499 F. Supp. 53, 1980.

[49] Id. at 78.

[50] Id at 93-94.

d) under the names "Mazeaud, Mazeaud et Mazeaud" there were 8 cases between 1973 and 1989. Five of these cases came from Puerto Rico, 1 from Louisiana, 1 dealt with the Warsaw Convention and 1 involved an issue of conflict of laws.
e) under the names "Planiol et Ripert", there were several references to federal courts of appeal cases but they concerned the Warsaw Convention.

As a conclusion on the use of foreign comparative law by American federal courts in the twentieth century, one can only corroborate the negative assertion that Roscoe Pound was making earlier in this same century with respect to the use of French law: "At present, citation of the authorities of the civil law, except in cases involving some point of international law or of admiralty jurisdiction, is usually the merest pedantry, and is seldom indulged in. When ... an American judge does see fit to cite them he does so in the manner of one who is displaying his learning, and not, as many American judges once did, in the same manner in which he cites common-law authorities."

[In August 1996, we were asked by our general Reporter to look once more at our report of 1993 to see whether it should be revised or whether the original manuscript ought to remain as originally drafted.

We decided to cast a glance at the 1993-96 caselaw of the U.S. Supreme Court and of the Federal Courts of that period. Once again, we decided to leave aside the federal courts cases involving Louisiana and Puerto Rico. Our research led us to a most important case of the Supreme Court and to some thirty cases from a variety of Federal Courts. However, in none of these cases did the courts concerned ever looked at a foreign legal system exclusively as a source of inspiration, guidance or support for a purely internal legal issue. There was no intellectual curiosity spontaneously engendered to look into the law of a foreign jurisdiction so as to rely on that legal system to provide a better and wider support or foundation to a legal solution determined exclusively by application and interpretation of the law of the case.

The U.S. Supreme Court case of Vimar Seguros Y Reaseguros, S. A. v. M/V Sky Reefer[51]*, concerned a foreign arbitration clause and its compatibility with the FAA, COGSA as well as the possible application of Japanese law. Thus, the use of Japanese law or, more precisely, the potential application of Japanese law was triggered by an arbitration clause and an issue of conflict of laws.*

The other some thirty cases from U.S. District Courts, U.S. Courts of Appeals, the U.S. Court of International Trade and the U.S. Tax Court, all raised issues either of conflicts of laws (and the application of German law, or Japanese law or Mexican law or French law), or arbitration or arbitral awards. In all these instances, therefore, the U.S. Courts were 'required' to

[51] 115 S. Ct. 2322, 1995.

look into the application of a foreign law; it was neither a matter of intellectual curiosity nor of enlightened cultural inclination.]

B. State Courts Cases

Restricting our investigation to the use of French law by State Courts (excluding Louisiana and Puerto Rico courts) during the 2nd half of the twentieth century, we were able to identify some 35 cases which did refer to French law in some form or another. This is obviously a very small number when compared to the thousands of cases handed down by the courts of the forty nine states since the year 1950. In addition, some of these 35 cases dealt with conflict of laws issues which compelled the US state courts to consider the possible application of French law under the particular circumstances of the case.

A run down of these cases would provide the following picture:

State of:	*Reference to:*	*Legal Issues*
California: 4 cases	Code Napoleon	guarantee
	French Civil Code	succession
		parents/child
		negligence
Delaware: 2 cases	French Civil Code	succession
	The Code Napoleon	
	(French Criminal law)	burglary
Georgia: 1 case	French Civil Code	mother/gestation
Idaho : 1 case	Napoleonic Code	succession
Iowa: 1 case	French Civil Code	easement
Maine: 1 case	Law of France;FCC	conflict/laws
Massachusetts: 1 case	French Civil Code	conflict/laws
Michigan: 1 case	French Civil Code	conflict/laws
Nebraska: 1 case	French Civil Code	damages
Nevada: 1 case	Code Napoleon	conflict/laws
New Jersey: 4 cases	Code Napoleon	succession
	French Civil Code	adoption/support
		evidence
New York: 5 cases	Code Napoleon	conflict/laws
	French Civil Code	Vienna/Convention
	Mazeaud and Tunc	Negotiable Instr.
		Criminal law
North Dakota: 2 cases	Code Napoleon	Property
		Liability
Ohio: 2 cases	Code Napoleon	concubinage
		legitimation
Oklahoma: 1 case	Code Napoleon	security/device
Oregon: 1 case	Code Napoleon	accretion

Texas: 3 cases	Code Napoleon	marriage
	Duranton	streams/rights
Washington: 1 case	French Civil Code	marriage/adoption
West Virginia: 1 case	Code Napoleon	property
Wyoming: 1 case	Code Napoleon	probate/will

[*During the period 1993-96*[52] *we found, again, a certain number of states courts decisions in which the judges were compelled to take into account some 'foreign law' because the conflicts of laws issues raised in those instances. In ten cases, at least, States Courts of Appeals, and some States Supreme Courts, had to consider legal issues that fell under the control of German law. In another set of sixteen cases of conflicts of laws, States Courts had to resort to Mexican law to render the required and proper legal decision expected of them. In four other cases, Japanese law was relevant to the conflicts of laws issues raised before the State Courts. Again, cases from Louisiana Courts and Puerto Rico courts were not intended to be included in our survey since the use of comparative law is a 'natural' and historical component part of these courts legal methodology.*

To our 'foreign' and intellectual satisfaction, we came across a few cases in which States Courts engaged in a truly scholarly use of comparative law to solve legal issues raised under the exclusive control of 'local law.' So instructive, and enjoyable, were these cases that we feel compelled to give, here, some credit to the judges by quoting from the Courts' decisions.

a: 'Defendants were indicted on charges of theft of white-tailed deer and deer antlers and criminal mischief ... We begin by flipping through the pages of time. History reveals a long recognition of common ownership in game and wild animals and its developing subjectivity to governmental authority ... Roman law recognized common ownership, but imposed its regulations on the taking of wild animals ... the legislation of Charlemagne, and later by the Napoleonic Code, ... The common law of England also based property in game upon the principle of common ownership, ...' [53]

b: 'Furthermore, whether the source of Louisiana law is the Napoleonic Code or the Code of Hammurabi is really irrelevant.'[54]

c: 'Moreover, ... , because the Mexican civil codes are based on the French civil code (Code Napoleon), Mexican scholars and commentators rely on authoritative statements written by legal scholars in France, Argentina, Spain, and other countries with a civil law tradition.' [55]

d: 'The general rule that accretion belongs to the upland owner is vener-

---

[52] As stated above, when asked to choose between updating our 1993 survey of the use of comparative law by U.S. Courts and merely leave the original manuscript untouched, we chose to look at the jurisprudence of these in-between years 1993-96.

[53] The State of Texas v. J. Bartee, 894 S. W. 2d 34, 1994.

[54] D. Webb v. T. D. , D. C. ; R. Ks, M. D. ; and C. H. A. M. D. , 912 P. 2d. 202, S. Ct. Montana 1996.

[55] H. Gardner v. Best Western International, Inc. 1996 WL 441663, Tex. App.

able. Over a century ago, the United States Supreme Court, in resolving a dispute over property in Illinois, traced it to the Emperor Justinian: 'In the Institutes of Justinian it is said: ... 'The rule is also found in the Code Napoleon.' [56]*]*

Conclusion

Despite these few illustrations of the use of comparative law by U.S. Courts, it remains that, if we leave aside the state of Louisiana where the influence of French law (and Spanish law) has always been most important, particularly at the level of the Supreme Court, it is fair to say that, by and large, the relevance of foreign (French) comparative law in American courts is almost nil.[57] American judges do not venture much outside the law of the land maybe because they already have an extensive field of comparative analysis available to them. In addition, a substantial amount of information on US law is made easily accessible to them by publishers of printed and on line materials. Furthermore, this information is available in the English language and presented in a form and style familiar to all those who have received their legal training in the USA. Few are the judges who have the knowledge of foreign languages required and the intellectual curiosity, as well as the time, to embark upon any research into foreign comparative law. One my also wonder how the practicing lawyers would react to citations of foreign sources of law by the judges! Drowning under this amount of American law, in a language known by all and immediately usable, it is no wonder that foreign substantive law is not readily used to solve *internal legal issues*.

---

[56] State of California v. The Superior Court of Sacramento County, 44 Cal. Rptr. 2d 399, Sup. Ct of Cal. 1995.

[57] On Louisiana law see, Pound, "The Influence of the Civil Law in America, 1 La. L. Rev. 1 1938; "The Influence of French Law in America", 3 Ill. L. Rev. 354 (1908-1909); A Levasseur & S. Herman, "La Circulation du Modèle Juridique Français en Louisiane," Rapport H. Capitant 1993 (Association Henri Capitant Journées Franco-Italiennes, Mai 1993).

Index

U. Drobnig and S. van Erp (eds.), The Use of Comparative Law by Courts, 335–341.